Encompassing Others

Encompassing Others

THE MAGIC OF MODERNITY IN MELANESIA

Edward LiPuma

Ann Arbor

THE UNIVERSITY OF MICHIGAN PRESS

Copyright © by the University of Michigan 2000
All rights reserved
Published in the United States of America by
The University of Michigan Press
Manufactured in the United States of America
⊗ Printed on acid-free paper

2003   2002   2001   2000   4   3   2   1

*A CIP catalog record for this book is available
from the British Library.*

Library of Congress Cataloging-in-Publication Data

LiPuma, Edward, 1951–
    Encompassing others : the magic of modernity in Melanesia /
Edward LiPuma.
        p.   cm.
    Includes bibliographical references and index.
    ISBN 0-472-11068-3 (cloth : alk. paper)
    1. Maring (Papua New Guinea people)—Social conditions.   2. Maring
(Papua New Guinea people)—Missions.   3. Maring (Papua New Guinea
people)—Religion.   4. Anglicans—Missions—Papua New Guinea—Jimi
River Valley.   5. Christianity and culture—Papua New Guinea—Jimi River
Valley.   6. Jimi River Valley (Papua New Guinea)—Religious life and
customs.   7. Jimi River Valley (Papua New Guinea)—Social life and
customs.   I. Title.
DU740.42 .L566   2000
305.89'912—dc21   99-051001

For my wife, Susan, my daughter, Laura, and my friend, Skip

Contents

Illustrations

Preface

Years ago, it seems like so many years now, I talked with my friend Skip Rappaport as we walked through the woods behind the house he had built on the outskirts of Ann Arbor. On this day, among other things we talked about anthropology, or more to the point how to be an anthropologist. Skip had several pieces of advice culled from his own life and beliefs. The first was that the essence of fieldwork was to follow the ethnography, to be very attuned to what was happening at that historical moment in the lives of the people with whom I was living. Research plans and agendas were less important than letting the ethnography make the ethnographer. In his own life in the field, he and his wife Annie had reached Tsembaga just as they were preparing for the now famous *kaiko*. So he had written about the ceremonial slaughter of pigs and the elaborate rituals that surrounded their sacrifice. His second piece of advice was to remember that if a writer expected his audience to spend part of their lives reading what he had written, he had an obligation to make the text as crystal and intelligible as his powers would permit him. The highest aim of the writing we call anthropology was to be deep but clear, faithful to the ethnography yet always sensitive to the audience. The writer stood between two sets of subjects, those he had lived with and those he wrote for, and so he had a responsibility to honor himself and his profession by respecting both. By this point in our conversation we had about completed the circuit through the woods. Skip hesitated by the stone steps leading back down into the house and offered a final observation. An observation as much about life as about science. That to be "good"—and I came to know that what he meant by this was to be a good ethnographer and to lead a fulfilling life—it was necessary to resist being buffeted and swayed by all the trends that sweep through the discipline. There was a difference between theoretical trendiness couched in unapproachable language and true depth based on a commitment to revealing the textures and experiences of people's lives through theory. Theory and ethnography must dance as partners, at times one leading, at other times the other: but always as partners.

I have sought, in this work, to put my friend's advice into practice. The study centers on the process of the encompassment of the Maring by colonialism, capitalism, and Christianity—what is known as modernity. If there was anything that characterized my stay in the Jimi Valley, it was the subtle though unrelenting progress of modernity. The reshaping of people's knowledge, wants, and expectations became inevitable as did the imagination of a new future and an equally new past. This was what was then happening, the work of culture in progress, and this is what now comes to center stage. My earlier study of the Maring, *The Gift of Kinship*, alighted on issues of modernization, but mostly only in passing and where the impact of modernity was transparent and magnified by the situation. Here, the analysis seeks to unearth the multiple levels of change, to confront the encounter between the Maring and the forces of encompassment. It is partly ethnographic, partly historical as it tries to spin out the processes and venues of the encounter. Central to the story is both sides of the story, the engagement of "others" from the perspective of the Westerners as well as the Maring, the vision of the Anglican priest from San Francisco in addition to the shaman from Kompiai. I have tried to let the voices of the station manager from Manchester, the nurse from County Cork, and the other Westerners be heard—to see the struggles alongside and in relation to the Maring. Theoretically, I am concerned less with the overt aspects of modernity—the building of a road, the advent of Western money, the physical presence of the Anglican mission—than the transformation of people's categories of knowledge and the structure of desire. My view is that these transformations are the most telling because they are generative. Changes in epistemology and desire are an engine that motivates other changes that in turn feed back on itself and motivates still further changes. Encompassment sets a dialectic in train, a new type of history is born, with a different trajectory, and surely a new direction to the Maring's story of themselves, a new myth of what it means to be a person and have a peoplehood.

Though the book is full of theory and method, I have tried to the best of my ability to write in everyday English, as it were, to tell the story of the Maring's adventure of the modern. My quest for simplicity of style should not be read as an effort to eschew theory. No, the web of issues defining the encompassment of Melanesia pushes anthropological theory to its limits, and so this is no simple descriptive journey. My argument is that for an account to be adequate to its object it must grasp the changes in the nature of knowledge and desire wrought by colonialism, capitalism, and Christianity. My argument is that for an account of the changes in knowledge and desire to be adequate to its object, it must focus on the encounter between the Maring and their others. And this encounter must not be thought of in terms of domination and resistance, however appealing this may be to our political sensibilities, but in terms of mediation and engagement. Capitalism is so much less an economic machine of domination than a means of seducing the senses, a carnival of goods, an image of the future, a call to arms for the younger generation, a license to express socially prohibited and repressed desires, the cultivation of a world of endless wants, endlessly fulfilled. Especially in the hinterlands of the Highlands, the power of capitalism and commercially driven mass culture derives much less from the coercive power of the state, Christian missions, and big business than from the enchantment of the senses, taste and touch, sight and sound. Finally, the book argues that there can be no theory of transformation without a theory and ethnography of generations, a concept often presupposed in anthropological discourse but rarely spoken about. In an intellectual universe focused on class, gender, and status, generation is the forgotten category. Moreover, theory and ethnography are linked by the fact that it was especially the up-and-coming generation of Maring that was eager for change, ready to embrace the new forms of value creation, new technologies of power, and ultimately new ways of being a person.

Each of these chapters advances these arguments across a variety of dimensions, from a number of angles. I imagine the chapters as a set of transparencies that, when laid one over the other, reveals a new and fuller picture. When I think that speed and information, especially snappy, predigested information, are the ecstasy of the modern age—a thought that inspires the kind of disenchantment that produces ethnographers—I remember what my friend Skip also told me on that day through the woods: that good ethnographers are slow, they take their time to think and write, and hopefully they will age like the '82 Cheval Blanc that we drank later that night.

(More than) Acknowledgments

Writing, and writing ethnography, are conversations that authors have with themselves about where they have been, who they have encountered, and what they have read. As such, writing is the site of so many reasons and relationships, memories and motives, that as I acknowledge those who have made this work with me, I am uncertain of what they have contributed even as I am certain that without them the work and its author would look very different. No doubt less. Much less. For it is only in the presence of others that we are able to uproot words from silence.

Though ethnography and writing have a tone of singularity, they are inherently collaborative and interactive—the ensemble of others, friends, colleagues, informants, that we incorporate within our bodies as dispositions to think certain thoughts and entertain certain reactions to the world. The focus of this book, the encompassment of others, grows out of more than a decade of association with the Social Theory Group, launched by the Center for Transnational Studies. The group introduced me to the critical theorization of the West in ways that allowed me to grasp the agents and institutions of encompassment better than I ever would been able otherwise. I would particularly like to thank Benjamin Lee and Moishe Postone who have been great interlocutors, and even better friends. From an ethnographic angle, I owe an enormous debt to Skip Rappaport and Cherry Lowman. Like poets of the field, they allowed me to apprehend the miracle of the concrete and also to find the spiritual undertow in the simplest fact. They taught me that the language of good ethnography honored its complexities, but was also direct and devoid of jargon. An ethnography should not be a menagerie of theoretical terms that, like circus animals that have forgotten their tricks, seem to shoot off in all directions at once. For this, I am grateful now and for all the sentences to come.

For all of my life, before I knew that anthropology existed, I read and wrote poetry. Some of my heroes are Wallace Stevens, Cesare Pavese, Pablo Neruda, and Octavio Paz: Stevens because he has more to say about ethnography and descriptions than all the books on methodology combined; Pavese because he understood that great cultural processes are manifest in specific instances and locales, as his beautiful realism of life in a small Calabrian village reveals; Neruda and Paz because each in his own way had such a concern for his homeland that he wrote passionately about the process by which the West encompasses others and its reverberations.

I also wish to thank Andrew Strathern, Pamela Stewart, and Viviana Diaz Balsera for offering comments that improved the manuscript. I also owe a special thanks to Susan Whitlock for her generosity of spirit in helping me to see the manuscript through. I have always felt that I was the most fortunate ethnographer alive—that Gou, Kiaya, Moses, Penga, and others not only befriended me, they taught me an extraordinary amount about their world in the process of being encompassed by mine, and they did so with a humor so scintillating that it still brings a smile to my face.

Finally, I would like to thank my wife, Susan, for her encouragement, intelligence, and courage, and my irrepressible daughter, Laura, who being as old as the manuscript, must think, and rightly so, that writing is inseparable from a lifetime. Both have provided constant reference points beyond the city limits of academe that allow sanity to creep in unnoticed. And so more than acknowledgment, I want to say thank you for sharing, in a true Melanesian way, measures of the only life we will ever lead.

CHAPTER 1

The Flight of the Cassowary:
On Subjectivity and Encompassment

When in the 1920s and 1930s gold prospectors and adventurers penetrated the Highlands of Papua New Guinea, they discovered that nearly half the island's population, some million people, lived on the slopes and plateaus cradled in the tall mountains. After World War II, the door of the Highlands opened to the world, and the West entered in force: evangelists hungry for souls and entrepreneurs for money, patrol officers bent on bringing civilization and ethnographers on recording culture. Each arrived with their own mission and sense of purpose, each so engrossed in their own concerns as to be only barely aware that the next performance in the theater of modernity was about to begin.

And in the beginning was the word as myth. The Maring have always lived by myths, archetypically stories of their primordial past. These myths on the origin of exchange and fire, the birth of kinship and the wages of war, all told how the world and its people came to be as they are. All, that is, except one rather singular, idiosyncratic tale about a time in the future when, all things cultural having been so transformed, today's customs reduced to cinders, that nature, the elemental order of orders, itself responds to these enormous changes in the world's fabric, and the cassowary, the flightless bird, takes flight. This is a "new myth," nothing more than a fabricated and amusing tale by Maring lights. But behind the laughter lies the invention of culture and the reshaping of expectations, the fact that a story of this kind, with its eyes fixed on the future, is possible and meaningful now. The story, as told to me one rainy afternoon by some young men, goes like this:

> There was a man who had much to drink, and falling asleep, had what he thought was a dream. For a long time, he had been residing with his wife's kinsmen who inhabited a very remote region. The man eventually feels lonely, and when he hears that there is to be a bride payment he decides to visit his "root" place. For two days he walks through the mountains to reach his natal village. When he gets there, he discovers that the road entering the town is paved. At the edge of the village he sees an airfield,

trucks, jeeps, and cars, and a whole array of paved roads shooting off in all directions. At the center of the new village are food
stores, a restaurant, and a store selling everything needed to
build a house: hammers, nails, finished woods. The man stum-
bles wide-eyed around his natal village. When he asks where he
is, everyone laughs, and then someone informs him that they
have become "white" ["though their skin is still black as ever"].
Shaking his head, he asks where are the pigs and gardens. His
true kinsmen tell him that everyone now has and eats as much
rice as they want, and that fish, pork, and even taro arrive every
day on the planes in tin cans. The man is so dazed and bewildered by these changes that he wanders off into the brush. There,
he is happy to chance upon two large cassowaries in a corral. He
assumes the cassowaries must be a part of the upcoming
bridewealth payment. But his comfort at finding a familiar reference point turns to shock when to his amazement the cassowaries, stunned by his presence, flap their stunted wings and
take flight. Now scared and disoriented, the man takes his own
flight back to his wife's village to the sound of laughter of his
own former villagers.

This "myth"—can we call it such—is as far from traditional mythos
as the metropole from the hinterlands. Traditional myths are about primordial events, ancestral times, and unquestionable truths. Our story is
about the future rather than the past. It is an imagination of what is to
come and what has been left behind in the encompassing gesture, the
uncharted cultural acceleration toward a future the Maring sometimes
refer to as "civilization" in contrast to the kingdom of kastam (tradition or
custom). Our story (according to a story about the story) is the twin of a
coastal tale; it is like the modern itself, simultaneously imported and cus-
tomized in the rites of retelling. The reenactment of another reality that is
fast becoming your own.

Whatever the status of the story, there's more at stake here than a
case of cultural eavesdropping. Like the tarnished secondhand clock that
hung on a wall of the mission school, it is a lesson in the remaking of temporality. Appropriately, the story abandons the cyclicity of traditional
time. How out of place to assume, as the Maring have always assumed,
that the clan as the main unit of reproduction will replicate itself from one
generation to the next, its continuity guaranteed by exchanges with ancestors and affines (see LiPuma 1988: chaps. 3, 4). The story recounted here is
also unlike traditional myth in that it is not about the heroic actions of the
ancestors or timeless truths. It is not about how societies remember, but
rather how they learn to forget. And indeed there is a growing number of

accounts of this type. From a Western viewpoint, these accounts spring up as myths, stories, and sometimes wild rumors of change. Above all, they are narratives of transformation. Who could not be impressed with the tale that "Skip and Annie" (Rappaport, the first anthropologists to work among the Maring, 1963–64) would soon return and deliver untold wealth from America to the Simbai valley (thus replacing local forms of wealth creation). Or that the sacraments of Anglicanism harbored a powerful sorcery that the attuned Christian could appropriate and direct at his enemies. Or that in the bowels of some unspecified building in Port Moresby there were mountains of wealth, now hidden and hoarded by the national elite. The myth of the flight of the cassowary, like other narratives of modernity, was part of an unending attempt to make sense of a world in which the structure of perception and desire, patterns of expectation and rewards, ways of speaking and listening, images of body and thought, the limits of travel and imagination, have all changed course rather abruptly, quite irreversibly. In their attempt to gain practical and conceptual mastery over this world-changing, the Maring have constructed these many stories, ranging from myths and cargo-cultish wish lists to descriptions of sojourns to Port Moresby and other cities, tales of life on labor plantations, and reminiscences about the varied Westerners they have known. These stories, devised and revised, edited and reformulated, are their way of progressively coming to terms with the encompassing process. Whether they are or appear factual or fanciful, singular or common, these stories are pragmatic attempts to experiment with the representation and meanings of the modern. The collective working through of these myths, tales, narratives, descriptions, and dreams is the Maring analysis of modernity.

So over and above its country-bumpkin humor the flight of the cassowary sings with the gravity of the matter: it announces a sense and feeling for change almost beyond imagination. The man in his own dreamtime has been away for less than a lifetime when all that has happened takes place. This mirrors Maring experience from the 1960s, which, in the limits of one lifetime and two generations, has gone from relative isolation to a burgeoning engagement with things Western. That the tale concerns a bride payment makes it that much more ironic and symbolically charged, for bridewealth payments not only antedate contact but have changed in shape and content in response to the advent of the modern. Bridewealth payments are a crossroads at which gender and domesticity, the immediate economy and wider politics, talk to one another. And insofar as they are inseparable from social reproduction, they are a marked index of societal transformation. It was also appropriate that the myth is a dream (or the dream a myth) in that the Maring, like other Melanesians, believe that dreams are omens of what is to come.

The symbolic density and irony of the story does not pause there: it locates our unknowing, bewildered visitor outside the space of "modernized" commercialized life. His spatial marginalization to the outer fringe of Maring territory parallels his cultural marginalization in the face of great change. The myth also plays with the intimacy between history and territory, conjuring this new village as a mediation between the metropole, the once and future city of modernity, and the bush hinterlands where traditional, ancestrally dependent clansmen dwell in some temporal warp. The story not only transmutes history into space but capitalizes on the Maring concept that differences in residence create differences in types of people. The distance between the new village and the hinterlands is thus measured in differences in identity and future trajectory. Even more, the myth invites its contemporary tellers to take their own grandparents and parents as objects of contemplation. For like this bewildered man, their own ancestors were culturally overwhelmed when they first encountered planes, cars, flashlights, and other Western technologies of modernity and power. The myth maps an imaginary frontier between generations, a promised height from which to look down upon their own past. So it was that Abraham, the son of Yingok, tells me (and a house of other young men) about the ignorance of his ancestors when faced with airplanes and white men, his local audience smiling in a bemused, slightly embarrassed way, aware of my presence, as though they were both confessing to this "genealogical" connection and letting it be known that they were now citizens of another more enlightened and slightly cynical viewpoint.[1]

From the tradition of a world that is at once spiritual and thoroughly personal, where the creation of value is as visible as a man burning a garden or a woman tending to her pigs, modernity is magic on its way to becoming miracle. On this understanding, the elder generation of Maring yearned to capture and deploy the magic lying behind the Westerners' ability to create value. And thus my old friend, Tipika the shaman, after teaching me his spells against illness, asked in return if I would teach him my magic for "pulling" things (without, apparently, my doing a lick of real work).[2] For Tipika and most of his generation, the world works by the old principles even if the players are new and the objects of desire come in cans and cartons. By contrast, the younger generation has no such illusions, simply the desire to indulge in the modern miracle of money and things produced from afar, the alchemy of turning gold flecks and coffee beans into *kina* (the Papua New Guinea national currency) and the kina earned into things of foreign origin. In this glittering light, it is not surprising that the myth of the flight of the cassowary should stand in marked contrast to other myths of beginnings. It has nothing to say about the creation of clanship, the complementarity between men and women, the inauguration of exchange relations, or the migrations of the ancestors. Thus does the story or dreamtime foresee a future so changed that the cultural anchors and sources of continuity have vanished. Here the myth cuts clear to the bone, for nothing is more central to the construction of Maring clanship and affinity than locally grown foods, which in the imagined tomorrow of the myth have been replaced by their canned, imported ghosts. In this and other stories of the modern, against the echo of their own laughter, the Maring have come to imagine their future as a great break with customs past even as, and this is the anthropological moment, their future must embody and simultaneously reinvent that past. As my friend and house-mate Gou once observed as we stood at a crossroads on the outskirts of Mt. Hagen, the provincial capital of the Western Highlands and for the Maring an exemplar of the urban, just because a road is paved doesn't mean that it goes where you want it to.

Themes and Theories

This book is a description and argument concerning the nature of cultural transformation and the way that it informs the lives of those who experi-ence it. I explore the themes and issues of encompassment that lay in the background of my earlier study *The Gift of Kinship* (1988). At issue is how these people of the Bismarck mountains or any people can reproduce themselves in the face of modernity: a catchall term for those processes by which a society reshapes itself as a consequence of being inexorably encompassed within a state (first colonial and then national) and inun-dated by Western capitalism, Christianity, and commercially driven mass culture. I employ the term *encompassment* (detailed later) to describe these processes, and indeed an aim of this study is to contribute to the theoreti-cal groundwork needed to produce an ethnography (that is also a history) of the encompassment of Melanesia. For my view is that we can only con-struct a genuine history of Melanesia, a history of the modern, from a communion of local histories—ethnographies that face both inward toward the meanings, strategies, and desires of the practical life and out-ward toward the encompassing universe. I accept without reservation the viewpoint of Fernando Cardoso, the anthropologically oriented political scientist who later became president of Brazil, who once observed that his-tory is where global forces touch everyday lives.[3]

The embrace of the West and the acceleration of modernity animated an encounter that was relentlessly dialectical. To begin with, the changes induced were dialectical because the presence of Western practices reshaped indigenous ones and simultaneously the determinate appearance of Western practices (schooling, medicine, Christian rites, elections), which were inseparable from, because mutually determined by, their local counterparts. For example, to the frustration of the mission men, the Mar-

ing conception of Jesus, his miracles, and his place in the social cosmology
has been inseparable from Maring conceptions of ancestors, magic, and
clanship. In the same spirit, their views of Western medicine and justice
informed and were informed by more indigenous concepts and practices.
Reciprocally, the weight of Western practices forever transformed the trajectory and meaning of indigenous practices to the point where the distinction between Western and indigenous becomes progressively rela-
tivized and the subject of its own discourse. The intertwining of thought,
desire, and practice in an endlessly reciprocal spiral is itself a hallmark of
the Melanesian encounter with the modern. And so we fail the ethnography when our theory and method fail to capture this dialectic, substituting
in its place simple lines of causation, such as those that imagine a world of
an imposing West and resisting Other. It sometimes seems as though the
anthropological nostalgia for Culture and the academic imperative to
defend our space by defending our concept blinds us to the reality that the
processes of encompassment neither leave others alone nor make them
Western. Rather, encompassment creates new terrain and terms for the
production of sameness and difference, value and meaning.

Importantly, to understand the modern as dialectical is to relativize
relativity. It is to acknowledge that what is considered (and contested) as
kastam today has been inflected by Western presence and pressures, just as
what is considered Western (parliamentary government, Christianity, the
use of Western-like money, etc.) now bears an unmistakable Melanesian
imprint. The modern is also intrinsically dialectical because encompassment is most determinative and inevitable at the level of the form of society. All encompassed peoples will become capitalist—but to what degree
and in what way is first open to and defined by the intersection of imported
capitalism with local practices, and then triangulated as international capitalism continues to interface with its domestic offspring (itself the product
of the first interaction), and also with what local agents come to define as
tradition or kastam. And what holds for capitalism is also true for the
nation-state, commercial culture, civic education, the mass media, and
much else. In a word, the modern is a dialectic of sameness and difference,
a negotiated terrain in which the absolute difference between Melanesians
and Westerners, that heavenly time before contact and encompassment, is
no more or less than an imaginary space, albeit a necessary space, that
allows anthropologists to construct the past and Melanesians the future.

Ethnography must honor this dialectic to avoid what has been a persistent problem in Melanesian studies. The tendency is to so fetishize how
Melanesians differ from Westerners that their similarities disappear. There
are no commonalities of conception and spirit. No points of commensurability that would allow a conversation to take place across cultures. What
we can understand of others is their difference and how, due to the weight

of colonialism, capitalism, and Western cultural imperialism, these differences are gradually and grudgingly being effaced. This vision tends to tell the story of encompassment in oppositional terms, reducing it to a war of Western domination versus local resistance. Indeed, the story is too often told as a machine of domination on one side and a history of small victories on the other, memorialized in stories (usually told with a wry smile) of how local agents outwitted missionaries, patrol officers, and other soldiers of modernity. Somehow, in a kind of backhand tribute to the "human" spirit, certain practices are thought to have come through the Western onslaught unscathed. More than theoretical, our attachment to this position has deep roots in the anthropological psyche (but that is a matter for another time, another chapter). The trouble with this way of thinking is that it cannot erase the realities of encompassment—the fact that big oil and various Christianities, the English language and the commercial culture of rock, democratic forms of governance and statutory law, the World Bank and the United Nations, are now so much a part of Melanesian history that the encompassment of Melanesia is part of our history. And African history and southeast Asian history and Amazonian history. This view also embraces a kind of romanticism that must see the modern as exogenous to the strategies and interests of local agents. It must pretend that people are not enchanted, seduced, and desirous of the modern,[4] and that, even more, the ground of enchantment and desire were not original conditions of the indigenous world. And finally, this viewpoint tends to see the purveyors of the modern, the missionaries, doctors, state officials, and the like, as a homogeneous class (the anthropologist excepted). As I will argue, none of these propositions is more than half true.[5] To keep the dialectic in sight seems the first job of modern ethnography.

The dialectic of the modern is also necessarily hierarchical because one of its principal turbines is the interaction among structures of different orders of magnitude, power, and intelligibility. More than anything else, this is a story of mediation. The ethnographic challenge is to document how the state, provincial and local governments, Christian missions and missionaries, health clinics, schools, the judicial system, the mass media, and commerce in the capitalist spirit, all mediate the relationship between the forces of encompassment and local societies, even as they come to embody both. This story involves not only how the Maring were encompassed and transformed but also how they, like local agents throughout Melanesia, reformed the institutions and agents of mediation. As the account unfolds, we will see that this relationship is self-consciously important to the Maring, and that they conceptualize mediation practically in terms of the now familiar concept of kastam. In this respect, the category *kastam* was triangulated. It was defined against things Western and those foreign forces that impinged on local lifeways, and also against local conceptions of what being modern is: what the Maring, like other Melanesians, call *bisnis,* a word of Tok Pijin origin that is now, appropriately and ironically, equally Tok Plas (the indigenous language). This triangulated category was part and product of the Maring way of knowing their world and was inseparable not only from an epistemology of knowledge but of desire and disposition.

The heartbeat of my account is social desire and epistemology. I am concerned with the new terms and conditions under which people represent and objectify their experience and define their wants. The question is, How does the advance of the modern change the very foundations of experience by reshaping people's notions and categories of knowledge, the means by which they grasp their world and the conditions of its representation to themselves and to others, and the forms of desire appropriate to this new world? My intent is not to grasp these changes in knowledge and desire in the abstract, but to locate them in two ways: first, to view them within the political economy of change, especially the rise of the nation and the influence of the state, the penetration of capitalism into rural areas, the internationalization of Western culture, the advent of affordable forms (e.g., radio) of mass media communication, and especially the emergence of generation as the critical social category; second, to locate the changes in knowledge, desire, and disposition within lived practice, such as going to school or a medical clinic, listening to a radio commercial about the virtue of a commodity or political candidate, or having to deal with anthropologists. These transformations also and simultaneously forged new conditions for the construction of personhood and peoplehood. For example, emerging local capitalism tended to endorse forms of interpersonal relations, such as acting "greedy," that were formerly unequivocally defined as antisocial and worthy of condemnation (e.g., ancestral retribution); simultaneously, the empowerment of these forms of relations and their embodiment as dispositions to behave a certain way in specified situations (e.g., when managing a trade store) tended to promote the development of indigenous capitalism. Changes in the way Maring define themselves and produce an identity go hand in hand with the transformations motivated by, and built into, new practices.

The book shapes an argument that is at once ethnographic and theoretical. To grasp the changes that beset the Maring requires that we locate their communities in the process of encompassment. This encounter unfolds dialectically as an intricate set of mediations and mediating institutions, such as the Anglican Church, that analysis must explicate in order to comprehend the shape of the encounter. The most profound aspect of this encounter is the transformation of Maring epistemology, desires, and dispositions because, once set in motion, these transformations touch off an endless wave of other changes. These transformations are embodied within, and especially apparent in, members of the junior generation who embrace and struggle with modernity as the key to their own future. The thesis is that for an account of modernity to be adequate to its object it must include an explicit account of encompassment and the externalization of social life; it must include an account of power and the conditions of its production; it must include a theory of generations, which is to say a theory of the interplay between the objective structure of practice and the cognitive and motivating structures that drive behavior; finally, it must include an account of the transformation of indigenous epistemology and desires produced by the modernizing process. The explicit claim is that the most critical, transformative aspects of the Maring encounter with Westerners and Western practices were the changes introduced in their social epistemology and the organization of desire. Though it is easier to focus on and catalog visible change, such as the building of a new road or attending church, these changes were ultimately more telling because they were generative; once they existed, they assumed a life and dynamic of their own; once they were ingrained, they redefined reality from the silent underside of practice.

On this account, each of the chapters develops the following perspective. What is critical about the appearance and local appropriation of Western practices and values is that these practices and values embody Western epistemology and desires. These Western exports are transformative because they (a) are imbued with power based on "indigenous" images of efficacy and modernity; (b) operate not only consciously but on a nonconscious plane (e.g., as presuppositions to action); and (c) become inscribed in the shape of thought, desires, and practice. The motivated changes are so generative because they become married to the remaking of subjectivity and peoplehood. The Maring's own conception of themselves as a collectivity, the possession of an identity that oversteps the limits of clanship and affinity, was directly bound to a notion and knowledge of kastam as distinct from, and generated in opposition to, what they understood to be Western ways of knowing, desiring, and living. What complicates the matter is that the local ways of "knowing" what kastam is, and what Westerners are, are themselves products of the encompassing encounter. In this regard, social epistemology is connected and homologous to language in that every change in content is also a change in form that, in turn, informs the interpretation of any future content. Moreover, these changes in knowing were inseparable from the self-acknowledged and visible changes in the production of persons. As Moses, the leader of the most successful locally run trade store in the Jimi Valley noted, what the new road demanded was people who know, and know how to discover what they need to know and do, to win in the time of the "white world."

What Moses left for ethnographers to say is that this "new" episte-

mology bears a family resemblance to its antecedents because it is a synthesis between that which is embodied in Western practices and local
means of apprehending, appropriating, and representing the world. A
"new" conceptual and emotional landscape comes into being that is not
Western, indigenous, or even some logical combination of the two. One
indication of this was that the "Westernization" of Maring epistemology
and desire varied from one context/practice to another. Certain practices
retained a semblance of traditional epistemology, whereas others, like
going to the health clinic, inclined greatly toward a Westernized set of concepts. The result was that people professed and depended on mutually
contradictory epistemologies. To the extent that knowledge is power, and
the power to know one's world is empowering (e.g., by speaking English),
these two epistemologies were in a state of struggle. The modern also buffeted most people, and most of all the junior generation, between a desire
for freedom—the chance to fly above the demands of kinship and community—and a desire to remake and reawaken the autonomy of that community. It was precisely this contention, discord, and ambiguity between the
modes of knowing and desiring-in-living that defined the modern era.

Though this account concerns the Maring, and only during one
specific if crucial period, it is also responsive to a wider set of issues affect-
ing the "culture area" called Melanesia and that theory of "others" called
anthropology (even when "we" are those "others"). The claim is that
global processes are made manifest in specific cases through the agents and
institutions of mediation. On this terrain, the ethnography deals with the
vexing problem of the way knowledge and desire, as rooted in cultural
practice and the infrastructure of the everyday (housing styles, treating an
illness, etc.), become transformed forms of what they were, and further,
how these changes in knowing and desiring inform the shaping and
reshaping of personhood and peoplehood. What are the processes that
encourage the emergence of the possessive individual? How do social relations mediated by kin and community become social relations mediated by
labor? When do the Maring cease to be a "culture" and become an ethnic
group? How do people deal with the confrontation between the binding
sociality of community and the unhinged freedom of modern lifeways? To
begin to answer these questions (and this is only a beginning) entails that
we travel analytically up and down among structures of different genesis,
degrees of transparency, power, and orders of magnitude. It entails finding
a space and language to expose the conjuncture of global forces (e.g., capitalism), the specific and often contingent appearance of those forces (e.g.,
as pressed by local missionaries), the structure and structuring principles
of local practice, plus the creativity and innovations of agents in these situations—their "experimental practice," to exchange a phrase with the
Comaroffs. The way that I see it, anthropology's devotion to (not to say

fixation on) the local sphere is now its greatest virtue and its singular limitation. The challenge is to incorporate the character of encompassment into our images of theory and ethnography without sacrificing our commitment and devotion to the local. This is not an original insight, but it does remind us that to grasp the reality of a world encompassed we need to rise above the methodological mud of localism.

Global, Local, and In-Between

The temptation is to frame my argument within the discourse of globalization, the understanding being that a work receives a better reading if the categories used to construct it match those that will be used to decipher it. The threat, especially with a subject as unwieldy and uncharted as globalization, is that the categories often seem to think in our place. Certainly, in much of the literature thus far, the analyses appear to simply ride the back of badly assembled categories. To begin with, the term *globalization* is a misnomer, a kind of deliberate disavowal of the politics in process. It leaves the impression that what we are witnessing is simply ever widening concentric circles of engulfment in the world (dis)order. The global swallows the local, creating sameness in the place of difference. As Robertson (1992) underlines, the growth of global institutions and movements, the speed and reach of communication, an expanding universal concern for the environment, a commitment to capitalism, the ascendence of the problem of individual rights, and a sense of "world citizenship" characterize the modern phase of globalization (59). The contemplated result is that the nation-state is a bystander in its own future, as the global flows and traffic in internationalized culture ignore national boundaries (Hannerz 1989), delivering a once unimaginable ensemble of representations, objects, information, and desires to unimaginably diverse peoples and places (Appadurai 1990). Or so the story has been told from the top down, from the insiders out.

For the Maring and the peoples of Oceania, like those of Black Africa, the Indian populations of South America, and a good deal of Southeast Asia, the modern age is the age of encompassment. The structures of economy and polity, the dissemination of culture and flows of information, the reach of the notion of individual rights, and everything else swept up by the term *globalization* unfold in a highly asymmetrical context in which they have, and have had since the age of empire, almost no voice. The people of Melanesia do not experience the radiating waves of globalization, they absorb, reshape, and respond to the changing face and forces of encompassment by the Western metropole. Guided by their own stars, they do this in ways that are never predictable from the charac-

ter of the encompassing agents and institutions alone. As the many species
of Catholicism, never mind versions of Christianity, should remind us,
even the powers of the Vatican (at once spiritual, institutional, and economic) are insufficient to guarantee that abstract signs—the Virgin Mary
comes immediately to mind—will possess even a semblance of universally
uniform local meanings and values. Equally important are the ways that
the modern Melanesian state, shorn of some of the original (for emerging
nations, only imaginary) powers, intercedes between the encompassing
world and indigenous agents, often creatively, sometimes capriciously,
and always particularly. However our epoch unleashes capitalism, it is
always as an intertwining with local markets, paths of circulation, modes
of production, and conceptions of consumption. "Macrocosmic moderni-
ties, in sum, [are] at once singular and plural, specific and general,
parochial and global in their manifestations" (Comaroff and Comaroff
1997:6).

The removal of the political, and hence critical, edge of analysis—
through the image of globalization—cohabits with a diffuse notion of
power. Power here seeps into the most remote corners of sociality and subjectivity, guided by unstable signs in search of even the most temporary of
homes. That sign systems may be porous and at times unstable, the value
of practices and action less than determinate, the expression of power
never exhausted by the political—while certainly true—is taken to mean
the absence of any larger social determinations. But such a perspective can
never account for the experience of those places and peoples who continue
to reside in the shadow of an encompassing West. Such a perspective can
never account for the forms of (historically determinate) totality that
motivate the production and reproduction of hegemonies that, despite the
instability of signs and actions, not to mention the everywhereness of
power, impose a substantial measure of order and stability on ourselves
and others. And have done so for at least the better part of two centuries.
The argument shaped here, which is no more than a literal reading of the
Melanesian experience, is that the intrinsic relationship between capitalism, the nation-state, and internationalized Western culture produces
larger social determinations.

In the framework of my analysis, the significant issue is how the state,
intranational regimes of production and exchange, and the appearance of
culture in specific locales mediate the relationship between encompassment and community. The concern is the construction of a particularity
that has critical threads of sameness in the face of apparently homogeneous and universalizing forces that, on closer examination, reveal critical
threads of particularity. On this score, the discourse of globalization is frequently uninstructive because of an overdeveloped sense of homogeniza-
tion. Too often the idea is that the globalizing capitalist economy is oblit-
erating local economies only to remake them in its own reflection

(Hopkins and Wallerstein 1987; Wallerstein 1990; Kurtzman 1993; among others). Either as an attachment or alone, there is the corollary notion of the disappearance of the state, as global forces progressively overtake and compromise its sovereignty. Never mind that most of the states of what is euphemistically called the Third World are very much alive, rapidly adapting to the modern shape of encompassment, even as they struggle to "regain" a sovereignty they never had. Finally, theorists of the modern have told us that, insofar as the globalization of culture expunges the conditions for the production of local images and identities, cultural localism will wither away (Gellner 1987). The problem with this take on globalization is not that capitalism has renounced its predatory march, or that missions and mass media do not proselytize Western culture, or that migration, electronic commerce, and the like are not dissembling aspects of the state. The problem is that the forces of localism, and the entrenchment of heterogeneity, are themselves constitutive of the globalizing process. Buttressed by its intimacy with the local, the anthropological thesis is that the encompassment and localization of cultural, economic, and political production are two moments of the same process (Foster 1991:235–36; Hannerz 1992: chap. 9; Comaroff 1996:194). Perhaps the most profound irony is that postmodern accounts of globalization reproduce the Eurocentric philosophy of imperialist expansion by portraying the relationship between globalization and localization as a struggle between universality and particularisms, thereby simultaneously misrecognizing the particularity of the West and the relations of power thus implicated in the process of encompassment.

Contrary to much of the grander theorizing on globalization, the anthropological thesis insists on the mutuality of local and global, and hence the absolute necessity of taking the particular seriously—the local in all its complications, manifold relations, and lines of mediation. The vernacular as a token that is more than a type. Objecting to the tendency to ignore the particulars in favor of the hegemony of "triumphant categories," Geertz writes, "matters are cast on a resolutely grand and abstract scale, a dialectic of mega-concepts heavily annotated with opportune mini-facts, assembled from here, there and elsewhere, rather in the manner of a lawyer's brief" (1983:517). But this will not do. Encompassment can only be grasped when analysis joins a theory of capitalism, the nation-state, and internationalized culture adequate to its object to an account of locality adequate to its.

Lines of "Influence" or the Sea of Coauthors

My project does not come out of the wilderness. It owes a debt of gratitude and builds upon the accounts woven by other ethnographers and historians. Though the focus is somewhat different, my analysis takes much of its intellectual and spiritual inspiration from the work done by Jean and John Comaroff (1991, 1992, 1997) on the relationship between Christianity, colonialism, and consciousness in South Africa, and Simon Schama (1988) on the origins of capitalism and peoplehood among the Dutch. Both Schama and the Comaroffs have written cultural history in the most complete sense of the term—histories able to bear the full weight of culture and ethnographies that live within their own temporality. Having done three years of field research in northwestern Spain (Galicia), I have drawn comparatively on my own understanding of Western culture and class (see LiPuma and Meltzoff 1989 and 1994), and from the European social theory tradition, most immediately from the work of Pierre Bourdieu (esp. 1962, 1977, 1987) and Moishe Postone (1993). My aim has been to join the sophisticated analyses of culture, class, and consciousness in the West with the historical processes now unfolding throughout Melanesia. Though those who study Melanesia have been slow to hear the drumbeat of encompassment, there has been a recent acceleration of interest, led by the pioneering studies of Robert Foster (1991, 1993, 1995b), Deborah Gewertz and Fred Errington (1991, 1995), and Andrew Strathern (1996), plus several critical edited volumes (Carrier 1992; van Meijl and van der Grijp 1994; Linnekin and Poyer 1990). What all these studies have in common is an attempt to thematize and theorize the issues surrounding modernity.

I am Western, writing for a mostly scientific audience, and so in keeping with my own cultural traditions I will assume full responsibility and also, of course, credit for what I write here. In a very non-Melanesian way, I will remove the social relationships out of which this work was created to footnotes, citations, and acknowledgments. I will detach this work from the body of others though I know on very good authority that it embodies their labor—my labor simply mediating between their labors and the production of the text. In the absence of these others, this book might not have come into being at all and certainly not in its present shape. Among other things, this practice of citation and acknowledgment insures that our ideology of the autonomous individual (the author) and the commodity form (the book) remain unchallenged. They remain in their misrecognized state because that is what is necessary to reproduce our way of life. Under the euphemisms of *influence* and *sources,* this practice externalizes the social and intellectual relations that are internal to the construction of the text—lest the individual and the individuality of the author be compromised. Let it be said immediately that no Maring would entertain these concerns. They assume that persons and the things they produce, from garden vegetables to flowery speeches, are joined to their sociality. A person is partly and only ever partly the author and cause of his/her own actions. If, as scientists of ourselves, we were to expose the highly social process of the construction of the ethnography, it would undermine the ideology of the autonomous commodity producer on which we base our notions of scientific production, presentation, and reward.

Or suppose we turn the tables and imagine that a Maring ethnographer of the West is examining our views of authorship and agency. To this imaginary eye, the claim that authors divine ideas that are wholly original and fully their own would be understood as neither more nor less than the Western ideology of the narrative construction of the Western self. Our commitment to the ideologies of the individual and the pure commodity guarantees that this book will appear to be extrinsic both to its producer, me, and the set of relations that have produced me. So it will go under my name alone and have a life of its own as a product circulated in the scientific field even though I deserve neither full credit nor full responsibility for what I say here. The joy and terror of the person in culture—especially in capitalist societies—is that we are given singularly rewards we have not won alone and punishments we do not singularly deserve. I highlight the relation between the ideology of the individual and that of the commodity form in respect to my own production because this relation figures centrally in my discussion of how Westerners would like the Maring to imagine the person and the object world. As I will argue, one of the ironies of the Maring encounter with the modern is that because they subscribe to a notion of the person that more closely resembles Western reality than Western ideology, the agents of modernity considered them tradition-bound and unmodern. I will underline the point by noting that the West considers Others never more "primitive" than when they resemble us in ways that we cannot, and mostly do not, admit to ourselves on pain of not reproducing ourselves as individuals of the capitalist nation-state. A critical irony is that the Western discourse of the "primitive"—or, in its more advanced anthropological form, the uniqueness of the Other—is a conversation about ourselves thought through the body of others. Luckily, Melanesians such as the Maring return the favor. They think of themselves through the body of Westerners insofar as missionaries, ethnographers, and the like socially exemplify those aspects of the subject that the Maring consider non- or antisocial.

Framing the Ethnography

The "ethnographic present" is no longer contemporaneous with itself, if it ever was. Recognizing this, we are (like those we study, like the Maring) enjoined by change to separate ourselves from our traditions—meaning that we must give our narratives a historical frame, a set of temporal brackets that define what we know and can say aloud. A big-man, Yingok, once enumerated for me everything that was novel since he was a young boy, counting off rhythmically, beginning with the appearance of airplanes and the stoppage of warfare, the cultural arrivals and departures of these years. What happened during his lifetime is the epicenter of the ethnography that follows. The historical period is the quarter century after the arrival of the patrol officers and the founding of an Anglican mission when the first generation of Maring, educated and exposed to Western practices, were coming of age. I wish to document their experience and convey something of their struggle to be a person in a world so changed in form and substance that little in their cultural memory could have prepared them for. The time frame is from 1955 to 1980, when the oldest generation could recall a life unfettered by foreign rules and interventions; the generation in power, aged thirty to mid-fifties, had been brought up in a traditional world but lived now wholly in the modern; plus a younger generation who had never known a world untouched by missions and government and capitalism. This process of encompassment ignited a struggle between generations, not least over the generation of generations. Where before the cultural memories laid down in the cycles of war and peace defined a generation, now the mode of generation would revolve on the nonlinear and often indeterminate interrelationship between the Maring and the agents and institutions of encompassment.

To focus on encompassment in Melanesia is to give an account of the conquest of consciousness in its embryonic phase. It is also a study of a people's consciousness of this conquest. These two moments are increasingly imbricated, bound in the cultural and psychic spiral toward modernity: what the Maring refer to as "the new road." Literally, new roads are signs of modernity. They connect places and people in ways that were barely conceivable prior to contact. They create new forms of relatedness, animating the flow of novel views, values, goods, and services—plus a swelling stream of "old" goods and services such as pigs and sorcery. The image of the interconnecting road or path has always had metaphorical weight, symbolizing marriage and military alliance between clans. As a conjunction of the old and new, there can be no more appropriate or strategic image than that of a new road. Metaphorically, the new road may be seen as connecting two overlapping topological spaces, each with its own habitus and generative principles, and hence forms of personhood and peoplehood. What happens when the objective structure that instilled the dispositions, desires, and senses of one generation has, by virtue of encompassment, become so transformed that different dispositions, desires, and senses are instilled in the next? There is a generation gap, a gap in the way in which humans are shaped into specific kinds of subjects. At issue is how subjectivity and peoplehood are constructed when the conditions of their construction undergo such a dramatic and overarching change. Two arguments, which are connecting threads throughout the book, are anticipated here. The first is that an account of generation, as category and practice, is essential to an ethnography of modernity adequate to its object. The concept of generation, long undertheorized and bracketed, must now be brought to the foreground. The second argument is that true understanding of the reshaping of subjectivity and identity entails an account of the relationship between encompassment and epistemology—or more precisely, epistemologies. At issue is how the frame of knowing of everyday life transforms in response to Westernization of the world.

Speaking in the Ethnographic Past

That period from 1955 to 1980 is a strategic time-frame for several reasons. It was during this period that the universe of goods and services for purchase, and even more for contemplation, expanded dramatically. By 1980, Maring were making regular runs (via the Christian air service to and from Koinambe) to Mt. Hagen, the provincial capital and primary Europeanized marketing center. Led by six men in their mid-twenties, two of whom were fluent in English as well as pidgin, there began a steady flow of consumer products into the western Jimi Valley. It was, as noted, within this epoch that the first generation that had grown up under the sway of encompassment came of age. With very few exceptions all were baptized Anglicans, with some believing, some understanding the doctrines of Christianity. They spoke pidgin well, had been schooled in a Western fashion, and were vibrantly conscious of the increasingly monetary nature of the world. In great contrast to their parents, they had uniformly sojourned to the coast to work on a plantation, experiencing new forms of social hierarchy, new forms of leadership, the politics of resistance and regionalism, and, of course, wage labor. It was also during this period that cash cropping for coffee became integral to village life, Western money forms (such as Papua New Guinea kina) replaced traditional shell valuables, and gold was discovered and panned for. By the mid-1970s, the Maring had also become well acquainted with anthropologists. By 1980, more than a dozen ethnographers had lived with various clan clusters. For their part, the Maring recognized that ethnographers were valuable economic and political assets, and they fast developed strategies to make the best use of them. By 1980, the signs if not the concepts of modernity had dug into the cultural landscape to the extent that its hallmarks, from fifty-pound bags of rice to the Christian cross, had become taken-for-granted features of life. Where before the Maring's own signscape was the unspoken and presupposed condition of seeing and being, now there was a proliferation of contesting signs, of alternatives for the gaze and stringbag. And thus it came to be that a certain species of Christianity, a certain arm of state power, a certain way of being the subject of inquiry, a certain concept of and desire for Western goods, an awareness of cultural distinctiveness (e.g., the difference between whites and blacks), and much more became inseparable from the local concept of modernity. On all fronts the period from the mid-1950s to 1980 was a time of unprecedented change in Maring lifeways.

It was also a time of erasure and forgetting. For the first time, exposed to the power of Christianity, people imagined that the sacred groves would no longer be used to worship the spirits. Like a sentimental object that no longer has any use but you also cannot bring yourself to destroy, the sacred groves were simply left to be consumed by rain and time and encroaching vegetation. Pressured by the Australian kiaps, the Maring realized for the first time that the rituals and weapons of war were things of the past. And all the powers of colonization let them know that their way of attending to their dead, left to decay on raised outdoor platforms, was profane (or, at least, unsanitary). Within this period, the traditional organization of marriage transformed, and shell money all but disappeared. Everything from the way they were born and married and cared for their young to the way they defecated and died was called into question. It is not just that colonization produced a break with the past in the sense that people acquired new practices and learned about other worlds; by its very nature it demanded that they forget, erase, and devalue, not least that they reconfigure the lights of self-understanding. Christianity, the modern state, and science were presented to the Maring as an explanatory scheme, a scheme that revealed how Melanesians were to appreciate nature, their own bodies, public life, and the culture of the subject. The reason that they had to devote Mondays to road building and other public work was that this was a state imperative; such work for the commonweal as good for the soul as it was for the local economy. In the same vein, the building of latrines at a safe, specified distance from living quarters, and the immediate burial of the dead, were health measures: they were explained by the science of disease, enforced by the state, thus to bring them through these acts of cleanliness that much closer to Christian godliness.

The cosmology of modernity seems an everexpanding universe; the continual increase in possible goods and services, access to new images and ideologies, the expansion of the public political sphere, the inflation of needs and wants, the emergence of novel technologies of power, and the rise of new forms of mass communication and conversation. And this is only for starters. The cosmology of modernity also seems to involve a contraction in local control, an imploding universe when viewed from the standpoint of social relatedness, certainty, and the security of everyday life. Unbalanced reciprocity rules. In exchange for the wonders of modernity the Maring, like others of Melanesia, must surrender their ways of being a people, their social identity. In this universe, the alignment of forces seems rather straightforward: capitalism, Christianity, Western commercialized culture, and the state imposing themselves on the small-scale societies of Melanesia. The contest here is between an imperial West—driven by the economics of capital accumulation, the politics of the colonial state, and the heavenly commandment to save pagan souls—and cultures that find ways to resist, fend off, and appropriate this Western advance. Or so it seems.

The ethnographic reality is more nuanced, more given over to complex struggles at all levels. The dialectic of encompassment generates a far more intricate tapestry, history conspiring with chance to produce a modernity stamped by its multidimensionality, internal contradictions, and unpredictability. There is no easy historical and ethnographic navigation. The oppositional logics of modernity and tradition, domination and resistance, the local versus the world system, though they come all too easily to mind, do not begin to capture the signs and substance of what is going on here. The transformation of Melanesia is not the result of a simple logical union between the imported and domestic models of reality (Meltzoff and LiPuma 1986:54). Rather, it is more akin to the improvisational dance, which is also a struggle, in which the participants, wittingly and unwittingly, continually respond and change over the course of a dance that does not, cannot, end. As it unfolds, the story of Maring modernity will bear this out. It will also testify to the force of the encompassing process.

The Encompassment of Others

Since World War II, the most powerful and insistent dynamic of societal transformations has been the globalization of modernity, or what anthropologists have more prosaically called social change. On this view, modernity represents a special kind of sociocultural transformation, moved by imperatives as diverse as the exportation of Western mass media culture and modern forms of electronic capitalism to the realization that the "ecological" politics of one nation-state may have telling implications for so many others. If there is a major feature of the globalization of modernity, it is the West's relentless embrace of other histories and territories. From island Oceania to the New Guinea Highlands peoples who have long stood at the epicenter of our discourse now join labor unions, form women's rights organizations, consciously engage in the politics of the nation-state, contemplate the nature of democracy and human rights, invoke the music and images of MTV and Christian broadcasting, attend Western-like schools, learn to speak English, appropriate a wide variety of Western technologies, and are increasingly immersed in mass commodity culture: and this is only for starters. The West has effectively othered others.

But being an "Other" is no easy assignment. Not for Maring or Melanesians generally. It involves a sort of cultural jujitsu in which people absorb and redirect the blows even as they seek to avoid being overpowered. So we find agents using "traditional cultural" sensibilities to deflect a modernizing gesture, such as efforts to relocate a village or introduce tourism (Errington and Gewertz 1996), even as the encounter subtly reconfigures these sensibilities. Even as the reconfigured sensibilities inform and thus alter the trajectory of still future encounters with the modern. Forbidden to bury their dead on raised outdoor platforms, the Maring began to bury them on raised underground platforms, thus preserving their moral geography even as they bow to the modern health code. The examples are as endless as the modern itself, but the point is that to grasp the nature of this dialectic, the anthropology of modernity[6] needs a theory of encompassment—a perspective that grasps the space in which modernizing forces and local communities become inseparable moments of each other's history.

I use the term *encompassment* to refer to those processes, at once historical and structural, by which the political economy of capitalism, the state (in colonial and national versions), internationalized Western culture, and interstate organizations (like the World Bank) progressively and simultaneously subsume, enchant, and engulf others. I refer to others in the plural to underscore that the "standardization and formalization" of life necessary to imagine an Other—whether the Other be the Orient, the Primitive, Black Africa, or whatever—is itself one of the ideological tropes of encompassment. Each of these aspects of encompassment has its own historical origins, animating force, and distinctive features. The contemporary conjuncture and codevelopment of these faces of encompassment in relation to local cultures and community is, for the peoples of Melanesia, modernity, "the new road," civilization, or simply the future. The issue here is not whether the "static" or "cold" structure of tradition will now become historical. The issue is that long bridge from already dynamic structures based on local, cyclical, and nearly determinate forms of social reproduction to a structure of externally motivated, perpetually indeterminate, noncyclical (and nonlinear) transformation.

This approach to Melanesian modernity marries the history of encompassment to the anthropology of culture. It recognizes that confronted with the exceedingly powerful and cumulative forces of encompassment, the cultures and people of Melanesia are tellingly transformed.

A dialectic is set in motion that forever changes their historical trajectory, and also (though less powerfully) the sources of encompassment. It is this interface and intersection, a power-infused, asymmetrical, mutually dynamic relationship, that is the engine of historical change. Ethnographically, this means that an account of modernity must focus on the encounter and interplay between the institutions, processes, and agents of both sociohistorical structures—the colonizer and the colonized, the embracing state and the local community. It is necessary that we tell both sides of the story. The story of the priest as well as the shaman; the story of the Western medical personnel as well as local healers; the story of the patrol officer as well as the big-man; and of course the story of the anthropologist as well as the informants.

These encounters were shaped by, and experienced as, partially interpenetrating and asymmetrical structures of signification and power. Up until 1980, the encounters were partially (as opposed to fully) interpenetrating because the Maring, ensconced in the hinterlands, still retained a good measure of autonomy. The autonomy allowed local agents to exercise some control over the personality and pace of modernity (as when, for example, some Kauwatyi expelled the locally residing Anglican deacon in 1977). The encounters were nonetheless asymmetrical because the degree to which the Maring could transform the West was nowhere near the power of the West to transform them. Finally, the encounters involved signification and power in that the existence of agents and institutions of encompassment could not but transform the context and content of the production of meaning and value. The local health station, to cite an example to which we shall return, combined, mediated, and arbitrated the tension between the Western forms of medicine religiously promoted by medical personnel at the Anglican mission station and traditional health remedies. In the Maring region, these outposts were part of a conduit that "Westernized" indigenous medical tenets and treatments and "indigenized" the Western practice of medicine—although the Maring did not, of course, request that their indigenous practices be Westernized, and their power to localize Western practice was circumscribed. Responding (at long last one might say) to these and the other changes animated by encompassment, Melanesian anthropology has begun to chart the ways in which power and signification are now being transmuted. Issues such as the mass media and commercialized culture, the production of national identities, the reorganization of desire, and the "cultural consciousness" of culture itself are now on the menu. This turn to the study of encompassment marks a critical refocusing, a sea change in our conception of the anthropological subject/object and consequently in the theories and methods that have oriented analyses. Importantly, it requires that we abandon the assumption that individual cultures or sets of cultures (like those of the

New Guinea Highlands) exist in some totalized state. It entails recognizing that there now exists an *intrinsic* (versus external) relationship between the structure of a culture and the encompassing forms. It tells us that if we (and the "we" here is all those who practice science) are to grasp the coming of modernity to Melanesia we must (re)locate ethnography to that partially shared world of historical experience. It means that we have to abandon the romance (and terror) of a divided universe, and locate ethnography in the interstitial space where the Western and Melanesian worlds overlap, collide, and make each other.

Under these sociopolitical conditions, Melanesian societies (such as the Maring) have no ontological autonomy other than that imagined, mapped, institutionalized, and contested in the public political sphere. The existence of these societies is inseparable from the totalizing project of first the colonial and now the nation-state, as this project has unfolded in the contexts of capitalism and internationalized Western culture. Less than fifty years ago the name, the category *Maring* had no real indigenous resonance, the Maring only "learning" that this was their collective name in the 1960s. By 1980, the Maring did exist, a notion of peoplehood having won considerable ground. They began to think of their own practices and language as an integrated, closed, and autonomous system—their "nomane" in contrast to that of neighboring peoples such as the Kalam and Manga. Gradually, at times grudgingly, the Maring came to imagine and construct a notion of sameness, of what they all possessed in common, in opposition to a white Western world that grasped the world in terms of peoplehoods and races. In other words, there is no way to talk about "the Maring," "the Enga," or "the Melpa" other than in the context of encompassment. The local subclans, clans, and clan clusters existed long before the first tall ships touched the Melanesian shores, but the Maring as a people, as a critical aspect of the construction of the subject, this is of modern origin. And for the Kauwatyi, Tsembaga, or Tukmenga to think of themselves also as Maring (not to mention as Highlander or Papua New Guinean) is to turn their own subjectivity toward the modern. The conception that the Maring have no ontological existence other than that imagined, contested, and institutionalized in the public sphere is radical only in the context of Western societies that, as a condition of their own production, must self-conceal the reality that they are so too constructed. Understanding this is critical because one of the primary ways in which the West naturalizes its notion of the social is through its power to create societies everywhere that it goes. It is through the "discovery" of "societies" in the most remote corners of the world—and few places are as remote as the Highlands of New Guinea—that the West assures itself of the naturalness of society. In essence, by imposing its historically constructed concept of society on Others, and then imagining that it has discovered what was always there, the capitalist, Christian, nation-state can naturalize its concept of society so successfully that the concept can become the doxic basis of its own structure and self-understanding.

This turn in the compass of study can also be read ironically in that anthropology is returning to the site of its own genesis: the fact that the birth of ethnography was inextricably linked to the march of Western capitalism, colonialism, culture. Even more and more personally, this says that our (and my) romance with the people of Melanesia is bound to modernity and the vast transformations inspired by the process of encompassment. All this has been well-confessed even as the consequences of encompassment have been sublimated, partly out of respect for others' cultures, partly out of fear that these other ways of being human were destined to disappear, and partly because it was undeniable that anthropology was and cannot help but continue to be a part of the encompassing processes. While the character and consequences of encompassment have been confessed (actually, overconfessed by a certain kind of mea culpa anthropology that forgets the good faith and good works of so many fieldworkers), they have not been adequately theorized or melded into anthropological discourse, in what might be called a kind of collective defense mechanism on our part. It is easier either to repress the implications of encompassment or to slap on a postmodern face and dismiss ethnography as beset by objectivist and logocentric leanings than actually to come to terms with the confrontation between the West and peoples of Melanesia. In this light, my objective is to begin to define an anthropology that is also a social history of what happened to the Maring during their initial moments of the advent of the modern. I operate under the assumption that the processes of encompassment are very telling at the local level. They inflect (and deflect) the practices of everyday life by changing the way people think and desire their world. They transform the habitus of senses and dispositions. It is this mediation between the systemic and local that is the ground of anthropology. It is where we have the most expertise and can do the most good.

The Power of Encompassment

It is sometimes said (accurately) that the colonization of Melanesia was a benign, civilized, genteel affair at least as compared with Africa and South America. By the time the colonization of Melanesia, and especially the Highlands, got under way, the heyday of colonialism had faded over the historical horizon, the attitudes and perceptions of those who came had become more tolerant of their others, and in any case, the thirst for raw materials by the industrial world had lessened since the advent of the technological revolution. Colonialism in the late twentieth century was not the same as its nineteenth-century ancestor. And indeed, few peoples of Melanesia have felt the exercise of power in its most crushing, overt, agentive mode. There is no Melanesian Montezuma or Australian Cortez, no imprisoned Mandela slowly wresting power from a belligerent white minority. Few attempts have been made to directly control the production, exchange, and circulation of signs and objects, or extract a surplus at gunpoint. Certainly the Maring have rarely experienced, and have not incorporated in their grasp of modernity, such forms of domination or hegemony—a point that apologists for colonialism in Melanesia (such as Sinclair 1981) have smilingly exploited.

But there exists another species of power that is mostly out of sight. It acts behind the backs of people, so to speak. This is the power to transform the habitus, the expectations, rewards, and dispositions of everyday life. It is the silent, muted, but authoritative power to suborn once marginal voices, subvert the hegemony of age, and inflect the very knowing of the world. All this is so transformative precisely because it entails no formal cultural surrender. There is a long roster of events that never happened. The kiaps never confiscated the Maring's pearlshells and replaced them with Australian shillings. They never came in force to round people up for plantation labor. The missionaries did not come and set the sacred groves on fire. No one compelled the Maring to plant coffee or pan for gold. No, the Maring have been accomplices of their own transformation.

What we are speaking of here is power in the passive voice, the gradual Western saturation of medical knowledge and justice, the aesthetics of dress and the sociality of food, the conception of thinking and the representation of the body. Thus, the everyday, the routines, the "givens" of life. These changes are, moreover, hardly experienced as direct power. There is only, for example, the displaced pain of the senior generation feeling the cultural ground move beneath its feet. Men sometimes flew into transports of pride when they recalled their wars prior to pacification, wars that were elements of an identity-making that no longer is. The silent indirect power of encompassment is felt as constraints on action, as new conventions and habits, and as changes in knowing and valuing objects and persons. "The silent power of the sign, the unspoken authority of habit, may be as effective as the most violent coercion" in shaping social thought and action (Comaroff and Comaroff 1991:22). It is through the repetition of the signs, practices, and desires of modernity that they come to be so deeply embodied in everyday routines that, even as they culturally transform and disarm a people, these signs, practices, and desires cease to be perceived and contested. The Maring have been drawn unwittingly and wittingly into the house of what they call "civilization" in contrast to "kastam." They have both cooperated and resisted in the encompassment of their world, finding the content of certain Western practices objectionable even as they accept the overall premise. The question for an account of modernity is to account for the practices that have vanished and also those (e.g., sorcery and compensation payments) that appear to have survived, albeit with transformed meanings and implications. Just why is it that some Western practices are clearly embraced by a people, some seem to insinuate themselves into the universe of the encompassed, other practices are objects of contestation and resistance, and others still are simply brushed aside? In other words, we must ask not only how capitalism, colonialism, and Christianity insinuate and impose themselves, but how they enchant the senses, stir desires, and carnivalize the world. We must ask how new forms of personal freedom blossom within the context of increasing objective dependence.

A critical although unrecognized aspect of the exercise of power by Western agents is that it is often unreflective power. Because the technologies of power, control, and influence are so deeply inscribed in Western practices, Western agents frequently understand their own actions only in the most instrumental sense (an understanding promoted by the bourgeois ideology of practice). Missionaries, patrol officers, station managers, nurses, and other Westerners seem to reflect upon their practice almost entirely in terms of what they seek to accomplish. Pushed into a kind of nether world are the forms of power and control, and the changes demanded of the local population, for them to attain these goals. Thus the Anglican churchmen saw their mission as the simple and virtuous act of providing the spark that would induce the Maring to find the light of God. Little did they appreciate the extent to which the realization of their project would change the shape of Maring culture or the extent to which the persuasion of God's word was based on the Church's economic power. In the same vein, the kiaps grasped the building of latrines and the burial of the dead as simple health measures—what, to quote one of them, "any reasonable society would do if they knew the risks"—rather than as a coercive challenge to local conceptions of the body and the afterlife. These examples could be multiplied; anyone who has lived in Melanesia could divine others. But the point is that the mission and state in particular, as incarnated in mission men and patrol officers, were unreflective centers of power. They influenced the trajectory of Maring society in more ways than they ever consciously understood or knowingly intended. The priests, patrol officers, station managers, nurses, and ethnographers who lived in the Jimi, however much they may have been agents of encompassment, were not simply gears in some machine of domination, though in some silly versions of colonialism they are so portrayed. They were mostly people who, in seeking to carry out their life, and because they operated from a more powerful vantage point, could not help but transform the others' practices, values, and epistemology. The power of colonization, for the Maring and for Melanesia generally, lay not in methodical and systematic efforts by the West to dominate them, but in the unreflective execution of its best intentions.

The power to change a people's cultural epistemology, to set it in historical motion, occurs in the liminal space between the contours of awareness and contemplation and the implicit, deeply buried, and unconscious structure of (semi-)shared meanings and assumptions. It occurs simultaneously, and this is a critical reason why the study of transformation tests the limits of anthropology, in the space between the awarenesses and unconsciousness of one generation and those of the next. The Maring were only partially aware of the changes in their epistemology, and this awareness was itself socially distributed as is people's implicit interest and investment in these changes. People grasped that the substance of life had turned in a new direction. The younger generation more than their parents. But they found it hard to place their finger and words on just what this was. This inchoate recognition, this partial vision, was a source of anxiety. There is an inescapable epistemological tension, inscribed in the possibility of epistemologizing itself, that, distributed across generations, is productive of new hybrid forms of subjectivity and peoplehood, of representation and desire. Everything that follows is simply a way of exploring and explaining this point.

Honoring the Complexities

Anthropology feels hard pressed not only to examine its tie to the processes of encompassment, but to review the institutions and agents that bring this about. Not the least of such problems is the tendency to treat Christianity, capitalism, and the nation-state as rather homogeneous forces. There is too little appreciation or analysis of the fact that the contingent appearance of each of these forces is constitutive of the encompassing processes. That is, the Maring are not simply influenced by capitalism, the state (first colonial and now national in form), and Christianity; they encounter very specific, usually rather unrepresentative versions of each of these agencies of social change. Moreover, one of the most characteristic and disruptive dimensions of encompassment is precisely that this contingency is its nature. To sketch but one significant example, Maring exposure to Christianity is irregular, heterogeneous, and unpredictable. Decentralized and idiosyncratic, Anglican missionizing often seemed like a random walk through the mountains. During this formative era, the religious doctrines that are emphasized, the intensity of evangelism, the degree of commercialism, the education and tolerances of the mission staff, and much more were different in the Jimi than in the Simbai Valley. The mission also varied in time due to the turnover in mission personnel, the wide latitude that the head priest had in determining local policies, and the gamut of accidental forces that might influence the existence and execution of such policies (e.g., the arrival of an anthropologist like myself who befriended the priest at the Koinambe mission and frequently argued with him about the need to tolerate and accept local practices). Further, some Maring clan clusters were exposed to Catholicism and others to the evangelical, Pentecostal Nazarene Church. In a word, peoples' encounters with Christianity were skewed, uneven, and subject to change without notice.

One reason such contingency has been ignored or bracketed is that the agents of encompassment (such as Father Bailey, a white, effeminate, bookish, middle-class man from San Francisco who oversaw the Koinambe mission) have themselves been considered either unworthy of our attention or a relatively homogeneous class that could be captured in a sentence or two. Similarly, ethnographers have not paid attention to health personnel, such as the nurses who worked at the Koinambe mission hospital. The implicit understanding has been that the agents of Western culture are immediate, unmediated reflections of the society that sent them. Their voices, motives, desires, and intentions have rarely been heard: what projects they imagined and how they responded to local agents. There is little data on how their encounter with Melanesians shaped the ways that they interacted with one another and represented themselves as a white, Western, gender-neutral collectivity to the local community. In order to present both sides of the story we must invite them back into the narrative, not as a homogeneous and faceless class, not as ethnocentric demons bent on destroying indigenous culture, but in all their complexities of organization and personality.

What the anthropology of Melanesia must take account of is that encompassment takes place only through the mediation of the practice, experience, and desires of agents differently situated with respect to capitalism, Christianity, and the state (colonial and national). The objectives and understandings of the clergy, state officials, ethnographers, and other Westerners have points of convergence, but also of divergence and conflict. Indeed, because these Western institutions and agents have occupied very different positions within their own society and with respect to indigenous ones, they have often been on different paths, and in some cases at each other's throats. In a very different way, the indigenous societies are also not homogeneous. Due to all sorts of "inequalities" (which can be as simple and contingent as proximity to a mission or government station) some people and groups are better able than others to capitalize on modernizing forces. Similarly, the upcoming generation often has the capacity and motivation to embrace modernity in ways that their parents cannot. The result is the existence of "unequal rhythms" (Bourdieu 1962:2) between groups and generations with respect to modernizing change.

It is much too one-sided to think that the missionaries and colonial officials, medical personnel and agricultural extension officers, transformed the Maring merely by interacting with them on terms not of their own choosing. The differentials of power in the hinterlands were never great enough to instigate wholesale unwanted alterations of local life. The power of capitalism, Christianity, and Western culture generally has laid greatly in the ability to enchant, to transform people's desires, to be spliced into local-level politics. On the others' side of this encounter, the various Maring clan clusters have influenced the terms of the meeting. Like an orchestra without a conductor, their collective actions and reactions, guided by their cultural habitus, have redetermined the ways in which priests, government officials, medical practitioners, and others consider and interact with them. They have seized and reconfigured the signifiers sent from the West even as these signifiers have changed them in more ways than the practical life can see. More, the reconfiguration of these signs and practices has, on the rebound so to speak, also changed the agents of the West more than their practice can comprehend. Any account must deal with the refractory nature of these processes, the tensions within both the Western and Maring camps, precisely because brute force and repressive inequalities have never been its dominant modalities. Signs of power and the powers of the sign appear at every turn. But they take the form of the carnival of new goods, the promise of new forms of wealth creation, the re-education of the young, the reshaping of desire, the assimilation of Western epistemology, and the transformation of the global context for the production of meaning.

This last point about context is particularly important and importantly overlooked in many ethnographies. Although there is no dearth of insistent and programmatic statements urging anthropologists to be sensitive to context, doing so is really against some of our most anthropological instincts. As I will argue, ethnography in Melanesia has been based on a distinction between modernity and tradition, embodied in the premise that we can parse practices into those aspects that are customary and those that are indigenous. The premise enters ethnography as a presupposition; it is not part of our customary discourse about what we are doing. Nevertheless, standard works on Melanesia will offer depictions of marriage, exchange, ritual, warfare, politics, body decoration, and so forth as though these depictions were more or less accurate reflections of traditional practice. Very often ethnographers will make the point by first describing the practice and then indicating how the practice has changed since contact. Reflecting on this ethnographic trope, the late Roger Keesing noted that even in those "parts of the Pacific for which it would be difficult to imagine pristine exotica—Fiji, Polynesia, Micronesia—many anthropologists still seem to have a remarkable bent for seeking elements of the old and hence genuine and filtering them out from present day realities" (1989:56). The problem is that for all our good intentions this method hides the hand of the larger context and celebrates the empirical at its expense.[7] A decontextualization of local signs and practices takes place. Ethnography lives and survives by example: so let me provide one.

Early in my field stay, Gou, one of my housemates, is suffering a mild fever and chills from a tropical ulcer. On the second day of the illness after what must have been an uncomfortable night, the shaman Tipika appears in the late afternoon. He is holding a string bag from which he removes a bamboo tube. He pulls the plug from the end of the tube to show me that it holds leaves and water, though of course not just any leaves and water. As he chants in a special ritual language (see LiPuma 1988:127–28), he passes the tube over the surface of Gou's body, then repeats the motion being careful to encircle Gou's head. On the surface, this event seems to be positively brimming with "tradition" (my fieldnotes say, rather euphorically, that this is a "real" curing ceremony as opposed, I presume, to that fake modern kind). More, the Maring claim to have followed this curing practice literally from time immemorial. Alas, its meanings and implications cannot be grasped at the empirical level alone. The appearance and possibility of Western medicine inescapably transforms the meaning of traditional curing even if the forms of the traditional practices (e.g., what words are said and who says them) remain the same. Now the indigenous practice is measured against and in relation to the Western one. Whether Maring who are ill visit the local shaman, the health clinic, or more likely both is read by others as an index of the extent to which they accept the vision of the world advanced by modernity. To chose any form of treatment is to make a political statement. Especially in a time of change, all social action and choices, even taking no action or refusing to make a choice, is condemned to meaning. As for Gou, he had a host of other motives besides getting better. Not the least of his modern motives was that he wanted me to "record" this rite, and to record the "correct" version of this practice. In other words, to write Tipika's performance as if it were "traditional" (read authentic) is to suck all of the meaning and intentionality out of the event. Or, to phrase this another way, we can neither define nor measure change by whether a custom has been retained or abandoned. The real issue here is the collaboration between the continuities of the observable and the transformations in meaning.

The Shape of the Narrative

The dynamics of interaction between Maring and the forces of encompassment are too complex, too multivalent, to be captured or rendered
sensible by a simple equation of colonialism, domination, and resistance,
or of social change as natural (e.g., inspired by the economics of want).
The quest, no matter the difficulty, must be for a nonreductionist account.
There is no safety any more in an analysis anchored only in the local.
There is even less value in the isolationism of the world systems approach,
which, through its addiction to mega- and triumphant categories, dis-
solves the local level. What possible joy is there is using a theory that
effaces what it means to have an identity? Perhaps these theorists have
never looked into the eyes of a Enga returning from a weekend war, but
they must at least have watched an Olympic athlete receive a gold medal,
their eyes swelling, their body visibly vibrating as their national anthem
sounds. All the signs of the modern "road" tell us that the substance of
modernity lies in the relationships (complex, multiple, and imbricated)
between what happens globally and what unfolds on local terrain. For
Melanesia, this means the many and varied relationships between the
Western embrace and the many interacting, variably overlapping, and
unevenly transforming localities. In this frame, our anthropology must be
to grasp how the interpenetration and interfunctionality of structures,
agents, and processes transform a people's categories and ways of knowing their world. What, we must ask ourselves, is the role of priests and
colonial officials, anthropologists and medical personnel, in the invention
of the "modernized" mind? What is the resonance of these agents, and the
practices they endorse, on people's notions of person, peoplehood, rights,
and privateness (as in privacy and property and singularity)? In what
respect do a people recapture a captured consciousness? What is the relationship between the generation of knowledge and the knowledge of a generation (versus another, for example)? The dynamics of encompassment
are anything but linear or straightforward. Nowhere is it simply the push
and pull of domination and resistance. Almost everywhere there is an
intrinsic, growing interconnection between modernized urban sites and
local places. That is why the interrogation of encompassment with respect
to people's categories and ways of knowing their world cannot but raise
issues of method, of our intellectual technology and epistemology, in the
investigation of theirs.

To compare cultures it is necessary first to understand them: against
this wisdom, Hocart, the great ethnographer of Polynesia, replied that one
must also compare cultures to have any chance of understanding them.
What Hocart knew is that all anthropology is comparative. The analytical
trope of explicitly comparing two or more cultures is only the most trans-

parent form of comparison and by no means the most important. Ethnography is inherently a comparative enterprise because it is founded on the commensurability of subjects, on the presumption that the intentions of others and the ethnographer are mutually intelligible. It is to assert that others' forms of subjectivity and personhood are comparable with and at least to some degree overlap with ours. This comparative tension is the normality of living foreign. When I interact with a Maring, I interpret the meaning of his/her words, gestures, and intonations against my own—an implicit comparison between my way of "knowing" what it is to be a *person* speaking and theirs. The corollary of this is that an account of a Melanesian society also entails an epistemological break insofar as the indigenous way of socially knowing the world is neither that of Western culture nor that of its stepchild, science. The process of knowing requires the self-conscious pairing and comparison of Western and Melanesian conceptions of reality in order to expose and destabilize our presuppositions—a project vividly addressed in the "new Melanesian ethnography" (Josephides 1991; Foster 1995b). The recognition of an opposition between the West and its alter is acceptable as long as we do not forget that all contrasts entail comparison, that the possibility of ethnography itself presupposes some degree of commensurability between Melanesian and Western cultures, and that the conjuncture of Melanesian and colonial histories is the history of the modern (see Carrier 1992).

Not the least of the problems in comparing Melanesia and the West is that anthropologists have not always understood their own society. The contrasts that are set up are all too frequently between an in-depth account of a Melanesian society and an ideological account of the Western lifeway. Accepting Western ideology at face value tends to exaggerate the opposition between Melanesia and the West because our ideology seeks to mask and misrecognize our sociality: to commodify all forms of social relatedness and to presume that we are the domain of the universal, free-willed, self-actualizing subject. This is, at best, a partial description of the West; it is also as far removed from Melanesian images of persons, actions, and history as can be imagined. Too strong a contrast between us and them also has a disadvantage in that it can never deal with encompassment, the ways that the structures of encompassment have braided our reality with theirs. What this means for ethnography is that there are multiple layers of comparison and comparability that we must come to terms with in order to write an ethnography adequate to its object. The comparative nature of the enterprise also implies that to come to terms with Melanesia we must come to terms with ourselves. The account of Melanesia must coexist with an appreciation of the West even if this latter dimension remains mostly in the background. The end product is an ethnography that is also partly a history, an account that even in its moments of thickest description is intensely theoretical, an attempt to tell all sides of the ongoing story of encompassment in a relentlessly nonreductionistic way.

The typical thought against such a perspective is that it is too complicated and complicating. There are few clean analytical lines; there are no singular and dominant determinations; and an uncluttered, linear narrative is out of the question. But it is also true that there are no linear narratives, dominant determinations, or clean analytical bottom lines to be found on the map of Maring modernity. But ultimately, the risk of complexity is small potatoes next to the risk of never knowing.

The Trajectory of the Modern

I have argued that one of the defining characteristics of the modern in Melanesia (like the modern everywhere) is that it is openly indeterminate and nonlinear. In this respect, the "new road" of the Maring has had a trajectory but not a destination. The changes wrought in the life of meaning and practice are never preordained though they are surely path-determined. Through their encounter with a motley and unrepresentative ensemble of Westerners, certain notions, desires, and practices have become canonized as representative of the modern. For example, there is no a priori reason why the Maring are Anglican as opposed to Catholic, Seventh Day Adventist, or Buddhist for that matter. External events and processes, a meeting of white colonial minds beyond their spheres of knowledge or control, shaped the color of their Christianity. Internally, the Anglican mission arrived on the scene immediately after a decade of the most severe warfare the Jimi valley had ever seen—that was the story related by the elder clansmen of both the victors and losers in these conflicts. Because they had been driven from their clan territories, the defeated clusters welcomed colonial rule and were quick to embrace Christianity as a new source of power, value, and political opportunity. Not to be outdone, the triumphant clan clusters, most notably the Kauwatyi and Tukmenga, also joined the ranks of Anglican converts. For both of these clusters, this was a self-conscious and calculated decision taken by the leading senior clansmen—what turned out to be a successful attempt to stay ahead of the political curve of modernity. The critical point is that once Maring big-men canonized their clan's commitment to the Anglican Church—probably for reasons that future generations know little about— the church of Henry VIII was effectively locked in. A contingent event at a crucial historical moment came to determine the Christianity of the Maring. And once the mission established itself, people became progressively more invested in the mission as a source of jobs, imported goods, transportation to urban areas, medicine, communication with their kinsmen working on plantations, access to the modern, and much more. Eventually, competing religions could make about as much headway against the Anglican mission as, say, Esperanto has made against English.

Modernity continually creates sociohistorical pathways that, once entrenched, no matter how contingent and accidental their origins, define the future trajectory of that people. In this regard, the trajectory of modernity is neither certain nor predetermined, and given the contingencies of its production, certainly not the same for all the societies of Melanesia. The making of these paths should also remind us that the agents and institutions of encompassment are not cogs of a machine that levels everything in its path, only to erect a new and monolithic Western world in its place. The progress of encompassment does not result in the unadulterated Westernization of others. It does result in the transformation of Melanesian cultures, such as the Maring, the state-run project of constructing a national culture in the singular (see LiPuma 1997), and, on the rebound, it also transforms the cultures of the West.

The Social Landscape

Before I launch into the more specific analyses, I would like to set out briefly the actors and groups that will be center stage in the story. I use the term *Maring* as a historically emergent category, aware that prior to colonization the designation *Maring* did not exist and there was certainly nothing resembling a Maring identity. I shall use the term transhistorically, then, merely as a matter of convenience. At the point of contact, the designation describes an assortment of clan clusters who occupy a more or less contiguous space, entertain similar rituals of war and peace, have similar forms of production, exchange, and consumption, and speak mutually intelligible dialects of a common language. There were never clear-cut boundaries, however, as the border communities were always and remain an admixture of practices and languages. For the most part, anthropologists have ignored these frontier communities because they threaten their image of a culture as a totalized, coherent vision of the world, focusing instead on more centrally located "core communities." As I will argue later, the existence of a culture as a bounded, self-animated, autonomous whole is an analogue of our ideology of the individual, and a more adequate theory would focus on gradients of difference. So at the time of contact, the existence of *Maring* as a collective noun was still something the Maring would have to learn, as they would learn in the ensuing era to begin to objectify their culture.

The stage on which this history unfolds is the Bismarck mountain range bisecting central New Guinea (see map 1). The Maring territory

consists of roughly 350 kilometers of steep, rugged, heavily forested terrain—as though a tropical rain forest had been lifted into mountain
clouds. There are at least twenty-one clan clusters, nine residing on the
northern fall of the mountain range in the Simbai Valley, twelve on the
southern fall of the range in the Jimi Valley, plus two mixed clusters that
are partly Maring and partly Kalam (see map 2). The Simbai Maring and
the mixed clusters are included in the Madang Province, the Jimi Maring
in the Western Highlands Province. This political boundary reflects the
reality that the Maring occupy the Highlands border and embrace some
features of the intermediate stepland societies lying between the Highlands
and the coast. For the most part, their cultural and linguistic affinities are
with the Highlands.

The Maring language is classified within the central stock of the Eastern New Guinea Highlands Stock (Wurm and Laycock 1961; Bunn and
Scott 1962). The Central Family includes at least fifteen languages, extending in a curved band through the Eastern and Western Highlands and
Southern Province. Consistent with its location on the Highlands fringe,
Maring is the most northerly outpost of this stock, belonging to the Jimi
subfamily of this Central Family. Their neighbors to the northeast (see
map 3) speak Kalam, an unrelated coastal language. The people at the
southeastern border of Maring territory, the Manga, speak a mutually
intelligible language (called Narak in the literature) and bear a close cultural kinship. In fact, it may well be an accident of colonial history—at the
moment of administrative intervention they were enmeshed in the war
with their western neighbors, the Yomban—that they were first classified
and then became recognized as a completely separate culture and language.

Maring clans are organized into clusters whose member clans are
integrated through a history of extensive intermarriage, trade, and daily
association. Prior to pacification, these clan clusters were mostly unnamed
associations of clans. They were subsequently assigned names by the colonial administration, and the Maring have since adopted these names.
Almost all clusters share at least one border with an old enemy, defined by
a history of contestation and quarreling that may range over many generations, and a border with a cluster with whom they are allies. This
configuration of enmity and alliance serves to localize warfare, and Maring have never engaged in long-distance warfare nor have they aligned
themselves collectively against other societies in military engagements.

My ethnography features the Kauwatyi clan cluster (see map 2),
though it aims for a much more catholic view of modernity. The Kauwatyi
are numerically the largest, traditionally most powerful, and, along with
the Yomban and Tukmenga, the most modernized of the Maring clusters.
The Kauwatyi cultivate alliances with the groups of the western Simbai,

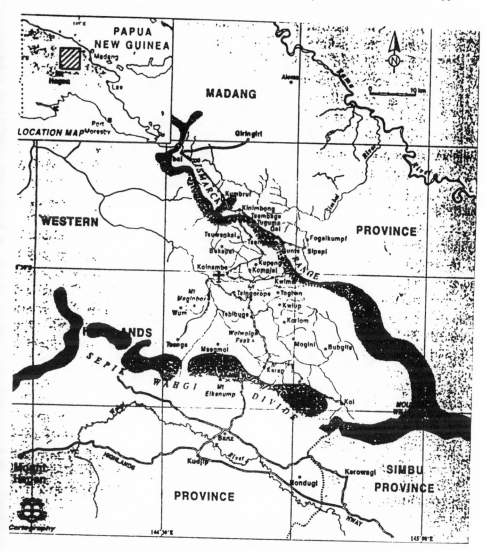

Map 1.   The Jimi and Simbai Valleys

especially the Tuguma and Tsembaga who reside on the adjoining face of the mountain range. In 1980, the Kauwatyi numbered in excess of 900 people; this number has swelled in recent years to well over a thousand. Political considerations have always encouraged population expansion since clansmen correlated political muscle with unit size. But despite the political and economic pressures to remain roughly equal in size, the clan clus-

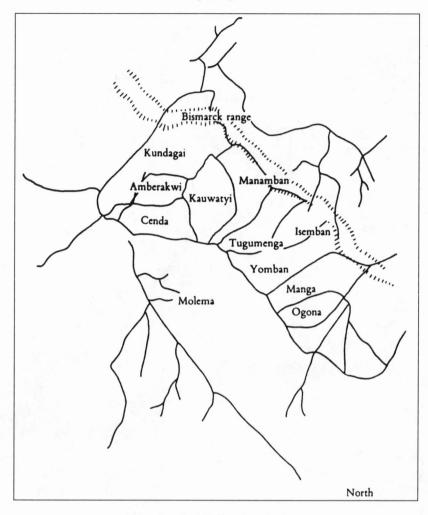

Map 2.   Jimi Valley clan clusters

ter varied considerably, ranging from a low of 150 members to more than 900. Prior to pacification, the Kauwatyi were the most militant and aggressive Jimi Valley clan cluster. Their collective memory registers at least five wars, the most recent being in the late 1940s and 1955. The dawning of pacification ended their military exercises but did not chill their aggressive bent. Influenced by the missionaries and persuaded by capitalism, they became strong proponents of modernity, seeking to win the new economic and cultural wars with an affable ardor that would have made

Map 3.   Linguistic boundaries. (Based on Healey 1990:14.)

both Carnegies, Andrew and Dale, proud. By 1980, most of the Kauwatyi aged ten to twenty-five had completed some school with about a dozen going on to secondary school. They were also ambitious in the planting of coffee, the opening of trade stores, and assuming jobs at the mission station. During the epoch in question, ethnographers also carried out significant research on the Tukmenga, Tsembaga, Tuguma, Kundagai, and Fungai-Korama clan clusters.

The Koinambe Mission Station

All of the Westerners (except the anthropologists, of course) were situated at the Koinambe mission station. The head of the station from 1975 to 1982 was Father Brian Bailey, an Anglican priest who had been born and raised in San Francisco. The only child of an older couple, Father Bailey was an effeminate, bookish intellectual, a portly man less accustomed to exercise than reading and thinking. He had been in Melanesia much of his adult life and made no secret of the fact that he felt more at home there than any place he had ever known. He read and talked about what he had read constantly—his own house lined wall-to-wall with books on history, religion, and especially military warfare. I interviewed him numerous times, often well into the night, our discussions of Christianity, his views on Melanesia and the Maring, and the role of the mission interspersed with discussions of the flanking maneuvers of the panzer division leader Heinz Guderian. Often unreflective and blinded by his faith, he was always kindhearted, good-natured, and sympathetic toward the Maring. Often discombobulated, given to mood swings, and uncertain of his destiny, spreading the word of God and saving the souls of others was his way of imbuing his life with meaning, a redemption song for having sinned seemingly for just being. During the period from 1979 to 1980, several other priests, all from England, stayed at Koinambe for periods of one week to three months, plus there was a visit by the Archbishop.

The other critical members of the white establishment were a nurse and a station manager sent by the Volunteer Service Organization of England (VSO). The nurse was a young and energetic Irish woman from County Cork who talked quite dismissively of life and the medical profession in her homeland. During her tenure in charge of the mission hospital, she ran it with singular devotion, animated by a degree of freedom and authority that she could not possibly hope to enjoy at home. Her relationship to the mission men was tenuous but cordial; she was a dispirited Irish Catholic who radiated little affection for England or things English. Moreover, she had the head and heart of a scientist, finding the good father's admonition to the Maring that they should pray for the remission of a disease at best a tolerable absurdity. Indeed, their relationship embodied the contradiction inherent in a missionary project that both celebrates the rationality of the West, especially its biomedical explanations and treatments, and also suggests to the penitent that they should pray to God for relief from illness and disease because He is the final arbiter.

Her VSO counterpart, the station manager, was a former policeman from Manchester who envisioned his stay to the Highlands as a change of scenery that would allow him to put his life together again. He had originally arrived with his wife, herself a former policewoman, but was soon on the road to divorce as she left him for a young Australian Talair pilot (who was not long after killed when his plane crashed and burned). Prior to his sojourn to the Highlands, he had never left England, and though a very competent station manager from a technical standpoint, he was hardly intellectually or emotionally prepared for the world he had to face. He thought the Maring lazy by nature and inclined to irrationality, they seemed unable or unwilling to adhere to schedules or rudimentary standards of punctuality, and their temperament resembled more that of a child than an adult. They seemed to show only the most grudging appreciation for what he was doing for them—leaving the comforts of his homeland to help them become self-sufficient in the modern world. He worked tirelessly to improve the Koinambe mission station, create new job opportunities for local men, and generally assist others in the best way he knew how. He, like many of the missionaries, had the unnatural, or more precisely uncultural, expectation that the Maring would become modern by first converting themselves into "modern" agents so that they might begin to appreciate and enjoy the wonders of modernity—not least the way those who were already modern or civilized were willing to help them, such willingness to help the lesser races itself a mark of the civilized man. This way of thinking the world could not help but to imagine the categories of the West as universal categories. The relationship between the station manager and the priest was strained both because they were endowed with different temperaments and because the former policeman was indifferent to religion.

The final group of Westerners who inhabited Koinambe was the Bible translator from the Summer Institute of Linguistics, his wife, and the Maring girl that he had adopted. Before receiving a calling to Melanesia, he had been a schoolteacher in a hamlet outside of Perth in Western Australia. He had attended school only through the secondary level and had little training, talent, or even special interest in linguistics. What he did possess was an unyielding belief in the might and right of Christianity to transform others for their own benefit. By 1980, he and his wife had lived for well over a decade in the Jimi Valley, making dogged headway in their attempt to translate the Bible into Maring. His principal assistant—who was in fact the actual translator—was a young Kauwatyi man he had semi-adopted, sent to secondary school at Ukurumpa (the capital of the Summer Institute of Linguistics, it resembles nothing so much as a cozy, middle-class, mid-American town replete with split-level houses and bustling supermarkets, though it is, of course, located in the heart of the New Guinea Highlands), and then to college in Australia. Like strangers trapped on an elevator (to heaven?), the Bible translator and the priest in charge displayed a situational solidarity, as the only long-term residents of Koinambe and the only white practicing Christians in a sea of black faces of dubious faith and white transient lapsed Christians. But it was always clear that the hard-wired fundamentalist from Australia could not bring himself to like or trust an effeminate, bookish, Anglican from America. And so days would go by when they spoke nary a word to one another, the translator holed up in one house and the priest in the other.

Though Koinambe was a mini United Nations with an Irish nurse, English station manager, American priest, and Australian Bible translator (not to mention visits from a "black" Indian nurse and a Chinese dentist from Hong Kong), the Maring viewed the white community as homogeneous. The community of Westerners encouraged this impression, maintaining a strict code of solidarity and harmony when Melanesians were present. In public, they always expressed a fondness for their native land even as they all confessed a fundamental unhappiness, of how coming to Papua New Guinea—"PNG" was how they always referred to it—was a reply to a feeling of dissatisfaction and estrangement with their homeland. Once in PNG, a reversal occurred, however. The marginality of the expatriates, their distantness from their own culture, was "corrected" in the Maring context: for in Melanesia they stood for precisely what they were alienated from, thereby reasserting their connectedness with their "home" by virtue of being spatially, culturally, and spiritually separated from it. What a task for the Maring to assemble a picture of Western society from this odd, psychologically distressed, and highly unrepresentative sample, made that much more peculiar by the occasional locally resident anthropologist. Nonetheless, assemble a picture of modernity they did. They transformed themselves in the face of transformative powers of encompassment. What follows is my attempt to capture one part of that history. My only hope is that it yields whatever truth is necessary for this historical moment; for as an anthropologist and a man, it is the only way I know of thanking the Maring for their generosity toward me.

CHAPTER 2

In the Fields of Encompassment:
Colonialism and the Advent
of Modernity

First it was messianic, then violent, becoming a long slow dissolve into the course of modernity. The first engagements of the Maring with Europeans were sometime in the mid-1930s. No one knows how often; these encounters were quasi ritual, the Maring mesmerized by what they beheld, some believing that the Westerners were ancestor spirits returned in transfigured form. The complexion of these invaders was pale and ghostly, their hair cropped and drained of color, their eyes alighting on each other promiscuously, their feet wrapped in some strange skin, their gait odd and unsure. Their bodies were abnormally large and they talked in a tongue that, to the Maring ear, barely sounded like language. They barked orders at the black bodies, mostly pairs marching in tandem, their heads tilted to accommodate the pole on their shoulders along which was strung a metallic box. And just as often there were no comparable witnesses from the colonial side, for the Maring were mostly watching the patrol party from behind blinds. The women and children had taken refuge in the deep forest while a band of men remained and witnessed the spectacle. Where in later years, the New Guinea Highlands would play spectacle to the West—lighting up its imagination and the covers of National Geographic—the first encounters were an inversion of that reality in the making. So early reports indicate that the patrols encountered signs of habitation but no inhabitants.

The next great moment was violent and revealing. A generation later, it underlined in blood that the Maring were vulnerable. In the opening months of 1955, a party of Yomban—the easternmost Maring clan cluster—chanced upon and killed a gardening group of Manga, apparently in retaliation for the theft of pandanus fruits and the rape of a Yomban girl. The entire Manga party—estimated at twelve—was slaughtered in the encounter. A patrol officer, R. I. MacIlwain, hearing the story of the massacre while doing a census among the Manga, then headed for Togban (see map 2 in chap. 1) to ferret out the Yomban "murderers" (MacIlwain 1955). But no sooner had he set foot on Yomban territory than he was met by a group of men who told him in no uncertain terms that their dispute with the Manga was none of his business. Believing that he did not command sufficient firepower to engage them, MacIlwain retired to the patrol post at Minj (Cook 1967:7). The Yomban then launched at all-out attack on the Manga, driving them from their land and leaving their homesteads in flames that could be seen for miles (Attenborough 1960:44–45). Determined to teach the Yomban a lesson and set an example, MacIlwain returned in May 1956 with a detachment of heavily armed police. They met a group of black-faced warriors as they entered Yomban territory and summarily opened fire. In a matter of minutes eight Yomban were killed, nine others badly wounded, the defeated Maring group now fleeing for safety. The patrol then proceeded to destroy all of the Yomban settlements, burning their houses, killing what pigs and cassowaries they could find, and leveling the pandanus trees. The use of direct, punitive, and summary attack on peoples who violated the Pax Britannica fit the colonial office's concept of "being firm." Watson (1960) reports that elsewhere in the Highlands the patrol officer, Ian Mack, accompanied by a police contingent, surrounded the men's house at Aiamontina (Kainantu) and opened fire on whoever might be within, killing at least nine and wounding others. There were numerous other killings and executions throughout the territory—though in the eyes of the administration, they were always justified and unavoidable. Peace would be achieved by whatever violent means were necessary.

For the rest of the Maring, especially the clan clusters to the west who had, up until this moment, only felt a touch of the colonial presence, the deaths at Togban and the rumors that flew around them were the beginning of a longer conversation with the encompassing universe. The narratives of the "red men"—first of the fear they provoked and then of their resounding firepower—became special episodes in the cultural history of the Maring as a group, as much a part of their collective memory as the wars they had won and lost. The red color of their skin, the smoke from their guns, their shirts that buttoned down the front, their supplies of tinned foods: everything conspired to make this a historical event in the truest sense, an oracular sign that a discontinuity between past and present was in the offing. After the original sightings, there was discussion among the Kauwatyi senior men about these disturbances in the field. Some argued that the "red men" were incarnations of ancestor spirits, red spirits who, enraged that their names had been forgotten and sacrifices were no longer made on their behalf, had returned to punish the living and reclaim their homesteads. Others argued that the intruders were sorcerers from afar, from the home of pearlshells and steel axes, their appearance in the manner of sorcerers, a transfigured form of their real persons. Just as a sorcerer could assume the form of a cassowary or pig, so he could take the form of a red spirit to fool and best his enemy. Another version of the aftermath of this initial meeting has the Maring as epistemological agnostics, of being unable to know who these foreigners were. Whatever the outcome of these collective ruminations, only the most incipient of cargo cults ever developed, and this was short-lived. What did occur was the collective recognition that the killings at Togban began a time when the Maring's traditional reaction to intruders would have to be placed in historical parentheses. Whatever and whoever these aliens were, they had conquered the Maring as much spiritually as militarily.[1]

Thus, on future occasions of encounter things would be very different. From 1958 to 1962 the colonial administration led by patrol officers such as Griffin, Worcaster, and O'Farrell made a more extensive series of forays into the Jimi and Simbai Valleys. This time the Maring issued no resistance; their fierceness had turned to anxiety, their defiance to a certain subordination and willingness to try to please. Gavin Souter, an Australian journalist who accompanied patrols into the Jimi valley, described an encounter.

> In 1958, I accompanied a patrol into the Bismarcks, a range of mountains whose green rococo folds of rain forest from the northern wall of the Jimi Valley. After two weeks of more or less comfortable walking . . . we climbed an almost vertical slope of mud and tree roots for three hours, then crossed a ridge of moss forest at 6,000 feet, and jolted downhill beside a hectic, nameless stream which our guides said would lead us to a rendezvous they had arranged with the Gants [actually, a place name called Gunts, the people were Maring of the Fungai-Korama cluster]. Ten minutes later we met the Gants; they were standing beside a waterfall, about forty men in grass sporrans and plumes and possum fur, and some were so nervous that they held each other's hands for comfort.
>
> They led us to a campsite, called their women and children out of the bush, and presented the patrol with two live pigs trussed to poles. After returning this compliment with steel hatchets and salt, the patrol officer, Barry Griffin, addressed the Gants in Pidgin English. Our interpreter relayed the speech in his own place-talk which, although not identical with that of the Gants, was intelligible to them. "I am the Kiap" said Griffin. "I am the Government. Many times I have heard you Gants people mentioned, and you have interested me. Now I have come here to your place, and I see all you . . . gathered to meet me, and I am pleased.
>
> When Griffin had finished telling the Gants that they must no longer kill or steal, and that they must help the government build patrol roads [i.e., do road construction for free on behalf of the colonial government], the time was 5:30 P.M. and the sun had

almost set. But there was still time to lower the Australian flag
which had been hoisted beside our tents earlier in the afternoon.
As the flag slid down its bamboo pole Griffin came to attention
and saluted; his police slapped the butts of their bayoneted .303s
and the poor bewildered Gants stood gaping. (Souter 1963:
235–36)

How different from the first encounters in 1955 and 1956 when the
Maring sought to fend off the kiaps. Here they are "nervous" and eager to
please, dressed in finery and offering two of their cherished pigs. A detachment of well-armed police accompanies the patrol officer, their .303 military rifles bayoneted as though they were expecting a firefight. But word of
the incident with the Yonbam has blanketed the valley, and the Fungai-
Korama appear more than willing to submit to government control.
Unlike the earlier episodes, this and future engagements would find the
Maring in a compromised position, willing to accept the verbal and sometimes physical abuse at the hands of the kiaps. Indeed, the Maring will give
the government little trouble for the next quarter century.

Pax Britannica and the Colonial Imagination

Those who hold that we should have left the primitive mountain
tribes of New Guinea to their innocent, idyllic existence would
change their views had they have been able to see the fear,
superstition and pain that dominated the lives of these people
before the government stopped tribal fighting, bound their
wounds and broke open the prison of their fearful isolation.
JAMES SINCLAIR, 1981

The patrol reports from across the Highlands talk incessantly about
"making contact" as though the brute act of making contact itself would
change the Other, projecting the morality of the West into a new geography. For many Maring, this was a gift that was at once unwanted and
unrepayable—that could only be acknowledged by submitting to the will
of the state and its agents. That many valleys of the Highlands remained
terra incognita well into the 1960s appears to have bothered the colonial
state no end; so it continually hatched plans and timetables to bring all of
the protectorate under control. There was more than a touch of magic in
all this. The mere planting of the Australian flag, a symbol having
absolutely no meaning to the Maring, magically brought once
autonomous peoples under the sway of the colonizer. The arrival of the
assistant district officer (ADO), the translated speech on the virtues and

law of the government, the ceremonial raising and lowering of the Australian colors, all of this was believed to be the first inaugural step in bringing the Maring into the twentieth century. The Maring could come willingly or reluctantly, but come they would. From the perch of the colonial administration, the history of the Maring was a Western concern. Having been granted the island in trust, it was a Western and specifically Australian responsibility to see that its people were marched into the modern era and onto the world historical stage. Maring, Melpa, Enga, and other Highlands histories would become moments of world history—minor stories on a larger stage produced and directed by the more advanced Western powers.

As one patrol officer explained to me in July 1974, the "civilization" of the Maring and all the peoples of the Highlands was a three-step dance: the initial step was contact, the second was pacification, and the third was the patient process of civilization. In the first encounter, the area was mapped, the "presence of the government" was made felt, and if possible a census was conducted. According to the patrol men, this instance of first contact set the stage for what was to come, and thus it was important to be muscular and determined. Flanked, as he was that day at Gants, by a phalanx of armed policemen, the tone and substance of the kiap's address underlined that this was not an encounter between equals—culturally, intellectually, or technologically. From that moment on, local lives and practices would be subject to a higher, Western, nearly omnipotent authority not of their own choosing.

In the next step, the "natives" were disarmed, and the firepower and authority of the government was driven home. In the colonial mind, fear and respect were fraternal twins. Often this display of firepower and authority took the form of the shooting of pigs, the burning of war shields, and punitive raids against "law breakers." In 1966, for example, officer Brown remanded most of the able-bodied Kauwatyi men to a two-week work detail as punishment for the "theft" of kerosene and food from a Western woman. Guilt or innocence was less the point than for the community to learn the divine right of kiaps—as it came to be called and enjoyed by those in stations of authority. From that period onward, the administration also demanded the nucleation of what were formerly more dispersed settlements. The rationale for the concentration of the community was that it would lighten the burden of the patrol officers' intermittent attention and make the Maring region easier to govern, although in the overall scheme of things this could not have been of much practical importance. But that was not the point. The concentration of once dispersed settlements was a permanent reminder of, and a memorial to, the power of the state administration. The nucleation also compelled and enticed people to congress on a more frequent basis, creating greater contact among distant relations. Particularly among the younger generation, it elevated the principle and possibility of friendship to a new level—a point to which we shall return in a few moments.

But Western influence was never simply a sequitur to Western policy. An unspoken aspect of the colonial presence was its influence on local house styles, especially its implicit opposition to men's houses. This aspect was unspoken inasmuch as the impact of the administration and the missionaries on the domestic sphere was never a matter of policy or doctrine. Rather, it existed as a presupposition, a given, that appeared in the attitude of the Westerners the Maring encountered, in those practices that won their nod of approval and those that provoked a shake of the head. The station manager, for example, once described the traditional, low-slung oval house as "more like a den than a proper house." So, desiring to be modern, the Maring began to replace their own low-slung, windowless, oval houses with what they called Papuan-style houses. The model and monument to this style was the kiap's rest house, centrally positioned by the administration on the clan cluster's common dance ground. The Papuan-style house was, first of all, large enough and meant to contain an entire family, this in contrast to a men's house semicircled by several or more women's houses. The Papuan house created a space for the family unit, husband, wife, and children, sanctified in matrimony and blessed by the Lord. Its design and size also permitted a fixed space set off from the outside world, divided internally into rooms allocated to specific domestic activities, such as sleeping, storage, cooking, and eating. This stood in contrast to the "traditional" arrangement that featured physically (though not conceptually) undifferentiated houses and that assumed a certain continuity between inside and outside (e.g., cooking). Just as the tropical environment with its "riot" of flowers and plants seem to dissolve into an indiscernible mass, so traditional housing did not appear conducive to proper sociality. To the Western mind, the A-framed Papuan house with its airy spaces, addiction to light, and internal divisions seemed infinitely more orderly than traditional arrangements.

Another invention in the management of newly "controlled areas" was the construction of a road linking all of the villages to the government station. The golden rule was that each Monday would be officially devoted to building and improving this main road, and its iron-fisted implementation (backed by beatings and lock-ups for defaulters) was that each cluster would "volunteer" to provide as much unpaid labor as the kiap deemed necessary to complete and maintain their section of the road. The big road, the new road, linking all the settlements to the government station was sacred to order, authority, and peace. The road was space out of "traditional" space, it belonged to no clan, and so all could walk along the road without fear of violence or intimidation (though maybe a little sorcery). "He ruled the Western Highlands like a principality," answerable only to his own inclinations, "one of his chief obsessions" being the construction of roads (Sinclair 1981: 208). So Sinclair describes Thomas Ellis, the district commissioner of the Western Highlands. The road, like the government and mission stations, the rest house and the medical aid post, were novel kinds of public space—spaces whose genesis and use was defined by the state (as impersonated by the kiap) rather than by kinship and marriage. Physically and metaphorically, it was nothing less than the simultaneous invention and expansion of the public political sphere, a new space in which categorical identities outweigh relational ones, orchestrated by men "whose skin we have never seen" (Maring elder in 1981).

The administration's aim was to imprint a Western standard of order and orderliness, to engrave on Melanesian bodies, minds, and landscapes an appreciation of Christian bourgeois discipline since this was assumed to be the grail of progress. This vision of evolution came with its own ontology. Just as fear led to respect, so an orderly village would produce an orderly mind. Cleared roads that ran by nucleated, evenly spaced houses with penned pigs and proper latrines would eventually produce subjects with clear, directed, and rational thinking. Subjects who would will their own metamorphosis. Diligence on the part of the administration was crucial; for it was the persistent impression of order that would eventually carry the Melanesian as close to the modern person as their nature would allow. The kiaps believed unquestionably and said emphatically that their fixation on "getting the settlements in proper order" was just what the Maring needed if they were to ascend into the twentieth century. This policy was both necessary and enlightened, even if the "natives" were only dimly aware of its eventual benefits. At some unspecified time in the future, they would be "thankful" for their guidance into modernity and onto the world stage. In the final step of the dance toward civilization, the local populace would cheerlead its own transformation, endorse the politics of citizenship and the nation-state, mature into God-fearing Christians, develop local business ventures and a sense of entrepreneurship, attend school as a matter of course, master the Queen's English, appreciate the values of money, applaud the miracle of science, and matriculate generally into prosperous societies composed of autonomous individuals bent on self-improvement. For the West, Papua New Guinea's peaceful and orderly metamorphosis into a democratic nation-state confirmed that the colonial intervention was not only necessary but ultimately salutary.

So many of the kiaps spoke of the three-step colonial project in terms that oscillated between a heroic and a thankless task, sometimes in the same breath. Particularly at night, when loneliness and a longing for home had set in and a melancholy had awakened in their eyes, when blind hours of drinking had disabled their superego and their conscience was allowed to vent the feelings their sober side would better repress, the kiaps told whoever was white and would listen how they loved and hated their job and "this place"—this place, this placeless referent, being both the concept of Papua New Guinea and their specific circumstance. For many of the Westerners who came to Melanesia, "this place," "PNG," and "the bush" were euphemisms. They described the terrain of their own psyches, the latitude and longitude of selfhood, more than cultural geography. "This place," "PNG," and "the bush" were sources of refuge from their own world, a challenge to prove themselves to themselves, a chance to restart their lives unencumbered by the weight of their own history—all of this and the possibility of redemption wrapped in the cloak of duty, adventure, and rational nationalism. And so the Melanesia they encountered was as much the projection of their own inner landscapes as a "real" place of the Other. Thus the profusion of geographic metaphors was no accident; for often the kiaps and "expats" (as the expatriates named themselves) spoke of "this place" or "the bush" as though it was uninhabited, as though one could speak of it independently of the people who had lived there for millennia. Thus the simultaneity of love and hate they felt for Melanesia could not have been more personal. And this most combustible mixture of human psychology, in its most unreflective state, often drove their behavior. My friend Penga, a lapsed seminary candidate at the Anglican mission school in Poppendeta, a man who knew astoundingly little about botany (at least for a Maring) but who spoke English fluently and was one of the most psychologically sagacious people I have ever encountered, summed it up this way: "If you can't live in your own place and you can't live here, you must live in a bottle"—referring to the fact that, in the long moment between nightfall and the click into sleep, all of the kiaps and expats he had ever known had bathed their psyches in whiskey and beer. On another occasion, this time in Maring and in a phrase that is almost untranslatable, he told me that they were people who did not like their own reflection.

   Sometimes the recruits were educated veterans, but mostly they were young men, too young and inexperienced for the complex task of interfacing between cultures. As Sinclair concedes in his most apologetic voice, officers of limited education and even more "limited experience at this time and for years after were often placed in charge of patrol posts or sub-district stations" (1981:15). To make matters worse, the department of Native Affairs never devised any formal, approved statement of its mission or operations. So these young men often seemed to be actors trapped in a recondite play with no inkling of purpose or plot, stumbling though their parts, nursing the bravest face they could muster. They were men whose public presentation of self as disciplined, manly, hard-boiled, and unflappable was part of a deception that was also and most of all a self-deception. The kiaps described their excursions into the local world in a way that was at once boastful and modest, a dance of tropes in which traversing a gorge over a badly weathered vine bridge or nearly air-crashing in the dense mist that overhung the mountains was told with a too casual humor, as though high adventure borne with good grace and measured modesty was the mark of a man. This was the convention. Their public self hid deep underlying senses of uncertainty and insecurity, fears that led them to be more punitive toward local offenders than was necessary, more condescending toward local leaders than warranted, more intolerant than inquisitive about local practices. Many kiaps harbored what they could not admit, least of all to themselves: a fear of powerlessness both in "this place" and when they returned home (denuded of the nearly absolute authority they exercised in the "bush," made doubly vulnerable because they had spent their lives learning a job for which there was no counterpart in Australia). And then there is the kind of alienation that visits a man who cannot be at home in so foreign a land but whose own home looks best when viewed from afar. Samuel Beckett, the Irishman who wrote of Irish men, but lived most of his life and all of his death in Paris, said of men like himself that, no matter where they were they were always far from home, and thus their behavior, in sympathy with their spirit, was often grotesque, angst-ridden, and laced with uncertainty.[2] Unlike the bookish and reflective Beckett, the patrol men were distrustful of anyone who put much trust in books—many of them swore to a deep anti-intellectual bent that they attributed to their working-class backgrounds. They were also deeply homophobic and would in private and for laughs accuse the seemingly more effete mission men of being "poofters"—Australian derogatory slang for gay men. From their perspective, it was hard to bring civilization and right-thinking to "bloody-minded kanakas," as I was informed more than once in a certain conspiratorial tone—as though I, as a Westerner, would understand such "politically incorrect" ethnocentrism as a truism that, given the heroic (read paternalistic) goals of the project, should not be said too loudly or publicly. The crime of colonialism was that these young men, hardworking but hardly trained, with honest intentions but conflicted souls, were the point men in the colonization of a people. So doing the best they could was a good day's walk from good enough.

The two central moments of Australian discipline and surveillance were the two yearly inspections of the villages and the patrol reports, the latter comprised mostly of what happened during these village inspections. These village inspections were fundamentally "rites of submission," reminders that local capacities and power paled before those of the colonial administration (see Gewertz and Errington 1995 for a discussion). The patrol reports themselves, though stylized and dry, and self-consciously "descriptive" in content—this was one of the admonitions given on how to write such reports—could not help but invent a particular type of native and native society. No matter which district officer was in command or who commanded the patrol, all the reports from the Maring region are remarkable similar in style and tone: short clipped sentences written in the third person omnipotent with the exception of the orders given ("The rest house latrine was in deplorable condition. I had them replace it immediately"). Local voices are vacant spaces, save on those occasions when a villager is responding to a question aimed at him by the patrol officer. Under no circumstances do the reports reveal anything of the "inner state" of the officers, except in a way that is so perfunctory ("I was happy to see that they had complied with my instructions") that its only function is concealment. Maring practices are depicted as timeless, as flowing upward directly from the natural substratum of our human natures. The implication was of a kind of precultural state in which the two controlling forces are human nature and nature itself, species and environment. What passed for culture was the routinization of the material and practical relationship between organism and environment, such as gardening techniques. The patrol reports are snapshots of the Maring universe in which the lens has little depth of field, the camera no memory.

The reports depict the Maring as obstinate and unfathomable from the perspective of the kiap, sometimes "stupidly" unwilling to act in their own obvious self-interest. They are also portrayed as being able to be hammered and cajoled into peaceful coexistence, even though a primitive, more instinctive, bloodier sentiment boiled just beneath the surface. In this self-conceived image, the kiap, essentially alone, but armed with his masculinity and civilization, stood between the natives, the colonists, and the outside world. It was his job to accommodate the interests of the administration, the various Europeans, and the local population. In kiap eyes, this task was difficult, more difficult than it need be, because the upper administration was overrun by bureaucrats; the colonists (Territorians as they were called) typically had only their personal interests at heart; while the local community, ignorant of the real shape of the modern world, did not know or understand what its real interests were. So the kiaps thought of themselves as standing at the center of this intersection of interests, "of keeping things going" on the frontier, accomplishing the kind of essential but "thankless" task that was often the work of those who "stood up" for their country ("like the boys at Gallipoli"). Those in the fields of encompassment, the men who were in "the line of fire" (as it was once explained to me), envisioned the colonial project as a policy of containment. They were to protect the colonists from the local population and the local population from the outside world. The patrol officer and the patrol report were to be the sole mediators between the local community and the outside world—specifically, the higher rungs of the colonial administration, the Western community at large, and the self-appointed army of international observers (who increasingly regarded the Protectorate as something of an anachronism).[3] The political control of these groups depended on the management of knowledge: the data gathered by the kiap and inscribed in his report. The international community would be kept at bay if only they appreciated how much work was still to be done before people such as the Maring were ready to fly on their own. The expatriate community needed to be contained and controlled in their intercourse with Melanesians. The businessmen especially, many of whom the kiaps thought to be unscrupulous and of questionable patriotism ("who else would leave Australia simply to make money?"), would take advantage of the ignorance of the indigenes to defraud them and in so doing retard local progress and compromise the colonial responsibility. In the vision of the kiaps, they were the rational and enlightened center, the only people who knew the whole story, besieged at times by bureaucrats and international pundits who understood nothing about life in the bush; by a local populace that was primitive, potentially violent, and slow to grasp the mechanics of modern life; and by expatriate businessmen who, though they shared a "mate" mentality with the kiaps, would not hesitate to place their own economic interests above those of God and country. The kiap was the only person on the scene who knew the world, knew the bush, and was loyal to his country and God.

Here is how one former patrol officer described the expatriate community that he had known in and around Mt. Hagen.

> There's not many good marks [honest men] here. Plenty of pointers [dishonest opportunists] looking for quick money, but mostly just spending hours getting pissed [drunk], getting wet [angry] over nothing at all, and looking at every other bloke's woman. They're always looking for an angle or two and have a down on [grudge with] too many people. I think many of them are Pommys [English immigrants to Australia] who just couldn't handle Aussie life, who just going to spend their life here go knocking along [doing nothing useful].

It is clear that the patrol officers drew a sharp distinction between themselves, men who had come to serve the interests of their country, and those expatriates who had migrated to New Guinea for crass economic reasons. In their eyes, the difference told the story even if, as it turned out, many of these same patrol officers would remain in Papua New Guinea after their service was completed and local independence had come (in 1975). The difference was a matter of mentality and morality, and it perpetually brought the patrol officers and the Australian administration in general into a subtle, submerged, but enduring tension with the expatriate population. For their part, the Territorians imagined themselves and their relationship to the "kanakas" in astonishingly racist terms, and they were thus contemptuous of the colonial administration for coddling the local population. In their vision, whites should never have to perform manual labor, were entitled to at least one "personal servant" apiece (Sinclair 1981:20), and had, by virtue of their superiority, the right to exploit the "natives" as they saw fit. This was a natural order that a too-liberal policy could only disturb. Not surprisingly, this "difference" between the kiap and entrepreneurial expatriate was lost on the Maring who saw them as two arms of the same body.

In addition to the odd missionary, the only other person who might be a threat to the authority of the kiap and the administration was the anthropologist. This was not of course intentional on either side, simply the circumstance of the colonial context. The threat stemmed from the reality that the anthropologist was the "other Westerner" on the scene charged with writing an account about that community. And the only other Westerner with the skill and the authority to act as a mediator between the community and the outside world. To complicate matters, the anthropologist was an intellectual, often non-Australian, and most significantly, did not share the goal of containment that was central to the administration's organization of the colonial space. Guided by their own stars, they were prone to overly liberal sentiments and unregulated speech, talk that in a frustratingly academic way seemed to be ignorant of the "real" problems pressing the kiaps in their governance of this colonial terrain. The anthropologist blithely ignored the intractable natives, greedy expatriates, and stodgy bureaucrats. Apparently intelligent and educated, yet soft and unsympathetic to the colonial cause, the anthropologist was, in the kiaps' focused eye, a threat to the control that they exerted through a monopoly on the textual production of that space and its public political presentation. There was an inherent conflict mitigated by a mutual, though unspoken, agreement: in exchange for the kiap's good office, the ethnographer would stick to academic concerns—the "kinship/cosmology shit" as one obviously knowledgeable kiap put it. In the practice of the field, no matter what they knew about how the patrol officers (or their national successors) had treated the local community, the ethnographer remained mute. As long as the behavior was not overly brutal and the violence mostly symbolic, they confined their observations to fieldnotes and the stories they circulated among themselves. And so clashes were infrequent, not least because anthropologists needed the cooperation of the administration to complete the most critical disciplinary hurdle of their profession—the fieldwork that would underwrite their dissertation, establish their place and credentials in the discipline, and constitute the foundation of future research and publications.[4] Twice strangers, with respect to the local community and the administration, and dependent on both for the realization of their project, ethnographers negotiated this terrain by helping the local community as much as they could without stepping out of line with the administration.[5] In the fields of encompassment, compromises were unavoidable, and all were compromised.

The kiap's image of their mission and themselves was also gendered. Western women in particular—female missionaries and Bible translators, the wives of plantation owners and businessmen, nurses, and the occasional anthropologist—were understood as particularly vulnerable. In their own estimation, there was a chivalrous halo to their role as the defender of the West's women—a role that many women ethnographers understood as patronizing and paternalistic (Reay 1992: 141–42; Buchbinder, personal communication). This gendered image was powered by the unspoken and unspeakable fear of miscegenation, sex and marriage between a local man and Western woman. The fear was not that local men would "force themselves" upon these women—indeed, that possibility was summarily dismissed with the comment that "even kanakas are not stupid enough to risk the thumping that would follow." No, the fear was that contact would spark intermingling. It would spawn fantasies of exploring the other sexually, thereby puncturing in the most threatening way possible (at least for the Western imagination) the containment of the two populations. So a very visceral sense of outrage was directed at Western women who, in associating "too freely" with Melanesians, violated the boundaries between the forms of racialized society. In their own frontier worldview, sexual relations between a kiap and a local woman was, given his seething virility and near complete isolation, understandable even if it did betray a certain weakness of character and was not something to be proud of. By contrast, a Western woman who was imagined to have relations with a local man had to have lost her bearings and sense of propriety. She had not only done something that was racially dirty, dangerous, and polluting; she had not only endangered the edifice of containment upon which colonialism was built; she had committed an act of cultural adultery, coupling with a local man when there were more than a few willing white partners.[6]

In the end as in the beginning, colonialism was always a bastard of its own inner contradictions. It sought to modernize and improve local communities yet conserve them as if in a state of suspended animation. It sought to civilize local cultures even while its own self-imagining depended on their otherness. It sought to erase the distinctiveness of the other on which the colonial project was itself founded, but also to identify and rank the differences between the West and its others, all the while ignoring the relations of power on which this exercise was based. It sought to fulfill its mission through agents who read the contradictions inherent in their own project as inadequacies of the other. It was grounded in the self-excusing notion, captured in Sinclair's epigram, that "primitive" cultures lived in the grip of a fear they secretly yearned to be freed from. Finally, it fathomed that it was changing the culture of the other through the nature of the West, thus to battle against the brute nature of the other with Christianity, capitalism, and the other instruments of Western culture. Perhaps the best that can be said of Australian colonialism is that its contradictions were its virtues, engendering enough indecision and offsetting actions that it caused less damage than it might have under other circumstances.

Fractured Politics and the Economy of War

For the Australian administration and the Anglican mission, Maring warfare was the essence of antisocial behavior. The acts of violence visited by one clan cluster upon another undermined sociality and prevented the Maring from rising to a higher standard of civilization—a Western standard. The Kauwatyi rout of the Manamban, the Yomban destruction of the Manga settlements, the descent of the Kundagai upon the Tsembaga, were all indicative of a prevailing state of nature. Under these circumstances, the worst of human instincts—greed, lust, pride, avarice—were allowed free reign. Warfare was the unbridled expression of nature and the suppression of society. In this view, pacification was absolutely essential in that it not only created peace and the conditions for prosperity, it allowed for the existence and advancement of the social itself. Forced pacification would move the "uncontrolled" areas of the protectorate from the state of anarchy—symbolically emblazoned in warfare, headhunting, cannibalism, and sorcery—to the progressive road of civilization.

For the colonizers, the coefficient of amnesia must have been as high as the Highlands itself. The correlation of Western civilization with peace and civility seems to have forgotten the series of genocidal wars that Westerners waged against one another in the twentieth century.[7] To hear expatriates and other Western commentators talk, cannibalism, sorcery, and head-hunting spoke to the very essence of Melanesian society, whereas nuclear weapons, genocide, and mass incarceration were marginal to the real character of the West. But even more than that, the idea that pacification would socialize the Maring misread the character of local warfare, which was defined precisely by its sociality. Like many of these peoples of Melanesia, the Maring make war only among themselves, never against neighboring peoples. There has never been a war between a Maring and a Kalam cluster, for example, and local fight leaders dismissed the idea that it was ever even a possibility. Warfare occurred exclusively between adjacent clan clusters (see map 2, chap. 1) and never for gross economic reasons such as the acquisition of garden land. Because land was part and product of the construction of kinship and the clan, the alienation of another clan's land, livestock, or pandanus was the appropriation of its kinship system. That an enemy's ancestor spirits could never be driven from their homeland symbolized that reality. So Maring warriors slaughtered the pigs and cassowaries, swept the houses into flames, uprooted the trees, and generally destroyed the territory of their enemies rather than appropriate it. To use the land or eat the food of an enemy was anathema because it would destroy the basis of kinship, expunging the instruments of similarity and difference upon which clanship itself was founded (LiPuma 1988:211).

Whereas interpersonal violence, especially between those related by kinship and marriage (e.g., within the family), is highly intentional and draws forth the individual aspect of persons, warfare was persuasively dividual and had little to do with the personal intentions of the combatants. Far from an example of anarchy, it was a kind of sociality, a modality of action between neighbors in which the value of collectivity effaced and sublimated the individuality of the actors—who may on other occasions have acted sociably toward one another. This was, of course, especially true in instances where, due to the pattern of marriage alliances, clans of the same clan cluster or even subclans of the same clan wound up on opposing sides of the battlefield. Harrison, speaking about Melanesia generally, puts it this way: "Amity and enmity, peace and war, help and harm, are contrasting aspects under which the same persons present themselves to one another" being "antithetical ways of envisioning, and acting within, the 'whole' of social relations" (1995:85). What this meant for the Maring was that the prosecution of war entailed practices, ritual and otherwise, that elevated and glorified the relational aspect of the person.

The practices that surrounded warfare assumed that there was no distinction between technical and ritual action. For example, the propitiation of the ancestors and the selection of weapons and enemy targets were inseparably instrumental in the success of the military enterprise. Warfare as a species of violence sought to efface and subordinate the individual aspect of the warriors. Or, to put this in a more Maring way, to be a warrior was not to be an individual but dividual in a pure and transparent way. The most public sign of the collective self was body decoration. All of the warriors had legs smeared with gray clay, black-painted faces, darkened headdresses encircled by cowry shells, and incised shields the width and sometimes the height of a warrior. Such decoration both symbolized and merged the *nomane* (spirit) of the clan with the *min* (life force) of the warriors. The warriors' individuality also disappeared into lineal time. As with their Melpa neighbors (Strathern and Strathern 1971), the decorations bespoke the presence of ancestral spirits—clan spirits, especially the souls of those who had fallen before the enemy's axe. In this vein, the war shields behind which the warriors hid were engraved with the abstract design of a fiery orchid, a metaphorical allusion to the hotness and habitat of the red spirits of war. From a Maring standpoint, warfare was not a way of channeling the aggressive instincts that lurk beneath the surface of civility. It was, along with marriage, exchange, trade (in plumes, axes, pigs, and salt), mutual avoidance, verbal jousting, and sorcery, the way that clan clusters orchestrated their braided histories.

The colonial illusion of an indigenously chaotic world lent support to the administration's notion that it was the author of order. But there existed of course another kind of order defined by the almost perpetual cycle of war and peace, symbolized by the uprooting and replanting of the rumbim plant, enacted in the great ceremony of the kaiko, and embodied in those who had been forced to flee their homelands and beg refuge with distant relatives (Rappaport 1968: chap. 4). The end result was that the Maring were always a "culture" divided, however socially, by fighting and feuding. And when the Australian administration appeared in the mid-1950s, the Tsembaga, driven from their land by the Kundagai, had sought shelter with the Tuguma and the Kauwatyi; the Manamban had been sent into exile by the combined forces of their eastern and western neighbors, the Kauwatyi and Tukmenga; and the Manga had fled eastward to escape the wrath of the Yomban. Entering a world that already had a shape and a distribution of people and power, the Australian administration was an exogenous force of untold power. For the defeated clan clusters and the diaspora of war, it was a stroke of serendipity beyond imagination, a way for them to reoccupy their lost lands immediately and gain an ally who would protect them in the future. So the more vulnerable the clan cluster the more likely it was that it would not only bow willingly to the colonial authorities, but would endorse the Pax Britannica as the road to salvation. As for the more powerful clan clusters, they were intimidated into submission by what appeared to them to be an arbitrary exercise of power—the verbal abuse, beatings, jail terms, work punishments, and shows of force. This was the kiaps' definition of being firm and authoritative. It was the Maring definition of the humiliation that befalls those who have been deserted by the their ancestors and defeated by their enemies. The elders' narratives of first contact report this reality, although, ironically, an aspect of the new road has been a cultural effort to erase and downplay these narratives. Not the least of the reasons why Westerners could not grasp the inherent sociality of Melanesian warfare was that their horizon of understanding began in a conception of human nature that, by its nature, was nothing less than culture naturalized.

Human Nature and the Other

Behind the comments and stances of missionaries, kiaps, and the expatriate community lay a tacit philosophy of human nature. This was a seat-of-the-pants philosophy, less a coherent viewpoint than a set of characterizations and explanations united by a common and underlying occidentalism. On this viewpoint, the nature of Melanesians, Maring in particular, was conceived as a layering, a number of tiers neither harmonious nor transparent to the uncritical eye. The first element was the concept that there is an inner core, an original sameness common to every human being. Listening to missionaries giving their sermons, the kiaps talking of their mission, or medical volunteers explaining why they chose Highland New Guinea left no doubt that these Westerners believed in a "generic human nature." In moments of liberal enlightenment, Westerners of all varieties, from the Anglican bishop to the kiap, would, referring to Melanesians, echo the phrase that "underneath we are all the same." This theory was of more than archaeological value; it was meant to suggest that, because we are all human, we all have the same potential. Here is an excerpt from a statement by the Anglican priest at Koinambe.

> People here [Maring] are different, but deep down, we are all really the same. What each person wants is peace and a chance at self-fulfillment. The people of the Jimi are just like people everywhere; they want to improve themselves; they want respect, and want to use their talents to make a better life for themselves and their family members. Everyone of us is equally God's children.

As if from central colonial casting, the good father's statement inscribes the double ideology of colonialism: that there exists a generic human nature and that this being is the bourgeois man in all his singularity. His words were founded on the conviction that fundamentally, in that first instance before God, there is no difference between Westerner and Melanesian. Conceived in His image, God has made all humans open to spirituality, love, faith, family, and the other virtues. Equally exiled from paradise, they must confront birth, aging, and death on the same footing. Attending a Maring funeral with Father Bailey, the wailing of the mourners piercing through the morning mist, he put his hand on my shoulder and offered that "one of the things that made us all human is that we cried at the death of a parent." There is a human condition, spiritual and physical, that makes us all, even in all our individuality, the same at the ground level of being. In particular, those who had come to Melanesia voluntarily to help or convert held this view as an unshakable ontological premise.

However noble this concept of heavenly and earthly equality, and however emancipatory it might be in principle, it was only one level of a heavily alloyed image of human nature. For at the same time, it was held that people have a set of base instincts—such as fear, lust, pride, aggression, avarice, and greed—that are common to all and constantly threaten the better side of Man. So the human artifacts of family and community, the ways that individuals come together socially to resolve the problems of the human condition, are constantly besieged by the forces of aggression, greed, and unbridled egoism. In this vision of human nature, life is an ongoing struggle between the part of us that reflects God's image and the sinful, destructive instincts that are part of our (fallen) nature. The Western view was that Maring, like people everywhere, are the same as Westerners at this base level. This human nature was transhistorical and transcultural. It was not bound by the tethers of time or culture, and thus one could take it for granted. A good indication of this was how the Westerners read, or presumed they read, Maring facial gestures. The idea was that there was a one-to-one correspondence between form and function, the gesture and its meaning, and that the source of meaning was the set of base virtues and instincts. The station manager remarked that he could see the glitter of greed in men's eyes when they were receiving money for their coffee or gold. The priest told me that although he could not speak to many of the woman parishioners (because they did not speak pidgin), he knew from their "look" who was "a virtuous and faithful wife." The goal of Church and the colonial administration was to create an environment—with a sense of order, peace, and godliness—that would elicit the positive virtues.

Overlying the sense of similar virtue and the scandal of basic instincts were culture and society. The inarticulate Western view was that by dint of these human virtues, a peaceful, harmonious, cooperative sociality could trump those disruptive instincts. Aggression, greed, and the other instincts could be kept at bay in the interests of society-making. Like a caged and cunning animal, these instincts could be held in check only with constant vigilance and surveillance. Only in this way was it possible to safeguard the social order and prevent it from reverting back to disorder and discord. Such vigilance required institutions and rites of community (e.g., civic associations and meetings) and the acceptance of the higher authority of God and State. From this viewpoint, the marvel of Western culture was that its institutions and practices were devoted to the suppression of the natural substratum and the celebration of sociality. Of course, violence and war sometimes erupted, aggression and greed bubbling to the surface, but the glory of the West was that civility and sociality soon reasserted themselves, driving the base instincts back into the hell from which they arose.

On this view of human nature, the "problem" and "failure" of

Melanesian culture was its glorification of the "wrong" instincts. Practices such as headhunting, sorcery, cannibalism, polygamy, animal sacrifice, institutionalized homosexuality, arranged marriages, and chronic warfare served to express, legitimate, and—worse—celebrate these base instincts. Headhunting was pride (i.e., trophies) and blood lust turned into a cultural sport. Warfare was aggression raised to the communal power. Sorcery was envy of others' success hardened as social practice, while polygamy was nothing less than a way of condoning untempered sexuality and lust. Even worse, institutionalized homosexuality was bestiality with a human face. Arranging marriages in which women were "sold" for money was an outpouring of greed writ socially large. These practices were not understood as fundamental to the character of Melanesian society but as universal human weaknesses that had become embedded in their cultural practice. The Western view was that Melanesian cultures were, and would remain, primitive so long as human weaknesses were socially inscribed and hence given a good name. The underlying premise was that Melanesian cultures, by encoding and sanctifying these universal human faults, stood between people and their better natures. Where the Western nations outlawed these sins, rendering them personal perversion (e.g., homosexuality) or crimes against humanity (e.g., cannibalism),[8] Melanesians made sin social. They seemed not to understand that these base instincts were something to be overcome not socially applauded. So Melanesian cultures were themselves the problem. Not only did they endorse immoral acts and practices, they were a barrier to becoming modern and the appreciation of its virtues. For the Westerners, it was precisely those practices that distinguished Melanesian from Westerner that retarded their progress. Modernity thus entailed, and was synonymous with, an erasure of those differences that distinguished Westerners from Melanesians. So in this Western theory of human nature, Melanesian man, in his encounter with and quest for modernity, was hobbled first by his race (which, with a few noteworthy and laudable exceptions, bequeathed him less than a European intelligence) and then again by their culture. No wonder that, from the Western heights, their climb toward modernity seemed all uphill.

Moreover, there were never any certainties here. No matter how long the installation of civilization, there was always the possibility of degeneration and devolution, an evolutionary reversal in which an individual or an entire people reverted back to headhunting, ancestor worship, polygamy, superstition, and other sins. Even when a people seemed to embrace capitalism, Christianity, formal education, medicine, and the state, vigilance was necessary because backsliding was part of the nature of Man. The ever-present threat of devolution was epitomized by the "European" who had gone "native," who had returned to the heart of darkness where people make the worst of our human natures the very foundation of social life itself. Nonetheless, within this vision of human nature all people are recoverable, redemption is always possible, because we all share a human nature and we can all endorse those customs that express its virtues.

This vision of human nature was also a method of interpreting others. As with facial gestures, it rendered seemingly exotic behavior in familiar terms. The ethnographic trick was to simply read backward from the cultural practice to the underlying instincts. Such was the case with the interpretation of ancestor worship—the sacrament in which the living community sacrifices pigs to the recently deceased in return for their help with material and social relations (bountiful gardens and fruitful alliances). The Western theory was that all humans, by virtue of their humanity, had some sense of the Almighty, some glimpse that there were supernatural powers that lay beyond their ken. Here in the summer of 1979 is what the Anglican archbishop of Papua New Guinea had to say on the subject: "That people worship at all shows me that deep down that they know God. They may not know Him in His true form, but they have a spiritual instinct, they sense His presence. By their nature, all people know God. The work of the Christian missions in PNG is to channel this spirituality in the right direction." A VSO worker involved in setting up the primary school education remarked, "If I was stuck out here in the bush and was far from any church, I might begin to worship my ancestors too." In this respect, the existence of local religious practice was simply an expression of a universal spirituality, a thirst for the divine shared by all humans. At the same time, the content of the practice was an expression of the fear that arises in those who do not share a scientific understanding of nature. So they confuse and conflate technical and ritual action. Ignorant of why plants and animals really grow, of the true causes of health and disease, some mixture of greed and fear drives them to look to the spirits for secular answers.

Understanding practice as an outpouring of instincts was itself a kind of policy of containment. True to the spirit of the West, it was a laborsaving device, a kind of cultural X ray for those on the frontier. For it meant that one only had to attend to the surface of indigenous lifeways. If it was difficult for Westerners to fathom why lust led to polygamy—as the Anglican missionaries observed more than once—it was transparent that the basis of polygamy was lust. If it was difficult to figure why envy led to the spells and magic of the sorcery, it was easy to see that the motive for sorcery was envy and greed. This theory of human nature rendered irrelevant any depth of involvement in the local world, any real search for the genesis and organizing principles of practices. So the goal of colonialism was to redirect people's instincts, create contexts for the expression of the most virtuous ones, teach people better practices for achieving the same results.

As a native son of Alabama, turned Baptist missionary in the Southern Highlands, once explained to me: "when you are cleaning out the closet [of old customs], it is not necessary to examine the throwaways too carefully." His maxim was a reply to my question as to why, if he had lived and worked with the same people for a decade, he did not know more about, and show more interest in, their culture. By the same token, the notion that one could glide along the surface of custom, that practice was self-explanatory, allowed the Australian administration to move district officers and other field personnel around swiftly and indiscriminately. Writing about the Eastern Highlands, Watson (1992) puts it this way.

> In recognizing local ethnic differences, an outsider might suppose that kiaps would be among the best informed. In fact, they were not. Plainly they were handicapped, among other things,[9] by the system of short-term posting. . . . This system put a man in one post for twenty-one months and then, upon his return from a three-month leave "down south" most often sent him next to a different station, not uncommonly a station in a remote or quite different corner of the country. The practical work of administering . . . could—or at any rate did—proceed without detailed ethnic knowledge of the local people. (185)

The same could certainly be said for the administration of both Simbai and Jimi Valleys. The notion was that for the kiaps, or for that matter any Westerners, to be successful all they had to do was use their common sense. This would lead from the surface of behavior back to the underlying traits that inspired it. The logic of administration was straightforward: social practices inspired by virtue would be condoned; those animated by vice would be extinguished with a firm, muscular response.

The Maring, like other Melanesians, had their own view of human nature, although, of course, there is no term in Maring that bears even a family resemblance to the Western conception. The founding reason was that humans by their nature have no nature, only the inscription of a thoroughgoing sociality. The social is never an artifact built on a natural substratum. Rather, as M. Strathern (1980, 1988), Harrison (1995), and others have argued, what Melanesians take for granted is the inherent sociality of life. To be human is to be cultural, to be immersed in a self-defining web of social relations in which different contexts for action require different modalities of sociality. Ultimately, what for Westerners were different aspects of our human nature were, for Maring, different levels of intentionality. The notion that sociality has inherently cultural roots has no place for "a generic human nature," and indeed the Maring understanding was that underneath different peoples are just that: different. The paramount example of this was, ironically, their conception of Westerners. I and other Westerners were thought to be immune from sorcery. Where sexual contact was debilitating for young Maring men—draining them of "grease"—I and other Westerners were thought to suffer no ill effects. By the same token, the Maring treated Westerners as though they had no gender: men and women ethnographers were on the same footing because, whatever kind of people they were, they sure weren't Maring. From the native point of view, Maring and Westerners were different in the first instance—a difference that the mission and the educational system would try successfully to change (see chaps. 7, 9).

Unlike the Western vision, the Maring did not believe that people had internal states. Accordingly, there was no way in the Maring language to assert that someone is intelligent, belligerent, honest, or whatever. What could be said is that they acted honestly; they hunted intelligently; or they fought aggressively. Persons did have biographies in the sense that others expected them to behave intelligently or give gifts graciously, but agents interpreted these as regularities of action rather than expressions of internal states. Contrast this with the Western construction of personhood. Because we imagine that persons have internal states, agents act toward others as if they did indeed have such states, which in turn motivates Western persons to construct their subjectivity and imagine themselves in terms of these states. In this respect, internal states are "social fictions" that are culturally and historically *true* in the fullest sense of the word because they inform the beliefs, desires, and judgments of Western agents. They shape the intentionality and meaning of behavior. The ideological aspect of this aspect of personhood is the Western notion that, because agents have free will and are the sole authors of their own actions, these internal states are the primary determinants of action. Open any Western newspaper and there will be stories of people who did well (on their job, on a test, in sports, etc.) because they are intelligent, courageous, hardworking, etc.; others who fair poorly because they are timid, lazy, corrupt, . . . fill in the adjective. What all of these explanations have in common is that they envision the results as the public expression of the internal state of the agents. The Maring did not, by contrast, attribute the results of an action to the internal states of the agents. Though feelings were embodied—anger in the abdomen, shame on the skin, betrayal in the liver—these locations were not states, but rather the incarnation of a relationship between the person and the social world. What the next generation would "learn" in school and church was that people did indeed have internal states. What they took this to mean was that the modern person was defined by having internal states. In the new-road world, no one should leave home without them.

A critical aspect of the Maring image of "human nature" was that the social capacities of people were inseparable from their physical being. The ability of whites—to "pull" all manner of goods, to receive letters and radio messages, command airplanes, etc.—these were taken to be part of their physical state, at least during the opening years of contact. By equal account, their inability to walk in the dense, rain-slippery jungle, negotiate the log and rope bridges across ravines, or carry loads on their back was also taken to be part of their physical capacities. What Westerners could and could not do were associated with their physiognomy. These physical attributes were common cause with their spiritual and mental qualities. One of the lessons of schooling learned by the next generation would be to separate the mental from the physical. As I was told more than once by this generation, "before the missionaries came we did not know that people had minds." In other words, because the locus of understanding of others was the conjuncture of relationships, the separation of mind and body as well as the conception that behavior is an expression of a person's internal states, though imaginable, did not figure in people's interpretation of these relations. Or, to put this another way, because Melanesians understood behavior as the crystallization and objectification of ongoing relations, what was in people's "heads," what states they may have, was entirely moot. They become important only when the world tilts so far toward modernity. And nowhere was this more the case than with respect to the up-and-coming generation of men *and* women.

The Generation of Modernity

"The *nomane* (spirit and culture) of my generation is entirely different from that of our fathers and mothers: sons go their own way and make new business; daughters speak their mind and marry the man of their choice; we show our elders respect but pay no attention to their wisdom because it belongs to the epoch of our ancestors." Spoken by a leader of the junior generation, the words encapsulate the birth of new relationship between reproduction and temporality. Certainly, if the Maring material underlines any point it is that to appreciate the dynamics of the transformation of Melanesia and beyond, anthropology must develop the theme and theory of generations. It must learn to appreciate those who, living on the social and existential edges of adult society, are most poised to change it. Such progress entails an anthropology that locates those who are coming of age, those who are in the throes of forging their identity, those who grasp history intuitively as the difference between the world they encounter and that portrayed by their parents—by any other name the youth of a society. Only too aware of their world-changing, the Maring senior generation also recognized that the beliefs, desires, and social trajectory of the junior generation were the oxygen of change. And they are not alone. Across the world, up and down the ladder of social class and consciousness, accounts of the clash between generations inundate media and mind. The reality suggests that an understanding of generations is essential to an account of encompassment and the creation of the modern. That at least is what I argue theoretically, amplified of course by the Maring ethnography.

Prior to their encompassment, the Maring, like other Melanesians, lived a different kind of social history. Locally produced oppositions and hierarchies (male versus female), cycles of exchange with ancestors and affines, and an elaborate system of rituals (see LiPuma 1988; Rappaport 1968, 1977 for detailed accounts) defined the overarching and objective structure of collectivity. Although the Maring had their own take on each of these, the social systems of Highland New Guinea and Melanesia generally were remarkably similar in the fidelity of their reproduction. This objective structure generated a world that inculcated in the living community a social epistemology, a structure of desire, and sets of dispositions (most prominently a sense of exchange and the desire to actualize it toward others). Because the objective structure at any given time tended to be similar to the structure under which these dispositions, desires, and knowledge were instilled, Maring tended to simply and positively reproduce themselves. This is not to say that change did not occur or even that change was not sometimes desired, only that change was animated by ecological and demographic fluctuations (Buchbinder 1973; Lowman 1980), the unpredictable outcomes of military engagements (Rappaport 1967; Vayda 1971), and the contradictions within the structure of clanship and affinity that engendered group fission, fusion, and migration (LiPuma 1988, 1989; Maclean 1984). The result was that Maring history was local, cyclical, and nearly determinate. The social distance between generations was, accordingly, relatively narrow. There was once a time, the poet explains, when all the generations "breathed the same air" (Pavese 1979:21).

This mode of simple social reproduction gave life to its own mode of generation. This was no more or less than a way of accounting for succession, the replacement of one person by another over the cascade of time. Prior to their encounter with the West, the tempo of Maring lifeways turned on two forms of social time: seasonal time or the rotation of gardens and weather, and the wheel of succession. These who were born and nurtured from the bodily substance of their ancestors in turn passed on and became incarnated through their descendants. In contrast to the West, where succession is an absent-from-mind anonymous relationship, here it was engraved in consciousness and interpersonal kinship. The Maring, like all those who refuse to posit a concept of society over and above social relations, saw the replacement of people as a rope of interlinked and interchangeable identities—a "line" of known and homologous persons whose "root base" begins in the founding of the clan that, in a kind of social tautology, was inseparable from, because defined by, the original "planting" of men on "this" land. The time of generation perpetually brought into convergence the relationship between mortal and social time—a mortality that the Maring transcended by designating a "line" of agents who, although they lived in mortal history, were conceived to transcend that history in the name of the reproduction of the clan. The function of ritual here, specifically funeral practices, was to form a bridge between mortal and social time. These rituals, as Foster (1995b) indicates, emancipated a chain of living ancestors to assume the place of the dead. For the Maring as for other Melanesians, living replaced the dead through transfers to the clan of the deceased, transfers that, by imagining the clans as collective individuals, allowed the participants to draw a homologue between one person/object and other (such as x's sons and y's daughter). The objective of replacement was the conservation of social relations; the production of a generation, bound by kinship and imbued with the values and dispositions of the ancestors, created a continuity that was more than meaningless perfection.

Encompassment changed this. Dramatically and permanently. It expanded the bounds of the public political sphere beyond the limits of the relations between clan clusters and set in motion a stream of external and indeterminate transformations. In the context of the new road, the connection between the objective structure and the installation of knowledge, desires, and dispositions became tenuous and disarticulated. Transformations in the objective structure brought about by the advent of Western agents and institutions meant that the knowledge, desires, and dispositions of the senior generation would be significantly different from those inculcated in the up-and-coming generation. More, what was instilled in this up-and-coming generation was itself becoming rapidly out of alignment with still further and continuing transformations in an increasingly global objective structure. No sooner had they mastered pidgin then it became apparent that to truly succeed it was necessary to know English. No sooner had they begun to adjust to the compass of the Australian state then a national state, moved by a different set of directives, emerged. No sooner had they obtained a primary education then it became essential to attend high school to obtain a job in the modern sector. In the fields of encompassment, the generation gap was as wide as could be imagined. Father and son, the senior statesman with shamanistic powers and his high school educated, trilingual, store-owning son, were defined by knowledge, desires, and dispositions that were worlds apart. Yet they were joined by semen and blood. By genealogy and identity. And by the reality that in the age of encompassment they would struggle over the character and creation of the world they had in common.

The junior generation grasped modernity as the unfolding of a new world of practices, as an invitation to probe the cultural possibilities once censured by kastam and now seemingly celebrated by modernity. In respect to social relations, most of the junior generation pushed for the relaxation of kin and community obligations. They continually explored avenues of escape from the embrace of their clansmen and affines—men and women who did not understand the logic of business, the individual rights of persons, and other wisdoms of the West. In their struggles with their seniors they were determined to amplify their personal freedom, to listen first and foremost to their own voice and that of their generation. The most able of the young politicians sought to create a respectful distance from their elders, listening to what they had to say but with every intention of following their own lights. This ascension of personal freedom was part of a progressive movement in which the individual aspect of the person began to overshadow its dividual or relational alter and the individual increasingly emerged as the locus of decision making and moral authority. This contravened longstanding conventions and helped to wrest power from the more senior generations. A paradoxical sign of its emergence was that the most successful senior leaders skillfully invented ways of both attaining their own ends and preserving (at least the appearance of) the independence of their juniors. Two of the dominant avenues for freedom, both requiring education, were a position in the civil service or with the Anglican Church. The ultimate assertion of personal independence was to move to an urban locale, a route that was taken by the most educated, especially those capable in English. A taste of urban ways went hand in hand with education because the only high schools were in the more urban settings of Mount Hagen or the Wahgi Valley. The more this group became accustomed to freedom, the more prickly they became toward the demands of kinship that would seem to spring up unexpectedly each time they returned home, dashing their plans for the immediate future. Some reluctantly surrendered to these obligations; others became increasingly sensitive to the increasingly infrequent call of their community. For a few who became emblematic of how modernity could deplete the strength of the community, this drove them to distant and more urban centers, ever farther from the tentacles of their relatives, spurring them ever more insistently toward the magnetic pole of the greatest possible freedom. The anonymity of life in Port Moresby and even more so in Australia epitomized this possibility, most visibly embodied in the Maring translator of the Bible who, educated in Australia, longed for the metropole more than the bush.

As the waves of encompassment washed over the Maring, two facts became impressed on the consciousness of even the most conservative adults. The first was that the socialization of children would be entirely and substantively different than under the more traditional regime. The construction of subjectivity would have a new basis because peoples' concepts, desires, dispositions, and life trajectories would have to be fitted to new objective conditions. And then refitted as these conditions changed. Not only would the phantom of socializing one's children have a new form, it would change suddenly and in barely predictable ways, producing in the senior generation a sense of disquiet and uncertainty, as though the heartbeat of social life had become irregular and arrhythmic. The senior leader Yingok observed that "I am like my father, but my sons resemble me less each day . . . because their bodies have been nurtured by your [Western] food, your medicine, your language, your schools, your religion and laws." His words capture the storyline better than any page of analysis. Spoken in the spring of 1980, they underlined the realization that socialization and succession would now be different from anything that had gone before. The second realization was that encompassment created a permanent divide between the time of custom and the time of law, the epoch of the ancestors and that of Jesus, the era of great shamans and the modernity of biomedicine. It was *the* historical event that founds and contextualizes all other events. One result was the genesis of a generation gap, articulated as a taken-for-granted distinction between those who had been born before the kiaps arrived and those born after. The more senior generations sometimes applied the term *kiap babies* to this generation; usually said with a measure of derision, it nonetheless acknowledged the temporal break in the succession of generations. Implicitly the Maring came to recognize that modernity produced a new mode of generation that was inseparable from the generation of new modes of knowledge and desire. So much was this the reality that irrespective of their position in social space, agents began to circulate a discourse that openly acknowledged generational divisions and assumed further that across a variety of contexts for action differences in generation would motivate and explain people's behavior. Thus, a distinctive feature of the first quarter century of contact was that generation became an increasingly visible and salient social category. As the modern became enmeshed in local lifeways so did the assumption that generation was always at issue. It emerged as a significant metadiscursive framing device, a presupposition that informed how agents would interpret a given instance of speech, especially when they used speech to characterize or explain behavior. Generation became a way of explaining everything from the way people spoke to the modes of dress and body decoration (e.g., pearlshells or a wristwatch) they preferred, from the way they liked to do business to the foods they yearned for, from whether their emphasis was on kinship and customary obligations or friendship and personal freedom. The circulation of a discourse about generation helped to engender the reality that it took as its object of linguistic representation.

In the first quarter century of contact, from the first encounters in 1955 to the ascension of the first post-contact generation in 1980, the Maring reconstructed generation according to four principles or criteria. The first was age grade which corresponded to, and was a proxy for, the major break in the objective structures of social life. As observed, they took the advance of the West as the epochal break in their history. However close in chronological age, it was assumed that agents who stood on opposite sides of this divide were almost sure to be generationally distinct. It commonly assumed that they would be imbued with a distinct *nomane* (denoting both spirit and customs) because their spirit substance had been formed in the crucible of their interaction with the West. The second principle was the internalization of those marked forms of knowledge, desire, and disposition specific to the character of modernity. Agents classified others and themselves according to the degree to which they had internalized these forms. Whether and to what degree a Maring spoke pidgin, for example, marked that person as belonging to one generation or another. Whether a person owned a wristwatch and whether they could tell and use time marked that person as belonging to one generation or another. Agents were also generationally classified by other agents according to their ability to operate within the Western sphere (e.g., opening a bank account, arranging for air transportation, and so on) and their ability to negotiate with its representatives (e.g., the Anglican administrators). The third principle was the exercise of personal choice. Historically, both ends of the phrase "personal choice" were new social determinations. The ascension of the person-as-individual as a critical locus of decision making and moral authority and an expansion of the rights of action of that emerging form of personhood were products of the Maring engagement with Western agents and institutions. They were founded on the dramatic increase in personal freedom coupled with the emergence of the individual aspect of the person brought about by the immersion of especially the junior generation in Christianity, formal education, plantation labor, and Western-style jurisprudence. Maring, like Melanesians generally, linguistically captured the ascension of personal choice as a legitimate mode of behavior by adopting the oh-so-appropriate pidgin phrasing "lik belong yu." It pointedly conveys the sentiment that the "you" embodies and is the cause of its own desires and action. This concept lives in stark contrast to the indigenous supposition that desires and actions were drawn out of a person by the relationalities in which he or she was inescapably immersed as a condition of the social. It was thus allowed that as a matter of personal choice agents might, through their own initiative and behavior, self-select their generation. The final principle was time or, more precisely, social trajectory. Agents gave themselves and others a position in the space of modernity by virtue of their trajectory of change over time. Those persons who constantly sought to become more modern were given a location in social space that tracked not only their outstanding forms of knowledge, desire, and dispositions, but what they were likely to become in the future. In this respect, the use of generation as an analytic/ethnographic category *relationally* unites the past (the source of measurement-from), the present (a person's presently embodied forms of knowledge, desire, and dispositions), and the *future* (what these forms may become given a notion of the future that is itself defined at the intersection of local and imported views of time) in a single moment.

The generational punctuation of what was, after all, a continuous demographic space became inscribed in the comparative discourse set up by agents when they classified someone as "too old" to speak pidgin or to want (desire) to travel to Mt. Hagen, or "too young" to show respect for the ancestors or the power of their elders. Certain people were "too hard" in their ways to appreciate the virtues of a saving account at the Bank of New South Wales, others too infatuated with the modern to appreciate the symbols of their past (e.g., implements of war and magic) other than as potential sources of income. Certain people were "too close" to the past to comprehend biomedicine, others too immersed in the present to believe in the powers of the shamans. What is clear is that persons who hold neighboring positions in social space, having been subject to similar agents and institutions of encompassment (e.g., education at the mission station by Christian teachers) and therefore subject to similar conditioning factors (e.g., emphasis on the individual at the locus of responsibility) have every chance of internalizing similar desires, dispositions, and forms of knowledge and "thus of producing practices and representations of a similar kind" (Bourdieu 1987:5). They have every chance of making the same choices and desiring the same trajectory toward the modern. The set of positions created by modernity were thus relatively stable because similar objective conditions impressed themselves on agents of a certain historical age. For example, in a survey of the Kauwatyi clan cluster (conducted in January 1980), all but 4 (out of 67) men aged twenty to forty had engaged the culture of capitalism through performing contract labor on a coastal plantation whereas only 6 of 42 men aged forty to sixty had done so. The positions were also relatively stable because each person (and hence each generation) was defined relationally, according to similarities and differences in respect to other persons. This produced a powerful and practical generational effect because agents with similar capacities, desires, interests, and dispositions were more likely to come together as a practical group. They were more likely to form social groups and coalitions to pursue their interests which, reciprocally, also tended to reproduce and reinforce their similarity. One result was that cross-generational groups tended toward hierarchy, archtypically a big-man and his subordinates, while the gravitational pull of intra-generational groups was toward equality.

But the ethnography also indicates that there is no absolute correlation between age and modernity; some persons who were over forty adopted a more modern perspective than those in their thirties. This appears unreasonable or contradictory only if we consider generation an age-dependent category and we forget that this social space was also intrinsically a field of power. In the flow of history not everyone inherits the same social leverage. Thus several men in the thirty-something age category chose to adopt dispositions and practices characteristic of more senior generations. Not having attended school, not having mastered pidgin, intimidated by the complexities of business, and thus deprived of the material and symbolic capital that "attached to the skin" of their contemporaries, they nominated themselves as critics of the modern and as young guardians of custom. In their own response to the modern, they recast kastam into a resource they could deploy in their struggles with other members of their generation. They once collaborated with several elders in a failed attempt to rekindle ancestor worship. And they sometimes joined their elders in publicly decrying the newfound independence of women. In their discussion with members of their own generation, they advised caution in approaching things modern. But history (and God) was not on their side and they were able to garner only minor and waning influence using this strategy and probably would have won even less except for the fact that honoring select customs was one of the few strategies available to the Maring to counter white privilege.

Simply because persons occupy similar positions in social space does not mean that they will automatically recognize themselves as a generation or that they will mobilize as a group to act in the world. Generations are "virtual" classes in that, due to the similarities among their agents, they will likely cohere as categories of self-conscious agents. In times of great change, such as the advent of Westernization, it is almost certain that a generational identity will emerge. Nevertheless, the emergence of this identity in any real life situation will always have to compete with other modes of identity, such as that of clanship in the Melanesian context and ethnicity in others. It will also have to compete with other, more practical divisions, such as the rivalries that spring up among members of the same generation. What this means is that a generation will emerge as a group only through the intentional action of agents who, in setting their generation off from others, both define and legitimize a new trajectory for that society. In the Maring case, I am talking about men such as Moses Winai. High school educated and fluent in English, a devout Christian who operated the most successful local owned trade store in the Jimi Valley, the true nephew of one the most powerful Maring big-men and the priest's handpicked candidate to manage the Anglican mission at Koinambe, a charismatic man who was imbued with all the forms of knowledge and desire characteristic of the modern man, Moses nominated himself to speak on behalf of the junior generation even as members of his own and other generations recognized him as a principal leader of this up-and-coming group of men. The relative emergence of a generation—its relative distance from other generations—is always the result of both a set of transformations in the objective structure of social life that, in turn, unfuses new modes of knowledge, desire, and dispositions into an age class, and the emergence of leaders who, on the basis of and inspired by these new modes of understanding and acting upon the world, strive to realize the forms of interest inscribed in this new vision and division of society by constructing a generation in and for practical action. The well-founded construction of a generation is one of the instruments—that is also a weapon—by which the junior generation wrests power from their seniors, and conversely, one of the means by which seniors claim privilege, in part by invoking kastam that, without hesitation, ceded power to them. Indeed, the field of encompassment was the site of complex struggles in which the senior generation sought to both claim its right of authority and co-opt the junior generation through the use of seduction and intimidation, all the while mindful of and seeking to create rifts within the junior division. For its part, the junior generation deployed its knowledge of the modern world to attain increasingly acknowledged ends (e.g., making money) and cited that knowledge as a way to disparage their seniors, solidify their own identity, and ascend to power before their "time," meaning customary time, the form of time characteristic of precontact society.

What was critical about this "modern" generation was that it stood precisely at the conjuncture between the forms of knowing and desire immanent in their parents and those forms that were instilled partly by these parents and partly by a world that played no part in the creation of their parents' habitus. Moreover this generation had to respond and adjust to the demands of a prevailing situation that increasingly exalted modern forms of knowledge and desire and disparaged customary ones. No wonder it was often difficult for them to maintain their sense of balance as they crossed a bridge (that they were also responsible for building) from one cultural world to another. This generation felt its predicament as discomfort and confusion, not least because (like all generations) much of what was happening with respect to the relationship between transforming objective structures and co-relative forms of knowledge and desire was happening beyond the pale of consciousness. So my friend says to me: "I am Gou by birth, Barnabas by baptism, and Barnabas Gou is the full name I go under—maybe I don't know who I am." "Not knowing who you are is a very Western sentiment," I reply, to which he just smiles a smile of amusement and resignation. What Gou grasped was that the practical consensus of meaning—the coordination of intentionality—that once came so easily to social life now seemed to be a struggle. For reasons that were hard to comprehend, the senior and junior generations usually found it difficult to see eye to eye (e.g., on how profits from the tradestore should be distributed, how marriages should be arranged and so on). Bourdieu (1977), focusing on the relation between structure and habitus, puts it this way:

> practices are liable to incur sanctions when the environment they must confront is very distant from that to which they are objectively fitted. This is why generation-based conflicts do not oppose age-classes separated by natural properties. They oppose habitus produced by different conditions of existence which, in imposing different visions of the impossible, the possible, and the probable, motivate one group to experience as natural or reasonable practices and aspirations that the other group finds unthinkable or scandalous, and vice versa (78, my translation).[10]

In the encompassment of Melanesia, the junior generation finds the ethos and practices of their seniors old-fashioned and passé while the senior generation finds the practices and dispositions of their juniors, if not unthinkable or scandalous, then simply an entirely new mode of sociality. The eldest generation of Maring—those in their late sixties and early seventies who had retired from public life—did see the ways of junior generation as incomprehensible. With a touch of derision and a hint of wonder they sometimes referred to them as "kiap babies"—children borne after the advent of the "new road." The agents and institutions of encompassment differentiated what I have called the elder, senior, and junior generations, but because the character of its effect was more pronounced on the young, the gradient of difference was much steeper between junior and senior generations than between senior and elder generations. The Maring themselves quite explicitly recognized this reality, conceptualizing it through the transparency of linguistic competence. This itself was a longstanding trope because the Maring always conceptualized differences between peoples in terms of language, professing, for example, to see earthshaking differences between Maring and Narak.

Of the junior generation it was said that both men and women were fluent in pidgin and that many of its leaders also spoke English (at least to the ear of nonspeakers). Of the senior generation it was said that most (though not all) of the men were conversant in pidgin whereas the vast majority of the women were not. Of the elder generation it was said that everyone was limited to tok plas with only a few even dabbling in pidgin.

But not only were all of the junior men fluent in pidgin, several spoke English and almost everyone in the junior generation knew at least a smattering of English vocabulary. The pattern of code switching and the introduction of English words were often intended to exclude members of the elder and/or senior generations. To index and mark their distance from the present reality. Repeatedly, for example, in a generational confrontation over the operation of a trade store, the store owner and other members of the junior generation not only sought to impose capitalist forms of knowledge and desire on the situation (i.e., to make and reinvest profits and use a bank account to accumulate capital to expand the business) but attempted to exercise control over the discourse by continually switching into pidgin, inserting English words and phrases, and inventing new verb-chains in Maring to refer to their new world (e.g., the verbs for repeat, gain, and grow were linked together to denote reinvest). Enos, a manager of Anglican trade store, when asked why he often used English and pidgin in talking to other Maring, observed that much of what needed to be said nowadays could not properly be said in tok plas. Or that it was necessary to twist tok plas in new directions. He knew what generations in change and the poets have always known: that because agents are condemned to speak a language already forged and immobilized by prior usage, to harness it for meanings and values beyond its horizon requires resources from afar and from within. As Proust reminded us over and over again, language is always trying but never quite able to cover all the terrain between the inner lands of emotions, the outer world of society, and the realm of the senses that lies between.

The typology was part of an indigenous comparative discourse about behavior in that people assumed that, since language was instrumental in identity formation, there was a correlation between linguistic competence and modes of sociality. This assumption was, of course, simply a specification of the original trope that Maring and Narak, for example, behaved differently because they spoke differently. Nonetheless, it is important to remember that the ideological door swings in both directions. And if we take the Maring's own discourse about language and the "new road" at face value only, we are liable to confer too much power on encompassing agents and institutions. We may end up believing that the mission, the schools, the medical system, and the other aspects of the modern shaped discrete and homogenous generations when the real story is that they were internally differentiated and separated by gradients of difference. This was especially true of the junior generation for reasons that were intrinsic to the very construction of the modern.

In practice, generation always intersects with other visions and divisions of the social universe and other principles of identity and practice populate the same space as that of generation. What leaders of any generation struggle against is this practical conjuncture of social principles that serves to blur the lines between generations and complicate the invocation of a generational identity. The resources of the modernity, while powerful, were still limited in their application after the first quarter century of contact, creating on these grounds a general division between urban areas and the hinterlands throughout Melanesia. Indeed, one could construct as a general principle that the closer a village is to an urban area the more control the junior generation has over its own destiny, this principle reaching its extreme in cities such as Port Moresby where the senior generation can exercise little or no control. But perhaps an even more critical point was that the geography of the modern redefined the influence and implications of gender relations. As throughout Melanesia, the Maring have always had a pronounced sexual division of labor that was also a division of sexual labor. A crucial dimension of this gendered division of life was the opposition between the inside, the domain of women and female initiative, and the outside, the domain of men and male practice. A consequence of this gendered view was that almost all of the Maring who attended school or worked on the Anglican mission station were men. Espousing the Western ideology of equality, the missionaries pressured the Maring to send more women to church and school, and the number of women associating with Western agents and institutions has increased steadily though slowly from 1955 to the present. Nonetheless, after a quarter century of contact, more than a few young women did not speak pidgin well and none spoke English. Only some of the women had been to urban centers and none had migrated out to perform contract labor, a modern rite of passage for men. The result was that the inculcation of the modern forms of knowledge, desire, and dispositions that depended on external experience was less pronounced in young women than in their male counterparts.

But this is only where the story becomes more interesting and complicated. Historically, the exchange of women, the alliances that ensued from the exchange, and the social, economic, and political implications of these alliances, elevated marriage to the single most important practice in local lifeways. Accordingly, the clan as a whole, especially the subclan, and most especially a woman's father and brothers, sought to control and regulate who, when, and where she would marry. Though the Maring did not treat women as chattel, this is how the mind of the missionary and the state administrator, imbued with the epistemology of the commodity form, imagined the situation. And so for this and other reasons, they set their opposition to Maring marriage practices. Maring women, and especially those of the junior generation, were quick to use this powerful and external resource, to add its weight to their own local inventory of resources, to check, modulate, and often nullify the desires of their family and clan. They joined the church and took up its gospel that marriage should be a matter of personal choice, an arrangement between the woman and the Almighty. With equal zeal, the junior generation of women began to occupy a portion of the economic territory staked out by men (e.g., cash cropping). So visible was this reconfiguration of marriage and economy that members of all generations often referred to the present as the "time of the woman."

Now this reshaping of gender relations, inspired by precisely the same agents and institutions of modernity that allowed the emergence and increasing independence of the junior generation of men, was often opposed by these men. Insofar as they perceived that "good" marriage relations and alliances were still important to their future success, brothers sought to retain control over their sisters. A principal reason was that not the least of their strategies was to use the production from the local, domestic sphere to enhance their position in the modern, public sphere. Where they might usually exemplify the beliefs, desires, and dispositions of the modern, on the issue of marriage they took on all the trappings of traditionalists. They seemed to align themselves much more with the senior generation than with the ideas and institutions of modernity. Thus men often took a progressive stance toward senior men even as they artic-ulated a much more conservative stance toward women of their own gen-eration in order to control them. And this in turn had a refractory effect on both the representation of the past by the junior generation and the orchestration of power relations between generations. On the one hand, there developed a rift between junior men and women on how they would appreciate their own past practices and imbue them with instrumental value for defining the future. Many of the men suggested that the Maring retain their customary marriage practices, critically because this nostalgia was essential to the preservation of their traditional cultural identity—an identity that, I have pointed out, was itself forged in the fires of encom-passment. Against this vision, their "sisters," in all the enormous polysemy that this term can muster, argued that (and acted as though) customary marriage practices deserved, as one woman put it, to be abandoned like "an old garden that no longer produces food." On the other hand, the tra-ditionalist stance of many junior men on the matter of marriage not only aligned them with their seniors, it often compelled them to solicit seniors' support. Young men would partially attach themselves to especially senior big-men, hoping to achieve that delicate balance by which they could retain as much as possible of their newfound freedoms yet satisfy the demands made of these big-men on their protégés. They would try to con-form enough to win the big-men's assistance in creating a successful mar-riage without compromising their beliefs or independence. The only mem-bers of the junior generation who were exempt from this contradiction were those who had obtained employment in the modern sector (e.g., mission station). Not surprisingly, it was this group who were the most vocal and uncompromising leaders of the junior generation.

In sum, the reshaping of gender relations allowed by the conditions of modernity and endorsed by the agents of encompassment (especially the clergy and schoolteachers) encouraged the emergence of a junior generation of women, who in the process of defining themselves through their control over marriage and its still powerful implications, created conditions that served to narrow the social distance between the junior and senior generation of men. Due to the cross-cutting category of gender, different factions of the junior generation emerged partly at each other's expense. Like viewing one transparency laid over the other, the social space occupied by women, and thus the value of those positions within that space, were influenced by and inseparable from, but were not the same as, the space and positions occupied by men. At the same time, these social spaces were themselves the result of the encounter between the Maring and the forces of encompassment.

A corollary dimension of the expansion of individuality at the expense of clanship and community was the fluorescence of a notion of friendship. Because generation has been an orphan category, anthropologists have failed to notice that one of the most important changes in postcontact Melanesia (and the encompassed world generally) has been the rise of the concept of friendship. There was always a difference between the total universe of close kin relations and practical kinship, namely those specific relationships that an agent chose to nurture and develop. One feature of indigenous society was that, other than the context of interregional trading relationships (LiPuma 1989; Healey 1990), the domain of practical kinship was relatively narrow. People primarily developed relationships with members of their own clan and those of their affines. The advent of Westernization has expanded the domain of practical kinship so that any two people who can trace a relationship can use this to establish a friendship. And since some kin connection can be traced with everyone but one's traditional enemies, the ground of friendship has been broken. The nucleation of settlements along the main thoroughfare (noted earlier) advanced the interpersonal contact that leads to friendships. Especially among the junior generation friendship became part of the cultural imaginary. This produced networks of friends, self-conceptualized and named in the pidgin term, *pren*. These networks cut across clan lines, practically disregarding kinship as a primary principle of the production of personal relations. Forged in the contexts of the modern—while doing plantation labor, attending the government school, working for the Anglican mission or an ethnographer—these friendships were practical, recognized, and often strong: More, these relations between friends were easily mobilized into groups based on their commonalities of knowledge and interests. Though fashioned within the indigenous paradigm of practical kinship, these relations had been given a decidedly modern turn. Certainly one of the distinguishing features of the junior generation was its willingness to promote friendship to a principle of group formation. The most powerful example was that the groups who sought to represent the junior generation in public forums were composed of men from a variety of clans. The notion of friendship was also important to ethnography insofar as it opened a space in indigenous social organizations for outsiders such as myself, allowing me to set up residence with two distantly related young men.

Examining the practice of agents, the schemes of practical classification, and their enactment, it becomes clear that generation is neither an arbitrary slice of an otherwise undifferentiated continuum of physical age nor a concrete category brought into being by a coalescence of the interests of members of the same age cohort. Rather, generations are relational and emergent, appearing as a space of differences based on principles of sociohistorical differentiation. These principles are continually forged and then reshaped in the interaction between the Maring and the West. Both the analytical concept of generation and the sense of generation felt by agents result from a space of positions whose relative distance or proximity to one another determines their values. What was (and still is) at stake in the tension between generations was the power to impose a vision and division of the social universe—in a word, to construct the reality that shapes the trajectory of the society as it pushes into its future. A future that is vastly different, objectively in its structure and subjectively in the forms of knowledge, desire, and dispositions inculcated within agents. A key concept and a stake in the contestation between generations, within a generation, and between the Maring and their Western encompassers, was the question, what was kastam. For the modern not only pushed away from the past, it also produced a social epistemology that helped to construct the past that it was pushing away from, not least by defining kastam.

The Customs of Kastam

Every discussion of custom is actually several overlapping discussions. Whether in a featured or supporting role, there is always a moral history that is also, among other things, a moral geography. Representations of, and reflections on, what custom/kastam/nomane was (and is) form a social conversation on the merits of the past for the future. The term *nomane* is Maring: it can be used to refer to local conventions and practices. Its ethnographic significance is that it is the most abstract word— that is, free morpheme—translatable as *custom.* It is certainly however not the only word or phrase. This moral history has had an increasingly kinetic quality with the expansion of the public sphere. Foster (1995b), with the intelligent clarity that graces his entire study, notes that the gloss "custom" is a paradox, a "claim about historical continuity expressed in a creolized form that bespeaks historical change" (1).

The Maring, of course, never knew they had customs until they engaged "civilization," or at least what passed for civilization in the personae of missionaries, ethnographers, kiaps, and the other creatures of modernity. The doubleness of language strikes here again. On the pragmatic side, speakers have access to a slew of terms to refer to, and so classify, a social practice. These can range from the creolized *kastam* to the English *culture* to local terms like *nomane* and *kopla* (balance). Semantically, each of the terms has multiple glosses (or metasemantic equivalence), these glosses partially overlapping with each other. The result is that these terms, like the modern itself, continually compose, decompose, and recompose themselves in mid-flight. Each context of use and each gloss conditions the meaning of all others. In order to grasp the significance of any usage we must apprehend the entire design for speaking. In their most embracing use, this set of terms took their bearing from the opposition between the "new road" and that of kastam. The Maring took this difference to be so transparent as to hardly require further comment.

KASTAM	MODERNITY
clanship	friendship (*pren*)
tok plas	tok pidgin, English
violence	law, court system (*lo*)
ancestor worship	Christianity (*lutu*)
sorcery	medicine
subsistence farming	business (*bisnis*)
valuables	money
men's authority	women's rights
inherited knowledge	education
kaiko (dancing)	Western-style "parties"

The construction of the category *kastam* involved the production and partitioning of historical time. The imagination of kastam in opposition to the modern entailed the invention of the past, a kind of time inscribed in practices and measured from the present looking back. This conception also transformed the present in that it was no longer imagined cyclically as a variation on an ancestral theme, but lineally as a discordant and radical break from a "traditional" way of life to its modern replacement. In this, there is also the beginning of the Western notion of objective history—a notion that parallels our theory of human nature in that the agents and institutions of social life are understood as expressions of larger and more enduring historical forces.[11] The Maring movement to conceptualize the past objectively as kastam entails the disembodiment and de-institutionalization of social practice. It entails a kind of reversal of the history produced by those whose history was inseparable from cultural practice itself. What I mean by this is that because indigenous history was embodied in people's dispositions and perspectives, and institutionalized in the practices of kinship and exchange, it was never encountered outside of itself. The world existed in a taken-for-granted state—what Rappaport, speaking of ritual, called the canonical.[12] There was no recognition of different or antagonistic practices—only different species of societies. Accordingly, agents (especially the junior generations and women) were not conscious of the power-distributing function of cultural practices. Under these conditions, the junior generations and women could neutralize a practice only by accepting it and then, through guile and insight, turning it to their own advantage (see LiPuma 1980 for a discussion of how Maring women practically negotiated their own marriages). The power of indigenous representations of reality derived not only from their capacity to shape a cultural logic, but their capacity to instill a sense of respect for the senior generations of men—to take but one important example. The advent of the modern and the construction of kastam brought the embodied dispositions, desires, and knowledge to light by creating a contrast within Maring society. Here was no longer the original indigenous contrast between the Maring and neighboring societies, but between those Maring who followed the cultural path of the ancestors and those who took the new and future road. This, in turn, raised to consciousness the power-distributing function of "traditional" institutions and classificatory schemes, setting up the possibility, even as Western agents and institutions provided the resources, for challenging the senior order. No doubt the epitome of such possibility was embodied in a young man named Ambrose who was paid handsomely for translating the Bible from English into Maring and who used his education, wealth, Christianity, and status to both expose the sources of customary power and to wrest power from the senior generation by systematically ignoring their wishes, denigrating their wishes to members of his generation and to his white audience, and "convincing" his seniors to go along with his. Though phrased in the language of self- and social interest—what he thought best for "his" people in their great march into the modern world (such as Christianity; in this he seemed to echo the sentiment of the kiaps)—his actions were nothing less than a moment in the reorganization of the structure of desire. Ambrose was helping, from a privileged position mediating both worlds, to redefine what was desirable for men his age at this point in Maring history. Put another way, the emergence of "kastam" as a social category was an index of the disruption of the once harmonious fit between objective and embodied structures that characterized the logic of local reproduction.

But the matter was more complicated than such a simple opposition would suggest. For the encompassing process served to parse kastam into those practices and beliefs that were wholesome, rational, and progressive and those that were telltale signs of the Maring's more primitive and asocial past. Ancestor worship, sorcery, polygamy, warfare, and animal sacrifice fell into the latter category. The patrol officers, missionaries, and medical personnel, backed by the weight of God and government, inveighed against these practices. Meanwhile, Westerners considered other indigenous practices as either positive or neutral. Westerners erected an implicit, practical, and situationally dependent gradient for assessing indigenous practices. If Westerners understood the practice of a strong familial life positively, they grasped the local language and the norms governing land tenure as unexceptional. Marriage exchange was more suspect in that it appeared to involve the purchase of a wife. More to the point, most Maring generally went along with this assessment of custom, though with a few notable and well motivated exceptions.

The struggle between the senior and junior generations—the forms of contestation and co-optation—were played out dynamically in the way that indigenous practices could be used to take advantage of modern opportunities, and the gains made in the modern sphere used to local advantage. In their struggle to build and insure their status, big-men and the senior generation had a number of weapons, symbolic and material, at their disposal. The primary strategy of the seniors, especially the big-men, was to enter the modern world where they could use their "traditional" leverage. This was particularly the case with respect to the cash cropping of coffee. In Maring land tenure, there was a hierarchy of rights conforming to the contours of the social structure. More inclusive levels have priority over less inclusive ones such that the rights of the clan take precedence over those of the subclan and the subclan over those of any individual claimant. Historically, this allowed for easy adjustments when gross inequities occurred, those who were strapped for land simply requesting grants in perpetuity from better endowed landholders. In the context of modernity, the senior generation and especially the big-men have used their authority as clan leaders to allocate significant tracts of land to themselves for coffee production. They then used their influence mostly over their own wives and junior women to manage and harvest these coffee gardens. The effect was to create a stream of monetary income for the senior generation. The seniors could not only use this income to buy coveted consumables, but to mount feasts and other public exchange ceremonies. This affirmed and augmented their status—in the Maring phrase, it raised their name—which in turn gave them greater discretion over the allocation of clan lands. Such actions also served to reproduce, with all of its new implications, the customary organization of land tenure.

For the senior generations of big-men, this also meant the continuation of polygamy, no matter how adamant the opposition of the Anglican Church. As men may receive gifts of land rights from their affines, multiple well-placed marriages allowed such seniors to increase both their effective land holdings and their labor power. The moral judgment of Anglicans was that they would not permit polygamists to be baptized and enter the house of God until they had renounced all but one of their wives. But not one of the fourteen polygamous men seriously contemplated this strategy. Punga, a big-man in his mid-forties, twice married and known for his coldly calculating political nature,[13] explained it precisely:

There is much to be gained from coming together with Father Brian [Bailey] and the other people at the mission. They have money and goods for those who adhere to their ways. But what would I do with my second wife and all of the exchange relations I have built up from it. Who would now attend to my coffee gardens? Who would help me when it was time to make a feast? Who would come to me and offer me money if I had none myself. What "bisnis" would I have? Who would know my name or listen to me when I speak? No, the young men make their way through the mission; those of us who were born in the time before [contact] have only land and wives.

Punga makes no bones about it. His logic was ironclad. In modern times, money was essential for feast-giving, and his primary access to cash was cash cropping and the labor power needed to produce it. His position and power, the control of his generation over reproduction, his promise of a future, turned on the degree to which he could harness "traditional" resources to garner cash that could then, as coveted consumables, be returned to the universe of feasting and exchange. In the same vein, the senior generation also exercised control through the management of bridewealth payments. Insofar as young men needed their assistance to satisfy their obligations to their affines—that was, to provide the pigs and raise the money required to consummate their marriage—the junior generation was dependent on their seniors, a dependence that the seniors cultivated practically through the timing of the payment.

A primary force motivating newly married men to conform to the standards and practice of bride payments set by their seniors was their wives. Because of the sexual division of modernity, women attended school and performed labor outside the village much less frequently than men and so were much more likely to harbor forms of knowledge, desire, and dispositions that resembled those of the senior generation than the junior one. Accordingly, a wife was likely to press her husband to remit a substantial bride payment to her natal clan, often by this act forcing members of the junior generation into the hands of their seniors. A way to avoid this complication was, of course, not to get married, and indeed, one of the primary characteristics of the leaders of the junior generation, men such as Moses, Pena, Gou, and Ambrose, was that, no matter how "eligible" they were, they remained unmarried. To remain unmarried was unthinkable in the Maring perspective such that their decision to postpone marriage was a provocation to the social order in the sense that it exposed the relationship between marriage exchange and the hegemony of the senior generation, a relationship made even more transparent, and thus also more threatening, by the public statements of these junior leaders that they were delaying marriage because of the difficulties surrounding bride payments. In this respect, what anthropologists have called bridewealth inflation was one of the symbolic weapons that helped to maintain the threatened and sometimes flagging power of the senior generation. The telling point, true across Melanesia and no doubt beyond, is that especially when the breach between generations is so great, the forms of contestation and co-optation crystallize in what agents say and what they leave in silence, in what they do, won't do, and undo, and in the opening up of a field of voices that engenders a novel cultural set of competing possibilities. Most radically, the generation then coming of age began to introduce a view of knowledge common to Western liberal thought (e.g., as inscribed in notions of democracy) that societies should not delimit the universe of discourse, that knowledge, including heretical knowledge, should be given a public hearing because even "bad" knowledge is a social good.

Finally, even as early as the late 1970s, there was an inkling of kastam becoming significant as a means of asserting the value of Melanesian ways of life and resisting white privilege. It began slowly enough with simply an increase in pride in the way Maring history had shaped indigenous lifeways. This newfound pride appeared in the transformation of the kaiko as first and foremost a dance of war to one whose distinctive dancing and costume, headdresses fashioned from the thorax of luminous beetles and crowned with pearlshells and plumes, symbolized the Maring as a people and the unity of each clan cluster dancing in formation. It was also "our" kastam for attracting wives as well as doing bisnis, such as selling plumes for cash. There also began at this time the crystallization of the big-man status as the modern political offices of councillor and committee. Accordingly, the instructions given by a councillor or committee on which candidate standing for election their clan members should vote for was a way of reflexively resisting the notion of the individual embodied in the idea of the democratic election, but also a way of asserting and validating this customary institution for modern use. As the councillor and committee were invariably from the senior generation, this was also a way of tilting power back in that direction.

Remembrance of Things Future

By the mid-1950s, the Maring had not only been conquered militarily, they had been conquered spiritually and socially. Though at different paces and rhythms, the various clan clusters moved, like an orchestra without a conductor, to the same music of modernity and collectively opted to embrace the modern. They felt the modern first through the power and authority of the patrol officers, detachments of young men assigned to pacify and begin the civilization process in the "bush." The process, by its colonial nature and persons, had a certain brutality to it, but one that was much less meaningful to the Maring than the reality that they were now on a new social trajectory. Central to their future would be to erase their past, particularly their penchant for violence, and indeed, by 1980 all of the war shields and fight stones were either in museums or the hands of anthropologists.

The Western community that the Maring encountered was rather idiosyncratic and often divided, though the Maring did not, of course, see it that way. I sometimes wondered what it must be like trying to imagine what the West was like from the motley collection of Westerners that visited the Jimi and Simbai Valleys—an effeminate priest from San Francisco, a disaffected nurse from County Cork, a Bible-thumping translator from Western Australia, a lapsed policeman from Manchester, young macho patrol officers, plus a series of rather nosy intellectualizing anthropologists. I imagined that it must be like trying to reconstruct "Eine Kleine Nachtmusik" after hearing a handful of sour notes played on a tuba. But construct an image of the West they did, as a military force, a carnival of goods, two new languages, and most of all, as novel modes of sociality that often seemed curiously asocial. Between the first sighting and the present, one generation and an entire world have passed.

To grasp this movement of generations, it is, I have argued, necessary to construct a theory of generations. Moreover, this theory must not only be relentlessly nonreductionistic, it must recognize that a generation is neither a ready-made category nor simply a statistical regularity apparent only to the anthropologist, but has gradients of difference that, embodied in inculcated knowledge, desires, and dispositions, and generated by changing social structures, separate generations. Because members of a generation will, having undergone many of the same experiences, tend to think and desire alike, there is every likelihood that they will coalesce into groups that are politically active. But this is never guaranteed because there are always other powerful principles of identity in play as well as a collision of practical interests. It follows that no generation will ever think or act homogeneously, but will have varying moments of strength and weakness, powerful realizations and equally apparent absences, depending on the situation and the charisma of its leadership. Nonetheless, there is no way of imbuing transformation with both structure and agency, of taking into account the many forms of contestation, cooption, and collaboration, without an account of generation. What I have presented here is at best a preliminary theory of generation, my intent being to open the discussion.

In the first quarter century after contact, there arose a generation that for the first time in Maring history sought to distance itself from that history and tie its fortunes and future to the modernizing gesture. This new generation took up a liminal space between a tradition with fixed reference points but no future and a modern future with few reference points. And from this liminal space, inherently dynamic and unstable, they began to fashion concepts, desires, and sensibilities that were neither Western nor Maring; nor were they some logical combination of the two, in that agents added large measures of creatively new forms, the shape of this creativity itself a product of the encounter between the Maring and the West.

CHAPTER 3

The Biography of an Ethnographer
in the Age of Encompassment

what we said of it became a part of what it is . . .
WALLACE STEVENS

If there was anything that attracted me to Papua New Guinea, it was the image of the frontier and that sensation of otherness—a certain conductivity as much bodily as intellectual, the simultaneous deferral and momentary collapse of being-in-the-world when I encounter another reality, honed from different principles and shaping other kinds of cultures and lives. But I also came to understand that I had been trained to this experience by an anthropology that, to constitute its focus, exalted the theater of culture by bypassing an account of the West's encompassment of Others. There was a celebration of culture as the backbone of a human spirit that could keep alive indigenous traditions against the onslaught of Western economy and polity. Small victory dances highlighted the words and works of those I admired, tales brilliant with how natives, armed only with their culture and on any punter's sheet a woeful underdog, fended off the predatory forces of colonialism, capitalism, and Christianity. Culture fought for the sanctity and recognition of the Other in a world in danger of losing its soul to the madness of cold war politics and the monotony of commercialized culture. More than another concept, it was the source of their salvation and our redemption—moral and analytical. Culture was heroic.

But these hymns to culture came with a certain loss of sight. Elided from theory and theorization was the effect of ethnographers on indigenous practice and the construction of the other, the relations of meaning and power that bound them to other colonials (especially missionaries and district officers), and more globally, the relationship between the possibility and methods of ethnography and the encompassment of Others. To make matters better and worse at the same time, the necessary critiques of structuralism, functionalism, and Marxism emphasized agency, resistance, and the discursive construction of reality in ways that make it more difficult for us to come to terms with the giant structural transformations that have reconfigured, and continue to reconfigure, the lives of the peo-

85

ples of Melanesia. Anthropologists have been reluctant to insert themselves in history and to take the contemporary history of Melanesia as intrinsic to their theoretical enterprise. But such reluctance cannot conceal the reality that our ethnographic isolation of the local universe is increasingly inadequate because the global processes now transforming Melanesia, although manifesting locally, cannot be explained by what happens within the rural communities that Melanesian ethnographers study and take as their center of analysis. This means that an anthropology that isolates the local level will, with every passing year, grasp less and less of the dynamics of local culture and practices—less, ultimately, of what it means to be a Melpa, Maring, or Mekeo in this age of encompassment. Reconceptualizing ethnography on these terms begins by reinserting the ethnographer into the processes of encompassment and coming to terms with how ethnography (of Melanesia, for example) has imagined its own project. What follows is an effort to begin conceptualizing how anthropology honed its methods in reaction to the realities of encompassment and the conditions of its own production.[1]

Anthropology Refocusing

Since the end of World War II and the age of empires, the most powerful and insistent dynamic of societal transformations has been the globalization of modernity. On this terrain, modernity beyond the Western frontier propels a special kind of sociocultural transformation, moved by imperatives as diverse as the exportation of Western mass media culture and electronic capitalism, with its extraordinary compression of time and space, to the realization that the "ecological" politics of one nation-state have telling implications for other peoples and nation-states. If there is any characteristic of the globalization of modernity it is the West's relentless embrace of Others. From insular Melanesia to the highlands of Burma, from the jungles of South America to the African savannah, people who for so long stood at the epicenter of anthropological discourse now enlist in labor unions, attend to issues of democracy and the role of the state in everyday life, form voluntary organizations (e.g., women's and environmental organizations), migrate en masse across national borders in search of economic opportunities, respond to the scripture and strictures of interstate agencies (especially the International Monetary Fund), create their own species of Christianity, immerse themselves in commodity culture, and invoke the music and messages of Western cultures for their own ends. And they accomplish this in ways comprehensible only from the analysis of the dialectic of Western encompassment and indigenous lifeways.

Even though anthropologists and fellow travelers have not developed a theory of encompassment, they have now begun to respond to its vibrations. Impelled by the realities unfolding before them, they have started to focus on its agents, institutions, and processes. Issues such as the spread of commercialized Western culture (Foster 1995a), the production of national identities (LiPuma 1995; Otto and Thomas 1997), the linkage between state and local communities (Polier 1994; Jorgensen 1996), and the creation of new regimes of subjectivity have come to the fore (Carrier 1992; Gewertz and Errington 1995). Animated by accounts such as those of the Comaroffs (1991, 1997), anthropology is slowly sliding toward the study of the forces and processes of encompassment. Like most scientific turns and reflections, there is an air of the obvious, the refocusing reality-driven as the accumulating facts and features of the "modern" Other seem to fall beyond the perimeter of conventional wisdoms. Here, anthropology, like the peoples that it studies, must find a way to both retain its traditions and reinvent itself.

This turn can also be read ironically in that anthropology is returning to the site of its own genesis: the fact that the birth of ethnography was inextricably linked to the march of Western capitalism, colonialism, and Christianity. Throughout Africa, Amazonia, Southeast Asia, and Oceania the possibility of ethnography was of a piece with the arrival of that primitive band of colonialists—the missionaries, foreign officers, adventuring businessmen, and the like. Perhaps out of a kind of collective angst and embarrassment, anthropologists seem to ignore their own history. Or they engage in acts of public contrition that, in the spirit of the Western saints (Augustine's *Confessions* comes immediately to mind), are also acts of hubris. By inflating the sins of anthropology, they exaggerated its importance to the colonial project. This view publicizes "the ethnographer as colonizer" even as it sublimates the dynamics of encompassment. This strange conspiracy of ignoring and confessing seems to have been crystallized partly out of a deep Boasian respect for the culture of others, partly out of the fear that these other ways of being human were destined to disappear (see, for example, Max Gluckman's foreword to *The Lineage System of the Mae Enga* in which he calls upon anthropologists "to record the social life of the inhabitants [of New Guinea] before it changed radically" [1965: v]), and partly because it was undeniable that anthropology was a part of that encompassing process. While the character and consequences of encompassment have motivated anthropologists to record the life of the Others and have been overly confessed by a certain kind of mea culpa anthropology, they have only begun to be adequately theorized and integrated into anthropological discourse. This failure might be called a kind of collective defense mechanism on our part. By the hair shirt of confession and the act of defending the Other— of "sticking up" for those who had to bear the burden of the Western

advance—anthropologists have felt that they were absolved of the obligation of coming to terms with the ambiguities and contradictions of their
relationship to a continuing process of encompassment. My argument is
that while anthropologists were (and remain) rather indeterminate agents
in the processes of encompassment, their response to their participation,
characterized by denial and defense, inflected the trajectory of anthropology. Ignored in theory and method was an account of encompassment,
the relationship between ethnography and the agents and institutions of
encompassment, and the influence of anthropology's history on its forms
of thought. Despite genuflection to history and the project of George
Stocking (e.g., 1987), the conditions of the genesis of the discipline have
done more to define its theory and methods than anthropologists have
been willing to let on. We must, at all costs and of all people, escape con-
fusing the entailed politics of our discipline with the manner in which history is actually made.

Also motivating the anthropological commitment to culture and
community—the "cultural logic" and dynamics of the local level—was the
abject failure of those who focused on world economy, politics, and history to connect their global visions to local realities. In the hands of liberal
scholars, such as Wallerstein (1974), Rostow (1978), Wolf (1982), Held
(1987), and Hobsbawm (1994), to cite some of the big-men of their respective fields, there arose a kind of *enlightened Westnocentrism*. While these
authors were universally sympathetic to the encompassment of Others and
often inveighed for their emancipation from imperialism and dependency,
they grasped the reality of the Others entirely through the prism of Western lights. This vision of the Other's world could not but efface local level
relations to the point where they vanished over the historical horizon.
These approaches, while extraordinarily different in many respects, had a
common point of departure in locating the historical dynamic and the
motive force of transformation squarely with the West. Missing in action
was the agency of indigenous agents. Also absent were those times when,
like an orchestra without a conductor, cultures that were similar had similar responses to Western encroachment, allowing them to produce a collectively powerful response. Untempered by a genuine understanding of
local cultures and communities, this Westnocentrism, however enlightened, failed to appreciate the ways in which indigenous agents and institutions inflected the face of encompassment. The Westnocentric view
conflated the construction of a world history and economy with the predatory and imperialistic aspects of Western nation-states. Against this blem-
ished Western approach to others, the manifestos of theorists like Sahlins
(1981, 1985) and Geertz (1983) and the unquestioned mission of numerous
ethnographers were to illuminate the categories, logics, and understandings of the local level—culture with a capital C. So anthropologists not

only sought to record the peoples encompassed, but were themselves part of that process; in the division of scientific labor, they were the anointed scribes of culture and community. There were surely multiple lines of determination, but the received product was an anthropology that bracketed the forces and effects of encompassment. To the genuine detriment of the project of comprehending the globalization of modernity, anthropology has removed itself to the sidelines.

That result initially is as surprising as it is detrimental. In the fields of encompassment defined by the encounter of cultures, it would have seemed, at least at first blush, that anthropology occupied a privileged position: What other discipline had devoted itself to understanding the peoples and cultures being encompassed? No other discipline has taken as its enterprise the art of others understanding others. If the encompassing West was to hear the voice of others above the din of wars, hot and cold, and the hum of electronic commerce and culture, anthropology had a mission and responsibility. The gift of anthropology as critical theory (and why I am proud of my profession) is that, whatever else its faults, it has never taken this responsibility lightly. Moreover, the globalization of modernity crosscuts and simultaneously engages fields from law, literature, and religion to economics and politics. The making of the nation-state implicates everything from economic policies and the politics of identity to state-sponsored religions and political rituals, nationalist novels and the arts, and the construction of legal, educational, and health systems (similarly with the infiltration of capitalism and Western culture). Here too it would appear that anthropology has a natural advantage because of its well-developed multidisciplinary perspective and because anthropologists were inherently sympathetic to world systems theory and the general project of portraying Western colonialism and capitalism. In a one line review, of all the sciences of the social, anthropology appeared most predisposed to be able to tackle the complex issues summarized by the notions of modernity and globalization. Nowhere more than in Oceania where ethnographers have developed an indispensable and necessary understanding of the structure of the societies being transformed. But there is alas an equally strong countervailing impediment. The concept of transformation current in anthropology is too compressed, undertheorized, and marginalized to grasp the character and dynamics of these multilevel transformations. It is a concept of transformation so mired in the immediacy of local life, so fixated on indigenous culture and community, that little room remains for a robust theory of encompassment. Why, we should ask, has anthropology been so hobbled? Why should the anthropology of Melanesia lack a theory of transformation adequate to societies whose fate is increasingly determined and mediated by supralocal structures. Having conducted fieldwork in Galicia, Spain, and the Florida Keys in

addition to the Solomon Islands and the Highlands of New Guinea, having focused on topics as traditional as kinship and marriage and as contemporary as the nation-state and European Community, the following
observations are more than a little auto-ethnographic.

Intellectual Capital and
Our Imagination of the Other

From the ethnography of Malinowski to modern-day writings, the anthropological imagination has linked the "Westernization" of the Others to
their corruption. The Melanesian missionary anthropologist Sir Walter
Ivans may have persuaded himself that a good dose of Western religion
and manners would propel "his" Islanders up that ladder of civilization
from debased heathens to God's gentlemen, but anthropologists saw capitalism, colonialism, and Christianity as corrupting indigenous traditions.
Certainly there is no doubt that confrontation with these empowered systems of economy, polity, and ideology motivated change and deflected
these societies from their "natural"—that is to say, mostly self-deter-
mined—trajectory. The unspoken sentiment that the infiltration of the
three Cs undermined and corrupted local culture went hand in hand with
a determination to document the thought and practices of Others before
they transmuted beneath the heavy weight of Western influence. Given
their mission and motives, anthropologists not only demonized their own
culture (and took a certain pride in doing so), they read this demonization
into their anthropological subjects. They wanted to attribute to indigenous   agents   a   rejection   of   capitalism,   Christianity,   and   the
commodification of social existence so badly that otherwise shaky ethnographies, epitomized by *The Devil and Commodity Fetishism* (Taussig
1980), became celebrated texts. To make matters worse, the analysis of the
globalization of modernity often bore an unhappy consanguinity with
development studies, thereby linking it to the chauvinistic, ethnocentric,
and self-serving programs of development agencies such as USAID and
the World Bank with their massive log, mine, and dam the indigenous people's projects.

   This image of social change shaped the theoretical habitus of anthropology. It was translated into the practice of everyday academia in a way
that was as forceful as it was silent. To begin with, those ethnographers
who worked in the most remote, primitive regions were awarded more
"intellectual capital," not only because of their triumph over physical and
emotional hardships but because they worked in unpolluted, still self-
determined cultures. A gradient of capital accumulation evolved with
Melanesia, parts of Black Africa, and Amazonia on one end of the spec-

trum, fieldwork in Western Europe and United States at the other end. Entire universes, like the Indian subcontinent and the high plains of the Andes, lay somewhere in between. The spectrum was always shifting and negotiated with agents enticed to exaggerate the remoteness of "their" people and thus the purity of their ethnography. This exaggeration of remoteness entailed bracketing of the agents and implications of encompassment. Missionaries, colonial officials, and sometimes the knowledge, desires, and dispositions of a whole generation needed to be redlined from the script. This was done mostly in silence with the understanding that the trained eye could scrape "modernity" off the ethnographic canvas to reveal the original picture of indigenous tradition. So we read (and assign to students) Victor Turner's fabulous description of Ndembu initiation rites (1967), aware only in another more remote region of mind that many of these men-to-be were the sons of transnational mine workers, that these Ndembu were involved in labor union organization at that time, that they were inundated with Christian missionaries, and that Ndembu had long been enslaved by, with certain lineages party to, a Portuguese-backed, transcolonial slave trade.[2] Given the dispositions of his discipline, Turner feels comfortable in omitting these realities or dealing with them en passant in the introduction. Both his original account and an endless parade of citations and reinterpretations have all assumed that the economy of encompassment did not inform the meanings and morality of the ritual. For anthropologists, the observation that modernity was overwhelming the world seemed to belong to a different region of the brain than that which wrote the ethnographies.

Along another vector, more intellectual capital accrued to those who wrote about social organization, subsistence economy, cosmology, religion, and local-level politics than forms of social transformation. It went without saying (because it did not need to be said) that someone who studied exchange in Melanesia accrued more intellectual capital than someone who studied the effects of the arrival of Wal-Mart on a mid-sized, mid-Western, middle-class American town; more intellectual capital was awarded to those who analyzed kinship and violence in the Amazon than social harmony in some Alpine village. I know this both because I live in the habitus of the field and auto-ethnographically: veiled and direct, seriously and jokingly, more times than I can possibly recall, other anthropologists have legitimated my project in Spain by reference to my having already done "real fieldwork" in Melanesia. Given these sentiments, it is hardly startling that for a long time within the field of anthropology, the polarity was away from the study of encompassment and those ethnographic venues where it was most visible. One result is that more ethnographers—at last tally, twelve— have studied and more has been written about the eight thousand Maring than the many million Galicians (northwestern Spain), with the studies of Galicia that do exist mostly focusing on small "isolated" villages where modernity has reputedly been held at bay and the ethnographer can go about the task of describing familial kinship, religion, smallholder production, and the micropolitics of class relations. Aware of the system of rewards of intellectual capital and endowed with theories and methods developed for small-scale non-Western cultures, the anthropology of the West did not animate changes in the anthropology of Africa and Melanesia, but has rather come to resemble it. The anthropology of ourselves did not form a bridge that would have allowed concepts such as democracy and civil society, as well as more sophisticated theories of capitalism and its epistemology, to cross over into the study of Africa and Melanesia. It should occasion concern but little surprise then that when the anthropology of Melanesia began to focus on capitalism, Christianity, and the emerging nation-state it did so the only way it knew how, indirectly as refracted through the effect they had on local communities.[3]

Epistemology and Ethnography

Concerned to uncover the reality of tradition in a world already touched by the West, anthropologists evolved a number of epistemological strategies that mostly entered their analyses as presuppositions. These were happy strategies in that by securing the concept of Culture, they secured the anthropological object and thus the place of anthropology in a division of scientific labor that was also a division of the academe. The presuppositions were not to be called into question on pain of a certain kind of betrayal of one's discipline.[4] The leading presupposition, alluded to above, is what one may call the transparency of tradition. It was, and to an enormous extent still is, assumed that ethnographers can accurately parse a practice into those aspects that are indigenous and those that are Western imports. There are key phrases that have entered the ethnographic lexicon. "Remarkably resistant to change" and "stable" are perhaps the most popular, though "retaining its inner core of traditional meaning" is my personal favorite. What does it mean when an ethnographer, speaking about an Amazonian people who have endured the vision and violence of contact for nearly a century, tells us that "while by *outward,* perceptible signs the indigenous population blended into its Brazilian settler surroundings, there was an *inward,* actively circulating discourse imbuing the world with a wholly different significance" (Urban 1996: 15; emphasis added)? Ethnography lives here by the metaphor of inside and outside, the inner voice and soul of a people versus the outer cloth of modernity. The unspecified claim is that encompassment and context do not inflect social meaning. As long as a practice, or aspects of that practice, appear to resemble their precontact forms, the ethnographer can infer a conservation of form, value, and ultimately power. Where the form has changed visibly—including obviously Western elements—this leads to an archaeology of meaning. Like levels of stratification at an archaeological site, practices accumulate layers of meaning as they evolve through the epochs of local history. By digging down beneath the surface, the ethnographer can uncover the original forms and values complicated by the advance of the West. Or so it was assumed as a kind of subtext. One corollary of this premise is that the ethnographer assumes that the traditional elements of a practice are the essential elements in contrast to the more contingent Western aspects, which, after all, were added on at a later date. This vision of the anthropological project brackets the objective structure of encompassment that, in its encounter with local lifeways, generates the context for the production of meaning. It brackets the desires and dispositions instilled in agents by the structuring effect of this encounter. And so this vision cannot help but ignore the practice of recovery itself in which the ethnographer, often through the memories of the elder generation and the stories handed down, reconstructs the past in the present tense—all the while assuming that this representation of the past will be, more or less, a pure re-presentation, a documentary unencumbered by immediate interests, the structuring effects of discourse itself, or the loss of knowledge entailed by the advent of a modernity of which the anthropologist is a part. We can clarify these points and dispel these assumptions by turning to a case on how ethnographers think, about ancestor worship for example.

It is the dry (actually less wet) season of 1980 and one of the Kukupogai subclans, commanded by a senior clansman, had decided to sacrifice pigs to their ancestor spirits in a "customary" manner. Bear in mind that, influenced by what the mission men portrayed as a "bad habit," the Kukupogai had abandoned ritual sacrifices in the sacred groves for more than a decade. In terms of performance, the ritual appears to be formally identical to the descriptions that other ethnographers (i.e., Rappaport 1968) have given of earlier performances, some performances antedating Western intervention in Maring society. The chanted invocation of the spirits in metaphorical speech, the sacrifice of the pig in the sacred grove (which needed to be cleared ahead of time because it had become overgrown with vines and shrubs from nonuse), its dissection with the ritual bamboo knife, and its apportionment and consumption seemed to replicate the precontact world. For the ethnographer this appeared to be a kind of enchanted scenario in which people resurrect their tradition intact, thereby providing a lens into the past. Making matters even better, my housemate swore to the authenticity of the performance. A reading of the ritual performance in terms of what unfolds before the faculties of ordinary experience (most Melanesianists as well as most Africanists practice substantialism without reflection) sees the cultural reproduction of the past.

Further investigation would reveal, however, that the meanings and values of the performance had transformed rather radically. To begin with, the agents grasped the sacrifice as a resurrection of their past, thus invoking and taking advantage of a distinction between the past and present that was itself a touchstone of modernity. The sacrifice was also held in the context of, and in opposition to, the Anglican Church, whose priests and especially lay catechists had expressly condemned such ritual, at times branding it satanic. But the ritual was held in opposition not only to the Church but to a related, rival clan that, in contrast to the Kukupogai, had endorsed and aligned itself with the Christian missionaries. The holding of the ritual by these senior Kukupogai was simply one more salvo in their perpetual political struggle with other clansmen. The ritual was also held not without a generous measure of intra-subclan dispute as many members of the junior generation showed their distaste by declining to participate. In response, several senior and elder Kukupogai accused them of betraying their clansmen and siding with their "friends" in the Christian-pandering clan. And whereas kastam restricted participation in traditional ceremonies to subclan members, this version included people from entirely different clan clusters, the point driven home by their stated desire to have an anthropologist present to record custom. Indeed, they were so concerned that I should record their ceremony correctly and in writing that several times my friend Gou chided me with a nudge for not taking notes on what he thought were important points. The result was that the ceremony included those who should have been excluded and was absent those who would have been included. Finally, the senior clansman who had organized the sacrifice was planning to run for local political office, leading some to speculate about the implications of the performance for the upcoming election (i.e., that unable to entice the support of the junior generation he had decided to appeal shamelessly to the senior and elder generations). In effect, though the manifest form of the ceremony may have remained more or less unchanged from precontact performances, its functional value and indexical meanings had changed so dramatically that calling it the "same" ritual was itself an ideological statement. Certainly, there is no way to write out of the current performance the collective notion that it was legitimate to include foreigners. There is no way to write out of the performance the collective notion that written texts—on the image of the Bible (see chap. 7)—have greater authority than embodied oral tradition. There is no way to write out of the ceremony the conflict between generations, the accusation of betrayal invoking notions of religious politics and friendship that were unknown to the past. There is no way to undress the participants and put them back in customary garb or eliminate the cross talk in pidgin. In other words, senior clansmen readapted the generative principles of ancestor-community exchange to the realities of a world encompassed. Despite its canonical fidelity to those old-time acts and utterances, these pigs for the ancestors were only and eloquent testimony to the encounter between tradition and encompassment.

Due to the unavoidable limitations of most field research, conversation and interviews between the ethnographer and local agents have been the dominant motif and method in the construction of the ethnographic object in Melanesia. Our custom of talking to local agents about their customs, coupled with our desire to recover what we could not witness, encouraged ethnographers to adopt a second presupposition: that there is an ontological authenticity to language, particularly narrations about the past. The premise is that the production of an ethnographic text from the discursive interaction between ethnographer and informants transparently encodes a past event, such that the process of entextualization, the contextual sensitivities of that event, and the production of a decontextualized ethnographic text have no bearing on our interpretation of the event in question. This premise was necessary because ethnographers have sought to recover the meanings and values of practices they could not witness or encountered only in a state of transformation. In no small way, the processes of encompassment that made ethnography possible censored some customs, rendered others obsolete, and instigated all sorts of substantive changes in content and context, meanings and motives. Toward this aim, ethnographers have assumed that the culture of a culture was made up of the relation between systems (e.g., kinship, ritual, and economic) that could be rendered as texts (epitomized by the kinship diagram, ritual cycle, and rules of exchange) and that the wording and structure of the speech events used to construct these texts did not inflect their construction.

A great virtue of what has been called the New Melanesian Ethnography is that it illustrates that the first clause of this theory—that a culture consists of a set of domains that are exterior to, and imposed upon, one another—relies on an implicit theory of Melanesian practice that, living an underground existence, is both ethnographically inaccurate and theoretically unexamined. In an illuminating page, Marilyn Strathern (1988) submits that in the practice of Melanesian sociality one domain or "area of life" is neither imposed upon nor an exteriorization of some other domain, and that, consequently, there is no supposition of a society that stands over and against the flow of persons in practice (102). The Melanesian materials seem to be trying to tell us that their social life does not consist of a set of discrete systems that react to, comment upon, or regulate one another. And if these difficulties were not enough, the second clause of this proposition depends on an equally troubled theory of linguistic practice. The problems intrinsic in this "folk theory" of speech became especially transparent when ethnographers asked different people to recount "the same" myth, inventory the presumably shared marriages rules, specify the general norms of exchange, or explicate the meanings of a ritual and its symbolism. Not only did different agents offer different accounts—difference here defined, of course, against the expectation of sameness—but often the same person offered "different" accounts depending on occasion and situation. The same myth was seemingly never told "exactly" the same way more than once, it was disquietingly difficult to get informants either to enunciate or agree on the "shared" marriage rules, the "norms" invoked to explain one exchange too frequently failed to tally with those invoked to explain an apparently similar exchange, and sometimes people would answer they had absolutely no idea what a certain symbol meant. What does it mean about the nature of knowledge and the context of speaking when some people inform me that, prior to contact, "we" settled all disputes by violence, other people assert that there were ways of peacemaking, and still others maintain that they do not know/recall how disputes were settled, this commentary distributed (but by no means perfectly) by gender and generation. Sometimes this information found its way into the published text (Schwimmer 1979), but usually it was something that ethnographers discussed among themselves. In writing cultures, they tended to create coherent, mutually shared, well-circumscribed texts— blueprints and maps of cultural lifeways. The method ironed out the discrepancies by systematizing the data on the pretext—literally and figuratively—that the task was to determine the grammar of the beliefs and practices in question. The method disconnected variability rather than integrating it as significant cultural and methodological data.[5] Left uncharted was the extent to which variability and its contemporary form, or inversely the nature of the sameness imagined about the past, were themselves the product of people's encounter with precisely those processes of which the anthropologist was a part.

In the meantime, studies in the ethnography of speaking were proving beyond a reasonable doubt that the structure of speech events bound representation to interests through multiple lines of mediation. The result is that descriptions of the world are systematically and usually nonconsciously bent because they were governed by a practical knowledge not comprising knowledge of its own principles (Silverstein 1981; Parmentier 1989; Bourdieu 1991). Other analyses of the ethnography of speaking indicated that the very act of giving a description of the past systematically skewed that description (LiPuma 1983; Silverstein 1987). Also complicating the process of entextualization was the reality of translation: either ethnographers translated the indigenous language—characteristically with a subject-object-verb format—into English or informants translated a speech event into pidgin at the ethnographer's behest and then the ethnographer translated the pidginized description into English. All of this should more than underscore that speech is never purely referential and that, accordingly, there is no guarantee whatsoever that people's narration of the past is ontologically authentic (Silverstein 1979 and 1996; Gumperz 1982; Gee 1985; Mertz 1988; Parmentier 1993; Hill and Irvine 1993; Briggs 1986; Hanks 1996; Silverstein and Urban 1996). The problem with inferring the character of the past from contemporary interviews is that it assumes, and seduces us into believing, that we can "know" the structure and meaning of a social practice apart from the contexts of its production. This in turn implies that agents can transmit meaning and value across social boundaries, such as generations, without incurring precisely the kinds of recontextualization wrought by the globalization of modernity. Though, as the preceding citations underline, there is now a small mountain of linguistic evidence demonstrating the impossibility of constructing or representing a practice independent of context, the premise was essential in order to bracket the ways in which encompassment had reshaped the indigenous context for speaking about practice and the ethnographer-informant context for speaking.[6]

The third strategy, already commented on extensively by Fabian (1983) and others, was the suspension of temporality. The sleight of time. Aided and abetted by the notion of the transparency of tradition and textual authenticity, this premise was embodied in the use of what came to be called the ethnographic present and in the notion that it was unnecessary to historically situate an ethnography. In his comparative study of the Highlands from the colonial encounter to the present, Feil (1987) is explicit: due to the character of his sources, his account is written in an ethnographic present that, in his own words, "makes scant mention of changes . . . wrought by colonialism, the penetration of capitalism, the cash-cropping of coffee, the rise of provincial government and the emergence of the modern state" (10). Like a public confession at a New Age church, the philosophy here is that if we own up to our mistakes and lapses, then God will wink his eye. Anthropologists would describe, and one could fill in just about any people and practice, Maring marriage rather than Maring marriage in some historical time frame, the assumption being that what the ethnographer gleaned from talking to contemporary informants flowed back indefinitely in time. As Feil observed in the same reading of the literature, "some authors describe events and institutions which no longer existed at the time of writing or reconstruct them only as they might have been" and "often" they do not make this clear or specify "the time period under scrutiny" (10). The success of this "strategy" declined with the duration and intensity of a process of encompassment that was not itself analyzed. The strategy may have had analytical traction in the first decades after the opening of the Highlands when many of these societies had felt only the first fire of contact, though speaking of his fieldwork among the Kyaka (in what is now the Enga Province) in the mid-1950s, Bulmer observed in a footnote that "my information on Kyaka religion is deficient" because of European contact, "particularly the impact of Christian mission activity" (1965:160). Nevertheless, bracketing the years of change and the comments of pioneers such as Bulmer, ethnographers have continued to commit themselves to the ethnographic present nearly a half century later (i.e., most of the ethnographies of Melanesian cultures published since 1990 speak about indigenous practices in the present tense and without clearly delineating the period under investigation). The understanding is that social practice can be parsed temporally into what is of "modern" origin—and can hence be omitted, placed in the far land of endnotes, or appended in a chapter on colonial influences—and what was traditional and went back indefinitely in time and space, even as it continued into the future. Left uncharted was what this temporal move entailed, theoretically and methodologically. What precisely was added and subtracted in the event of recovery under the determinate social conditions of encompassment? What kinds of information shine through clearly, and what kinds are subject to re-presentation? Why do members of different generations sometimes recount different stories about their past? How, under the conditions of encompassment, does controlling the past help one generation to maintain or wrest power from another, and how does controlling the ethnographer's ethnography figure in this project? The questions are complex and critical, but they can only be broached once we take them seriously.

It is impossible to appreciate the place of these presuppositions in the ethnographic imagination or the almost religious commitment to them—which often entails that ethnographers deny to themselves their own experience—unless we grasp that these suppositions provide a solution to the contradiction inherent in an implicit, that is to say inadequate, theory of the relationship between ethnography and the conditions of its own production. Like a refuge for our collective psyche, these presuppositions enable their users to bring all of the technologies of Western power (state authorization, science, money, writing, etc.) to bear on the other without having to acknowledge their transformative powers. The ethnography of Melanesia, like that of Africa, the Amazon, and beyond, ranged from unbridled endorsement of these epistemological strategies to grudging acceptance. But that is, of course, not the point. The crucial point is that anthropology, born in the midst of encompassment, defined its project as the description of "Otherness" and crafted an epistemological perspective to meet this objective. However successful this endeavor, the epistemology that underwrote the ethnography—that these societies were transparent in their traditions, spoke to the ethnographer in a purely referential language, and were suspended in time—hindered the creation of a genuine understanding or theory of encompassment. Insofar as the thrust of ethnography is to factor out, bracket, and transcend the agents and institutions of Western encompassment and the resulting transformations, there are no ways or incentives to construct a theory of them. This was (and remains) especially true for Oceania and the New Guinea Highlands in particular, which (like the Amazon) became privileged ethnographic venues precisely because here it was easier to bracket the processes of encompassment.

This is not to say that there was no anthropological awareness of the penetration of colonialism, capitalism, and Christianity. Only that the received epistemology, in concert with the system of rewards and incentives, led to a constricted theory of transformation and a narrow ethnographic focus. For the most part, studies of change and transformation were told entirely from the perspective of the local culture and community. And they were filtered through the politics of anti-imperialism and the defense of the Other as told from the perspective of anthropology. The perspective inspired a number of writers to reduce the globalization of modernity to coercion, resistance, and appropriation: that is, capitalism, colonialism, and Christianity pressured local peoples into adopting Western concepts and practices, and in response these societies did their best to fend off the advance of the West and to appropriate things Western for their own ends. Ethnographers celebrated the ways indigenous peoples fought for the return of the native lands, outwitted the colonial tax collectors, boycotted the plantations and mines, sidestepped the wishes of the kiaps, excommunicated Christian missionaries, secretly engaged in forbidden practices, gave false names to census takers, and created counternarratives that deflected imperialism and helped to preserve their identity and dignity. This vision of the encounter between the West and Others was consistent with the foundational epistemology. The notion of resistance is the consort of the notion of the conservation of the forms and values of pre-encompassment culture. The underlying and unidimensional philosophy is that, despite the presence and pressures of the West, indigenous concepts and practices remained as they were because local agents chose to conserve their customs and slip those the West imposes. Accordingly, the ethnographer can discount the presence of missionaries because people still appear faithful to their customary religion. By the same logic, the notion of appropriation goes hand in hand with the supposition that Western influences can lay like trousers and T-shirts over the still intact body of local practices. Thus an archaeology of meanings and values is ethnographically justified because it is already inscribed in indigenous intent. Accordingly, an ethnographer can analyze a marriage exchange involving money the same as an exchange involving pearlshells because the former is an appropriated substitution for the latter. Not to belabor the point, but this understanding of the encounter between the West and Others—fixated as it is on resistance and appropriation—is inadequate because it is entailed and constrained by the original epistemological presuppositions.

This take on encompassment also seeks to restore the history and validate the culture of the Other by joining them to our own demonized history. But conceived as a tale of resistance and appropriation, their histories turn out (alas!) to be stories of victimization and heroism. Their agency is that of the oppressed. Their culture is a culture of self-defense. They have finally been cornered even in the most remote corners of the world—their final source of salvation, isolation, now removed forever. What is more, all of the action unfolds at the community level: the penetration of capitalism, the sects of Christianity, and the colonial and postindependence state regimes are conceptualized as exogenous, homogeneous, and distant forces, and are thus not themselves taken as objects of analysis. The Comaroffs (1991) note that

> white colonizers, if they are thought worthy of attention at all (cf. Beidelman 1982:1), have more often than not been treated as a homogeneous class—in and for itself. The divisions among them, and the often acute conflicts between them, have been largely ignored in the history of the Third World. At best they are regarded as instances of . . . "non-antagonistic contradictions." (10)

Resistance and appropriation surely do occur. But the story has only begun. What is sorely missing is an account of the complexity of the encompassing agents and institutions, the complex process of mediation by which capitalism, Christianity, and the modern state influence local communities, and the concepts, logics, and practical structures of vision and division within these communities that inspire appropriation, enchantment, carnival, imagination, novel identities, refurbished political strategies, improvisations of all sorts, and the forms of knowledge, desire, and dispositions that make the social world work. Foster (1995b:15) is right when he maintains that, taken alone, neither the symbolic innovations, logics, and operations of simple reproduction nor the imposition of the forms of modernity, such as the commodity and the possessive individual, can account for the changes in the practice of the encompassed. Only an account of their relationship will do. For an anthropology of modernity (has there ever been any other kind?), accounting for transformation requires the community project of articulating a theory of encompassment. This includes the reinsertion of ethnography and the ethnographer back into history.

Ethnography and the Genesis of the Maring

At the turn of this century, the poet's intellectual, Wallace Stevens, wrote the now legendary poem "Description without Place," in which he contemplated the character of inscription and desire. He observed that, caught between memory and emotion, description

> is an expectation, a desire,
> A palm that rises up beyond the sea,
> A little different from reality:
> The difference that we make in what we see

With a poet's grace and good Kantian manners, Stevens tells us that a description is not only not the thing itself, but that it is bent by our desires; and further that the memories that are formed become the ground of still further descriptions. What Stevens is saying is that the epistemology and interests of the observer cannot help but to inform the description, and more than that the ground of describing itself. The poet then goes on to wonder whether there might not be a description that is more "explicit than the experience" itself. Wonder no more: for the Western narrative of Melanesia, of which ethnography is a part, has done precisely that, by first creating a description of others that embodied our epistemology and desires, and then watching as this description became the reality itself.

In the process of inventing itself, of delineating an object of inquiry that distinguished it among other sciences, anthropology defined and developed two notions of culture. The first was culture as that ensemble of concepts and practices, material and social arrangements, that permeate and orchestrate people's lives. All humans have culture much the same way as they have language. On the most common interpretation, the power of culture to orchestrate the relations between agents turns on the reality that they share these concepts and practices, material and social arrangements. By extension, this allows a second and ultimately different concept of *culture as peoplehood.* The notion is that culture as a system of understandings, concepts, and logical operations circumscribes and delimits the universe of the shared, thereby producing culture as peoplehood. Because the concepts, practices, and arrangements of one people are distinct from another, the form of peoplehood created is sovereign and totalized. Accordingly, it is possible to talk not only about culture but the exis-

tence of "a culture." Transported to Melanesia (among other venues), the
implicit idea has been that this shared set of structures and practices leads
to the crystallization of a peoplehood that transcends a people's own sense
of the limits of identity, defined by kinship and marriage. While local
agents might accept that kinship and marriage define the limits of sameness and solidarity, in reality a cultural sameness unites a much larger
group of people. While, for example, Maring consciousness may imagine
no relationship whatsoever between two clan clusters—because they neither fight nor intermarry—in a deeper reality they are all members of the
same culture. Thus, it is possible to talk not only about the culture of the
people of the Jimi and Simbai Valleys but Maring culture. Or Navaho,
Ndembu, Tuareg, Kachin, Innuit, etc. culture. And to represent these cultures in mutual opposition to neighboring cultures. In this image, anthropologists perceive a culture as an autonomous, self-animating, and
bounded collectivity. The assumption is of a kind of cultural sovereignty
and individuality, psycho-symbolically linked to and reflecting the individuality of the ethnographer through the concept of "my people" and all
the dispositions and desires thus entailed, not to mention the Western epistemology thus revealed.[7]

There is, and has long been, theory and evidence to the contrary.
Thus, to sustain the illusion of a primitive peoplehood requires some
denial, which, in turn, requires the work of invisibility for which science is
justly famous. The work is not disputed or disproved, simply consigned to
the dark. In the Melanesian case, the most obvious example is "Visible
Sociality," an article that is ignored, even by the author's friends and intellectual neighbors.[8] In what he considers perhaps his best analysis, Roy
Wagner (1988) argued that "the ethnographic literature is founded on a
necessity to fix either groups or units (or both) as a beginning point in
analysis" (39). This occurred whether an ethnographer wished to treat a
people descriptively or theoretically, or even to reduce them to a materially
self-interested horde (will the cultural ecologists raise their hand!). Referring back to our society and the inherently comparative character of
ethnography, he notes that the "isolation" of these groups and/or units is
the analogue of the "Western juro-economic idea of the individual agent,"
emanating "as it does from a society based on abstractly defined roles, currencies, and contractual obligations," not to mention time, space, and
labor itself (40). Calling this "the negation of social inclusiveness," Wagner argues:

> In a society in which both social units and the relations or
> alliances among such units are articulated through social rela-
> tionships, a unit *in its constitution* is never really alienable from
> its relations with others. It reproduces itself through alliances

> with others, and allies with others through its own mode of
> reproductive constitution. But this very fact argues for a much
> stronger statement of contextualization than has heretofore been
> made. (40; emphasis in original)

Indeed it does. For it suggests that all forms of community are emergent in that they crystallize and become visible only under specific historical conditions. To prove the point, Wagner demonstrates in amazing detail that the Daribi community was protean by design, its borders permeable, its very structure animated by a logic of exchange and interchange with other communities. In this respect, the forms of solidarity produced, such as community and peoplehood, were "much the opposite of the kinds of strictly bounded units that anthropologists have elected to identify and model" as basic to the social (59). A critical aspect of simple reproduction is that boundaries come into being only as they become practically necessary because they are not inherently necessitated by the practices of sociality. For any scale of collectivity, such boundaries are potential, not elements in its table of organization. The realization that boundaries in Melanesia are emergent calls into consideration the larger implications for ethnohistory, especially because people such as Wagner's Daribi imagine themselves as "intercultural" communities whose various parts have migrated from different locales in the Highlands. This evidence and argument is a challenge to the notion of culture as peoplehood, a challenge that anthropology sublimates in the interests of finding a totality. It is worth asking ourselves why we have collectively ignored a virtuoso performance by one of the best and most famous Melanesian ethnographers. Why "Visible Sociality" has been made invisible.[9]

Although anthropologists have been a tad uncomfortable using the idea of culture as peoplehood in the metropole (for example, what exactly is "Spanish" culture? Some hypothetical soup of Galician, Gypsy, Basque, Catalan, Andalusian, and Castilian cultures?), it became the touchstone for the analysis of Black Africa, Oceania, the aborigines of the Americas, and rural neighborhoods of Southeast Asia. While anthropologists applied the concept of culture as peoplehood everywhere (this is the premise behind the *Atlas of World Cultures* [Price 1990]), it was in these locales especially that this concept of a culture seemed to work naturally. The natural history of a culture was to become autonomous—to shape principalities of meanings and values that were distinct from their neighbors. From an evolutionary perspective, migration, adaptation to the new environment as culturally perceived, and the symbolic logic and practices of social reproduction would cause an original protoculture to fission into two new autonomous cultures. And presumably, each of these cultures would in turn divide—the metaphor springing inescapably to mind that of

cell division. This perspective is a direct outcome of a reading of an archaeological and linguistic record that strongly suggests that all the "cultures"
of mainland New Guinea are the result of several waves of migration, followed by processes of expansion and diffusion (Foley 1986; M. Strathern
1988:46; Wagner 1988). By this process, the once empty Highlands became
full of separate cultures.

In the Jimi Valley, this ethnographic logic entails the existence of a
proto-Maring/Manga culture that over time separated into Maring and
Manga culture. Subsequently, the neighboring cultures would sustain
their integrity and respect their distance by virtue of the reproduction of
these differences. The ethnographic logic presupposes (and one could
devise) similar sequences for related cultures through Melanesia. Application of this logic to the Strickland-Basavi region, for example, would show
that, despite their portrayal in the ethnographic literature as distinct "cultures," the "Etoro, Onabasulu, Kaluli, Kasua, Kamula, Bedamini,
Gebusi, and Samo are [so] similar in economy, social organization, and ritual [that they] represent historically linked variants of a regional sociocultural system" (Kelly 1993:27). Linguistically and culturally, a regional
sociocultural system is also evident for the peoples (e.g., Tairora, Auyana,
Awa) of the eastern Highlands (McKaughan 1973; Robbins 1982; Watson
1983). Beyond the Highlands, Gewertz (1983) has explored the extraordinary intercultural connectedness that characterizes Sepik sociality. Jorgensen (1996:193) observes that the ensemble of Mountain Ok "cultures"
conceptualize their relationship in terms of descent from a common ancestor and kindred ritual, dietary, and kinship practices. The idea that the
Highlands have always been populated by numerous sovereign cultures is
based on the marriage of an evolutionary metaphor with a comparative
typology. What is missing is actual historical knowledge of regional relationships (Lederman 1991), the generative principles of the production of
difference, and the determination as to the significance of these differences. Against this, it is all too easy for ethnographic description to
advance the conception of the sovereign culture through the trope of the
nominalized subject. Statements that predicate about these cultures (e.g.,
that depict the Maring as more warlike than the Manga, the Etoro as having sexual practices distinct from the Onabasulu and Gebusi, and so on)
prospectively absolve the ethnographic community of having to specify
what the worldly referents are for these cultural names, to whom "these"
nominals are meaningful, and how their genesis informs their meaning.
This is especially true in that favorite framework of Melanesian anthropology, the comparative generalization (e.g., big-man versus great man
societies [Godelier 1986]). By substituting a product, namely, a culture, for
the generative principles of its production, the ethnographic trope assumes

that Melanesia has always been composed of a multitude of sovereign cultures. Or so it was conceived and presented ethnographically.

Given their relatively small numbers and rather remote location, the Maring should exemplify this use of the term. Maring culture should produce the Maring as a culture. This assumption crumbles under the weight of the ethnography. It is only recently and increasingly, with the development of their relationship to the agents and institutions of encompassment, especially the national state, that the Maring have progressively self-recognized themselves as the Maring. In a reversal of the supposition that a culture was a sovereign unit, the evidence indicates that it is only in the context of encompassment that the Maring begin, indeed have the reason and motivation, to conceptualize the existence of a categorical identity (as opposed to traditional relational ones) or, further, a pan-Maring solidarity. One of the great virtues of Kelly's (1993) *Constructing Inequality* is that it recognizes that the indigenous situation was not characterized by anything resembling sharp boundaries and cultural sovereignties (see also Knauft 1985b). That the people of the Strickland-Basavi region (like those of the Western Highlands) were rather remote should be enough to underline that a paradoxical aspect of the simple mode of reproduction found in Melanesia was that it encouraged fluid community structures. Based on relations of exchange, kin assembled, detached themselves from local groups, migrated to other areas, and reattached to other kin groups. The identity of persons, being inherently relational, responded to the generative principles for the construction of relatedness (such as intermarriage, sharing food, etc.) in ways that were both endlessly creative and faithful to these principles.

The notion that the Maring were not originally a people was itself inscribed in Maring mythology and the oral histories of the formation and fission of communities. Myths of origin of clans often centered on the travels and migration of the founding ancestors. These sagas depicted clans and clan fragments as mobile and labile, attaching and latching onto other groups even as the social entropy of dispute motivates a part of that group to fission off and migrate elsewhere. The picture drawn was of communities whose composition was protean, as unstable as the explosive tempers of big-men. The founding myths of several Kauwatyi clans depict their ancestors as migrating into the Jimi from somewhere in the Mt. Hagen region. Beset by warfare and famine, they followed shimmering stars that led them out of Hagen and across the perils of the Jimi River to their present homeland. Other clan myths of origins (e.g., Isemban cluster) suggest that some of the founding ancestors migrated from due east—from the Kuma or Kandawo regions. The adventures of the ancestors, enshrined in sagas of searching and migration, tell of their attachments to kin-related clans and of their detachments and subsequent journeys. More recent oral histories tell a similar, if more local, story of the flow of subclans between clan clusters. These histories and myths of origin notwithstanding, Maring clans still imagined themselves as the true and rightful inhabitants of the territories they occupy, a conception that stemmed from their notion of the relationship between land, eating the foods gleaned from that land, and the production of identity (LiPuma 1988). If the Maring do not seem to pay much heed to their ancestors on the question of the origins of community, then again anthropologists have not paid much heed to theirs either. Quite a while ago, at the tail end of *Elementary Forms,* Durkheim observed that "cultures have no fixed frontiers" and that social life tends to "spread itself over an area with no definite limits" (1915:426). True to this observation, when we reach the "borders" of Maring territory we do not find sharp edges, only complex gradients of difference. On the western side are communities that were bicultural and bilingual in the best historical senses of those terms. These communities were composed of both Kalam and Maring clans—the Maring migrating from the Highlands proper to the fringe and the Kalam from the coast upland. Though the languages are genetically unrelated (Foley 1986:237, 243) social practice in the "bicultural" clan clusters appeared to interweave aspects of both Maring and Kalam with a measure of invention thrown in. To complicate matters further, some clans (e.g., Ambek of the Kandambiamp cluster) were "mixed" in that they were comprised of Maring and Kalam subclans. The ethnographic doctrine that each culture must be sovereign here produces an impasse: anthropologists cannot unambiguously classify these clusters as either Maring or Kalam. So especially in the age of the glorification of cultural identity, pity the clansmen and -women of Kandambiamp. Ethnographers who focus on the Maring classify them as either non-Maring (Rappaport 1968:10) or Kalam (Healey 1990:14), while ethnographers who study the Kalam (Reibe 1974) assume that they are Maring. They were not only on a cultural frontier but in ethnographic limbo.

On the eastern frontier lay communities that were culturally and linguistically very similar to Maring communities. Their languages, especially at the border, are mutually intelligible, differing only at the dialect level, and social practices are nearly identical. That they have been classified as a distinctive culture certainly has more to do with the fact that the Yomban and Manga were traditional enemies than with any cultural reality. Due to their animosity, there were no border settlements, leading the colonial administration to interpret this spatial discontinuity as indicative of cultural difference. Ethnographers such as myself have concretized this difference, produced by encompassment, as indicative of a peoplehood, by identifying the Yomban as the easternmost "Maring" cluster and the Kundagai as the westernmost "Maring" cluster. Based on this same scheme, the

Anglican Church at Koinambe created its parish to end at the Yomban-Manga border, and accordingly, Togban, the rest house and dance ground of the Yomban, was the westernmost stop on the circuit of the medical outreach program and the Anglican clergy. The final result was that on the western end of the valley there were two clusters that combined very different languages and converging cultures while on the eastern end there were two similar clusters divided into different cultures and languages.

No one knows for certain where the name *Maring* comes from, though it does begin to crop up in patrol reports in the late 1960s. The best guess is that it is derived from the Kalam term *malng* (Healey 1990:28), which means "others." What is certain is that *Maring* was not originally a Maring word and that, prior to the advance of colonialism, it had no referential, let alone self-referential, content whatever for the Maring. In the initial years of mission and schooling, sojourns to the coastal plantation and ethnographic visitors, the local focus was still entirely on relations of kinship and marriage. Beginning sometime in the mid-1970s as the first wave of the junior generation emerged from school and returned from the melting pot of the plantation, those with the most exposure to Western ways began to conceptualize themselves as a people. During this time, those from the Simbai and Jimi Valleys first began to refer to themselves collectively as the Maring in contrast to Kalam, Melpa, Manga, and other peoples. Especially in conversations with Westerners, the junior generation began to use the word *Maring* referentially to differentiate themselves from other "native groups," as one school-leaver phrased it. As was explained to me in 1980, the ignorance of the ancestors was not only that they did not know the names of other peoples, but, worse, they did not know their own name. In this reflective light, the awareness of a peoplehood that always existed but was—like money and writing—only discovered through the Western mind was itself an index of being modern. As a corollary of the emerging concept of peoplehood, and in response to the missions and the state (in both forms) that continually opposed the "native" way of being with that of the Christian, they began to think of their own conventions and practices as an integrated, closed system. The very construction of a past that the new road transcended presumed the existence of a fixed and defining roster of beliefs and practices that constituted that past. Anthropologists played a part in this process. The dozen or so ethnographers[10] repeatedly inquired about the character of local practices and, especially by "training" informants, began to teach the Maring to take their own culture as an object of contemplation. Moreover, by 1980, the Maring not only had a name for themselves collectively, but the junior generation began to deploy an indigenous term, *nomane,* to refer to their collective culture, to a Maring peoplehood. Where before the range of denotation for nomane embraced will, intentionality, custom, and manifest soul, it now assumed the new valence of peoplehood. Both this use of *nomane* and the adoption of the nominal *Maring* were abstract inventions, a retooling of the lexicon to accommodate the changes of modernity. Thus began the progressive movement from the relationality of clanship to the category of our culture. What began as hegemony is ending up as consciousness. In a recapitulation of the evolution of other colonialisms, Melanesians are beginning to reflect back to contemporary Westerners the very image of themselves they saw reflected in the gaze of the patrol officer, missionary, and ethnographer.

As history unfolded in the 1970s and into the 1980s, it was clear, not least to all those concerned, that the recognition of peoplehood was a matter of generation and part of the mode of generation. The elders continued to ignore the existence of the name and, in response to my questioning, claimed that it was impossible to share an identity with those they had fought in battle, either directly or as allied to other clan clusters. They were adamant that clanship and affinity defined the social universe, even as they had begun to lament the passing of their own world. The senior generation in power was thoroughly ambivalent about what the acknowledgment of a pan-Maring identity might mean, as though they were beginning to understand it cognitively but still could muster no emotional commitment or attachment to the concept. They viewed it positively insofar as it was associated with the modern but saw few contexts in which it seemed to make a difference. By contrast, a number of the junior generation professed to having a Maring identity. Indeed, the representation of a Maring identity, even though in embryonic form, was one of the hallmarks of the leaders of that generation. Here is a comment by Abraham, the son of a leading bigman and himself a leader of the junior set, on Maring peoplehood.

> Before you [meaning Westerners collectively] came, we did not know that all the clans of the Simbai and Jimi Valleys were related. We thought of this thing like our ancestors did: people were related because they were of the same ground or because they gave each other wives. But now we know what a wontok is, and recognize that whether someone comes from Gai, Nimbra, Togban [all place names associated with various clan clusters], or whatever, we are all Maring. We learned this the first time when the labor recruiters came and took us to the plantations. People were housed according to their group identity. All the Highlanders were in one house, the Sepiks in another, the Maring had one part of the house, other groups had other parts. On the plantation, it was important to stick together because fights occurred all the time.
>
> In school at Koinambe, the teachers are from the coast

[coastal New Guinea, primarily from Oro and Milne Bay Provinces]. They draw contrasts between their customs and ours, between Maring customs and language and those of their place. One of the things we learn in school is where everyone is from in New Guinea. Who is Orakavia and who is Binandere [culturally and linguistically interrelated Oro Province groups].

As our speaker explains, the modern not only brings others into opposition with one another, but retools the concept of otherness in the process. Given the asymmetries of the encounter, the Maring could not help but reflect back to the plantation manager the image of themselves they saw in his eyes. The organization of space on the plantation assumed and inscribed a Western vision that, for all agents, peoplehood was a critical and defining identity. Explaining the layout of worker housing on his plantation, one manager noted that each compound was "its own country." A giant of a man from a tiny town south of Darwin, with huge fists and leathery skin, he confirmed that part of his job was to break up fights before they escalated. On his view, what he called Coastals, Sepiks, and Highlanders comprised the Melanesian world. Speaking of the Mountain Ok—a term that has no indigenous resonance—Jorgensen (1996) notes that on the plantation men soon discovered that, as far as the outside world was concerned, they were all "Sepiks." Internally, "grouped together in common barracks and supporting one another in the inevitable urban scrapes, the sons of erstwhile enemies or strangers" learned, at least parenthetically and in this context, to re-imagine themselves collectively in opposition to the peoples of the coast and highlands (195). This notion of identity was also the hinge on which Abraham's comment made the transition from life on the plantation to that at school. After national independence in 1975, the staff at the Anglican school became more Melanesian and the curriculum was transformed. One of the lessons in civic education of the reformed curriculum that made a deep impression on a number of Maring was heralded: "Kantri Belong Yumi" (pidgin for Our Country). The heartbeat of the lesson was that "our nation" was composed of culturally and linguistically separate peoples who all possessed a common origin, purposes, and philosophy of life and nature. Whether expressed in ancestor worship or Christianity, all Melanesians had a spiritual nature; they all approached and respected the earth in much the same way; and they naturally understand one another no matter their cultural and linguistic differences. In a rehearsal for the concept of nationhood, the lesson espoused culture as peoplehood in order to underline the notion of the nation as an embracing form of peoplehood. In the same light but from a more celestial angle, Father Bailey and his catechist preached numerous sermons across the Maring clan clusters on nonviolence and tolerance toward others. The two threads of their argument were that peace was something that God wished for all the Maring people and that all Maring should show tolerance toward each other precisely because they had a common identity. The constant and underlying theme was the Maring as the collective children of God. That Jesus was their common ancestor symbolically exemplified this peoplehood. Here is a comment by the manager of the mission trade store.

> Before we knew about Jesus everyone thought they had their own ancestors. The missionaries taught us that Jesus is above all of them. That he is the ancestor on top of all the ancestors. This means that we are all related and that we cannot and should not fight with each other. The mission teaches this but old men don't understand; they still revel in the glory days of war, when the axe was used on our enemies [the axe was the privileged method of killing one's enemies]. And though their stories are very good, their time is as dead as the ancestors.

The young Christian avows that the Maring are all related because they are all the descendants of Jesus Christ, thereby providing a charter for the revision of the traditional genealogical calculus. In seeking to establish the place of Jesus, to connect Him to local forms of descent, and explain why God was their father, the mission unconsciously invoked forms of peoplehood. Also implicated in this process was the translation of the Bible into a language called Maring. A Kauwatyi who had been adopted by the Summer Institute of Linguistics translator, Lance Woodward, and then educated in English did the translation. Naturally, he translated the bible into the dialect spoken by his people of the western Jimi, thereby not only establishing the existence of Maring as an autonomous language but standardizing a particular dialect as that language. As a closer look at any of the major studies of Melanesian languages should suggest (Franklin 1981; Foley 1986; Lynch 1998), a language is a dialect with Western friends. Moving eastward along the Jimi across Manga terrain and into the world of the Kuma, at no point along this continuum can we draw a clear line between mutually unintelligible languages. Ethnography can best analogize this linguistic pattern as a series of overlapping circles in which the degree and dimension (semantically, phonemically, etc.) of overlap were uneven, thus creating variable gradients of difference. The value that agents attached to these differences varies over time, space, and contexts for action. For their part, ethnographers from Rappaport to myself have continually assumed that Maring were not only a culture but a peoplehood. Ethnographers never justified this perspective. Here as with other Highland societies, it was so deeply inscribed, so much the unmarked understanding, that, as a matter of tradition and convenience, ethnographers did not see what they already knew. They found it difficult to imagine any other choice.

What was not hard to imagine is that modernity creates new contexts for action that both presuppose and encourage the conception of peoplehood. The assumption of the plantation manager was that every Melanesian who spoke a mutually intelligible tongue possessed a solidarity born of collectivity. The categorical identity of Maring was assumed to trump the relational identities of clanship and kinship. Moreover, the conditions of life on the plantation invested this new form of identity with great practical value. In a less violent idiom, the Westernized teachers—Western precisely and in part because they had internalized a modern notion of peoplehood—presumed that a Maring peoplehood must exist, and that, accordingly, a pedagogical tool was to compare and contrast cultures. Similarly, the mission men and Bible translator presumed the existence of a Maring peoplehood and language as a condition and product of their own efforts. Thus modernity continually introduced new contexts for the production of a notion of a sovereign people, a notion that played no part in indigenous thinking prior to pacification.

The story of this encounter between the Maring and the West is by no means unique, either to Melanesia or the history of encompassment generally. It underlines that only outside agents in the role of observers can fix the boundaries of local cultures—that is, transform the relationality of culture into an objective boundary. The missionaries, kiaps, teachers, and ethnologists were all partly responsible for concretizing as a "tradition" fixed limits to Maring society. Everything in the epistemology of the West—the presumed sovereignty of the national state, the autonomy and self-containedness of the commodity, the imagination of the person as a self-animating bounded individual, and the conception of nature as disenchanted from culture—conspired toward the notion of the sovereign culture. The Maring as a people with fixed borders appears in ethnographic, administrative, and missionary maps of Simbai and Jimi Valleys. These borders rest on acts of objectification that are also acts of scientific, cultural, and state power—the power of the modern to constitute all Others in its own image of self and otherness. In the same vein, Young (1997:101–2) observes that there is a sense in which missionaries "invented" the Dobuans as a tribal category by extending the anglicized nominal to include surrounding groups who spoke similar dialects. Speaking from another continent and colonialism, Abercrombie (1991) demonstrates that, for Bolivia, both the concept of "being Indian" and the specific Indian ethnic identities were produced in dynamic opposition to Spanish domination. From still another continent and colonialism, Wilmsen (1989) argues that the Herero, Khoi, San, and Tswana become separate cultures only after British colonial policy had severed their lines of mutual sociality and definition. All of these accounts testify that, for both Western and local agents, it was the encounter itself that determined the cultural whole, critically because they experienced this encounter as a partial and asymmetric intertwining of multiple meanings and values.

Perhaps somewhat more abstractly, they also testify to the fact that modernity, of which ethnography is a part, produces a social inversion that corresponds negatively to an already inverted ethnographic stance. Where in the past the assumption of simple reproduction (the cyclical, nearly determinate, replication of relations) was generally justified, the assumption of closure on the frontiers was not. The reason was that, because the agents of simple reproduction understood the world relationally and doxically, they had no need to construct cultural boundaries by objectifying culture. They also had no reason to imagine a totality that had no practical necessity or significance. There was no Maring peoplehood and consonantly no name for this imagined community within a bounded and imaginary space. By contrast, with the encroachment of the modern, the assumption of a Maring peoplehood was increasingly justified as a direct consequence of the operation of modernity whereas the assumption of simple reproduction was not because of the very process of encompassment instrumental in producing that peoplehood. The process of producing *a culture* historically, one both in and for itself, presupposes a process of complex reproduction. The character of the modern is to connect intrinsically social reproduction to external agents, institutions, and processes; to a field of internal opinion created by the self-consciousness of groups based on principles as diverse as class, gender, and generation; and to an internally differentiated political and moral economy. So from the moment of its birth, the anthropology of Melanesia was based on a immanent contradiction—the coexistence of simple social reproduction and cultural sovereignty. A contradiction veiled by the erasure of frontier communities and an epistemology determined to bracket the effects of missionaries, kiaps, businessmen, ethnographers, and other agents of encompassment on indigenous society.

Part of the story of encompassment in this part of Melanesia was that Western agents, institutions, and practices fixed the boundaries of Maring culture, capitalizing on their external position to instigate a form of identity that was beyond the purview and interests of indigenous society. That does not imply, however, that these boundaries were entirely arbitrary, determined only by the caprice and power of the West, or that once established they did not make sense to the Maring and their neighbors. The borders drawn had a certain historical rationale because indigenous conceptions of otherness—which take wing on an entirely different ontology than ethnicity and other Western classifications of Others—mediated the relationship between culture and peoplehood. Local notions of otherness stand between the transition from overlapping spheres of relationality to bounded, self-referential entities. In the Maring story, the agents of encompassment thought that they were simply codifying naturally occurring borders, when, in reality, they produced these cultural boundaries by virtue of their relationship to the Maring, a relationship that, operating in an implicit state, interrupted the cycles of local history (such as that of war and peace) to fix "borders" as permanent that were only temporary moments of a longer and larger process, and that in any case were constituted on entirely different grounds. Nonetheless, the boundaries were fixed in the encounter or interface, even if, due to the asymmetries of power, the Maring had to learn to appreciate these boundaries whereas the Westerners could continue to live in an implicit state.

Melanesian notions of otherness appear as a comparative discourse about the beliefs and behaviors, perspectives and practices, of others.[11] Members of indigenously named and constructed groups, such as the clan cluster, create a discourse about the otherness of other groups. Although the principles of this discourse were entirely different from their Western counterparts, the forces of encompassment appropriated and recast them in order to bring the Maring into conformity with the Western conceptualization of what a people is. The Western concepts of otherness met a Maring comparative account of others developed along four intersecting lines. Looking out from the perspective of any group, people would classify others according to the mode of sociality. At the most inclusive level, Maring divided other clan clusters into those with whom they intermarried and shared kinship, and thus served as allies and exchange partners; clusters with whom they had been at war and, by definition, shared no kinship relation, past or present; and clan clusters with whom they had no sociality. From a Kauwatyi perspective, they intermarried with the Tsembaga, Tuguma, and Tukmenga and accordingly considered them allies; historically, they waged a series of wars against the Cenda and Manamban and counted them plus their allies as enemies; and they had a blank relation with the Irimban and Fungai-Korama—small clusters in the far eastern end of the Jimi and Simbai Valleys with whom they neither fought nor intermarried. When I asked a Kauwatyi elder if he was connected to the people at Irimban, he responded rhetorically: "How can I be related to those with whom I have no relations?"

A second line of difference that people cited was language. Professed language differences ranged from those who had an accent to those with whom communication was next to impossible. Not having heard of Saussure, the Maring do not make a distinction between langue and parole, but rather have a single concept, *tep,* that encapsulates everything connected to human discourse. Domestic animals, specifically pigs and dogs, have a lower species of tep. This allowed for an equation in which speakers classified other humans and domestic animals as having similar levels of tep. What distinguished other humans were higher planes of *min* (bodily consciousness) and *kandep kani* (sentience), thereby allowing them to master new talk. As a Maring man indicated, his audience smiling in agreement:

> When I was working on the plantation and those around me were talking English or "Sepik" [Sepik tended to function as the residual term to denote all non-Highlanders], I was like *the dog* because I could know very little of what they were conveying. Of course, when I was talking to [two young men who were with him on the plantation], they were the dog. That is how pidgin [Neo-Melanesian] came about. (emphasis added)

In a way that was never intended to be self-derogatory, the speaker equates himself with "the dog"—that is, he does not equate himself with a dog but with the difference between humans and dogs with respect to tep. Accordingly, the polarity of the metaphor was fully reversible. Moreover, our speaker in an added flourish (that amounts to a metapragmatic tour de force) attributes the genesis of pidgin to the symbolic vacuum spawned by intercultural contact. His perspective underlines that both Western terms, *language* and *speech,* used alone or bundled, were inaccurate glosses for *tep* because speakers do not objectify language/speech itself, but the interrelationship between agents. Thus, a better translation for tep was the transmission of intentionality through the body. In this concept of communication, not only is the verbal grammatical channel simply one dimension of conversing among others, but the sounds of speaking were of the body because there existed no distinction between body and mind, the physical self and the thinking subject, least of all with respect to communicating. As such, the concept of tep embodies no distinction between kinesic processes and language/speech. Culturally, prior to Westernization, the Maring did not have a conception of language as a closed, autonomous, and isolatable system. *Tep* denotes larger and more inclusive practices of communication.[12]

When translated into a comparative discourse, the Maring did not distinguish themselves from others on the basis of speaking a different language or dialect, but rather on a break in intentionality. The reason why Kalam was more distant than Narak was not that these were separate languages conceptualized as such, but rather that the possibility of conveying one's intentionality to a Kalam was so much more difficult than to a Narak agent, speakers of Melpa lying somewhere in between. The asymptote of difference was when two agents, unable to understand each other's talk, were reduced to the communication of gestures, skin, and intonations. In the language of our storyteller they were "like dogs"—domesticated but unable to animate the instruments of human communication. From this perspective, the world of others existed as a continuum of communication punctuated by gradients of difference that sometimes, as when a Maring crossed over into Kalam land, became steeper.

In concert with images of kinship and speaking, there was a discourse of others that focused on practices and behavior. The inference was that others were governed by customs or nomane that were regular, intelligible, yet different. The people of the Jimi Valley would, for example, cite some clearly defined distinctions between them and the peoples of the Simbai. Even when speaking about those with whom they had an affinal connection, and there was considerable intermarriage between Jimi and Simbai clans, they would note that there was a difference in the relative status of big-men and in modes of public display and dress. As Lowman (1968) pointed out, the status of big-men in the Jimi depended on ceremonial exchange, the orchestration of the asymmetrical transfer of women, oratorical ability, and their stature in compensation payments that substituted a special class of goods for people. Their "political role before contact was sanctioned by supernatural powers they [were] believed to possess" (199). By contrast, the big-men of the Simbai were "much smaller," their power less connected to ceremonial commerce and the orchestration of marriage exchanges and compensation payments than with their ability to serve as intermediaries between the living community and ancestral world. Along these lines, the Kauwatyi estimated that the Kalam had small big-men, the Manga of similar size, and the Melpa even bigger as exemplified by Moka exchanges. Another man, commenting on the difference between the Jimi and Simbai people, noted that Simbai groups "have acquired practices from the coast, such as wearing beetle bonnets during a kaiko or dance [woven helmets adorned with the green iridescent thorax of a local beetle]."

There was, of course, another category of otherness created by the process of encompassment itself. How to conceptualize the otherness of Westerners. From the start, no matter whether they wanted the role or consciously responded to it, the ethnographer was a critical person for the Maring process of thinking the Western other—the ethnographer being the only Western other who was immersed, if episodically so, in the cradle of everyday life. Their most obvious characteristic was their physical size, taken as a hallmark of practically created and magical-aided nurturing, and their ability to command goods through the projection of their intentionality—the power of their nomane and tep. Further, speaking as an extension of their Western self, ethnographers claimed to be the cause of their own actions and to cause other actions to happen. The Maring learned not to be amazed by the confident and matter-of-fact expression of individuality—a point my housemates made to me through our long hours of conversation and mutual questioning.[13] Another telling characteristic of Westerners was that they were a kind of people with whom the Maring had relations of sociality, but based on neither kinship nor enmity. That was a departure in that, at least by premodern standards, all forms of sociality fell within this compass. The Maring did not understand the Westerners' willingness to live without their kin as indicative of a racial difference, but as a peculiar choice. As to why they "adopted" me, Kuku-pogai clansmen would reply that they "felt sorry" (*kobeluai kani*) for me. Said in descending tones, the speaker's head nodding slowly, the term implied that the gift one gave to another by "feeling sorry" on their behalf was a willingness to assume some of the weight of their loss. Another crit-ical (and at first very puzzling) aspect of the Western other was their demand for privacy. "When white people first came, we kept asking our-selves, why would anyone want to be alone, what could they be doing that they did not want us to see?" (Kaiya, 1980). But at least some of the Mar-ing would learn that their own implicational logic equating privacy with secrecy, and that with nefarious behavior (e.g., archetypically, eating food without sharing, which was perforce a denial and denigration of sociality), was not an accurate portrayal of the Western person. Their Western oth-ers were also immune from the effects of sorcery because they were outside the web of social relations and intentionalities animating it. Westerners were others who could summon goods, lived without kin, reveled in pri-vacy, and stood outside the circle of indigenous powers and influences.

These notions of ethnicity differed radically from Western notions in that the Maring conceptualized diversity as a continuum of sameness embracing variations. Moreover, the features of difference were performa-tive and acquired, focusing on knowledge and the coordination of inten-tionality. Contrast this vision of difference with Western conceptions of ethnicity that imagine that a fundamental biological sameness grounds the recognition and reality of a cultural and historical identity. History mat-ters in that the presumption is that the recognition of this identity—self-conscious and named—leads to endogamy. The result is an essentialized discontinuity. Only notions of a common humanity—itself constituted by the disenfranchisement of nature—link these islands of difference. Like the other categories of the modern, which separate the modern from other periods and from the primitive, the magic of its success is that ethnicity cloaks the social and historical conditions of its own genesis by construct-ing, in terms of an empowered and legitimated discourse produced by the West for universal consumption, cultural and historical inscriptions of itself as natural and transhistorical. Ethnicity is thus the cultural realiza-tion of a cross-cultural discourse that imagines itself as noncultural. In a move unknown to the world of simple reproduction, the self-misrecognition of itself is a necessary condition of the reproduction of ethnicity. In addition, through the process of misrecognition and accommodation, a process that always unfolds as a struggle, ethnicity must align itself with the commodity form, the individual, the nation, and the other epistemological precepts of the modern. This surfaces in the struggle, especially visible in emerging states such as Papua New Guinea, to align peoplehood, the nation, and subjectivity. In this conception of ethnicity, performance is canonical and iterative. Performance does not create ethnicity, it dramatizes, renews, expresses, celebrates what already exists.

The Maring of the precontact epoch would not have recognized this conception of peoplehood. Much of what they understood as the ground of sameness and difference was a result of acting in the world: understanding another's speech, eating food from the same clan lands, sharing ritual knowledge. The relationality of kinship also produced understandings of fundamental difference between peoples. The space between subject and other was not a question of biology or bounded, autonomous categories of people—a form of thinking that can come into existence only in concert with notions of race and peoplehood. Accordingly, the spectrum of clans, ways of communicating, practices, and behavior produced gradients of difference on different grounds. That the people of the Jimi, Simbai, and beyond imagined sociality as a song that never dies explains why—though well acquainted with the process of naming—they did not name themselves or name others. And it was these gradients of difference that the advance of the West concretized and codified. So on their Western frontier, the colonial authorities divided the Maring from the Kalam on the basis of language, translating this gradient of difference into a peoplehood. The Maring naturally understood the existence of a difference, though not as peoplehood until the socializing processes of the West began to educate them to this newer reality. On the eastern frontier, recalling the opening sections of chapter 2, the Manga were divided from the Yomban on the basis of their continuing intertribal warfare and the spatial discontinuities at the borders that it produced.[14] Ultimately, the Manga emerged as a separate culture and language not because of great differences in language or culture but because of an increased gradient of difference produced by the historical consequences of warfare, a form of interaction that the Maring understand as a specific mode of intracultural sociality. To assume that the indigenous comparative discourse of otherness invariably led to the crystallization of a peoplehood is to take as the indigenous state of affairs precisely what encompassment created. Prompted by war and demographic expansion, the historical flows of migration and community have situated Maring culture, like that of the Manga, Kalam, and their neighbors, in a permeable field of difference, encompassed first of all by a regional cultural economy and then by the agents and institutions of modernity. Modernity has imbued existing differences with a significance that tradition could never have imagined. It imagines them as bounding a culture, an entity that could take its place alongside the other imaginary bounded entities of the modern—the individual, the commodity, the nation-state, and nature. Neruda, Pavese, Paz, the poets are right: the wings of identity are never folded and never the same.[15]

The Maring material informs us that the production of the people-hood that Westerners have presumed to have always existed arrives as a highly mediated historical product of the encounter between the Maring and modern. Modernity constructed the Maring by reusing indigenously constructed differences in a modern way. The practice of recycling the history of others for our own ends has, incidentally, long been "our" tradition. Since the adventures of Columbus and Cortez, Christian missionaries, colonial administrators, and ethnologists (from Sahagun to Livingstone) have provided the West with the raw materials for articulating its self-identity through its relationship to an other—an other who was not only created symbolically as a figure for the Western imagination but who emerges from the encounter in a form that is unlike either its original culture or that which the West has sought to impose. God has forsaken the details; he now lives in the mediations.

Ethnographic Interlude

As ethnographers investigated the Maring, the Maring performed their own ethno-ethnography on the investigators. This inquiry, a companion to the weaving of histories and mythologies of the modern, was part of their attempt to make sense of the Western other, to revise their comparative discourse to embrace those who, not a short time earlier, they had not imagined. This kind of story—the kind that might appear transmuted in Benitez-Rojo's luminous *Sea of Lentils,* rarely finds its way into an ethnographic script, though perhaps it tells more, and more wonderfully, than the hand of the ordinary description ever can.[16]

In the summer of 1974, while living in the Simbai Valley with the Tuguma Maring, I conducted fieldwork on sexuality and marriage as part of a larger study on gene flow. The practice I inherited from the other ethnographers of the Maring was to pay those informants who had spent the better part of the day with me in goods and cash: three Australian shillings to be precise. One night at around nine as I was going over the fieldnotes of that day, there was a tapping on the door, a low tapping on the slatted wood as though revealing a reticence. The man was middle-aged; I had talked with him several days before as he was one of only two

Tuguma who had gone and returned from a stint on the coastal plantations. I had asked him about his impression of Europeans for an afternoon
and then in the usual manner paid him three shillings for this time.

Older than most of the men who had since left for contract labor,
Banyon was a leader of his subclan. He entered gingerly, on the slow heels
of anxious curiosity, and immediately sat down on the floor in front of the
sawed off tree stump that I had been using alternately as a seat and work
bench. He asked if I have liked my stay with the Tuguma: I reply yes in a
way that I think will reassure him, though I sense (from the movement of
his body, his tone?) that this is not the question he wants to ask me. Then,
as if starting the conversation from scratch, Banyon tells me that he would
like to ask me a question. I counter that that was only fair in that I had
some more questions I wanted to ask him. There is a pause and then he
asked, "Is it true that where you come from they chop off the head of a
man's penis?" Maring were usually skittish about talking about sex but I
remained unruffled, if you put aside that I bit into my lip so hard I nearly
drew blood. On the plantation, he had seen several circumcised Australians and, showing an interest in comparative anatomy, wanted to
know if this was the kastam for Western men. I said that "for some but not
all," beginning to compose my thoughts on what more I should say. But
before I could go further, he interjected, "Is the head of your penis
chopped off?"—the pause on and lengthening of the pronoun unmistakable. I slowly nodded. In the backlight of the lamp dangling from a cross-
beam, his eyes were lost in the frame of his cheeks, and I could not quite
make out his reaction.

But I did not have long to wait. "Can I see it?" he asked, his tone
inquisitive, my senses simultaneously mesmerized and spinning. I said
nothing, quietly hoping that he wouldn't repeat the request, that the world
would return to its "normal" size and shape with me asking the ethnographic questions, the Maring displaying their cultural practices. He asked
again while I remained perfectly still, imitating a survival strategy for any
number of species. Then all of a sudden Banyon brandished a smile of
insight—like Archimedes in the bathtub I imagined even then. He spoke
with an edge of triumph: "I will pay you three shillings"—certain now that
he had clinched my consent as he upended the small pouch that hung from
his waist, the money I had given him the days before tumbling out onto the
floor. Though I did not accept his money, I did show him my anatomy to
which, in a characteristic show of astonishment, he put his ear to his shoulder, rattled his hand, and made a whooshing sound from his tightly pursed
lips.

There was a pause that endured even after I had rebuttoned my pants.
Then he asked who had done this to me. I replied that my parents had
authorized the circumcision when I was born. Given his comparative

interests I should have anticipated the next question: Why? Why did Westerners engage in such a practice? Before I could answer, Banyon sought to broaden his study. "Was Skip [Rappaport, who had studied their allies and neighbors, the Tsembaga] circumcised?" I answered that it had long been the custom of Skip's people to circumcise their male children. I pointed out that some, but by no means all, Westerners were circumcised. He then returned to the issue of why, to which I replied that body carving was a powerful and enduring way of marking a person's identity. Adopting a more anthropological composure, I compared it to a once prominent form of Maring body mutilation: chopping off the last segment of a finger to commemorate the death of a close relative. He nodded in understanding, and I thought that this might close the matter, again underestimating his comparative instincts. Then, on the issue of identity: "If you see someone wearing pants, how can you tell if he is circumcised?" He now started laughing in anticipation of his own whimsy saying rhetorically, "everyone doesn't carry around a bag of shillings to find out each other's identity." By turns serious and funny, off and on, with no obvious ending, this conversation continued for some days over a range of subjects as he sought to place Westerners in focus.

Besides the humor, what was evident was a cultural capacity and interest in defining a comparative discourse of otherness. What was also evident was a certain reversibility to the ethnographer's position. An ethno-ethnography was inevitable, a turning of the tables, insofar as modernity compelled the Maring to redesign their discourse of the other. Where the traditional object of this discourse was other Melanesians, the rise of modernity not only motivated the emergence of a new discourse of otherness, but one that had to integrate Westerners as a kind of other. A result was a deep indigenous interest in the ways that Westerners were different beyond their obvious access to powerful technologies and unlimited materials. Part of the conversation between the Maring and the West, on both sides, was how to conceptualize these differences of relations to others. For the Maring, it was also part of a process by which they learned that all Westerners were not alike even if "their skins" appeared so much the same. Employing their nonracial conception of otherness, the Maring gradually evolved a concept of Westerners that, by 1980, stressed that Westerners could live comfortably in the absence of kinship, hoarded material objects, desired privacy whenever possible, embodied greater power/intelligence than local agents, spoke another language, and imagined themselves in terms of an opposition between local agents taken collectively and Westerners. In this composition, Westerners were both a source and model of freedom from the strictures of kinship and community, and equally an opportunity, especially for those of the junior generation caught between the homelessness of freedom and these strictures, to reconstruct their notions of community and place. Ironically or not, the matter of circumcision was never mentioned again.

Biography in Ethnography

A creature of ethnography, of the singling out of key informants, is the creation and imagination of biography. The story of persons over time, and the events of their lives, that the ethnographer may add up to create a global picture of what a culture is about. And without thinking about it as an inherently comparative exercise, not least because it is their own order-ing mechanism, ethnographers explore the memories of those they encounter to fashion a chronological accounting of their lives, beginning with where they were born, who their parents were, the various stages of their life as marked by momentous events—initiation rituals, the advent of Westernization, marriage, and so on—to construct the person that stands before the ethnographer, imbued with knowledge, interests, desires, and judgments about the future and past.

It takes only a little reflection to realize that biography, the creation of narratives about the self, in its many inner states and public presenta-tions, lies at the center of the modernist project. Our biographies, in their more or less inchoate practical state, in the situationally specific pragmatic narratives that we construct (e.g., for a job interview), and in their formal written forms, are thought to be indispensable to the making of the social itself. Biography is the self made public through language, the story we tell about the story of our lives. This is critical to the modernist project because it begins in the premise that society is a collection of individuals who have through their recognition of the pleasures and benefits of mutual association agreed, contractually, to cooperate and collaborate in the interests of the common good—a common good defined by a general will that is itself the sum of the individuals wills. Like all the fictions upon which social reality is built, there is a wonderful circularity to the vision—a logical tautology that appears to ideology as coherence and closure—that is as the convention naturalized. With this in mind, most ethnogra-phers create biographies of those whom they live with; they request and elicit patterned information that traces the sequence of actions initiated by agents to produce a particular event, such as a marriage ceremony on the grand scale and the harvesting of coffee on the small. The assumption underlying the biographically based ethnographic method is that agents are individuals whose free will is constrained by the nature of their culture. But what if the nature of this culture is, as in the Highlands, to assume that the individual dimension of the person is far from the epicenter of social life and that agents do not have fixed properties and states? Then it becomes clear that the biographically constructed ethnography is a trans-lation—a way of rendering their lives in terms that are meaningful to us. Biographies as such are the products of individuals, and it is safe to say that since the individual aspect of the person is not prominent in Maring society, the Maring did not indigenously have biographies. At least not in that Western sense and sensibility as a linear and cumulative narrative of how the autonomous agent selectively incorporates and rebuffs environ-mental influences on their path from birth to last breath.

The making of biography always implicates a politics of memory and forgetting in the service of the creation of the self in the present. As such, Western biography is an opportunity to recast the most oppressive memo-ries and memorialize those thought to epitomize and emancipate the self. Biography thus consists of accounts of the past projected into the future in the interests of the present. Toward this end, the West has specialized in creating a narrative framework that presupposes that the (person as) indi-vidual is the uncontested and natural ground through which a person becomes an individual by re-presenting the self through the arts of memo-rializing the significant and setting aside the inconsequential moments of a life. In keeping with the overall framework of a society that envisions itself as universal—as the people with and creating history—and driven by the commodity, the person in biography has both an abstract and concrete form. Abstractly, the person appears as the transhistorical and cross-cul-tural individual. Concretely, the individual constructs a biography from the brute ontological facts of their past—their family life, education, occu-pations, marriage(s), and so on. Rather paradoxically, this framework assumes an essential and essentialized opposition between collective and individual aspects of remembering, consecrated as an opposition between biography and history. Individuals have biographies, societies have histo-ries (or fail to have histories). This conception—to which children are edu-cated by, among other things, the very organization of the library—ideo-logically severs that which the character of Western culture links structurally. Namely, the social processes and metaphysics that create the indispensable fictional structures through which persons individualize their lives as biographies. And also conversely the equally indispensable structures through which agents and instruments of the public sphere (newspapers, novels, movies, etc.) transform the sum of these individual biographies, great and small, into a collective history. The reification of biography thus goes beyond the fact that a life constructed socially and historically appears as an individual and personal product. Even the onto-logical categories that generate the very essence of Western sociality—here the person and society—are reified, not merely their forms of appearance in the marketplace of ideas (e.g., biography). If science is the art of tran-scending the ideological, what this compels us to do is to relativize relativity by discovering the relationship between the construction of persons and sociality on one hand and the construction of remembering and forgetting on the other, and to expose how this relationship is specific to each people and now united historically in the process of encompassment. Recognition of the relationship is essential to avoiding an analysis that ends up comparing Melanesian reality with Western ideology. The comparative enterprise runs aground when analysis draws its contrasts between Melanesian realities and capitalism grasped only in terms of its illusionary appearance. The object is rather to set the comparison between Western realities of which ideology is a very necessary dimension (of the reproduction of those realities) and Melanesian conceptions of how persons remember. Lattas observes that we need to place memory in history, treating it not as the "free product" of individuals, but as a critical structure "for producing historicised subjects; that is subjects with particular ways of apprehending time" (1996:258).

The Western convention for linking the person to temporality, and in the process contributing to the creation of both, is through the narrative of biography. The mandate, as inculcated through numerous processes from schooling to worshiping, is to imagine our life (and the lives of those around us) as a coherent and integrated whole. At its highest expression, an agent's life unfolds as an expression of an objective and subjective project (and so I tell people that, raised in a Sicilian household in an American society, I was always an anthropologist inasmuch as I was always aware of cultural differences, thereby transforming a finality into an original intention). We demand of each other that the temporal unfolding of our lives appear as logical progressions—as, for example, on employment forms, curricula vitae, obituaries, and informal narrations of self. To imbue their lives with meaning, Western continually transform successive states and positions in social space into predestined steps in a developmental sequence. This creates a set of intelligible linkages, which is our way of projecting the past into the future in the service of the present. Of apprehending the time of our lives. The primary convention is to highlight a few significant events and then to imbue them with a certain telos, although it could just as easily be said that Westerners highlight certain events—that is, these events become significant—because they permit the production of such a telos or unifying purpose. Western agents are their own ideologists to the extent that they fail to see that the ontological forms (the person as individual and biography) that appear to ground and naturalize the personal ones are themselves social. Through a set of conventions, durably installed in Western institutions and habitus, a lifetime that is fluctuating, often discontinuous, subject to untimely and unpredictable chances, obtains a shape that allows the production of a very particular type of social being—and collectively, a very particular type of collectivity that is both Western and society. Not surprisingly, the modern novel and novelists, and poets, have called attention to the conventional character of this relationship by creating characters who live nonlinear chaotic lives, absent an inherent logic or overarching purpose. The construction of a biography through the conventions for the use of personal memory and forgetting also requires that agents abstract themselves from the relationality definitive of their lives and the fields they inhabit. This allows Western agents to think of themselves as conceptually distinct from the relations and fields of experience that draw them together thus creating a narrative picture of the unique, self-sufficient individual in a world unfinished. In essence, through the construction of memory and the abstraction of agents from the relationality of their own self-production, biography is one of the principal Western means of relating persons to temporality and social space in such a way that the results foreground the individual aspect of personhood. I will return to an explicit and comparative theory of the person in the next chapter.

Because Western societies have historically evolved such that the categories of the person, commodity, and society are organically bound to one another, it stands to reason and reality that Melanesian peoples did not, as a matter of practice, construct life histories because they never imagined life to be a history. This does not imply that Melanesians cannot learn to imagine a life as a sequence of successive events and relations—as indeed the agents and institutions of encompassment would begin to teach them to do. It does imply that even when Melanesians crafted a biography, epitomized by Strathern's (1979) wonderful account of the Melpa big-man Ongka, it has nothing resembling the same implications for the making of the person, economy, or collectivity. The absolutely critical, and critically overlooked, essence of differentiation between the West and its others has been this: in Melanesia, the form of appearance of a practice is only, and only sometimes, masked by an ideology that attempts to paper over a contradiction between that and other social practices. In the West, the form of appearance of a practice (such as biography-making) conceals the structural categories that produce it (e.g., sociality, person, and value), such that those dimensions of the practice that contradict the categories are the necessary forms of their appearance. So, for example, the construction of biography as individual narrative contradicts the underlying reality that, among other things, the successive states of the field(s) through which a person has progressed determines that agent's trajectory. The Maring certainly do shape memories and recollections of their own actions and the actions of others, and they can recount their own and others' pasts (as exemplified in portraits of warriors), but these biographical acts did not lie at the core of the construction of persons, they did not appear as a regimented narrative of any type (let alone imbued with a linear teleology), and they were connected to objects of economy and the objectification of collectivity in a way that emphasized the relations between persons above all else.

When Maring agents speak about themselves and others—when they use the metapragmatic resources of their language—they seek to expose or make visible the sociality defining a given relationship. Speakers may, for example, characterize others in regard to their ability to attract, entice, embolden, empower, and motivate an audience through their command of speaking (*tep*). The description visualizes and acknowledges the power of the orator's speech (as opposed to the orator) to cause others to enact a specific kind of sociality. Noticeably absent from the cultural logic was the notion that powerful orators (in contrast to successful academics, for example) are defining their selfhood through the ability to influence others' subjective states by virtue of their personal qualities. This example from speech held true across the board, in the domains of exchange, kinship, and the politics of everyday life. When speaking of themselves or others, Maring never arrange a person's life as some sequence of logically ordained steps. In recounting the past, thereby constructing a selective memory of that past, the relationality between speaker and audience determines the ordering of events, emotions, and responses. There was no compulsion to place the events of a person's life in a chronological order on the understanding that earlier events would somehow illuminate the reasons for subsequent actions. The primary tropes and images were spatial and relational, so much that the conflation of the naming of a relation with a space defined a critical way in which agents would verify their statements. Without pursuing a more detailed discussion, the point is that the Maring relation between time and the subject was transparently different from what the West imagines. Ultimately, the quest is to grasp how the Maring and other Melanesians created images, memories, and accounts of persons that were never biographies in the Western sense.

However, one of the hallmarks of the West was to impress upon people the virtues and processes by which people have biographies. The Western notion of life as biography was exemplified by the story of Jesus—a story that, as a touchstone of Christian missionizing, was repeated over and again. And then again still countless other times, a mantra of the good and godly life. The immaculate birth, the wandering in the desert, the teachings, the death and resurrection, glorified in the stations of the cross imprinted and pictured in a kind of primitive catechism, imagined the life of the Savior as the highest form of telos. His beginning already inscribed a specific conclusion. The life of Jesus, a model for all lives always and everywhere, was to inspire the Maring toward the proper behavior, especially the expulsion of violence and the other deadly vices from their kingdom. In the portraits of other Melanesians that were part of the reading lessons of the school, there were invariably stories told as biographies of their lifeways. The life and trials of Michael Somare, drawn from an auto-biography that charts step-by-step his ascendance from rural villager to the first postindependence premier of Papua New Guinea, exemplified this new way of envisioning a person. The birth of the nation was linked to the biographies of its leaders, their examples of personal vision and determi-nation. Westerners, placing their own cultural psyches on display, would introduce themselves, explain to themselves as much as to the Maring why they came to Melanesia of all places, by constructing a history of their backgrounds. Why being a priest from San Francisco by way of Milne Bay, a nurse from Ireland by way of the United States, or a policeman from Manchester by way of a failing marriage, somehow explained their present and presence in the Bismarck Mountains. Because Westerners had completely internalized the notion of the biographical person, the story of their individuality and the logic that threaded their life together, they pre-supposed the same in their encounters with Melanesians. While the philosopher (Ricoeur) may recognize that there is no self at the start and the poet (Paz) may realize that the deepest reality is the illusion that the "I" writes alone (stepping through the shards of its own shattered image), the ideology of the person in its fully naturalized state was the simple, time-defined, unadorned biography presented to the Maring by all of the agents and institutions of encompassment. Perhaps the ultimate and most unreflective irony of encompassment is that the West seeks to transform others' realities so that they are structured in the form of our appearances.

The Maring did indeed recognize progression (e.g., that agents mas-ter some things cumulatively over time), they did make comparative gen-eralizations about the relations of others (e.g., that some people seemed to fashion exemplary exchange relationships while others made relationships that seemed perpetually to flounder), and these observations surely figured in the construction of intentionality. But they were not fragments of biog-raphy in any Western sense: they neither expressed nor did they have the effect of creating any underlying structural relationships. The crucial point, and what ultimately separates biography in the Western world from kindred depictions in Melanesia, is that the structuring principles of biog-raphy are aimed at creating the person as individual, even as they function to render this person a homologue of society and the commodity, and they do so in such a way that the form of appearance of the person and of the homology of the person, society and commodity, conceal the relations of sociality and value that are their constituting essence. The great weakness of comparative accounts of the encompassed world and the West has been that, whether they take the economizing and maximizing rationality of the West as a universal logic (typified by ecological anthropology) or they assume that there is a radical alterity between the West and its others (typified by postmodern anthropology), the point of origin of both viewpoints and those in between is *only the form of appearance* of Western society. The epicenter of comparison and entrance into the Melanesian world, seemingly eclipsed by the processes of encompassment, is the subjectivity of persons.

CHAPTER 4

The Modernity of the Person
in Melanesia

To speak about the making of a generation is to speak about the shaping of subjectivity in a world defined by encompassment. In this arena, the construction of the person figures centrally in any understanding of the forms and implications of the conversation between Melanesia and the West, not least because the concepts of personhood indigenous to Melanesia and Papua New Guinea in particular are significantly different from those embodied in Western practice and texts and presupposed by the colonially inspired political institutions that define the emerging states of Oceania. Concepts such as nationhood, liberal democracy, civil rights, and electoral politics presuppose at least a Western-like image of the individual (ideologically defined as an autonomous, self-animated, and self-enclosed agent). The emergence of the nation-states of Melanesia, oriented toward and encompassed by Western culture and capitalism, entails the evolution of Western-like conceptions of the individual (embedded, for example, in World Bank policy about how these nations should organize their economies in terms of a free market [LiPuma 1996]). To so speak of modernity is to place the construction of identity in the path of desire, not least being the desire of Melanesians to internalize the modern, to consume and be consumed by the goods and services of the capitalist economy, to entertain "rights" not known or needed before (e.g., the right of privacy), and the desire to redefine the political so that the polarity of power reverses course and flows back from the white West to black Melanesia.[1] All of these motivate the emergence and increasing visibility of the individual facet of personhood *because the individual is the main and mythologized locus of those types of desire particular to modernity.* To connect the study of the person to the evolving of modernity and the larger set of forces reshaping life throughout Melanesia is to carry the ethnography of personhood onto a terrain rarely visited by anthropology, and certainly not the anthropology of Melanesia—which in theory and description has long been bound to the local level. To approach the construction of the person in the context and conflicts of modernity is to problematize the interpenetration and interfunctionality of levels: for the people of Melanesia, the ongoing dialectic between the construction of subjectivities at a local level and the encompassment of Melanesia. If there was any single feature that characterized the up-and-coming generation of Maring it was the emergence of the individual aspect of the person, the knowledge, desires, and life trajectories of these agents increasingly attuned to the world beyond the walls of kinship and community. For their part, the agents of Westernization glorified and naturalized the individual aspect of local persons, rewarding those Maring who "used their own initiative," "thought for themselves," "were their own person," "took care of their own interests," and so on.

More than anything else such an account of personhood requires a sense of proportion. Studies that overemphasize or underestimate relations of sameness and difference between Melanesian and Western societies hobble our efforts to understand how the dynamics of encompassment reconfigure local forms of personhood. The necessity is to clarify the character of relativity. And also to relativize relativity: for what is considered (and contested) as "local" today has been influenced by Western presence and pressures, just as what is considered Western (parliamentary-style government, capitalism on Bougainville, the use of all-purpose money in bridewealth payments) bears an indelible Melanesian imprint. In other words, a theory of relativity is crucial because all scientific and most public sphere discourse about Melanesia (even when Melanesians are themselves the authors of such discourse) is comparative.

The concept of the person also has another and different hold on anthropological understanding. The reason is that ethnography—and one could go back to Malinowski and the mythological origins of fieldwork—has always held, indeed been founded on, if not an overt contradiction, then two positions that want careful negotiation and management of perspective. Subsuming itself to the universe of the Other, anthropology has argued for the unique and special character of each and every culture. At least in part because the genesis of anthropology was inseparable from the encompassment of the Other by the "West," anthropology has positioned itself against all versions of ethnocentricism (including in-house varieties) that would otherwise reduce the others to some version of the West. And, as I have argued elsewhere (LiPuma 1998), this defense of the "otherness" of the Others led ethnographers to ignore precisely those conditions of encompassment that made their own enterprise possible. Within the academic field of anthropology, a much more positive political value was placed on an ethnography of difference than on sameness. Certainly a primary trope of anthropology is to criticize others' studies (especially by the preceding generation of ethnographers) on the grounds that they have been compromised by ethnocentric presuppositions. This is the basis, for example, of Marilyn Strathern's critique of Leenhardt's study of New Caledonia; namely, that though Leenhardt recognizes that the person is highly relational/dividual, he cannot break free from his Western bearings, leading him to posit a residual individual aspect or center (1988:268–70). For Melanesia and beyond, there has been imagined a theory of anthropological "progress" based on increasing epistemological awareness of the uniqueness of others' cultures.

In the same breath, or at least the same texts, anthropologists have been making equally strong claims for the psychic, linguistic, and biological unity of humankind. The foundational claim is that whatever differences may exist, however much indigenous notions and practices were bound to their context of production, no matter that local cultures had their own epistemology, ethnographers could work their way into the habitus of the other, they could understand what lay behind local practices[2] and translate and reproduce this for a Western audience of, minimally, peers.[3] No less a student of other-ness than Stanley Tambiah began his Morgan lectures (1984) with the statement that the ethnographic project begins in the understanding that there are human "continuities of experience" as well as common "existential problems" (e.g., death) that engender a "psychic unity" across time and culture (1990:1). If the rationale for an anthropology rested on the first claim, the possibility of a viable ethnography adequate to its task rested on the second. In practice, anthropological claims of distance and the "uniqueness" of cultures coexist and co-occur with claims of proximity and sameness (although the latter claims have not been the subject of the same theoretical reflection). In the absence of these claims, anthropology would be drained of purpose, ethnography of meaning: the enterprise would be nothing more than self-analysis exoticised. Nowhere are these twin claims brought into relief or contested more than in reviews of the character of persons. In sum, there is no way to grasp the journey toward modernity by the nation-states and cultures of Melanesia or the anthropological project itself without clarifying the character of personhood. Moreover, the two are linked inseparably because an account adequate to an understanding of modernity in Melanesia must be able to grasp the conditions of its own construction.

Reconceptualizing Personhood

I would like to begin by setting out the primary argument, not least because of the complexity of engaging an issue that crosscuts so many dimensions (e.g., linguistic, political, juridical, medical) and social levels. The perspective developed here takes issue with theories of personhood that posit the self as fully individualized and defined in terms of internal attributes, thereby presuming that the "individual" is an ontologically privileged transhistorical and transcultural (meaning noncultural) category. From this viewpoint, the difference between persons in Western and Melanesian societies is a function of the content given this category. Though this view dominates Western social science, it is a minority report in the anthropology of Oceania that has progressively stressed the difference between our images of the person and those indigenous to Melanesia. In this light and against this background, I would also like to take issue with the view that Western and Melanesian images of personhood are fully incommensurable because the West constructs individuals while the societies of Melanesia construct dividuals or relational persons. Though this theory is politically appealing to an anthropology that fetishizes difference, it is ethnographically, theoretically, and, in the context of the emerging nation-state, also politically troubled. In making this argument, the analysis cannot help but promote a dialogue with the relational position staked out by Marilyn Strathern (1984, 1990) and others. The intention is to clear a theoretical space to better explore the conceptual and historical relationship between Western and Melanesian persons. The goal is not to refute the relational position as much as to embed it in a theory that enshrines its insights and strengths while allowing us to transcend its weaknesses.

In all cultures, I will argue, there exist both individual and dividual modalities or aspects of personhood. The individual facet emerges in the use of language (insofar as speech metapragmatically[4] centers itself through the use and/or presupposition of an "I"), in the existence of autonomous physiological systems of the human body, and by the fact that the body serves as the ground and signifier of the person, most importantly as the locus of an intentionality that is shared between, and thus presupposes, agents (Lambek 1993). By equal account, all societies encode relational, dividual aspects of personhood. This is true insofar as the identities of subjects and objects vary across contexts (domesticated animals can both be treated as members of the family and be "put to sleep," eaten, used in medical experiments, etc.), each language inscribes the use of a "you" as well as an "I," and identity and self-construction are the result of socially created relations (ethnicity, ritual, etc.). The foregrounding and hence transparency of individual and dividual aspects of personhood will vary across contexts for action within a given culture. More, cultures differ critically in the ontological status, visibility, and force granted individual/relational aspects of persons, especially as these appear in the construction of their own comparative discourses about persons, such as justifications or explanations for actions. From this view, it is a misunderstanding to assume either that the social emerges out of individual actions (a powerful strain in Western ideology that has seeped into much of its scientific epistemology) or that the individual ever completely disappears by virtue of indigenous forms of relational totalization (such as those posited for certain New Guinea societies). It would seem rather that *persons emerge precisely from that tension between dividual and individual aspects/relations.* And the terms and conditions of this tension, and thus the kind (or range) of persons that are produced, will vary historically.

In this regard, encompassment and the progress of modernity in Melanesia simultaneously create and capitalize on the foregrounding, affirmation, and promotion of the individual aspect of this tension thus leading to a greater visibility and public presence of persons as individuals (see Foster 1995b). To assume, in other words, that there exists an opposition between societies based on substance and those based on relations, cultures of fully dividual persons versus a Western world of individuals, is not only to accept Western ideological notions of the person (which sees the person as undividedly individual), but to use that ideology to construct the Other as its opposite image. Indeed, a general problem in the conceptualization of the relation between Melanesia and the West (taken collectively) is that accounts of Melanesian thought and practices are contrasted not with equivalent accounts of Western notions of personhood, but with Western ideology. Because our understanding of Melanesian persons takes place in that field of contrasts with Western persons (in theory and in the practice of ethnography), an adequate analysis of Melanesia is inseparable from an adequate account of the Western construction of persons. Unfortunately, I would argue, many recent analyses define the Melanesian person against an inadequate account of the Western person, which leads them to overstate the differences, a failure that, quite consonantly, is most apparent in the contexts of ethnography and of modernity.[5]

Those who hold a relational view of Melanesian personhood, who in Josephides (1991) words practice the "new Melanesian ethnography," read the following contrasts from the ethnography.

WESTERN	MELANESIAN
Persons are conceptually distinct from the relations that unite them and define them.	Persons are the compound and plural site of the relations that bring them together.
Collectivity is grasped and symbolized as a unification of pluralities. Singular person is an individual.	Collective sociality/life is defined as an essential unity. Singular person is a composite.
Society and the individual are in a relation of opposition, contestation, and hierarchy.	The social and the individual are parallel, homologous, and equivalent.

Social life consists in movement from one internal/external state to another.	Social life consists in movement from one mode of sociality to another.
The person is the subject of an explicit and visible ideology: individualism.	There is no explicit ideology of persons, only contextually situated images.
An individual's behavior and intentions are interpreted as the public expression of inner qualities (greed, honesty, etc.).	An individual's behavior and intentions are interpreted in terms of his or her actions in context.
Persons mature biogenetically as a consequence of their own inner potential.	Persons grow transactionally as the beneficiary of other people's actions.
Persons depend on themselves for knowledge about their internal selves, i.e., self-knowledge.	Persons depend on others for knowledge about themselves, and they are not the authors of this knowledge.
A person's power lies in his/her control over others; power is a possession.	A person's power lies in his/her ability to do and act; power is a relation.
Persons are axiomatically same-sex; social identity should fully replicate one's natural physiological state.	Persons alternate between same-sex and cross-sex identities; social identity is detached from one's physiological state.
Society stands over and against the individual as an external force that imposes norms, rules, and constraining conventions.	Society runs parallel to the individual; it is embodied as a disposition to think, believe, and feel in a certain way.
Its commodity logic leads people to search for knowledge about things and to make an explicit practice out of knowing the nature of objects.	Its gift logic leads people to search for knowledge about persons and to make a practice out of knowing the person-making powers of objects.

The contrast here is between the West's own self-understanding, which exists both ideologically and normatively (as embodied in constitutional and statutory law, ethnoviews of aesthetics, economic reasoning, the relation of individuals to the government, etc.), and an account of the foregrounded elements of personhood in traditional, nonencompassed

Melanesia. The Western notions of the person against which the Melanesian ethnography appears are ideological inasmuch as they privilege and
foreground individual elements of Western personhood while masking,
subordinating, and sublimating the more dividual facets. For the West, the
notion of the person as wholly individual (as an autonomous, self-contained, self-moving agent) is constructed historically, contested, at best a
partial description, and critical to forms of "misrecognition" (Bourdieu
1984) and abstract domination (Postone 1993) common to capitalism.
Although I can only gloss here what is implicated in the Western production of the person, it is nevertheless necessary to at least locate the Western
person because it constitutes the background and presuppositions for our
discussion and ethnography of the Melanesian person.

    The person in capitalist society has two defining features: (1) the per-
son is composed, historically and culturally, of dividual and individual
aspects; and (2) paradoxically, the person appears as the natural and transhistorical individual. The double character of the person is intrinsically
bound to, and homologous with, the character of commodity-determined
labor. Unlike Melanesia, where products are distributed by ties of kinship
and community, and overt relations of power and domination, in capitalist societies "labor itself replaces these relations by serving as a kind of
objective means by which the products of other are acquired [such that] a
new form of interdependence comes into being where . . . one's own labor
or labor products function as the necessary means of obtaining the products of others. In serving as such a means, labor and its product preempt
that function on the part of manifest social relations" (Postone 1986:6–7).
So it is that commodity-determined labor is mediated by structures such as
that of personhood (and also class) that it itself constitutes. The social
relations of capitalism are thus based on a quasi-independent structure
that stands apart from, and opposed to, persons understood as individuals. Labor, here, as socially mediating activity creates relations among persons that, though social and containing dividual elements, assume a quasi-
objective and individualist character. And as capitalism develops, as now
throughout Melanesia, the mediating function of labor slowly but
inevitably reshapes the cultural form of the person.[6] The person becomes
progressively reified as a self-contained, self-shaping, independent agent.
What this means is that a defining feature of capitalism is that the ontological forms, such as labor and the individual, that appear to underlie the
social ones (individuals' actions) are not only themselves social but have
their sociality disguised. The extension of this view is that an ideology of
the person as fully individual is a necessary feature of the form and reproduction of the person in capitalist society. Certainly one of the major features that distinguishes Melanesia from the West is the absence of a
sanctified ideology of persons that is necessary to their construction.

Nonetheless, the ideology of the Western person as fully individual only partially conceals the reality that Western persons are interdependent, defined in relation to others, depend on others for knowledge about themselves, grasp power as the ability to do and act, grow as the beneficiary of others' actions, and so forth. Most of the features of Melanesian personhood cited above also apply to the West, however much they may be misrecognized or pushed into the background.[7] It is at this depth of sociohistorical construction that we discover that the true ontological form is not, as the West would imagine it, the individual; it is the dual person delineated by both dividual and individual facets, the basis of what anthropology knows as the psychic unity of humankind, which opens the possibility of an ethnography of Others.[8] Simply phrased, it is because persons are inherently dual that an ethnography of Melanesia is possible.

Once we grasp the character of personhood in societies defined by the commodity form, it becomes evident that our real danger is in understanding the preceding inventory of differences as a totalizing opposition: as indicative of two incommensurable forms of personhood and sociality, rather than as two socially and historically variable ways of relating dividuality to individuality. The contrast between the West and Melanesia is telling because along this epistemological divide Western cultures place the greatest emphasis on individuality whereas Melanesian cultures stress dividuality. My argument is that we should not replace the "ethnocentric" notion that Melanesians are sovereign unified subjects who operate as causes of sociohistorical effects with the idea that they are partible subjects who operate as effects of multiple lines of determination: neither notion is a productive description of personhood for either Melanesians or for Westerners. The ethnographic goal, I would argue, is to uncover the conditions (e.g., encompassment by the West) under which dividual and individual aspects of personhood emerge and are hidden.

Ethnographers, of course, have assumed all along that whatever forms personhood may take there are sites of commensurability and the possibility of translation. The very practice of description assumes that between we and they, Westerners and Melanesian/others, there is never absolute separation of substance and agency, individuality and dividuality. No matter what is argued theoretically, ethnography as intercultural communication and experience presupposes at least the partial unification of person and agency. To juxtapose a theory of Melanesia that separates the person and the agent to a Western image (ideology) of the unity of person and agency is to render these two forms of society incommensurable, to push relativity to the point at which ethnography is no longer possible. It is to say that there is no point of essential similarity, no sameness between Melanesian personhood and Western personhood that would allow translation: the "I" of the Melanesian sentence would have no translation into English or any other non-Melanesian language for that matter. Perhaps the case that ethnography as anthropology has known and practiced it is truly impossible, and perhaps the sadness of that understanding is a function of the encompassment of others by the West: that "we" can understand others only to the extent we make them like ourselves. But I think (and would argue) not, one key reason being that a too-strong claim of cultural relativity is politically disabling and disempowering (to Melanesian women, rural populations forced to deal with mining or logging operations, etc.). Because such relativistic positions rely on a positional epistemology, they shear away the ground of critique itself, a crucial political point that many anthropologists in their desire to honor difference seem to overlook.[9]

Ethnography and the Person

Though an earlier anthropology assumed that Melanesian cultures were comprised of Western-like individuals and a later anthropology denied the existence of such individuals, ethnography all along has presupposed both a critical element of difference and a fundamental sameness. For however cultures construct intentionality, and those of Oceania clearly imagine intentionality differently from the West (LiPuma 1994), they must always link agency to personhood. That is, the sentence must always have a speaker, the agent must always have a name (even if that personal name is fully bound up in a system of relations),[10] and bodies perform acts (e.g., observe taboos), acquire habits and language, and undergo changes independent of one another (e.g., birth and birthing, illnesses, and death). What I am getting at is that a Westerner can have access to Melanesian intentionality and a Melanesian can have access to Western forms of intentionality because both operate in terms of dividual and individual aspects of personhood. Whatever else ethnographers have said in statements of theory and method they have always presupposed (1) that persons are the locus of intentionality, (2) that every agent (the ethnographer especially) has an identity that is neither reducible to nor wholly predictable from his/her position in a system of relations, and (3) that a person's identity is more than culturally inscribed; it is continually reshaped in a life-world that is never reducible to a fixed system of social relations and values because people are confronted with, and encompassed by, unpredictable circumstances (like crop blights and plagues) and foreign phenomena (like colonialism and capitalism) that, transcending and transgressing the limits of understanding, elicit new ways of being in the world. Accordingly, the succession of generations is never a mechanical process, the production of identity never a finality. Ethnographers have assumed this to be the case in a double sense.

The first is that every ethnography presupposes the conditions and possibility of coordinated intentionality. This is the premise that the people with whom ethnographers live and interact have beliefs, desires, and judgments, that is to say, intentions to act, and that we as ethnographers have access to those beliefs, desires, and judgments—sufficient access that we can grasp and understand the action of others as deliberate and meaningful. For example, if an ethnographer witnesses a curing ceremony (a Maring shaman places leaves and water in a bamboo tube, bespells it, and then passes the tube over the body of the ill) the ethnographer must presume that those involved hold global beliefs about the form and value of curing and specific beliefs about the form and efficacy of the particular cure; that they have the desire to cure the ill individual; and that they have made the judgment that this curing ceremony is appropriate to the illness in question. Even the simple and seemingly transparent act of watching a woman and her young daughter plant taro, which we may take as commonsensical and demanding no explanation (even a note in our field diary), presumes beliefs (about the value of taro and when it should be planted), desires (to be productive, help and support kinsmen, etc.), and judgments (this is the appropriate time and place to plant), and takes as axiomatic that ethnographers can and do have access to them. Ethnography is founded on the idea that a coordination of intentionality is cross-culturally possible; that a person from one culture has the bases to grasp and interpret the actions of a person from another culture.[11] The actions may be no more or less than a report about the past action of other agents or what ethnographers do when they interview someone about what has happened previously. To put this differently, ethnography rests on the assumption of the ontological existence of the person; an agent defined minimally by the fact that he/she has beliefs, desires, and judgments, thereby constituting intentions and thus the possibility of coordinated intentionality or shared meanings (with, for example, the ethnographer).

The second premise of ethnography is that it can be transcendent in a social sense: that ethnographers can overcome both the social and the epistemological separation that almost all ethnography, the study of New Guinea societies being where such separation is at its zenith, is condemned to. The premise is that the accounts produced by ethnographers will not simply be an objectification of their own culturally and individually defined beliefs, desires, and judgments. On one hand, they will not simply understand, thereby reducing the Other's categories to their own epistemology. The idea is that the ethnographer can find points of convergence that allow him/her to determine, explore, and relate the shape of indigenous epistemology in a way that does not do violence to that epistemology or the acts and events that presuppose it. On the other hand, ethnography must assume that its agents, by virtue of taking up a position analogous to local agents or capitalizing on indigenous means of integrating strangers, can make a place for themselves (a social position) in the societies they study. The integration of the ethnographer into any society, even those with highly relational images of the person, is possible only through the space of individuality, precisely because an ethnographer has no socially, locally created identity. In this respect, ethnographers resemble, at least for Melanesia, big-men or chiefs: namely, agents who possess the power to express and enforce their individuality. In terms of modernity, the ethnographer (like the missionary and the health official) is a locus of individuality and an instrument and index of historical change. Or, to note this a different way, the dividual is to the individual as culture is to nature, as the social/ritual order is to entropy, as the clarity of custom is to the epistemic murkiness of modernity. For Melanesians and others, the conundrum is that Western notions such as democracy, freedom, and civil society (because they are founded on the concept of individual rights) foreground the individual facet of personhood in societies in which sociality, order, knowledge, and indeed the entire structure of intentionality have been mostly (though never exclusively) defined in terms of the dividual facet of personhood.

What this means is that ethnography as social action presumes the existence of an intrinsic connection between individuality and social dividuality. Ethnography in Oceania has long been based on, and taken advantage of, the fact that the very incorporation of a Western ethnographer into a society that privileges the relational aspect of personhood is itself a privileged position from which to see social life. In other words, ethnography not only presupposes an individual aspect to Melanesian personhood but uses that aspect as an entrance point into indigenous lifeways. This individualist aspect would be much more transparent if anthropologists routinely deconstructed the space of being an "informant" in a society that does (or at least did) not recognize such a "role." Certainly, in the era of modernity what needs to be analyzed is the construction of the practice and position of information mediation and mediator (i.e., informant) in the face of requests for social information by anthropologists, colonizers, missionaries, government officials, and other emissaries of Westernization.

The encompassment of Melanesia is simultaneously objective and subjective. Further, it underlines that these objective and subjective moments of encompassment are intrinsically connected. Agents interpret transformations in the objective structure through the prism of the concepts, desires, and dispositions already instilled within them even as these transformations redefine these concepts, desires, and dispositions. Nowhere is this more telling or socially transformative than in the construction of the subjectivity of the up-and-coming generation. The condition of modernity under which the junior generation has been raised calls for, elicits, valorizes, and ultimately rewards a new kind of subject, a new kind of person. A consumer, a citizen, a Christian. On these grounds, the chapter has developed two interrelated arguments with respect to Melanesian personhood. The first is that there has always been an individual aspect of personhood, even if this aspect was traditionally in the background and on the margins of practice. The second argument is that this individual aspect is becoming more important, visible and foregrounded with modernity. In this respect, modernity seeks to move what was traditionally marginal to the Melanesian person to the epicenter of social life. The move entails not only the foregrounding and valorization of the individual, it entails the construction of the modern Western concepts of a culture and a society because in the cultures of capitalism the individual and the social receive their values from their mutual opposition. The individual is defined in opposition to the social just as society is perceived as an integration of individuals. The remainder of the chapter sets the stage for grasping the emergence of the individual by tracing a kind of history of the Maring person.[12]

The Person in Maring Exchange

The assumption, long made by ethnographers, that there exists a necessary and universal connection between substance and agency, dividuality and individuality, is more than a methodological trope or a descent into ethnocentricism. For most ethnographers, it has its basis in their ethnographic experiences. We could retrace our steps back to Leenhardt and the founding of comparative studies of the person (1947) to see that even as he explores the character of relationality, he is aware that there must be a connection between agency and cause. The connection becomes apparent when we examine the construction of persons in, and across, practices and contexts for action, which are also instances of self-(re)presentation. To do this, I would like to explore the Maring concept of the person; specifically in the context of exchange that appears to exemplify the relationship between dividual and individual aspects of personhood. The evidence suggests that the "person" in exchange emerges precisely from the tension between dividual and individual aspects, and that is particularly true in instances where the exchange goes awry and there is no coordination of intentionality. Moreover, I would argue that tension between dividuality and individuality has long been a common refrain in Melanesian society (see Kulick 1992), though it goes under other names (such as the contrast people make between agents whose intentions are transparent and who act

openly and in public versus agents who operate secretly and privately and
whose intentions are easily imagined as nefarious).

The Maring concept of truth holds that truth has an inner and outer
dimension and that it is inscribed in the act itself, an idea that has been
explored in the context of "veiled speech" (Strathern 1975). The surface or
appearance of an action, its skin to use the Maring's own metaphor, characteristically manifests deception, lies, and dissembling. Its aim is to
manipulate the beliefs, desires, and judgments that surround the presentation and reception of the gift. By contrast, the inner core of the action is its
truth and power to pull or bend others. Language is thought to lie on the
skin of the action; it is the primary (though not only) means of disguising
the "true" intentionality of an actor. In this respect, the importance of
exchange lies in the virtue that gifts are indexical; they are a part of that
which they express. Nevertheless, the social practice of gift-giving is still
infused with manifold intentions and active dissembling. When agents
evaluate a gift, they expect a difference between its surface or "skin" and
its more "interior" truths. This inside-outside schema is the Maring way of
organizing the hierarchy of intentions that will be embodied in a given
action. For example, the presentation of a gift will include a verbally
stated intention (e.g., the gift is because you are my affine), a presupposed
though unstated intention (e.g., the gift helps to discharge my outstanding
bride-payment debt), and a disguised intention (e.g., the gift will be followed by a request for use of your garden lands). Conversely, every
request for a gift can be seen as the maintenance of a social relation, repayment for a gift given previously, or as an extortion based on power, such
as the power to harm through sorcery and magic. The intentionality of a
gift is such that the beliefs, desires, and judgments of the recipient concerning that gift are often read onto the donor. If a recipient "feels" subjugated by a gift, he/she may well interpret the subjugation as intrinsic to the
gift-giving, and thus part of the intentionality of the act itself.

Maring locate intention in the relationship between an action and its
influence rather than in the "mind" of the agent. There is no means in
Maring to speak about someone's intentions or judgments apart from
what they do and other people's experience of those acts. There is no way
to differentiate between the mental dimension of an act and the act itself;
rather the action is understood to embody a hierarchy of intentions.
Determining the meaning or intent of some action, "digging out its root"
to use local metaphor, is a function of understanding and assessing its
inner and outer layers. In this respect, the agent is the fulcrum of the relationship, the cause of a specific response inscribed in the relationship itself,
such that the agents appear passive in the sense that they are constituted
by that momentary crystallization of relationship—what we refer to as an
event. The actions of agents appear to be sucked out of them by the com-

plex of relationships with others in terms of which they act (M. Strathern 1988:272–74). Agency and cause appear to live separate lives.

At the same time, however, agents are also aware that nothing can guarantee the execution, meaning, interpretation, or aftermath of a specific act of exchange. The structure of clan affiliations, relations of affinity, the history of exchange between the parties involved: none of these can guarantee the actions of the participants, and, more precisely, the unfolding of intentionality. There is always a possibility that one of the agents will back out of the exchange or interpret/intend the gift as an act of violence or extortion. There is always the possibility that the agents, as the body and embodiment of intentionality, will tell (cause) a lie or dissemble. There always exists a degree of uncertainty that is at least partly brought under control by representing persons. So it is said of certain persons that they "see gifts badly," meaning that they often ascribe malevolent intentions to the donor; other persons are portrayed as tolerant and inclined to be generous. In the same spirit, some ancestors are portrayed as generous, to look favorably on the gifts (of pig) offered to them and to reciprocate by helping the living; a smaller number of ancestors, by contrast, are depicted as ungracious and unwilling to help their descendants. And, just as a man will cut off an exchange partner who sees gifts badly, so he will refuse to propitiate an ungenerous ancestor. In this respect, people classify the behavior of others. They create a comparative discourse about interpretation of the intentionality of gifts that is inflected by, but never reducible to, the complex of relations shaping the event. The "scandal" of the gift is that there is a thin subjective line between generosity and treachery—even in some cases between brothers, what Maring ideology lauds as the most presupposed and predictable of kin relations.

The Maring not only thought and talked about people comparatively, but also created and recognized person's biographies. How a person exchanges—simply and practically, that person's pattern of action over time—was a central element in the biography. The performance of giving objectified the affinity between exchange partners. But the act of objectification, that performance, was undertaken by the "singular subject." This was exemplified by the language of giving that centers itself indexically in the I. Thus, the presentation of a gift will use such ritualized phrases as: "I give this to you nothing" (without expectations). No matter how set the field of relations, no matter how regimented the exchange context, the inscription of intention/meaning was not necessarily transparent or predetermined. The individual aspect emerged because performances were individuated, and the history of these performances generated a person's biography, name, reputation. And the history of people's performance was circulated, becoming part of collective memory such that the memory itself becomes an aim and presupposition of future exchanges (e.g., raising one's name). Though, according to Maring, the reasons why others were the way they were can never in principle be known, and those I talked with were unwilling to even speculate about why some agents often "see gifts badly," there was always the possibility that a person would be the basis of his/her own actions, and that some agents were comparatively more likely to be the basis/cause of their actions than others. There was always the possibility that individuality would help to shape the meaning and implications of an exchange event. So it was not only that the person comes into being in the context of relationships: to some degree agents always act as their own cause because they always had the option of doing so or not. It was not just that agents come into focus with respect to their relationships to others but that they do so as a matter of choice, however presupposed and overdetermined this choice may be.[13]

Within Maring society, the individual aspect of personhood had little visibility in many contexts for action, such as exchange and production. There was no ideological endorsement of individuality, as occurs in the West generally and especially in the United States. People did not simply valuate others by the way that others activate relationships (i.e., successfully or unsuccessfully), though this was surely critical; people evaluate others also through their personal biographies of activation of relationships. And the difference between the way different persons activated relationships, and more precisely, the memory of these differences as instantiated in people's comparative discourse about action (e.g., the way people are represented by others), *was* their individuality. For the Maring, there was always the presence of individuality, though a notion of unknowableness masked its presence. One way to interpret this evidence was that the difference between the West and Melanesia did not lie only in the respective emphasis they place on individuality versus dividuality, but also on the way in which they objectify and represent persons' actions. The objectification of behavior in the West converts acts that are both dividual and individual into pure individuality, whereas the objectification of behavior in Melanesia converted dividuality/individuality into a knowable set of relations and unknowable reasons for action.

The corollary to the involvement of persons in exchange was the relationship between these persons and the things that flowed between them. The possession of an object like a bird plume engendered a partial and contextualized identity (affiliation) between the owner and the object owned, a partiality that was revealed in the reality of the enjoyment of its use values, even as that object was destined to be alienated by decay, loss, theft, or sale. The product can be separated from its producer, the plume from the man who captured it, with a partial though recoverable loss of self. For Maring, as for Westerner, there was never a one-to-one correspondence between owner and object, producer and product, although in certain situations it might appear that way. What distinguished Westerners from Maring and Melanesians more generally was that Westerners presumed ideologically that there was an identity between an agent and what that agent owned and that persons were the sole authors of their own actions, whereas Maring presumed, but did not submit to ideological reflection, that a partial connection existed between owner and object, and that agents author their behavior in relation to, and with, others. For Maring and for Westerners, persons are least like what they are, have, and do in the domestic sphere, and more so along the avenues of exchange and circulation. The error here would be to assume that the one-to-one relationship between owner and object, the necessary and highly inculcated form of capitalist epistemology, accurately reflects the structure of Western life, and to then conceptualize Maring society as its opposite, thereby ignoring or having to "explain away" those instances where Westerners act as if no correspondence existed, and Maring act as if one did.

The direction of an intention away from the "self" revealed the intention in the act (of giving) and the coordination of intentionality, each agent acting as the other's effects. The gift a person created was evidence of his/her effort in relation to an "other" who in that sense incorporated that effort. At the same time, however, the form of the gift (its size, quality, form of presentation, etc.) and therefore its intentionality was never fully predetermined (meaning that the gift was indexical and hence a statement about the current state of this relationship). The result was that in the act of exchange the person emerged—became visible—as dividual and as individual because that effort both belonged to the recipient and was never totally predetermined by virtue of existing relations. This tension revealed itself when there was an absence of a coordination of intentionality. Donor and recipient may have different interpretations of the gift: the beliefs, desires, and judgments of one may be very different from the other. The attempt to reproduce or grow relations through exchange may or may not be successful. A clear example is a case described by Riebe (1987) where an exchange misfired due to a lack of a coordination of intentionality, leading to accusations of sorcery and an eventual murder. Similarly, it was sometimes the case that a gift earmarked to support one relation was redirected toward another. Here is an example.

> Yingok has three wives, the middle wife having been with him for seven years and the youngest wife two years. The kin of the youngest expect a payment of cooked pork from Yingok and indeed Yingok seems to have intimated that two of his larger male pigs are destined for them. However, he slaughters the animals as part of a ceremony for his second wife's clansmen, in payment, he says, for her children. The relatives of the youngest

wife are miffed at the outcome and threaten to take him to court. Yingok readily acknowledges the claims of his youngest wife's clan, but disparages them as greedy and says that they did not "hear him properly."

The case in question clearly indicates that the gift or effort cannot be self-consumed, but also that its destination and thus its intentional effects are neither preordained nor free from ambiguity. The problem with a purely dividual reading of this event is that it leaves no room for contingency or creativity. Interestingly, given the fact that the Maring have a rather deterministic ideology, this event, when recounted in the past tense, was portrayed as inevitable and very presupposed, as though Yingok's decision was simply called forth by the relational field in front of him. Just as a "Western" ideological reading would see only the individual—Yingok trying to strategically maximize his resources to improve his social status—so Maring grasp his behavior as predetermined by obligations toward his affines. Analysis is lost here if it forgets that the power of these ideologies to construct reality is simultaneously their power to disguise it, to produce forms of misrecognition essential to the reproduction of that reality.[14]

The Practice of the Individual

If local representations of exchange masked the presence of the individual, there was another practice in which the individual facet of personhood could not be more transparent. Indeed, it is the one local practice defined by its expression. The practice in question is, of course, sorcery.[15] Whereas other local practices presupposed constraining relationships that consume and devalue the individual, sorcery devalues the social through the wanton consumption of other members of the social body. It could be said that until the progress of Westernization sorcery was the indigenous name for instances and acts of individuality. So a person who was inordinately successful in relation to others (in hunting, pig-raising, etc.) was suspected of sorcery. And just as sorcery was the expression of individuality, so those persons who rose above others could only have managed this through some form of sorcery. The argument is that the Maring knew the individual element of personhood in two ways: in practices such as exchange in which the individual element was ideologically masked and in the practice of sorcery where it comes to the fore and in this respect challenges the indigenous image that the social is the paramount cultural value. Further, I would suggest that one reason that the advance of modernity has been accompanied by an upsurge in the practice of sorcery (LiPuma 1998) is that they share the same underlying epistemology.[16]

For the Maring, sorcerers were as powerful as they are marginal. They expressed that facet of all of us that is better left sublimated and mute. While ethnographers frequently grasp sorcery in terms of cause and effect, viewing it as the prosecution of physical ends by symbolic means, the Maring focused much more on the personhood of the sorcerer. They spoke first of the sorcerer as someone who wantonly disregarded the limits of kinship and thus of morality. All social relations had the propensity to be violent or peaceful, reciprocal or nonreciprocal, mutually beneficial or predatory. A moral person was someone who modulated and controlled these propensities in respect to social distance. But the sorcerer could not. Greed overcomes him, envy "eats" him, and so he turns on his own kin. The sorcerer does not "walk on the road"—a description that was equally a metaphor of the public and visible paths that join residential hamlets. Rather, the sorcerer "walks in the bush," hidden and hiding from the comings and goings of everyday sociality. Where normal people made "noise" to announce their presence, the sorcerer treaded silently to conceal his movements. Sorcery was the inverse of wealth creation; it was selfishness carried to its most profane result.[17]

Sorcerers thought only of themselves, casting aside their social obligations to others. They "want things only for themselves," thus expressing a possessiveness, a sense of greed, that was the opposite of sharing and reciprocity. The sorcerer "throws away" the kinship relations that defined him in social space, and becomes the sole and only cause of his own behavior. The intentionality of the sorcerer was opaque and unfathomable because he acted only in his own interest. Whereas the ancestor spirits (including nowadays Jesus) might attack a wayward man to punish him for having spurned his social commitments—not least the imperative to share food with kin—sorcerers attacked their own kind for self-aggrandizing and malevolent purposes. They acted without regard for the well-being of their community and in this regard defined themselves in opposition to it. For this reason, the sorcerer must be stopped at all costs, and indeed he was the one type of person who may be killed and killed justifiably by his own close kin: for his uncontrolled individualism threatened the nature of the social itself. A sorcerer's *nomane* (sentience and culture brought about by the socializing influence of kin) was "twisted" and "crooked" (see Strathern and Stewart 1996 for the parallel Hagen concept of *noman*). So the Maring said that "sorcerers are not part of us though we know they live among us"—or at least so it was told in indigenous ideology.

But this was only one of a number of stories that people related about sorcery. They also knew that it was very reckless to discount the reality that someone living nearby, even though they may appear oh so normal, could be deeply engaged in sorcery. In this sense, the sorcerer as a "species" of person was an abstract personification of a set of actions and relations. And so people admitted that anyone, a man, a woman, regardless of age or social position, may and can use sorcery if overcome by greed, anger, or envy. The sorcerer led a secret double life. My housemate Gou put it this way: "You believe all along that this man you know, even one of your own near kinsmen, respects the customs of reciprocity, but actually he wants to take and destroy what's yours without giving anything in return." Sorcerers almost always "saw things badly" although they pretended to "think straight." The duplicity lay in the fact that the "skin of the behavior" of someone who practices sorcery simply disguised its twisted intentionality—an intentionality defined by possessiveness, a quest for accumulation at the expense of reciprocity, a disregard of kinship in one's own interests; in short, the sorcerer takes himself as the primary value. Note that what the Maring perceived to be the worst traits of the sorcerer—such as his compulsion to possess power, accumulate things, and live in privacy—the West understands as the natural and universal attributes of persons qua persons. In acting as agents, sorcerers internalized or consumed the relations of which they were composed. They literally cannibalized the life force (*min*) of their own kin. In this respect, sorcerers exhibit, but in the most false way known to Maring, the knowledge of their internal compositions and capacities in the response of others.

What Maring said about sorcerers indicates that they used to be, and in 1980 to a great extent still were, the most visible, telling, and forceful expression of the individual aspect of personhood. Though markedly antisocial, sorcery was the exemplar and name for the articulation of unbridled and transparent individuality at the expense of social relatedness. It was the surfacing of the should-be-sublimated dimension of the human psyche. In this regard, the Maring have always had much more than a casual acquaintance with the individual aspect of personhood.

Politics and the Emergence of the Individual

Within those societies that privilege the dividual dimensions of personhood, the individual has a critical political moment, not least as a resource of negativity. Even before the arrival of the colonial officials and missionaries people imagined the individual as the obverse of dividuated personhood. And especially since the advent of modernity (read encompassment), agents have been enabled to protest the "traditional" order by organizing action around the individual aspect. Modernity has allowed the individual to become visible, the tension more explicit, and the expression of individuality more legitimate. In the precolonial epoch, there were two recognized sites for the emergence of the individual facet: common acts of sorcery and rare cases of "wild man" behavior.[18] In other words, the other transparent form of individualism was insanity (*pym*) in which a person, for no apparent reason, became disconnected from his social moorings. Both were instances in which a person's secret or unknowable individual desires overpowered their sense of social limits, leading to the inward direction of violence against their own kin. The encompassment of Melanesia has generated a new and much more powerful context for the expression of individuality. This individuality was personified by missionaries, anthropologists, and local "informants"; it was objectified in new institutions such as schools, trade stores, and courts; it was broadcast by television, radio, newspapers, and other forms of mass media as well as by the constant migration of people between town and hinterlands. What Western modernity has in common with the traditional contexts for the expression of individuality was that it also often involved violence.

In a series of articles, Robert Foster (1992, 1993, 1995a) has examined the structure of media and communications at the national level. His enquiry underlines the extent to which the politics and practices of modernity stress individuality. Billboard, print, and radio commercials peddling soft drinks, petrol, and a symphony of other products are also on an ontological plane, advertisements for the ascendence of the individual. They emphasize that in the world of modernity the individual is the privileged site of desire and interests. In a similar though more muted and retarded sense the same thing has been happening at the local level, and for a longer time. The persons and practices of the church, health care, business, school, and the state do not simply motivate change in the way people worship, manage illness, use money, or educate their children; they inaugurate a reformation in the location of knowledge, desires, and dispositions. Perhaps the most subtle and powerful change has been the creation of local contexts for the expression of the individual aspect of personhood and the legitimation and empowerment of that aspect and its expression. All the chapters that follow, each in their own way, illustrate that in the contexts of the modern, from prayers to the Almighty to the paradise of consumer choice, the underlying and unquestioned premise is that knowledge, desires, and dispositions are embodied in, and properties of, the individual. In this image, the universe is populated by self-animating, self-enclosed, and self-interested persons who, from the bastion of their individuality, recognize that they have interests in common with other individuals and, accordingly and contractually, join with them to create a society.

The process of foregrounding the individual aspect began with the arrival of white Europeans. It was advanced through permanent contact with such Westerners in the person of district officers, missionaries, medical personnel, ethnographers, traders, and sometimes their respective families. From the Maring perspective, these Westerners had two telling characteristics, taking as normal precisely those ways of being that indigenous life saw as aberrant. The first oddity was that these Westerners were clearly willing to step outside of social relatedness and inhabit a world where they had little or no connectedness to anyone. From the Maring slant, they appeared to be beholden to, and trusting, no one. Many Maring, in fact, found it hard at first to believe that the Westerners on the Koinambe mission station (Jimi Valley)—the VSO nurse from County Cork, the Anglican priest from San Francisco, the former policeman from Newcastle, the Summer Institute Bible translator from Western Australia, as well as the anthropologist who lived with them—were not somehow related. They believed there must be some kinship or community connection not because they were all "white" (the Maring were more than aware that all similarly colored people do not have a kinship relation) but because no one would be so individualistic. Such people seemed to have approached the world as if it were a canvas for the inscription of their own desires. Nothing symbolized this relationlessness more than the Western quest for privacy that the Maring, especially the senior generations, equated with secrecy, that, in turn, was equated with nefarious behavior (such as that of a sorcerer).

The second oddity was the Westerners' attachment to things. They seemed so attached to their possessions that they appeared blind to the possibilities of exchange and immune from the obligations of sharing. What the Maring did not know was that they were encountering people who embodied the culture of capitalism. What they did suspect was that these people apparently defined their subjectivity in terms of their possessions. They would inexplicably tire of their clothes long before they were worn out; they purchased new watches while the old ones still happily ticked; they raised houses seemingly large enough to shelter a whole subclan and then lived alone; they accumulated large quantities of rice and meat but rarely held feasts. Filtered through the logic of sociality, the evidence presented to the Maring led them to misinterpret the actions of the Westerners. Some observed that the reason these Westerners had removed themselves far from the sphere of kinship was precisely so they could accumulate gifts without having to share them. Some thought that the Western pursuit of privacy (read secrecy) was the hidden source of their magic over objects, their ability to attract an unending stream of material goods. What all these experiments in understanding had in common was their attempt to make sense of persons who imagined themselves as individuals.

The lesson, inscribed in Western practices and embodied by its agents, a lesson that time and experience would reinforce over and again, is that desire is personal. The mission school, the nature of Christianity with its belief in a one-to-one relation between a person and God, the behaviors and sermons of the Anglican minister, an introduced system of trials that focused on the culpability or guilt of specific persons, the operation of the mission trade store and other agents of capitalism (e.g., coffee buyers), and the biomedical view of illness have gradually created the understanding that the individual aspect of personhood and its expression is what modernity is all about. Persons as individuals receive grades in school, God saves individuals, not whole clans, biomedicine's singular mission is to heal the bodies of individuals, the individual who commits a crime must pay for it: all these reinforce the concept and legitimacy of the individual facet. There is no small irony that the "progress" of modernity has coincided with a growth in sorcery and sorcery trials (LiPuma 1994), a critical reason being that sorcery was one of the primary traditional sites for the expression of the individual aspect of personhood.

The pressure brought to bear on the local notion of the person is remarkable for its unevenness, with the consequence that agents must necessarily practice, if not endorse, a bivalent epistemology, using one image of the person in rural settings and another in the context of urban, capitalist, Western-like interactions. But even in the rural locale, there is a dynamic not only between urban and rural notions but also in the way in which different aspects of modernity intersected variably and contingently with local practices and were imbued with variable degrees of legitimation. Indeed, if we take the Maring as an example, an implicational logic runs from the appearance of the trade store to the emergence of the individual aspect of personhood. The trade store implies the right of private property, exemplified by a decline in the obligation to share, and private ownership in turn is a metaphor for privacy or the self-containment of the person that is an index of individuality. The emergence of a notion of private property is exemplified by the emergence of interclan and even immediate kinship (e.g., between a man and his mother's brother) trials for property theft. In such trials, it was typical for defendants to claim that they were only sharing/borrowing the objects in question whereas the plaintiffs argued that certain forms of sharing were no longer possible. So one plaintiff argued that "the time when no one cared who took what is over; now is a time of business, a time when individuals own things and have a final say in who can and cannot use them." What is increasingly clear is that, under the conditions of modernity, different levels of epistemology become metaphors for, and speak on behalf of, each other, thus opening the way for the construction of a new politics of personhood. This was nowhere more true than at the crossroads of generation and gender.

The emergence of the individual aspect as a political resource, empowered by the institutions of modernity, had a telling generational effect. The existence and validation of extracommunal opportunities allowed members of the junior generation to pursue new forms of freedom at the expense of kinship and community. They could now cut the tendons of dependence by working on the mission station, going to high school, and generally availing themselves of opportunities outside the community. But the effect of the modern was also to compel the Maring to recalibrate the relations of obligation, duty, and compliance within the community. And no more so than with respect to women. The Maring called the modern age the "time of women"—using the pointed pidgin idiom of *tim belong meri*. The possibility of freedom allowed women to extend their sociality beyond the walls of the domestic enclave and into the emerging space of the modern public political sphere. More than their mothers could have imagined, the junior generation of women expected their beliefs, desires, and judgments to matter. They gained newfound control over the marriage process, especially in the choice of spouse and the timing of the union. In contrast to their mothers, many women of the junior generation expected to have a resonant voice in the initiation and developmental cycle of the family. They embraced Christianity because they believed its tenets were more favorable to women and because its agents gave them additional leverage in the pursuit of their individual interests. The Anglican priests inveighed in private, print, and pulpit for the "rights" of indigenous women, the locus of these rights being, of course, the individual. In particular, the Anglican clergy and the most Christian Maring of the junior generation fought against what they saw as the traditional acceptance of domestic violence against women. The Christian argument was that domestic relations were subject to the laws of God and state, for God had a one-to-one relationship with each of his children and the state protected every one its citizens. The entrance of women into a public sphere that was itself being created by modernity allowed them to participate more actively in exchange and bisnis. For women in the kingdom of kastam, the individual aspect of the person functioned as a resource to negate the existing order of power and as a doorway into the modernity of the future. Especially the elder generation of men rued this emancipation of women, however modest, and would sometimes (particularly for the benefit of foreigners like myself who knew them only in an emasculated state) wax nostalgic about a time when women knew their place and men were warriors endowed with the gumption, the fire, the presence to maintain the social order. But this time had passed. So one young woman, as her grandfather made such a speech, a speech that she had surely heard before, simply pursed her lips and smiled at me, indicating that she was as respectful of his age as she was certain that the landslide of history would bury the sound and fury of such sentiments.

Beyond the Person

As a theoretical preamble to the chapters to follow I have argued that the Melanesian person, like persons everywhere, has both dividual and individual aspects. My argument is that to grasp the transformative influence of biomedicine, Christianity, and Western legal and educational systems on the construction of Melanesian subjectivity (and one could also include Africa and other traditional haunts of anthropology), it is necessary to understand that the crosscultural ontological form is the dual person and that the process of encompassment engenders an extraordinary tension between the dividual and individual aspects of personhood. The danger is that the project of relativizing our metaphors can too easily be carried to the point where the relations between Melanesia and the West appear so incommensurable that we have no way to account for the possibility ethnography and the emergence of the individual person in the modern era. It thus seems that if the notion of the composite person or dividual is to be integrated into the modern history of Melanesia, it needs to be relocated or repositioned in ethnographic space. In this reading, the person emerges from the tension, itself always variable and culturally and historically shaped, between these two aspects of personhood and the ways in which they are objectified and embodied. And further, the marginalization of individuality in Melanesia and the sublimation of dividuality in the West are necessary for the creation of the kind of person that each of these sets of societies attempts to produce (LiPuma 1995). It is precisely this individual dimension of Melanesian personhood, traditionally subordinate to the dividual image of the person, for the most part ideologically unarticulated, almost invisible in the context of "traditional" social practice, that is now beginning to emerge with modernity. A critical reason for this history is that individuality is central to modernity not only conceptually but as the locus of the forms of desire that define the modern. The true irony is that the overemphasis of the individual that was the hallmark (and error) of the original encounter between Western ethnographers and Melanesians has turned out to be an omen of things to come.

The encompassment of Melanesia is simultaneously objective and subjective, transforming in an endless dialectical dance both the concepts, institutions, and practices of the objective world and the kind of subjects or persons who enact and reproduce that world. In the first quarter century of contact between the Maring and the West, this change appeared most dramatically, to the senior generations disturbingly, in the kind of persons that were the junior generation. Western agents and institutions came to dominate Maring even as they provided some of the objective political resources and validated the expression of the forms of subjectivity that would allow for the greater emancipation of the junior generation and especially women. There is here a political conundrum for anthropology. The "liberation" of women, ethnic minorities, etc. from conditions that we would find intolerable is accomplished through a process of cultural violence, the encompassment of the Other, which, in turn, permits the emergence of new and powerful forms of interpersonal freedom, but, as is intrinsically the case under the culture of capitalism, at the expense of new forms of abstract and impersonal domination (such as those imposed by the market). The view from the cultures of capitalism is that abstract domination is inherently preferable to overt interpersonal domination because the latter is an insult to the individual in a way that the former is not. Indeed, a significant lesson of modernity is to appreciate greater freedom in the context of diminishing autonomy. One result is that Western observers are often perplexed by the fact that those who are emancipated from kinship and community-based domination seem less thrilled with their newfound freedom than their Western saviors think is warranted—a reaction that they attribute to the persistence of tradition rather than the loss of identity that accompanies diminishing autonomy. But my friend Gou knew better. He observed that "civilization allows us to leave home and attend school so that after we graduate and can't land a job we have no choice but to return to a community where we no longer want to live." So throughout Melanesia (and the world of Others generally) there are floating bands of young men who inhabit the violent space between the dividuality of a community that they can no longer tolerate and the individuality of a modern society that has no use for them.

CHAPTER 5

The Logic of Sorcery and the
Justice of Modernity

Just before daybreak on a moonlit night in July, Kam was attacked in his sleep by a sorcerer in the guise of a cassowary. Invisible slivers of knife-sharp bamboo penetrated his liver, and taros and sweet potatoes from the night's meal now blocked the flow of air to his lungs. In three days, Kam, a man in his mid-forties, embattled in a land dispute, disowned by and willing to disown the ancestor spirit of his paternal grandfather, lay dead. On his deathbed, or so it was said, Kam cried out that he was the victim of an ensorcelled packet of food; Kam's clansmen, drawing on the social logic of revenge and redress, implicated Tenga. An imposing force from a neighboring clan, Tenga was a senior clansman who had aligned himself with the junior generation and had become increasingly influential in the process. The medical diagnosis was pneumonia compounded by chronic malaria; the social diagnosis was sorcery and within the month a long and tortuous trial would begin. This trial, which so divided the community, was only the most notable of the seventeen sorcery trials that occurred during my fieldwork. Many Maring tell and take as self-evident that the gravity and frequency of sorcery and sorcery cases have accelerated since pacification, a not uncommon result throughout Oceania (Lederman 1981:20; Westermark 1981:90–91; and Lattas 1993:55). As will become evident as the case study unfolds, modernity was simultaneously conducive to the advance of sorcery insofar as it created new forms of violence and inequality that people must deal with and explain, and also antithetical to its perpetuation insofar as modernity endorsed those forms of knowledge and power, such as positive science and Western religions, that have little tolerance or use for indigenous wizardry. Modernity engenders novel problems for explanation, unfathomable problems from the lights of traditional insight, even as it seeks to delimit the compass of common sense.

The advent of modern law and its technologies of power and justice represented the intersection, sometimes the collision, of the moral economy of local life, its vision of right and wrong, the amplified presence of Western agents and institutions who assumed that the social itself was a legal arrangement, and the emerging Papua New Guinea state. If law and its forms of reasoning are ways of orchestrating the relationship between persons and/in the collectivity, if morality, justice, and the practice of law rest on a common set of assumptions about the foundations of social life— What is a person? What is sociality and relatedness? What is the connection between action and intention? What is truth and to what purposes should it be put socially?—then the construction of Melanesian modernity must consist of experiments, improvisations, and innovations, all intended to reconcile the distance between these assumptions. And like an endless series of portals and thresholds these foundational fictions of social reality (and also social science) lead to other questions. How does the creation and circulation of new forms of discourse inflect the knowledge, desires, and dispositions of those who dwell within it? How are new objects of understanding canonized or removed from the roster of approved cultural images? Are sorcerers on the endangered species list? How does the abstraction of law from context, the Western move, allow it to subsume all contexts, this in contradistinction to the Melanesian concept that neither decontextualizes law and justice nor assumes that they supersede or stand above social relations. What, ultimately, is the interrelationship between knowledge and power; how is it systematized, legitimated, and circulated in the context of the mediated relationship between the West, the state, and local agents?

The objective of this chapter is to draw out the concepts and conflicts behind the sorcery trial as a way to begin to answer these questions. Both the Maring court and Western anthropological theory will be put on trial, their testimony taken, so to speak, in an effort to understand the evolution of local notions of knowledge and truth and their relationship to the practice of justice. As sorcery trials lie at the intersection of power and knowledge, these trials were about the construction of cultural reality and, going further, about how Maring modernity was both a condition and consequence of a reality that was increasingly heterogeneous, contested, and uncertain. The interrelationship between knowledge and social transformation centers on three issues. The first issue is about sorcery as a form and use of knowledge and its relationship to power. How did this unfold within the framework of a sorcery trial, a practice that fuses an indigenous structure of action and experience to an imported process? To frame this question, the analysis begins with the ethnohistory of the notion of justice and the evolution of the rural court system. Of particular importance here will be the role of law in the construction of history itself, the imaginative divide between a past in which society made subjects according to the ways of war and a future in which the modern makes its agents according to the ways of business. Second, what counted as evidence? What was the moral/epistemological basis for its evaluation? On what grounds were accounts about an agent's previous actions and intentions judged to be true? This is critical because sorcery is a crime that has material results—short-windedness, fever, and sometimes death—but leaves little direct physical evidence. So assessing the truth depends on how reports about a defendant's intentions and covert actions, as extrapolated from his public behavior, inform the way in which the court interprets the evidence. Speech is central here because sorcery trials were comprised of a series of linguistic representations of, and presuppositions about, cultural reality. Thus, the trial process and sorcery trials in particular were major venues for the progressive and strategic reinvention of local epistemology in light of the encompassment of the indigenous world. The final issue is the extent to which the contestation of social hierarchy (e.g., men versus women; senior versus junior clansmen) was carried out as a struggle over the character of cultural reality itself (Zelenietz 1981:6). The argument I have been making is that the Maring encounter with Europeans and the appropriation of Western practice has created the social and epistemological conditions for a cultural critique on a level, and with a force, unimaginable in the past. The evolving encounter compelled the doxic world, what was always on the hither side of contemplation, to confront itself in the reflection of a competing discourse, an empowered discourse that not only was imposed by the agents and institutions of encompassment but found its way into the mouth of their own children. So it was that these sorcery trials were part of a revolution in the trajectory of cultural life brought about by simultaneous and mutual transformations in epistemology, practice, and the character and distribution of power. Though there are seemingly infinite ways to approach these issues, such complexity itself a gift of modernity, the present analysis focuses on the epistemological foundations of these trials and their internal dynamics before turning to the ways in which trials served as an index, representation, and site of struggle over the form and implications of the modern.

The Context of Law

If encompassment has transformed the ambitions and ambit of collaboration, it has done even more for contestation. The public political sphere within which clan members exercise power now extends well beyond the clan and clan cluster; in some cases, like the struggle over where and who will construct the road from district headquarters at Tabibuga, it embraced every Jimi Valley Maring. The advent of a public sphere was the claim that for the first time in Maring history the universe of kinship would no longer be coterminous with the political universe. It opened up the possibility and also created the necessity for political affiliations and ad hoc groups that, though they more than superficially resembled indigenous ones in that they could not help but incorporate customary relations, could not have been more different in principle. Whereas indigenous groups have always presupposed a kinship that predates the group's formation and lives on after its demise, the voluntary associations of modern politics exist only so long as they satisfy the functions for which they were intended. Immediate interest, sometimes overt self-interest, defines participation to the extent that agents envision the group as a vehicle for the realization of their own interests rather than, as was customary, assume that a person is (and should undertake) the realization of the group's interests. So while it seemed that there was nothing unusual in the group of Maring leaders, senior men from a variety of clan clusters who traveled to administrative headquarters in Tabibuga to plead for a new road (upon which they could more easily export their coffee), the reality was that this group, whose reason for being lay outside of itself, was as emblematic of modernity as the tinned fish and rice that they ate that night. Moreover, standing before the district officer the coalition argued that provision of a new road was an issue of justice. They were entitled to the road as a matter of social welfare. And, if the provincial government did not allocate the money, the next step would be to take the matter to court. As one of the leaders so beautifully put it, they were no longer bush people who did not know how to make war in the courts. There is a prima facie case that modernity has created a new and expanding political landscape based on an innovative chemistry of custom and modernity.

But the story here is ahead of itself, a story that begins in 1955 when the Maring first encountered Western law in the person and personality of the Australian kiap. If Pax Britannica meant anything it was that the rule of law, albeit as interpreted in the rough and tumble style of the frontier, was to replace or at least supersede customary means of dispute settlement. The point of reference and power for law and order would heretofore lie beyond the walls of local sociality, beyond the reaches of the Jimi and Simbai Valleys, to a foreign haunt ruled by men the Maring had never seen. There was here a moral geography in which the state sought to remove the logic and sense of right and wrong, perpetrator and defendant, reward and punishment, from the hands of local agents. Peter Hasluck, the minister for territories from 1951 to 1963, viewed the British tradition of justice as "a gift we have brought to" the native, and thought it was imperative to instill in them "the idea that the Queen is the fount of justice and that the courts are the Queen's courts" (1976:189). More than an instrument and institution of dispute settlement, the law became a means of managing and controlling the relationship between people, the state, and the agents of encompassment. Indigenous dispute settlement, especially when it overflowed into combat, challenged the monopoly on violence that the modern state imagines is part of its birthright.

Especially from 1955 to national independence in 1975, the kiaps were the gods of law. They were feared and respected, despised and obeyed. Just as Jesus had displaced the ancestors and money had replaced pearlshells, so the time of law vanquished the tradition of violence. The pidgin term *tim belong lo* (time of law) became the metonym of modernity, a representation of the reality that foreign agents and institutions now governed the Maring. Not least, the kiaps tried to teach the Maring that the law is the property of the colonial state rather than an emergent relation of group interaction. From the colonial perspective, the disorder and paralyzing uncertainty of indigenous society was a direct and obvious fault of lawlessness (in both senses of the term), chief justice Mann advocating imposition of the Queen's law on the grounds that Melanesians "recognize in the law something that their society sadly lacked" (1966:84). Submission and resignation before the colonizer, yes; recognition and sadness, absolutely not. The wings of ethnocentricism spread easily and glide over the surface of lives, assuming that the world of Others is hollow and that all of its meanings can, as Octavio Paz once noted, be discarded into a shallow grave. What the Maring did recognize was that the trajectory of colonial law combined with the high culture of the kiaps preordained what would count as evidence and fact, when "history" began, what was equitable and just, and who in native society was worth listening to. One immediate effect of this legal system was to empower the junior generation of men who, knowing pidgin and having observed white culture during contract labor, served as translators and mediators between the senior clansmen and the kiaps.

The standing instructions encouraged kiaps to settle local disputes on the spot rather than refer them to district court. And they were perfectly positioned for this process, being magistrates, police, and wardens all encased in the same skin. There was in this a certain efficiency in that a patrol officer might apprehend, arrest, try, sentence, and punish an offender before his afternoon tea and vegmite. Due process had no more meaning for the kiap than it had for the Maring. There were no appeals as the kiap's decision was final and unquestionable. In their own ideology, the kiaps conceptualized the most important elements of dispensing justice as being decisive and strong, and never appealing or reversing one's judgment. The kiaps were, after all, self-declared men of action who, in their own eyes, nurtured on a marriage of rugged Australian individualism and European civility, embodied the legacy and power of civilization plus the will, the know-how, the moral authority, and the civic responsibility to implant the rule of law in the body politic of the Other—to set an example of how the Maring should maintain law and order. Given the local and explosive character of land disputes, the kiaps were especially anxious to resolve squabbles before they got out of hand. They accepted the principle that the legal boundaries of local territories were those reported at the moment of colonial intervention in the region. Given the perpetually shifting nature of these boundaries, the kiaps' principle essentially froze the flow of history. What were once inherently fluctuating frontiers entered a colonial state of suspended animation. Nonetheless, the resolution of land disputes was done with an air of informality and superiority—much, one imagines, as the lord of the manor resolved such disputes among his serfs. Speaking about the Enga, though his account could just as well be about the Maring, Meggitt (1977) explains:

> kiaps devised their own modes of rough and ready arbitration, in which they briefly visited the disputed tract, summarily heard out both groups, and then with a compass and chain marked out a boundary that seemed reasonable to him and gave something to each side. This . . . was technically an out of court settlement reached by the litigants themselves, a procedure that did not conform to the rules of the CNA [Court of Native Affairs] and hence was not entered in the court records. Instead, the kiap usually make an entry in an unofficial, ad hoc register, cursorily identifying the locality in question (not always accurately) and the groups concerned, and noting his decision (1977:158).

This rule of law varied from enlightened despotism to unenlightened tyranny, depending on the kiap in question. Their disempowerment aside, Maring of all generations still found considerable virtue in Western-style justice. Even if they did not always understand its epistemology, logic, and conventions, they could see real merit in its results. The kiap, whatever else his faults, produced the kind of visible, swift, and decisive resolutions that restored all-important balance (*kopla*) to a divided community. In a sense, the advent of the kiap solved a problem indigenous to Maring justice, engendering two immediate effects on the process of dispute settlement. First, it fully triangulated the mediation process. In the precontact era the main persons negotiating a resolution were those kinsmen who were related to both of the embattled parties. This process presented two drawbacks: the kinsmen-in-between often had an interest in the outcome of the intervention and thus their motives and manners were sometimes suspect, and by definition the most serious disputes occurred between parties who had no common relatives. The kiap expunged both drawbacks in one stroke in that his relation to indigenous agents was not defined by relative sociality, but rather the absence of relatedness altogether. Neither the sociality nor the intentionality of the kiap was at issue. Second, the kiap empowered the middle term. Where the local arbitrator could promote a resolution mostly by persuasion, the kiap was able to morally and militarily enforce his decision. His uniform of white skin meant that behind his decisions lay the institutions of colonialism. Reflecting on the frontier justice offered by the kiap, several senior clansmen observed that because it focused on settling disputes it was closer to the local system and sense of justice than the formal judicial structure given its preoccupation with procedures and the application of otherworldly rules. From the start, rural justice was an odd yet rhythmic mixture of Western and Melanesian senses; the already deeply-inculcated concepts, desires, and dispositions of local agents impelled the kiaps to indigenize the Queen's law even as they compelled the locals to submit to it.

In the years after contact, a tripartite court structure emerged: incidents settled locally by locally selected or elected officials, those settled by the kiap either during a patrol inspection or at the district outstation, and those that were filtered through the Western court structure (principally district courts overseen by kiaps who had more advanced legal qualifications and then in later years increasingly by magistrates). Although the Australian administration chronically tinkered with the judicial framework, the changes were barely noticeable from the bottom up. Following independence in 1975, the structure of the legal system began to metamorphize. For a variety of reasons, the Papua New Guinean kiaps who replaced the Australians rarely made patrols. According to Maring sources, from the years just preceding independence to 1980 the kiaps made no tours of the Maring territory and thus adjudicated only those cases that were brought to district headquarters. A primary consequence was that even before independence local officials began to assume the judicial duties formerly handled by the kiaps. There was, in effect, a de facto process of decentralization and increasing hybridization of the judicial system. The government institutionalized this transformation with the introduction of village courts in the Jimi Valley in 1977–78. These courts were the first tier of the national judicial system and imbued local elected magistrates with official judicial powers. By 1980, these local courts were trying all but the most serious felonies, including cases involving theft, adultery, disputed land, the destruction of property, delinquent compensation payments, and, as the introduction of this chapter made clear, sorcery.

Law and the Imagination of the Modern

The Maring's conceptualized radical break between the time of custom and that of modernity was never more telling than in the field of law. Phrased in pidgin as *lo,* it was consciously understood as a touchstone of the objective and subjective difference between the past and the present. The past was represented as a time in which disputes were habitually settled by violence, the disposition and desire to even the score through the use of violence entrenched in the manner of men. The less clan-related the disputants, the greater and more lasting the violence. One violent act precipitated another until cut off either by formal truce in the case of true warfare or by compensation payment in the case of conflict between relatives. But there was enlightenment. And though the qualities associated with warfare were central to producing cherished images of clan power and manhood, people also recognized that violence and warfare were disruptive, disruptive not by the lights of an abstract normative morality, but because it interfered with gardening, productive exchange relations, visiting affines and trade partners, conducting what was now called "bisnis."

Implicit in the antinomy between the epoch of custom and that of law is a moral relativization of custom into those practices and perspectives that were good and thus should be carried into the future and those aspects of custom that were ill-suited for contemporary life. Maring say that prior to their contact with Europeans, they adhered unquestioningly to the customs of the ancestors because these customs were "all we knew." It was not only that people's sense of right and wrong were more enacted than thought, but that the difference between what was conscious and nonconscious was immaterial. Accordingly, the law was no more a topic of discussion than their conception of time or the intricacies of their pronominal system. As Gou once pointed out to me with startling clarity: people think about law because it applies to everyone. The metamorphosis from war to law was an index of a transition to a new concept of the past, a past that was no longer desirably reproduced in the present, but rather was conceptualized as separate from it. The break with the past, inscribed in the lessons of the mission school and in the history that the mission has constructed of its intervention in Maring society (namely the leap from pagan unawareness to Christian enlightenment), was for the Maring nothing less than an introduction to the notion of history as lineal, progressive, and externally animated. The field of law especially was an arena in which the Maring learned to separate themselves from their own past, periodize or delimit this past, and then render it up as an object of representation and judgments. But this objectification of the past contained a contradiction because the senior generation and their elders also experienced their history directly as personal and collective memory, a contradiction that, I suggest, sorcery trials, with their allegiance to local categories of belief and experience and yet clear demarcation between old practices and modern, help to accommodate and transcend.

Western-style justice also changed the relationship between the ideal of political balance (*kopla*) and conformity and their conceptualization. Before contact, there was nothing that even resembled the field of law. On numerous occasions, elders would preface their testimony with a statement about how settling a dispute in court was far removed from anything that they knew as custom. Prior to the advance of the modern, there were simply two ideals: the ideal that the will of in(dividuals) should more or less conform to the general clan will and the ideal that the goal of dispute settlement (revenge and redress) was to restore intracommunity balance. These ideals were not objectified as abstract and formalized principles, but felt as dispositions to follow custom and maintain harmony within the clan cluster and with allies. As is often the case, the indigenous world only appeared as a system of classification and a chosen way of life just as it vanished over the horizon to be consigned to a past that it was instrumental in creating. The evolution of a local court system was part of, and instrumental in furthering, the emergence of a jural field, together with the objectification of ideals. The field of law removed an infraction to a new space that stood apart from the relationalities of the whole. Traditional images of justice did not fixate on either of the agents—the perpetrator or defendant—because their individuality was incidental to the event and immaterial to the outcome. What mattered most was that an action threw the relationalities of the collectivity out of balance. Untoward behavior disarticulated the relations so carefully constructed through the exchange and sharing of food, land, labor, and people. So the object of litigation was to restore the totality. On no account did the Maring conceive the reality of a transcendent social from which the acts of persons could be detached and removed to a field possessed by its own rules of inquiry, judgment, procedure, and punishment. This was a lesson of modernity that the Maring absorbed through a cultural membrane whose form and function transformed Western justice in surprising ways.

The Transcendence of Kinship

Like all peoples who live within the compass of kinship and community, Maring notions of right or wrong in a universal moralistic sense were less significant than the consequences of behavior for the clan as a whole. Maring leaders made the point that a person's behavior was constrained by fellow clan members. They would take umbrage at him if his untoward public behavior undermined intraclan unity, valued affinal relations, or trading partnerships, or caused the clan to become embroiled in an unwanted conflict, suffer ancestral retribution, or have to pay an onerous compensation payment. Archetypical crimes were physical violence, stealing food from another's garden, eloping (the word in Maring literally denotes to abduct) with a young woman without her clansmen's consent, and sorcery. Prior to pacification and contact with the West, Maring used the compensation payment as a major means of resolving disputes.

Though precontact negotiations of compensation bear a historical and logical resemblance to payments awarded during modern trials, they differ in several ways. The guilt or innocence of defendants with respect to specific crimes was never the critical issue. People's accounts of compensation payment (circa 1950–65) characteristically presuppose the defendant's guilt (at least when viewed from a Western jural perspective). The reason was that justice did not involve either individuals or the application of a general rule to a specific instance but the particular relation between groups. If a person's actions had a negative effect on others—if the food they served caused others to become ill for example—then that person was guilty of a crime regardless of their intentions because their actions destablized community relations. The relationalities between agents were of a higher epistemological order than their individual intentions. Persons could be genuinely guilty of crimes that they did not commit as an individual. By the same logic, the assessment of a compensation payment was a perceived loss of balance or equality within the community, meaning that the actions of a member of one clan compromised the reproduction of another. As men, women, pigs, and gardens were the essence of reproduction, any action that harmed them demanded violence, compensation, or both. Punishing an offending individual was not the purpose of compensation or an end in itself; the object was to restore balance. Thus, a man convicted of homicide in 1978 was released two years later when his clansmen paid compensation. Most people viewed the jailing not as a punishment, least of all punishment aimed at reforming the offender, but as a means of forcing his clan to raise and render compensation.

For Maring, the practice of the trial itself was critical to, and an index of, how far they had traveled down the new road of modernity. Where customary compensation payments were always negotiated by representatives (i.e., senior clansmen) of the clans in dispute, the local court was supposed to be supervised by individuals who transcended their kinship relations. Because the indigenous system fused kinship and law, the same code dictated very different responses depending on the kinship connection. The "theft" of food by an affine animated a very different response than the same act by a member from an unrelated, or worse, enemy clan. Recall that the violent confrontation between the Yonbam and the Manga that led to Australian retaliation began partly over the theft of some pandanus fruit. When I first saw the working of the local court, I was puzzled that a dispute between a Baigai and a Kamjepakai would be heard by the local Councillor, a Kamjepakai, rather than by one of the other big men who often presided over trials and were connected to neither. My initial thought was that the choice of judge itself represented the use of power by the Kamjepakai litigant to predetermine the outcome. However, the

Baigai man won the case handily (over a pig ruining his garden) and was awarded what he saw as generous compensation, some fifty kina. As I would soon find out, the Baigai litigant had willing agreed to let the Kamjepakai Councillor decide the case, noting in response to my question that this Councillor "was a man of the new road" and that he "had a reputation for fairness." Indeed, it turned out that the kin and clan affiliation of the judge(s) was not a noteworthy issue. Big men who desired to be judges but who could not transcend their kin and clan relations were simply not accepted by litigants. The power and authority vested in judges was thus dependent on the transcendence of kinship—a modern inversion of the customary pattern of socio-political relations.[1] There was, in this, a critical epistemological turn in that it began to insinuate the Western distinction between the person and the position, here the kin-constructed agent and the office of adjudication. It also called for a restructuring of the terms of desire in that the desire of the kinsmen to help his own kind under any circumstances was being displaced by the desire to render a fair judgment, and by doing so reap the symbolic rewards awarded to those leaders who led the charge toward the modern.

This change is revolutionary in at least three ways. First, it was part of the increasing "externalization" of social life. The trial's power and authority derived in large measure from a nation-state over which the Maring have little control. To accept the trial as a legitimate social practice was to accept the fact that the local community, to survive and prosper in the modern era, must adopt and adapt to imposed practices. Second, as a corollary and just as importantly, the advent of such a field of law began to introduce the kind of enduring and quasi-objective domination that characterizes the capitalist nation-state. Indigenous modes of domination were always interpersonal and fragile precisely because there were no permanent or impersonal means of controlling others. The influence exercised by the senior men over women and the junior generation was inseparable from their status as leaders of the clan and adepts in the exchange system. Under these conditions, dominance never appeared as something that stood over and against agents but was manifest in the speech, bearing, and other attributes of the big-man. It was precarious because seniors and especially big-men were dependent on others' dependence for their power, a dependence, moreover, that was not mediated by labor or law but by the neverending work of building and tuning interpersonal networks. Third, from an internal standpoint, the trial process gained a great measure of its power and legitimacy by representing and producing distance from the past. Little could be more indicative of this distance than the introduction of practices in which agents were expected to neutralize kinship and commitments tied to it. This displacement of kinship was a companion to the notion of friendship that also tempered the power of kinship. Finally, modern trials were part of a general transformation away from a community based on kinship and exchange to a community based on political hierarchy and civil authority (e.g., police). The result was a "generation gap" insofar as the clan, kinship, and exchange structures that produced the practices and dispositions of the older generations now had to co-exist with, and partially give way to, a new set of structures that, especially in the younger generation, engendered new practices and dispositions that, inevitably, made those of the previous generation seem increasingly out of time and place. In this regard, the trial of Tenga for the sorcerization of Kam marked a change in that two men in their mid-twenties mission-trained and practicing Anglicans, argued (clearly for the first time in local history) that Tenga could not be culpable because there was no such thing as sorcery. To grasp what was at issue here it is necessary to reconstruct as greater depth local concepts of truth, knowledge, and agency.

Truth as Revelation

The local concept of truth held that truth had an inner and outer dimension and that this was inscribed in the act itself, a notion that has been explored in the context of "veiled speech" (Strathern 1975). The surface or appearance of an action, "its skin" to use the Maring's own metaphor, characteristically manifested lies and dissembling. Its aim was to manipulate the beliefs, desires, and judgments that surround, for example, the reception of one's gift. By contrast, the inner core of an action was its truth and power to pull or bend others. Language was thought to lie on the skin of an action; it was the primary (but not the only) means of disguising the "true" intentionality of an actor. In this respect, the importance of exchange lay in the virtue that gifts are indexical; they are a part of that which they express. Nonetheless, the social practice of gift-giving had an element of dissembling. When people assessed gifts, they expected a difference between the "skin" of the gift and its interior. The inside-outside schema was the Maring means of organizing the hierarchy of intentions that may be embodied in a given action. So, conceived practically, the presentation of a gift may include a verbally stated intention (e.g., the gift is because you are my affine), a presupposed though unstated intention (e.g., the gift helps discharge my outstanding bride-payment debt), and a disguised intention (e.g., the gift will be followed by a request for use of garden land). Conversely, agents could view every request for a gift as the maintenance of a social relation, repayment for a gift given previously, or as an extortion based on power, such as the power to employ sorcery. The intentionality of the gift was such that the beliefs, desires, and judgments of the recipient concerning the gift were often read onto the donor. If the recipient felt subjugated by the gift, he might well interpret this subjugation as intrinsic to the gift-giving and thus part of the intentionality of the act. Maring located intention in the relationship between an act and its influence rather than in the mind of the donor, the gift in no respect a reflection of the internal state of the subject objectified through its qualities. There was no way in Maring to speak about someone's intentions or judgments apart from what they did and other people's experience of those actions. There was no way to say or interpret statements such as "I thought that the gift would help you and strengthen our relationship, though I now realize that it has placed you in a compromising position." Actions were never an "expression" of a subjective intention, but rather the ground of intention. There was no way to differentiate between the mental dimension of an act and the act itself; rather the action was understood to embody a hierarchy of intentions. In relationship to speech, intentionality was interior and invisible; the sounds of words, exterior and sensory. Determining the meaning of an action, or "digging out its root" to use one local metaphor, was a function of understanding and assessing its inner and outer layers.

The archetype of the outer dimension was speech, which Maring understood as a way of disguising the layers of intention inscribed in action. As Rappaport (1979: 227–29) has argued, language's reliance on symbols imbues it with a special capacity to deceive because what is said and what is referred to (be it a concept, desire, or object) need not be copresent. Maring understood speech as a way of disguising the layers of intention inscribed in any given action. Here is one informant's comment about the nature of language in social exchange. Note that his commentary contains metapragmatic rules[2] for interpreting what people say in this type of speech event. Characteristically the metaphor used is horticultural, its oppositions are above ground/below ground, inside/outside, and the generative scheme betrays an economy of logic that, grounded in the senses, dispenses with overt concepts and inner states that, from a Western perspective, it cannot fail to encode (i.e., deceit and a ubiquitous mistrust of the Other).

> When people talk, we listen with only one ear, we look with only one eye. The other ear is to hear what they have said to others privately (e.g., gossip); the other eye is to see/know the root of the gift. Talk is like the flowers/leaves of a plant; it captures the eye and is pleasing but there is also much that lies below the ground. You know the truth of someone's gift when you have gotten past its outside. People are fooled/taken-in all the time by the words that surround gift-giving.

Few people consider this view of speech as anything more than common sense. Paradoxically, oratory and the aesthetics of speech are made all the more important by this view of language. People say a good orator has a "smooth and shiny skin" to his words; the enchantment of eloquent and powerful speech-making is that inside and outside become virtually indistinguishable. Caught up in the orator's powerful persuasive speech, his audience "forgets" to delve beneath the surface and discover the underlying truth. There is no contrast here between language and action; rather, language is a type of action or mode of doing that possesses its own special properties and advantages. Like a person's skin, to which it is equated metaphorically, language mediates between the interior of an action or person and others' appreciation of that action or person (Strathern 1977:109; Goldman 1983:268; Frankel 1986:55–56). The words, intonations, and gestures of a good orator weave a cloak of enchantment over the hierarchy of intentions inscribed in an action.

Ironically, Westerners assumed that they immediately grasped this notion of speech and intentionality because it encapsulated what for them was "bad faith"—words whose basic and intrinsic purity has been corrupted by dishonest intent and desires. For the Anglican priest and the mission staff, government officials, and even for anthropologists (who should know better), speech was imagined as an analogue to commodity circulation. On this conduit model, a speaker invests and articulates his thoughts in words that, it is hoped, reflect those thoughts and then, through speech, convey them to an audience who unpacks or decodes them. As the priest explained to me, "because I put a lot into my sermons I expected my parishioners to get a lot out of them." It was only through a lack of Christian values and civility that agents—like peddlers of snake oil at the state fair—would load their words with deceptive ideas whose decoding or deciphering, being neither fully possible nor expected, would engender a pervasive distrust of the other. In this Western image, words can reflect the universe they were invented to represent—there can be a unity of form and meaning—only if the hearts of the speakers are pure, their minds are clear and rational, and they have a well-founded faith in the honesty of others. Thus, if the Anglican Church was successful in its attempt to inculcate Christian values and the state imposed order on village life, the result would, among other things, lead to speech that faithfully encoded what people thought. There was, moreover, a leap from speech to language. The unarticulated Western notion was that the Maring language itself leaned, more than English or other Western languages, toward the darker side of human nature because it had never been exposed to positive influences. The Bible translator observed that to translate the word of the Almighty into Maring it was necessary to invent words for faith, hope, love, and charity, but not deceit, anger, or envy. The underlying concept was that inasmuch as Maring had so long expressed the worst side of our human spirit, it was not surprising that it could all too easily accommodate and resemble sorcery. To put this another way, all languages have veiled speech. The difference is that the West professes an ideology that visualizes such veiling as a departure from the ideal (the plain-speaking man of common sense) caused by an upwelling of bad faith and conflicting motives. Melanesians like the Maring simply assumed that this was the "nature" of speech as a modality of action. There was neither a human nature to suppress nor an ideal to live up to. Simply language in its practical state.

The Cultural Logic of Sorcery

To foreground the trial and further contextualize the substance and sense of Maring lifeways, it is necessary to describe their conceptions of sorcery and sorcerers. Like societies across Melanesia, the Maring believed that at least some misfortune was caused by ancestor spirits disenchanted with a person's behavior. Sorcerers too could turn on their own kinsmen. The actions of ancestors and sorcerers who turned on their own kin stood at opposite ends of the social spectrum. Ancestors attacked those who had abridged the norms of the community—persons who had failed to share pork or perhaps had committed acts of sorcery—whereas sorcerers attacked their own kind for self-aggradizing and malevolent purposes. Sorcerers acted without regard to the fortunes of their community, and so people felt that they must seek protection from the ancestors/Jesus and root out intracommunity sorcery through whatever means available: murder, countersorcery, and litigation. Sorcery had been unambiguously permissible only against traditional enemies, though even this concept was not endorsed by mission-trained Maring. As in other Oceanic societies (Nachman 1981; Tonkinson 1981; Knauft 1985a), sorcery has variable, contested, and ambiguous legitimacy: variable because its legitimacy was situationally specific; contested because what counted as sorcery and its appropriateness in a particular context were open to debate; and ambiguous because often some agents were uncertain about its presence and/or legitimacy in a given situation.

The sorcerer was a form of personhood, a mode of subjectivity. As illustrated in the last chapter, there were two moments to the Maring conception of personhood and identity. The first was that a subject's identity was a synthesis and objectification of his or her social relations. That is (the oddness of my language is an attempt to be faithful to the local phrasing), a person was the accumulation of the relations that he or she inhabited. The second moment was that each of these relations had the potential to be aggressive or peaceful, reciprocal or nonreciprocal, mutually beneficial or predatory, sharing or greedy, physically nurturing or enervating, relation-making or destructive of personal networks. A moral person was someone who modulated and controlled these propensities in respect to social distance. Between subclansmen, for example, the aggressive dimension of the relationship should remain "veiled by a smooth social skin." At the opposite end of the social spectrum, violence, negative reciprocity, and sorcery typified relations with enemy clansmen. All three represented forms of violence because they directly compromised the victim's social reproduction. Accordingly, death and illness through physical violence and sorcery as well as the failure to "back" a marriage exchange were all equally actionable in local court. The ever-present threat was that individuals would violate the limits of kinship and the predatory, violent, greedy propensities of relations would surface close to home. While all forms of violence fracture genealogical space—historically, the commission of murder within a clan has led to the clan's disintegration—sorcery is a special kind of threat because the sorcerer leads a secretive double life. Unlike violent persons who cannot control their behavior and explode publicly without regard to its consequences, the sorcerer uses his control over esoteric knowledge to destroy his own kin. Secrecy and premeditation define his actions. For this reason, sorcerers are the only persons who legitimately may be betrayed by their own clan members. Thus, on occasion, a sorcerer's own clan members have delivered some of his exuviae—nail clippings, hair, and the like—to an enemy clan. A sorcerer may harm not only by using the exuviae of the intended victim but that of anyone connected by substance, principally the victim's parents. Because the accumulation of esoteric knowledge is the basis of sorcery, a prominent shaman observed that since pacification the ability to do sorcery had increased. Sorcery techniques tend to be imported, and the opening up of public life had provided new opportunities. Stints on coastal labor plantations, the freedom to travel through traditional enemy territory to visit other groups like their Kalam neighbors, and the introduction of Christian rites have all provided novel sources of empowering knowledge.

Sorcerer attack the *min* of their victims. Min, the life force or shadow substance of a person, is like an immaterial spiritual double insofar as it replicates an individual's speech, physical form, intentions, and behavior, but possesses no bodily substance. Speakers used the word *min* to denote a person's shadow, reflected image in a mirror or pool of water, and the echo of one's voice off the valley walls. These were the concrete manifestations of a person's min in everyday life. For the most part, a person's min resided within the body, though in certain states, such as dreaming, intoxication, and at death, it could act independently. Its movement was limited to the immediate environs, and it usually did the same types of tasks that people normally do: gardening, hunting, lovemaking, etc. In one court case, an adulterer said that he had first slept with his younger brother's wife during a dream. The min of a "normal" person did not venture into the spiritual realm. Only the shaman, by quickly inhaling native tobacco and chanting monotonously, tried to release his min into the spiritual domain in order to communicate with the ancestor spirits. The critical concept was that a person's min was not inalienably housed in that person's body, but could be released, drawn out, retrieved by a number of (other)worldly forces (e.g., the magic of the sorcerer), forces that must themselves be controlled.

A sorcerer is someone who leads a secretive double life. In the everyday world, the sorcerer perpetrated nefarious acts such as offering poisoned food to clan members and affines while pretending to be upstanding. The duplicity lay in the fact that the surface of a sorcerer's actions only disguised the underlying intent and truth. While the sorcerer pretended to be inseparable from the social relations that should cause his actions, his dividuality only disguised an overweening individuality. Only by being the cause of his own actions could he go against his own kind. Like a clear and odorless acid, the sorcerer corroded the "whole" of social relations by alienating himself from the relations linking him to others. In the spiritual world, the min of the sorcerer could act apart from his/her physical body, taking on different forms such as inhabiting the body of animals and birds. The sorcerer's spirit double was invisible to others in his normal state, and thus he could conduct his nefarious activity unnoticed and unidentified by his victims. Nevertheless, the objects he used, such as food and axes, were visible. People could hear the sound made by a sorcerer moving through the underbrush, the splashing of water when fording a stream, or a gate creaking when entering a residential compound.

A sorcerer attacked the victim's min by feeding the victim ensorcelled food or by thrusting a knifelike object, archetypically a sliver of bamboo (traditionally used to dissect ritual pigs), into the liver. The bespelled food refused to dissolve, thereby blocking the passage of food and air through the victim's body. Sorcerers were reputedly cannibalistic (though not everyone believes this), first dismembering and then eating the "body parts" of the victim's min piece by piece. The victim experienced the diminishment of his life force as labored breathing, fever, pain, and eventually death. Sorcerers may pursue their deadly hobby either as a matter of conscious intent or non-consciously in a dream state. The Maring did not use this distinction between conscious and non-conscious states, their assumption being that conscious acts and dream images were different modes of a unified reality of thought and practice.

As was true across Melanesia, there was a logic to sorcery suspicion and accusation that can never be reduced to its sociological function. It was a practical and implicational logic that cut across numerous domains for action. This logic was the basis for understanding the intentionality of the other and the comparative discourse about the behavior of such others. If a person had an unusual or unexpected accident or a family suffered the death of a marriageable woman, the first question asked was, Who could have caused the calamity? The next question was, With whom have we reneged on a social obligation or who has so indicated this to us by asking for a gift? In particular, have we refused a gift to someone or deprived someone of a reproductive good? As each transaction or exchange presupposed a previous one, a disruption of an exchange cycle opened several logical possibilities. One was that this request for a gift implied that the asker had already proffered a gift, and our denial was met by the use of sorcery. A second possibility was that our refusal to present a gift had motivated them to seek revenge because our failure to give shamed them by "denying and making waste" of the kin link. Another possibility was that others were jealous of our success because they feel that our increase must have come at their expense; thus they have used sorcery to damage us. The implicational logic linked accidents or deaths to revenge and redress by means of an exchange system that shaped and permeated almost all interactions.

Riebe (1987:220) offers an example of this logic among the Kalam who intermarry and share the Simbai valley with the Maring. The case involves a man named Maklek who asked his cousins to continue providing him with stone axe blades after their father had died. But the cousins denied any obligation to supply the axe blades, thereby denying any good reason for Maklek to continue asking. By Kalam logic his asking implied that there was some unfulfilled obligation. The cousins thus postulated another more secret reason: "He was claiming (by implication) to have killed someone for them with witchcraft and was demanding pay for this." From here, it was a short step to: Maklek asked us to pay for his earlier killing on our behalf, we refused to render compensation, and thus he has taken revenge by killing our father. That Maklek was subsequently killed for his sorcery indicates the extent to which this implicational logic grounded indigenous concepts of intentionality and motive. A repeated request in the face of a refusal implied that the request was based on some past action that had not been taken into account when the refusal was made. It was in fact a fundamental principle of Maring exchange that the first request for a gift served to initiate an exchange whereas a repeated request was a performative; it presumed, presupposed, and thus brought into existence, a debtor/creditor relationship. Such relationships were of three kinds: my immediate subclan ancestors gave help/gifts to your ancestors; I have given help to your immediate kinsmen; or, I have given aid to you of which you are unaware or forgetful. It goes without saying that the flow and request for gifts (often through an intermediary) could devolve into a tense, ambiguity-ridden calculus of give-and-take, of classification and probing of an undisclosed hierarchy of intentions. The possibilities for misunderstandings that fomented anger, symbolic and physical violence, and not least sorcery were ever present.

The Structure of the Court

The Maring court was a formalization that was also necessarily a trans-formation of indigenous dispute resolution. Despite the Maring's repre-sentation of their own past as one of unmitigated violence, there was a long-standing tradition, almost inevitable in kinship-based societies, of using common kin to mollify the aggrieved and negotiate a settlement. As of 1980, the objective of Maring litigation was not to identify who was in the wrong, or even to determine that a law had been broken, but to restore balance to the disrupted community. Thus defendants sometimes agreed, or were forced, to pay compensation even as they continued to deny hav-ing committed any crime. The mere fact of the court indicated that social relations were askew and need to be righted. The crucial concept that Mar-ing have drawn upon from their tradition and adapted to the trial situation was that of social balance or *kopla;* it was generally believed that justice was based on a restoration of equivalence between clans and persons. Accordingly, most trials began with a pronouncement that its objective was to restore balance by "straightening" the matter. Still, trials, like pre-contact efforts at dispute resolution, may fail to restore balance, at least in the sense that some people aver they were worsted in a settlement they only grudgingly accepted. As is common in non-Western systems of justice (e.g., Knauft 1985a), the Maring still placed little value on discovering an offender's state of mind or why the crime was committed, though this was clearly not the case for all Highland societies (Goldman 1993). A claim of insanity *(pym),* for example, did not offer a legitimate defense, mitigate an offender's punishment, or change the amount of compensation.

In contrast to the logic of Western justice, local litigants (especially the senior and elder generations) made little attempt to reason by example. They treated each crime as a communally and historically specific rupture of sociality. There was no idea that there was a "society" whose integrity depended on a rule of law because persons were ontologically inseparable from the images and institutions that brought them together. The notion that the regimentation of law furthers the construction of the social pre-supposes as the ideal, the integration of ontologically primitive individuals into an equally irreducible society, what the Maring understood as the dissolution and dissembling of sociality. To put this another way, the most criminal aspect of sorcery is that the sorcerer posited himself in opposition to the collectivity. Given this view of sociality, the Maring also did not appeal to the concept of precedent, and there was no effort to transpose some proposition descriptive of one case into a general rule of law and then apply this rule to other cases. In a cultural sense, every case was unique because people assumed, without ever being aware of their assumption, that persons and circumstances were never identical. Because the objective was to ensure that a crime did not impair the ability of the victim's clan and kin to reproduce, no distinction existed between criminal and civil cases, that is, between the behavior of a defendant and the social and economic consequences of a crime. By the mid-1970s, many Maring courts had incorporated jail terms into the legal process, although it was· generally acknowledged that jailing was a pointless form of punishment because it did little to restore harmony or compensate the victimized clan/person. It was hardly surprising, then, that even those who were convicted of serious crimes never had to do hard time.

All of the trials I witnessed or obtained information about had much the same pattern. A court convened on notice of the most senior clansmen who were themselves responding to the pressure and logic of community sentiments. On the day of the hearing, those interested in the case or had testimony to give convened at the dance ground, a neutral space. Depending on the gravity of the case, one or more magistrates would be chosen to preside. Invariably, they were senior clansmen of stature who had developed a reputation for adjudicating disputes. The local practice was to allow all those who appear at the trial to speak as often as they wish, for as long as they wish, on any subjects they wish.[3] Often the testimony served as a character reference for the defendant or plaintiff or as a moral appeal to the clanspeople to cease their squabbling. The deeds and misdeeds of defendants and plaintiffs were also raised, no matter how far removed they may have seemed from the trial's basic issues. A person's generosity with his relatives, for instance, was seen as directly relevant to understanding whether he was a likely sorcerer, as was how hard he worked generally. A great deal of the trial practice was a test of wills played out through the intricate speech event that was the trial. The participants mobilized every linguistic resource from body postures and demonstrative posturing to verbal declarations and narratives of the past. A defendant typically sat very still, eyes cast downward, the face muscles motionless, thereby indicating that the testimony being given against him was untrue, shaming, or unacceptable. The same defendant might in the next instant launch into a violent tirade, others having to hold him back forcibly as he grasped for a club or spear, his screaming speech denouncing what he saw as the defilement of his name and that of his clan members.

Local courts received testimony in an informal though orderly sequence. As a speech event, one of the most distinctive aspects of the trial was an attempt to create a documentary narrative. In contrast to other forms of negotiation and conversation, the trial pioneered the grafting of a Western narrative of facts onto an indigenous explanatory logic. Most Maring understood this as the discursive nature of the imported practice. As is evident in the case cited earlier and the example to come is that the trial encouraged people to link a sequence of events via an implicational logic. Most trials began with an opening statement by the big-man chosen to oversee the case. His speech typically approached the issues before the court in an indirect or veiled fashion. A significant purpose of the speech was to motivate the litigants and community to resolve the problem at hand and restore harmony. Next, the plaintiff, members of his clan, and all others who wished to give testimony spoke. They related what they heard, saw, knew, or believed about the litigants and their actions. Then one or usually more of the senior clan members intervened. They attempted to sum up the testimony and through persuasive, cajoling speech tried to convince the court and community to adopt specific courses of resolution. In important cases, this portion of the trial continued for months, the court meeting again and again in an effort to reach a consensus. As testimony was heard over several hours, days, or months, the court and community eventually reached a consensus. This process of indeterminate length was less an attempt to explore all the facts of the case than to awaken publicly the incorporated state of the community so that it might collectively restore its collectivity.

A characteristic turning point in many cases was when a defendant admitted to the crime; almost all cases ended with an explicit confession by the defendant or the acceptance by the defendant of his/her guilt. Rarely did trials end inconclusively. Stalemates were unsatisfactory, provoking further accusations and recriminations and usually leading to violence. Of seventeen sorcery trials recorded over a fourteen-month period, eleven produced what the local court determined were confessions. These ranged from outright admissions of guilt in nine cases to tacit acceptance in the other two. Because of their notions of personhood, the Maring conceptualize guilt rather differently than Westerners do, focusing much more on the contextualized effects attributed to persons, such as the communal disruption "caused" by sorcerers, than on the intentionality or internal state of the defendant. Twelve of the cases involved serious illness in which the victim was saved through a combination of Western medicine and indigenous healing, three involved an apparently healthy pig struck down by illness, and two involved human deaths. In the cases involving illness, the court awarded the victim from one hundred kina in cash to five hundred kina plus three pigs depending on the damage resulting from the sorcery assault. In four of the six trials in which a defendant did not confess, the judges ordered the clansmen of the sorcerer to pay compensation.

Case Study: The Trial of Tenga

The trial began in early August 1980. The first statement was by the principal judge in the trial. He was seated on an overturned twenty-gallon kerosene drum between two other judges; directly in front of him was the defendant, Tenga, and immediately to his left was Kam's half brother and father. Due to the seriousness and notoriety of the case nearly a hundred men and a handful of women attended, sitting on the ground in a semicircle. The principal judge got to his feet and, talking in a modulated cadence, began the familiar refrain about how the modern era was time of strong law. He then recounted some of the virtues and advantages of the new day, citing among other things the presence of an anthropologist (meaning me) who was going to record the trial the way it was done in Port Moresby. His talk then turned to the issue of sorcery without mentioning the current dispute.

The first to speak in the case was Pint, Kam's half brother. He related how Kam's wife had come to him to report that Kam was ill. At first, he thought it was only a mild sickness (many people suffer from chronic malaria), but the fever raged worse with each passing day and when Kam refused food and water (such a refusal was a customary reaction to illness) he realized that sorcery must be the cause. Kam's deathbed statement confirmed this suspicion. Although some elder clansmen had said that Kam had died at the hands of an angered paternal ancestor (presumably the one he had disavowed), Pint claimed that his death was clearly a case of sorcery. Both he and his brother were, on several occasions, awakened in the full of the night by the sound of snapping twigs in the underbrush behind the encircled compound they shared with Kam. Pint's wife said that she heard the thrashing of what she initially took to be a cassowary, but now knew was a sorcerer. It was this transfigured sorcerer, pointing a finger at Tenga, who had poisoned Kam's food. In addition, they cited two further signs of Tenga's involvement. On the path leading from his house there were discovered bamboo knife filings, purportedly from the knife used to penetrate Kam's liver. Moreover, when first approached about "poisoning" Kam, Temga simply turned away, disdaining to give even a reply to the accusation. When I asked informants whether they had personally examined the bamboo knife filings, they replied that they had not seen such filings, but knew that the filings existed because: (a) carving a knife from bamboo always leaves filings; (b) the filings must have existed because this was how Kam died; and (c) if Tenga (or anyone else) were angry he would have used sorcery now that violence was "taboo." Thus, an implicational chain was created between the intention to harm and the physical evidence.

At this point, one of Kam's clansman launched into a tirade saying that Tenga's subclansmen were known for sorcery, and that they had recently obtained some new, potent sorcery from, of all places, the Anglican Church. But midway through this diatribe the chief councillor interrupted him; he stated that though Tenga's subclan would be held responsible for compensation, the reason for this trial was to determine if Tenga was guilty, not to rehearse whether or not his fellow subclansmen practiced sorcery. The councillor then turned to me and nodded as if to confirm and legitimize his distinction between who was culpable (an individual) and who was responsible for compensation. Several other clansmen then argued that the past behavior of Tenga's clansmen was extremely relevant and that, further, people had always considered such information cogent. The debate provoked by the attempt to create a court was over what counted as evidence. To follow the procedures prescribed by a Western-like court system, that had long been on display in the behavior of the kiaps, was to incorporate without explicitly seeking to do so the notion of the plaintiff as a singular individual. The older and alternative stance was that the behavior of Tenga's clansmen was relevant because he was a product of the social relations that created him (not as the West might hold as a matter of character reference).

Kam's clansmen constructed Tenga's motive for the sorcery in this way. Tenga conducted an exchange relationship with Kam, who was his brother's wife's younger brother. Kam had assisted Tenga in harvesting and carrying the coffee some nine miles to the Kionambe mission station to be sold. This was not the first service that Kam had done for Tenga, gifts that Kam felt were not acknowledged or reciprocated. As a consequence, there existed a smoldering discontent on Kam's part, who felt that he could not refuse a request from his sister's husband's brother, yet received little or nothing from Tenga for such efforts. This culminated in a vituperious outburst by Kam; he raged against and shamed Tenga by saying that he had no intention of helping him in the future. That Tenga felt no obligation toward Kam meant that Kam's help was payment for an already existing debt, specifically Wai's death two years earlier. Wai and Kam had been involved in a bitter land dispute before Wai fell ill, presumably as a result of Tenga's sorcery, and died shortly after. Now, because Kam had refused to recognize his debt to Tenga and had shamed him, Tenga sorcerized Kam as he had Wai. In such fashion, Kam's kinsmen constructed the implicational chain that established what most people thought was plausible and possible. Other people now testified at some length that Tenga was generous, to which it was replied that if Tenga was generous and did not repay Kam (in fact, he did give him several gifts, but clearly not what Kam thought he deserved), then it could only be because Kam was already in his debt—that is, Tenga's alleged sorcery of Wai.

The story is complicated and the logic implicational, but by virtue of this analysis Tenga was now linked to both the murder of Kam and the "unsolved" death of Wai. Wai's widow, sitting on the periphery of the circle, passed along the comment that the reason that Wai's death had not been investigated more thoroughly was that his brother was "too Christian" to ask questions, that working for the Church in Koinambe had moved him to accept that Wai had "just died." Although not part of "official testimony," her comment was audible to everyone. At this point, Tem, a senior member from a group affinally linked to the clans of the defendant and plaintiff, intervened to observe that Kam had been seriously ill on other occasions and that these previous illnesses had been attributed to retribution on the part of a paternal ancestor that he had spurned. Tem then went on to discuss Kam's public behavior, offering examples of Kam's often cunning if not dishonest behavior. Tem cited those instances where Kam had been stingy in sharing bridal pork, had failed to treat his affines fairly, and had been overly successful in trade relations. Although Tam played out these examples to the approving nods of those gathered, he concluded on the ambiguous note that people such as Kam attract sorcery, thus suggesting the likelihood that Tenga did commit sorcery, that Kam had in the past paid for the aid of a sorcerer, again suggesting that Tenga might have worked sorcery on Kam's behalf, and finally, that sorcery is inevitable and not necessarily bad, implying that men like Kam invited retribution and usually got what they deserved.

Those testifying also gave commentary on a simmering antagonism between Tenga and other senior clansmen. More than most, Tenga had extensive holdings in coffee which he had translated into a substantial pig herd. Some of his own clansmen suggested that Tenga could acquire such a great herd because he accumulated more than he shared. As one man put it, Tenga had made friends with money. That he had a passbook savings account at the Bank of New South Wales in Koinambe proved the point. Several people testified that they had on at least one occasion seen his red passbook in a plastic sleeve, the unspoken argument being that a person would open such an account only if he intended to renege on his obligation to share. Such a person has no shame insofar as he/she lacks the morality, the propriety, the sense of relatedness to others that would preclude such behavior. The view still held by senior and especially elder clansmen was that persons were supposed to evidence and exemplify the social, not merely reference it. But the story had even more twists and complications. A significant reason for his success was his relationship to the young men who worked for the Anglican mission. They helped to transport his coffee and to bring back consumer goods from Mt. Hagen on his behalf. Reciprocally, he had supported them in their Christianity and on several occasions sided with them against the most senior clansmen. In particular, the trial elicited testimony to the effect that he had contemplated starting a business in Mt. Hagen and manning it with his proteges from the junior generation. To this was added a further allegation that, insofar as Tenga was fixated on bisnis, he must have been jealous of Kam's success.

When the court reconvened two weeks later, the trial took an unexpected turn. Two men in their mid-twenties stepped forward to give testimony. One was the councillor's brother's son, the other the son of his matrilateral cross-cousin. Both men had worked in and around the coastal city of Popondetta for nine years studying at an Anglican preparatory/religious school for indigenous clergy, although neither of the men completed their course of study. The first argued that Tenga could not be guilty of sorcery because it did not now exist; sorcery was something that people believed in before they knew about Jesus Christ and the "truths" of Europeans. The only real evil power that existed was that of the devil Satan, who alone could harm people magically. To believe, they argued, that mere people can become pigs and cassowaries in order to harm others was part of the customs of the ancestors, but this was not true any more.[4] Kam's death was most likely a punishment from God because Kam was neither a good person, often cheating others, nor a worthy Christian. They argued further that there was a surefire way to determine if Tenga was innocent. Let him take an oath on the holy Bible, swearing that he did not commit sorcery or cause Kam's death. If he was lying about causing Kam's demise, the sword of the Almighty would strike him down.

Before they could finish several elders (men in their late fifties and sixties) then replied, incredulous that anyone would say that sorcery did not exist. Their argument was that they knew from experience that sorcery did exist; kinsmen that they had known had died from ensorcelled food and they knew people who practiced sorcery. One of the elders then recited several examples of people who had succumbed to sorcery. How, he inquired, could anyone find bamboo filings if someone had not indulged in sorcery? Other senior clansmen then testified that they knew sorcerers and that sorcery had been openly practiced in wartime. Moreover, how could one explain the recent outbreak of disease without recourse to sorcery? The almost-catechists responded that poor sanitary conditions caused the recent outbreak of malaria and influenza, people and pigs defecating upstream from the main settlements had contaminated the water, punishing those who had disobeyed the modern commandment to use the latrines. Lapsed hygiene rather than sorcery was at the root cause of the problems. Several younger men then offered tentative support for their contemporaries, acknowledging that the Anglican priest had given a sermon in which he pronounced that those who were true Christians should question the existence of sorcery. To this, a senior clansman retorted that the sermon was nothing more than talk and launched into a discussion about how the local Anglican Church had promised much but delivered only words. The trial adjourned until the next weekend. But words wreak havoc, epistemological havoc, when, moved by changes in the objective and subjective structures of social life, they name the nameless or expunge a name. The two young men, in calling the very existence of sorcery into question, were undermining a given of Maring reality by removing sorcery to a field of contrasts in which it was not only pitted against empowered Western thought but exposed as one version of reality among others. The senior and elder generations reacted so viscerally to this proposition because they sensed, oh so correctly, that it undermined their authority in favor of their juniors. The junior generation amplified their assault on traditional realities by claiming that poor hygiene was to blame for the outburst of sickness. The pattern emerging here is not restricted to Melanesia. The junior generation does not so much remove their seniors from positions of power as they began to remove the reality over which they exercised power. They approach the flow of practice with the skeptical irreverence of one estranged from yet still attached to their world. What results is not a betrayal of tradition but a revelation of transformation. The footprint of modernity had become a size larger with the calling of sorcery itself into question.

That week the community began to divide into those who believed, or more precisely, presupposed that Tenga was guilty and that the court should move forthwith to the issue of compensation, and those who contended: (1) that Tenga was innocent; (2) that there was no such thing as sorcery; or (3) that no clear verdict had yet emerged. These positions reflected the politics of modernity as much as an evaluation of the evidence. In particular, a number of young men supported the two almost-catechists publicly, even though they confessed to me that they found it hard to believe that sorcery did not exist. Moreover, as the trial progressed the actual death of Kam seemed to slip further and further into the background. For the senior and elder generations, sorcery was a understandable way to condemn and punish what they perceived as immoral and antisocial behavior on Tenga's part—the brand of antisocial behavior that could inspire sorcery. The individualism that marked the sorcerer was now appearing in another modality. In contrast to expectations, the community not only failed to reach a consensus, but became increasingly polarized as the trial evolved.

When the trial reconvened, the two young men reiterated their contention that sorcery no longer existed, knowing well that their provocation had shaken the court and community. Both now appeared, armed with Bibles, seeking to refute the view of senior clansmen that the priest's sermon was just talk. The young men alternated speaking but with the same message: the words of the Christian God are written down and exist in material form; they are thus unlike the words of a speech, which are simply lost. Where is it impossible to trust ordinary discourse, we know that the words of the Bible are true. If the psalms and parables were not true (as opposed to merely talk), the servants of the Lord would not have written them down. Their point was that codification guaranteed the identity of the inner and outer dimensions of an act; it proved that there was no hierarchy of intentions because, in contrast to speech, the author was not here identified indexically by the mere act of speaking. In this way, the almost-catechists not only challenged the modernday existence of sorcery but, based on their evangelical training that stressed the absolute truth of the Bible, they argued that the truth value and validity of written language was intrinsically higher than spoken language. This was also a powerful claim that modernity introduced forms of truth and knowledge that were different and better than those of the past.

When the young men concluded, Tenga stood up and said that it had not occurred to him to work magic against Kam and that he did not usually think of sorcery. He said that the accusations against him were false and that he could prove this. He then began an extended and animated discussion of his relationship to Wai, listing the times that he had shared pork, the many exchanges of goods, the help they had lent each other. During the course of discussion Tenga reiterated that he was proving that he did not kill Kam. That proof consisted in severing the implicational logic linking Tenga to Kam through the death of Wai. But even more, Tenga went on to defend his business ventures, the luck that Jesus had brought him in raising pigs, and the help provided by a junior generation who was more in tune with the modern ways. At the end of this session about a half-dozen young men went to the councillor's house to ask him to terminate the trial, threatening to boycott the trial if their request was refused.

When the court reconvened, none of the young men who had sided with the two almost-catechists was present. At least half had returned to the local mission station at Koinambe, saying that they intended to recruit the white Anglican priest to intervene in the trial. Before this could happen, the councillors announced that even though not everyone was in agreement, they had reached a verdict. When everyone was assembled, the lead councillor asked if I had the trial recorded, to which I replied that I did. He then said that all the witnesses had been heard from, the evidence had been evaluated properly the way it was done in Mt. Hagen and Port Moresby, and that a trial record had been taken. He justified the verdict not in terms of community consensus, but that the right procedures and protocols had been followed, a departure from tradition in that this validates the verdict by reference to a jural domain, rather than to community sentiments and interests. He then said that there was insufficient evidence to say for sure that Tenga was guilty of sorcery. However, it was clear that sorcery played a strong part in Kam's death, and by the same token, no one was sure that Tenga was innocent. What there could be no doubt of was that Kam's clan had suffered material loss and needed to be compensated. He then ordered that Tenga's kin pay Kam's clansmen the sum of two pigs and 200 kina—extremely low for a homicide payment (another payment in 1979 was 30 pigs and 3,000 kina) but reflecting the ambiguity that surrounded the trial and the struggles that it embodied.[5] The trial outcome satisfied few people. There was no consensus or unanimity, and in difficult cases of homicide and sorcery there might well never be unanimity again because the convergence of views was secured by the givenness of a world now permanently disturbed and challenged by Western culture.

Knowledge, Contestation, and Change

Sorcery trials were remarkable because they tested, contested, and transformed the character of cultural life and its epistemological grounding. For those who participated in such trials nothing was more real or of greater moment than the immediate struggle and verdict, and sorcery trials were one of the few arenas of Maring life where the scent of laughter was rare. Nonetheless, the struggles between plaintiffs and defendants were only the skin of deeper changes and challenges. Not least was the means by which in such an egalitarian kin-based society, agents, their desires and dispositions swayed toward the modern, create the moral authority so that the court can pass and then enforce judgment on someone else's kin. Possibility of legal and hence nonviolent redress rest on the flowering of a new and broader vision of community and cultural integration, captured in the words of a big-man: "We speak one language, have the same high ancestor [Christ], and vote in the same election; though we would have fought in the past, we must now find legal and peaceful solutions when there are problems." In this context, the trial has emerged as a form of practice in which those who adjudicate are required to bracket their kin loyalties in order to reach a verdict that will be accepted by the community. From the deep pool of indigenous sociality, a distinctive field of jural relations began to emerge, endowed with its own logic (validity claims), history of practice (the setting of precedents for adjudication), and identities (claims of authority founded on fairness and impartiality). There was a shift characteristic of capitalism and the modern polity from relational kinship-based identities to categorical identities (e.g., plaintiff), in particular identities that neutralize kinship and take the state as their point of reference (e.g., citizen), in the process helping to pave the way for the new road of "deep, horizontal comradeship" that underwrites nationality (Anderson 1983:4). It is fair to say that the trial in concert with the other modernizing agents and institutions, was responsible for *re*-inventing sorcery. The express objectification of sorcery demanded by the trial—especially the effort to create a documentary narrative of what happened—and the vision of sorcery proposed by the Anglicanized commentators presupposed a distance and opposition between the physical and spiritual worlds that had no place in the traditional understanding. So even as the crime of sorcery inflected the meaning and methods of Western-style justice, the epistemology inscribed in Western practices began to infect local notions of sorcery. Or, to put this another way, the Maring were now on the road to being introduced to the forms of sorcery and magic that inundate Western society.

Let me develop this point from a Melanesian point of view, especially because Western society has specialized in concealing and misrecognizing the extent to which sorcery and magic determine its character. In the West, sorcery and magic are particularly significant in fields of medicine, law, and business. The world-producing difference is that Melanesians take the unity of spiritual and physical realms as their reference point, whereas Westerners legitimize sorcery and magic by reference to science. Science, I should add, not as it is conceptualized and generally practiced by the scientific field, but science as a mythology and mysticism of the concrete. A good example is the professional investment community on Wall Street. Because investors, brokers, and underwriters would profit from predicting the future price of stocks they own, they hire what the trade calls technical analysts. These analysts use all sorts of quasi-mathematical and statistical tools to divine the hidden pattern in the price history of a stock and then use that to foretell its future. From the crystal ball of science, they discover patterns with names such as double bottom (an omen of a future advance in price) or head and shoulders (a sign of a future decline), and then issue forecasts that motivate investors to buy or sell a given stock. Statisticians have long pointed out that the methods are invalid while others from the ivory towers have shown repeatedly and conclusively that such forecasts are no better than chance. Nonetheless, the allure of being able to predict the future is so great, the mythologized god of science so powerful, that the West spends more money each year on technical analysis (approximately seven billion) than on physics, chemistry, and mathematics combined. Many in the investment community base their beliefs and judgments about stocks on such analysis, thereby directly influencing the ability of firms to raise capital and thus the course of capitalism generally. There is here a secular magic of the concrete founded on the supreme being of science.

If the business community is partial to divination, the legal community has always found a friend in sorcery. Consider, for example, the pending litigation on silicone breast implants from a Maring point of view. A class of persons came to embody a substance that unbeknownst to them was poisoned. The result was the proliferation of diseases and ailments connected by the fact that the same entity "caused" all of them. Like sorcery, breast implant litigation attempts to explain and account for real sickness and suffering. And like sorcery, a wide assortment of diseases and ailments—the litigation has indicted everything from lupus and lung cancer to narcolepsy and back pain—are linked by the fact that they are all the result of a malicious, self-serving, and antisocial behavior. That biomedical studies demonstrate that someone is no more likely to contract lung cancer from breast implants than they are of contracting malaria from consuming sweet potatoes has only slightly impeded the litigation's progress. The difference is that Western sorcery bases its case on some yet undiscovered impairment to the body's autoimmune system. The junior generation was, of course, beginning to internalize this logic in their claim that lapsed hygiene was the cause of the recent outbreak of illnesses. The foundation for the belief in the impairment of the autoimmune system is one that Maring of all generation would find very intelligible, namely the yearning to explain sickness and suffering. Both Westerners and Melanesians recognize that many of the individuals who ate the poisoned potatoes or received the breast implants did not contract any illness. But this does not come close to explaining why those who did, did. How to account for the outbreak of disease in young and otherwise healthy individuals? For this, other explanations are necessary and the victims, both Melanesian and Western, require compensation to restore the imbalance in the social universe. In other words, part of the process of the transition to modernity involves the new forms of magic and sorcery that will emerge from the encounter between the indigenous system of socio-spiritual magic and sorcery with the Western system of secular scientific magic and sorcery.

From its inception, the trial as the instrument of justice has foregrounded the issue of individual responsibility and culpability for a crime as against that of the clan as a unit. Tension arises because the trial process, as extrapolated from its Western context, cannot help but focus on the individual in a society in which the very notion of the person and of agency was historically bound up with a person's kinship relations and clan identity. In the trial at hand, the trial process mediated a potential contradiction by assigning culpability to the individual qua individual and responsibility for compensation to the subclan. At least within the context of the trial and an emerging jural field, the Maring seemed to be moving toward a quasi-Western image of the person—that is, the concept that demonstrated qualities (from intelligence and perseverance to anger and deceit) are internal properties of individuals and that individuals objectify and express these properties in and through their actions. Some Maring expressly acknowledged this by noting, as during the trial, that before the arrival of white missionaries they did not know that intelligence, shame, envy, generosity, and other properties of actions originate within the mind (itself housed in a person's head) and flow outward. This ideology of the person was opposed to the customary image that actions embody a hierarchy of intentions and that a person's skin was the bodily locus of human agency. The trial in concert with the other practices introduced by Western encompassment were inducing a shift toward a concept of intentions as the mental objects of individuals.[6] In this respect, the internalization of Western legal practices was helping to lead the Maring to reinvent their notion of the person, specifically by gravitating toward a notion that sees persons as more self-moving, self-sufficient, and self-contained agents.

The evidence of the trial underlined the emergence of a distinction between oral and written language in terms of their relative authority and believability. Where spoken language was instrumental in disguising the layers of intention inscribed in actions and thereby masking the beliefs, desires, and judgments of agents, codified language was suggested to be transparent and authoritative. By erasing the text's author, acceptance of this distinction relocated intention from the relationship between an act and its influence (the traditional view) to an unspecified point outside of, and therefore not instrumental to, the strategies and judgments of practice. This leads to a transformed conception of truth, and signals the emergence of a context in which the identity of the inner and outer dimensions of an action is guaranteed. The question becomes what does the text mean on the premise that the text has an objective meaning that can be decoded by those in the know. In the trial context, this could only mean the young men who had been educated at the Anglican missionary school. This view of written language also transformed and masked the shape of enchantment and mystification from the spell cast by an orator (through a use of tonal modulation, inflection, repetition, alliteration and other techniques) to the displaced, omnipotent, and unanswering voice of a text. Powerfully, the erasure of the author is especially true of religious, medical, and government documents that, like their Western counterparts, are written in the third person and then typically left unsigned. For the Maring, the advent of written, third-person documents was part of the social invention of the disembodied, anonymous person—the individual who is not known either from personal experiences or from knowledge of their clan affiliation and kin.

The trials also exemplified a tension between generations whose dispositions, priorities, and beliefs about their place in the world were inculcated under very different circumstances. At issue was not merely the production and distribution of power, but the power to define and assert a view of social reality. The trials of 1979–90 played out the struggles between the legion of important senior clansmen, aged 40 to 55, and the newer generation of Maring men who have attended the Anglican-mission school, done contract labor, speak pidgin and a smattering of English, and see themselves as wise in the ways of the West. This struggle was not limited to maneuvering at the social level (the guilt or innocence of the defendant) but concerned an epistemological struggle as the Western/Christian-educated men challenged the very existence of sorcery and sorcerers, and sought to mobilize support for their view. While this challenge was (temporarily?) beaten back by the combined weight of senior clansmen, that it was argued seriously underlined an enlargement in what may be called the resources of negativity. The concepts and institutions of the modern were emerging as a means by which the junior generation could deny the senior generations by denying the reality to which they were attached. The sorcery trials were social contestations between generations over what should constitute the cultural imaginary, this conflict played out both above and below the surface as a relationship between magical forces and the moral body.

The encompassment of the Maring world has led to the emergence of exogenous and powerful voices, most critically those of the national state and the Western churches. Through various forms of education, from public schooling to religious instruction, they familiarize people with other viewpoints and practices. Even more, by virtue of the power of the state and religious institutions, such viewpoints and practices became saturated with authority. This, in turn, afforded agents, such as women displeased with arranged marriages, historically subordinated subclans, and young men chafing under the control of senior less-Westernized elders an opportunity to reposition themselves politically by reference to a recognized, exogenous, and clearly powerful voice. In other words, a major change wrought by the imposition of Western forms of polity and religion, and the new forms of media such as radio, movies, and writing that accompany these forms, was that it began to give agents the conceptual and political leverage to produce critiques of their own society on issues, and with a power, unheard of in even the recent past. Moreover, these critiques were both ways of readjusting to the modern—experiments in epistemology and ontology so to speak—and defining the kind of modernity that people desired to live in. The clash over the very reality of sorcery and the sorcerer as a type of person was an exemplar of just such a critique.

Because sorcery trials lie at that intersection of knowledge, power, and the character of persons, it is hardly productive to rely either on unidimensional approaches, such as conflict regulation (e.g., Patterson 1974–75), even though sorcery does sometimes regulate conflict. No better are approaches that depict sorcery beliefs, accusations, and trials as an encoding of, and commentary on, the violence and inequalities that permeate the social order, particularly social orders undergoing fast transformation (e.g., Le Roy Ladurie 1987). These approaches are only partly satisfactory because, as Tambiah (1990:105–10) observes, they are too heavily weighted toward causal, representational, and instrumental orientation, thereby bracketing the participatory and performative character of spirituality in kin and community-based societies. As Leenhardt (1982) realized, participation (as opposed to causality) was the center of gravity of Melanesian notions of personhood, sorcery, and knowledge. To this he could well have added intentionality, truth, and speech. In contrast to the West, the causal aspect of Maring sorcery (like many other Melanesian as well as African societies) was founded on an implicational logic that was itself deeply connected to their participatory orientation. The Maring materials suggest that Western practices encode Western epistemology and notions of subjectivity and that these interacts with local categories and concepts of knowledge to generate new and mediated forms. These forms bear a family resemblance to other domains of indigenous practice and to Western practice, but are identical to neither. New forms of thought emerge out of the encompassment of the indigenous world and the strategies that its agents devise to improve their position and gain political leverage. On another level, the encounter between the Maring, the West, and the emerging national state engendered a system of transformation that began to organize a discursive field of legal discourse whose effect was to erode the performative and relational aspects of customary dispute settlement. If this is the case, then an ethnography of truth, intentionality, and agency is critical to an understanding of Melanesian modernity. And nowhere was this more the case than with respect to the two bedfellows of Western life: money and Christianity.

CHAPTER 6

Money and the
Representation of Life

A signature event in Maring history was the introduction of Western money. The importance of this event has, ironically, been masked by the ease with which the locals integrated Western money into the economy of everyday life and ritual politics. Within the first decade of sustained contact, money came to figure critically in everything from the purchase of trade goods to payment of bridewealth and homicide compensation. No other Western product, image, or institution has had such resonance or been granted such an open reception, save perhaps what amounted to much the same thing: the person of the Westerner.

Despite the apparent ease with which Maring have accepted and integrated Western money into social practice, its penetration has animated a process of change and accommodation that is as critical as it is hidden from the ordinary eye. The primary engine of this process was the infiltration of the commodity, as the type of goods and services associated with the encompassment of Melanesia by the West (i.e., imported goods bought for money in a trade store) and as a form that inscribes the epistemology and social presuppositions of capitalism. Most Maring, as well as most other Melanesians and expatriates, imagine this as a transition from a "traditional" form of wealth to a modern one, an evolution from the "kastam money" of pearlshells to a Western-type specie. Whatever money is, it falls under the spell of an ideology that offers the clarity of surfaces in trade for a deeper, more complex view.

Ideology aside, this transition from pearlshells to money is never simply the replacement of an indigenous form with a foreign alternative. As elsewhere in Melanesia, this is the case for the Maring. The money that emerges is a hybrid; it is the product of the skewed image that the Maring have of "Western" money, defined differentially by the contingent character of contact (e.g., the view toward money of the Christian ministry that happened to be in their territory) in relation to local images and practices of use. Moreover, intrinsic to the emergence of "local money"—which is the shaping of a quasi-Western money form—is the emergence of an ideology that conceals the local contribution to the new money form, not only as part of its production, but the reproduction of the modern itself. It

is precisely the form and progress of this imbrication of practice and ideology that an ethnography of money in Melanesia must sort out. Indeed,
as the story unfolds we will see that the Maring imagine that they have
appropriated a Western form in its pure Western state, the purity of the
form understood locally as an index of the degree to which they have
embraced the modern.

To view money as a form of hybridity is to recognize that even as it
advances the commodification of the local world, it is infused with a complex of culturally specific meanings. Thus the meaning and functions of
money for the Maring are not necessarily the same as for other Melanesian
peoples. Another way to look at it is that, due to its social saturation, currency in the West is nearly homogeneous nationally in meaning. This contrasts greatly with the highly culturally variable meanings of kina. The
result is that to treat the Australian dollar and kina as parallel money
forms is, at least at the present moment, an ideological exercise or viewpoint. Money in the West has numerous social meanings and functions
that are shared nationally though denied ideologically whereas money in
Papua New Guinea has numerous local meanings and functions that are
not shared nationally. In contrast to nation-states in the West, the Papua
New Guinea state can exercise scant control over the construction of the
subjectivity of its citizens, especially in the hinterlands of the Highlands.
What this means is that for us to understand the nature of hybridity, it is
necessary to come to terms with the character of the Western money form,
as an aspect of a continuing process of encompassment, in relation to the
changing attribution of meaning and use at the local level. Only thus can
we ground an ethnography and analysis that is inherently comparative.

In this light, I argue that money is the perfect instrument of modernity not because, as formal economics would have us think (e.g., see the
listing under *money* in the *Encyclopedia of the Social Sciences*), it has form
without content, but because its defined and often definite content is so
contextually specific and dependent. This means that transformations in
social practice and contexts for action will transform the meaning of
money. It means also that there will be an evolution of the meaning of
money that traces the trajectory of modernity. And it means that there will
be bifurcate epistemologies, the way in which persons engage money in
one setting, such as town, differing from its engagement in the hinterlands.
To accomplish this requires an understanding of the apparently simple
horizon between money and pearlshells.

Thematizing Money

There are two general viewpoints that have guided the story that ethnographers and other travelers tell about the introduction of money into

Melanesia. The first is what we may call the steel-for-stone view. The notion is that labor the world over produces commodities that people circulate and exchange in order to improve their living standard. Money is that special commodity that helps to grease the wheels of trade, be it primitive or modern. Just as Melanesians quickly shifted from stone to steel axes, so they also quickly adopted Western money because it is more efficient, easier to manage, and more durable. The easy virtue of this idea is that it has an answer as to why Western money was readily adopted. The steel-for-stone view is, however, problematic because it can never account for those societies that continue to use shells (e.g., Akin 1996; Liep 1996) in concert with money. As importantly, it cannot adequately theorize the character of capitalism, having reduced it to a universal human motive. Labor, the commodity, and everything entailed by them are imagined as transhistorical and transcultural categories. The end result is that this view cannot deal with the encounter between Melanesia and the West, the economic violence of colonialism and Christianity, or the profound changes in knowledge and spirit animated by capitalism. The view is chained to Western metaphors and cannot help but ground itself in our epistemological presuppositions about the nature of agency and action. The result is that everything that is Melanesian vanishes (as does everything that is historically specific to capitalism). This is the idea of money that was championed by the Australian state and is currently being advanced by the Papua New Guinea state in collaboration with the World Bank and other interstate agencies. The steel-for-stone thesis is a distillation of Western ideology, bearing in mind that a peculiar and necessary feature of capitalism is the construction of an ideology that masks its essential social form.

The alternative position fixates on the cultural and economic space that separates Melanesia from the West, arguing these points from two complementary angles. The "economy of difference" theory begins with an understanding that there is an enormous gap between capitalist and primitive economies, the bridge between them shaped by the history and consequences of colonialism. Labor, value, the commodity form, money, and the other categories of capitalism have no parallel in the primitive world. They have no abstract döppelganger as a necessary, intrinsic, and masked feature. There was no abstract labor or value in precontact Melanesia. So the commodity as the West knows it cannot exist, money cannot be the exemplar of the form, and thus whatever the pearlshell is, it bears no lineage with capitalist money. Money and shells are the exemplars of that qualitative difference between societies in which kinship mediates social relations and those societies in which labor itself mediates social relations.

On the cultural side of the ledger, generally with little thought to economic issues, there is a new Melanesian ethnography that calls for a radical alterity between the West and its others. It self-consciously, if not always self-reflectively, endorses an opposition between us and them, and presses the thesis that there is an essential and inalienable space that divides Melanesia from the West. The method with the theory is to relativize our images and metaphors in order to destabilize the Western (and capitalist) presuppositions that too often underwrite anthropological inquiry. Because of this perspective, this view cannot help but romance the opposition between commodities and gifts, between commodity-based and gift-based societies (even if the ultimate objective is to destabilize this opposition). While the focus of this ethnography is usually issues such as agency, intentionality, and local concepts of time and space, it has no problem with, and implicitly endorses, the idea that there is a radical separation between Western money and pearlshells. The critical virtue of this distinction and the "new ethnography" that lends it support is that it can come to terms with the vast and deeply inscribed differences between Melanesian currencies and Western money. While I am sympathetic to this view, indeed in most respects I embrace it, I also recognize that it cannot easily account for the ease and rapidity with which the Melanesian world adopted Western money—thus the conundrum that the steel-for-stone thesis, by overestimating commensurability, cannot account for the encounter of cultural differences, whereas the economy of difference thesis, by taking a highly relativist perch, cannot easily account for the eager, uncoerced adoption by people like the Maring. The view that colonialism and the nature of encompassment are forcefully imposing the capitalist money form on Melanesia is only a starting point; if taken too literally, if we mistake this bald descriptive overview for a theory of what is happening, the inherently comparative account of the relationship between money and pearlshells becomes derailed because we are led to undervalue the force of Melanesian agency and to overvalue the capitalist ideology of money.

In this respect, this chapter also takes issue with the position advanced by Parry and Bloch (1989). They call into question what they view as the anthropological assumption that the introduction of money animates rippling changes in the institution of exchange and the epistemology of personhood. Westerners, they argue, view money as an "acid" that corrodes social relations by arousing the individualistic, possessive, and materialistic instincts that are buried in each of us. It elicits the worst of our human natures. Those people who imagine the devil's face impressed on every note have an inside track on understanding the power of money to dissolve the lineaments of social life (see, of course, Taussig 1980). For the societies of Melanesia, those who subscribe to this position think that the money form itself leads to a shift from gift to commodity exchange, from a world in which relations are valued over things and per-

sons are defined by these relations to a world in which objects trump relations and persons are defined exclusively as individuals. Parry and Bloch
question and contest these notions on the grounds that the introduction of
money often does not lead to a dismantling of the exchange system and,
conceptually, many peoples do not equate money with the loss of social
relations. Their reading of the ethnography leads them to conclude that
anthropologists have overestimated the extent to which money transforms
others.

Their perspective is, however, troubled on several counts. To begin
with, it confuses the ideology of money of the West with an account of
money adequate to its object—that is, as an aspect of a capitalist economy
that necessarily masks and misrecognizes the social relations that constitute it. The result is that they envision the money form only in its fetishized
state, as invested with agency, autonomy, and animation, and so enabled
to institute change on its own. But the force of money is different from,
say, pearlshells, not because there is anything "inherently" different about
money, but because it is part and product of a capitalist set of relations
that are embedded in everything from the nature of colonialism and Christianity to the polity of the nation-state and internationalization of Western
culture (e.g., the adoption of Western juridical and educational system
across Melanesia). The countercultural claims that Parry and Bloch make
about money for other societies are also true for the West. Westerners do
indeed use money in relations based on "diffuse enduring solidarity"; no,
they do not always associate money with the pursuit of short-term individual gains; yes, they do sometimes direct their personal ambitions
toward the reproduction of the group. The underlying reason for this is
that there is, as I expressly argued in the discussion of personhood, a
"dividual" dimension to the Western person, a dimension that is concealed
by, among other realities, our ideology of money. The ideological image of
money in capitalism—although necessary and intrinsic to its form as a
commodity—not only is not true for Africa, Amazonia, and Melanesia, it
is not true for the Western world either (though, of course, the character of
this mystification always has a certain cultural-historical specificity).

The Parry and Bloch position is troubled not only because it founds
its comparison on an inadequate account of capitalism, but because it subjects the ethnography to an overly objectivist—not to say empiricist—
reading. The fact that the inflow of Western money has not led to the
demise of "gift exchange" or that money has been excluded from the
spheres of exchange thought to be critical to social reproduction (i.e., kastam) does not mean that the indigenous exchange system has somehow
escaped its influence. The existence of money reorders the context for the
production of meaning and value; the copresence of the two alternative
spheres of exchange and the two forms of currency mutually inform each

other's meaning. Simply to choose a sphere of exchange is itself a commentary on the state of the exchange, its modern-day purposes, and its objects. Indeed, as we shall see in the Maring case, it was precisely the introduction of money that permitted a new equation to emerge in which money was to bisnis as pearlshells were to tradition, with pigs the mediating category. Money has redefined the nature of pearlshells just as the customary use of shells helps to define the social meaning of money. Moreover, as was pointed out earlier, strategies for obtaining money constantly defined the trajectory of social organization and relations, especially between generations. The general error of the Parry and Bloch viewpoint, which ethnographers have repeated across a spectrum of domains, is that because they base their analysis on the Western ideology of money (as opposed to its structure in its demystified form) they cannot formulate a comparison adequate to its intent or object. Like so many other analysts before them this led them to overstate the difference between Melanesia and the West even as they understated the effects of modernity on the production of meaning and value, not least as a favorite symbolic weapon in the struggle between senior and junior generations.

Comparison and the Money Form

Somewhere in *Capital,* Marx remarks that money is a god among commodities. To this we should append Durkheim's observation that what is interesting about gods is that even when they are imagined as universal, they are always culturally and historically specific. And so it was necessarily with the Melanesian encounter with money, this money being the capitalist money form, materializing first in the Australian shilling and later the PNG kina, and introduced by a particular and idiosyncratic core of Western agents. There was an inseparable relationship between the adoption and meaning of money for the Maring and the circumstance of its introduction. Taken at face value—the practical and ideological mode of its apprehension—money reveals solely its practical and ideological aspects. Its relationship to labor, its epistemological underpinnings, its link to subjectivity, embodiment, and indeed the commodity form all lie beneath the surface. Hence an understanding of money in Melanesia must begin with, and ground itself in, an account of the submerged dimensions of the Western money form in relationship to the differences between capitalist and noncapitalist societies. So far, this relationship is all but untheorized; what follows is a preliminary attempt to begin to write an account adequate to its object(s?).

Money in capitalist societies (however it may be defined) is significantly different from what has been called money in other societies.

This difference derives from the reality that money is the externalized, visible, and most quantifiable expression of the commodity. Existentially, money renders commodities commensurable by allowing the exchange of qualitatively different goods, services, and information. More importantly and at a deeper level, money is the expression, index, and measure of that commensurability. This contrasts dramatically with the role of pearlshells or shell money in exchange. When a Maring man gave an affine a gift of shells to compensate them for having helped him, the objects involved in the transaction were in no way thought to be commensurable, nor was it thought that commensurability was necessary. The reasons for this was that gifts engendered overt social relations bound by spatial and temporal realities and shaped by the terms of kinship and marriage—what capitalism grasps as barriers or constraints on trade that only inhibit the circulation of commodities. Unlike the commodity, the use and exchange values of the gift had no abstract dimension, the gift was not part of a quasi-natural system that appeared to lie beyond the control of agents, and thus the commensurability needed was between the agents rather than the things. To put this another way and avoid confusion, shells in Melanesia were forms of currency (so too are pigs and plumes), but they were never money—not at least until they encountered the Western money form.

The dual character of the commodity in capitalist societies insures that money will have a dual character. The first is money in its concrete or practical form. The meanings and uses of money in its concrete guise are determined by the concepts, institutions, and ideology of specific societies. On these grounds, the various capitalist societies of the West will imbue "their" money (dollars, francs, lira, etc.) with their own social meanings, functions, and values. So Zelizer (1994) argues that there are numerous kinds of currency in use in the United States (paychecks, food stamps, gold coins, etc.) and that the meanings and uses of a currency are inseparable from the social history of the nation. This means that money is not as advertised. It is nowhere near as homogeneous, liquid, fungible, or lacking in sociocultural qualities as purely economic stances make it out to be. Certainly, one of the defects of the ethnography of money is that, influenced by formal economic theory, it has too often assumed that there is a dichotomy between primitive and modern monies because the latter has been freed from its social moorings. The notion is that, released from the fetters of spheres of exchange and ritual control, the economy of the gift and the politics of compensation, capitalist money can function as a universal medium of commodity circulation. This image buys into a Western theoretical ideology of money, not least by shutting its eyes to the reality that, at the existential level, both money and shells have numerous (though, of course, different and differently constituted) social, socially defined uses and meanings (Parry and Bloch 1989). On this level, there is a family resemblance between money and shells. Indeed, an economistic view of money aside, the Westerners who approached the Maring always assumed that money had a social calling. By injecting money into the local economy, they thought that they were not only introducing a better lubricant for exchange, they were introducing the Maring to the moral economy of modernity. Thus, the Anglican Church ran a corresponding branch of the Bank of New South Wales as part of an effort to teach the Maring among other things how individuals could save money in their own name for future purchases. Implicated in this simple practice was an entire epistemology and economy of desire: that persons were first and foremost individuals; that they needed signs of possession, a passbook bearing their name, as part of the construction of their subjectivity; that their actions should be organized and measured against time, an indefinite time in the future when the sum of money corresponded to their material desires; and that placing it in an anonymous institution of saving, distant from one's kin and one's own nature, was a safeguard against the temptation to spend it frivolously.

The second side of money is historically specific and general to capitalism. So constituted, money is a commodity in a world of commodities (money as one type of commodity), the form of the most abstract expression of the commodity, and equally the sign of that form. These qualities allow money to mediate the relation between producers and consumers in such a way that this relation, although social at its core, takes on a quasi-objective character. And, as capitalism evolves, its abstract character comes to overshadow and inflect its existential overt social character. Money becomes progressively reified, though in a culturally/nationally specific way. A paycheck or food stamps, for example, are kinds of currency with specific social meanings and functions (they may be earmarked for certain purposes, understood as an index of industriousness or idleness, regulated by government agencies, etc.), but these overt meanings and uses are shaped by the socially mediating function of labor, which, as Postone (1993) argues, is the key defining feature of capitalism. The mystification of money goes beyond the crucial fact that money appears to have an existence (e.g., it can compound in value) independent of relations among persons. In a capitalist society, money thus has two features: it is produced, historically and culturally, in a concrete and abstract form; and its abstract form appears so natural and transhistorical that its concrete form appears to be an extrinsic aspect of money. The ethnographic goal is thus to grasp how the social meanings ascribed by Maring to Western money intersected with the social meanings of pearlshells, and how the gradual infiltration of money into their economy helped to engender a gap between the concrete and abstract dimensions of the objects of local exchange, especially money.

The Social History of Money

Let us take as a given, because the elders and ancestors say so, that gifts of shells were vital to those exchanges that create sociality (LiPuma 1981). Their exchange mediated key relations of social reproduction, particularly marriage, and they thus stood as tokens of these relationships. The most valuable shells, bestowed with proper names, objectified relations between clans and served as a memory of the embodiment of commitment toward others. Given their centrality in the orbit of social relations, the question is why people's confidence in the indigenous media evaporated; why, within two decades of intermittent contact, did pearlshells all but disappear in bridewealth payments? Why, generally, do people give up the given for the unknown?—assuming of course that we refuse to imagine there is that wonderful little soul, the rational economic manchild, peering out from inside of each Maring and spurring them to embrace the greater, transparent efficiency of Western money. Indeed, in the eye of the Australian administration as well as the expatriate population, a battle raged across Melanesia between that universal human instinct to act rationally and the veil of culture that could easily lead to irrational behavior, explicitly between the adoption of money or the continued use of shells. On this score, the Maring deserved a round of applause, if only the authorities knew.

Objects of exchange did not comprise a homogeneous or unified field within which there is "free" convertibility. Until the mid-1960s, pigs and pearlshells were the two most critical objects in a special category of goods called *mungoi* (LiPuma 1981:271). The things of this category had cultural preeminence because they were not merely consumable but reproductive goods; people identified them with the clan and subclan, and used them to sustain those relations deemed necessary to social reproduction. However close the parity between pigs and pearlshells, however much they were implicated in the same sphere of exchange, they had radically different fates in the modern era. Pigs became increasingly significant in all forms of compensation while pearlshells all but disappeared. Even when a small number were included, this was done for the benefit of the "old men out of respect for their sorrow about the past"—that is, as a nostalgia deep enough to serve as an emotional touchstone for a distinction between kastam and modernity.

Prior to the European infiltration into the Highlands, circa 1930, pearlshells in the Jimi and Simbai Valley were scarce, their scarcity imbuing them with power. Possession of a named shell was an index of the extraordinary man; the big-man who had the charisma, magic, and extralocal relations to attract or pull the rare shell. The shells were exemplars of externality, of the passage of things across frontiers from an alien unknown and other into the heart of culture. In the Maring's own comparative discourse, there existed clear and telling differences in thought and practice between them and all other peoples. They embodied this in the symbolically charged opposition between the cultural, domesticated world of the inside, and the untamed, mysterious, world of the outside. At the same time, however, the flow of shells across borders was grounded in exchange relations and thus presupposed a certain sameness and sociality, the communication of intentionality across the frontier. So defined, the pearlshell was a kind of indigenous fetish because it combined the categorically opposing values of sameness and difference, and because it simultaneously expressed and veiled both of those values. The shells were obtained from (I want to emphasize the term) *exchange partners,* even as their exotic, alien qualities conveyed "a magical aura of beauty, power, and mystery" (A. Strathern 1996:1). However, and this is the heart of the difference between money and pearlshells, commodities and gifts, the fetish was never itself fetishized. The ontological forms, such as exchange, that underwrote social practices, such as trading for pearlshells, were always understood in terms of overt, personified, social relations rather than as the naturalized categories, such as those intrinsic to capitalism.

Beginning in the 1930s, the flow of Australian colonists into the central Highlands dramatically, though indirectly, altered the availability of shells in the Maring area. The colonists injected an extraordinary number of new shells into the Hagen region to pay for local goods and labor. These shells then filtered through the trading routes to the Maring region where they led to an inflation of exchange rates. During this period, from the late 1930s until the early 1960s, shells that the Europeans used as commodities, as a species of money, were absorbed into the local economy as wealth objects. The onset of shell inflation started to chip away at its indexical force: the practice of naming shells died, the frequency and number of shells in wealth payments spiraled upward (from one to several dozen), causing a certain indeterminacy in their value as signifiers of extraordinary relations. There evolved a kind of struggle between those who, having shells for the first time after a life of unfulfilled longing, wanted the pearlshell to retain its customary value, and the entropic forces of the social economy that dissipated its value.

But the turbulence engendered by the flood of new pearlshells paled before the next phase of contact. Beginning in the mid-1960s, money, first shillings and pounds and then dollars, began to enter the local economy. The Maring obtained Western money via contract labor on coastal plantations, working for the Anglican mission and visiting ethnographers (of which there were thirteen over a twelve-year period), panning for gold, and the sale of coffee beans grown on the steep and shaded slopes of the hillsides. By the birth of the 1970s, those clan clusters located in proximity to Western outposts had all but replaced shells with money in bridewealth and homicide compensations. A new regime of values was evolving. Now compensation payments would revolve entirely around pigs and money, with pearlshells defined exclusively as body decoration to be used when a kaiko or dance was held. The value of shells fell in local eyes, and many were sold to Westerners of all stripes, the greatest number purchased by the Anglican mission that then resold them to a retail outlet for tribal arts in Port Moresby. By 1980, in what was surely an ironic turn, the number of shells in the Jimi Valley returned to near precontact levels. But few people, save perhaps the ethnographers, took much notice.

Pigs, Pearlshells, and Modernity

The receptivity of the Maring to Western money was part and product of a more global transformation in their social life, not least being a reformation of their worldview. The Maring came to imagine a radical break between the time of kastam and the modern economy. They re-presented their past as a time in which people were limited to subsistence goods and there were periodic bouts of hunger in the rainy months between the planting and the first harvest. In particular, men's garden work, felling the trees and clearing other secondary growth, had been much more difficult without the aid of steel axes. Ignorant of money, every critical compensation implicated only pearlshells and pigs. Where capitalism produced a carnival of goods, the older economy was defined at every turn by its limitations, limitations that only seem so, of course, in the perfect hindsight of the present. As was pointed out repeatedly to me, in times past everyone was the same, and the demand for conformity guaranteed that what was inevitable would happen. If in the rare instance, a man distinguished himself by acts of production and accumulations that appeared ostentatious, no doubt as much by good fortune as by good effort, he was likely to be accused of sorcery not because anyone imagined that there was a direct connection between the number of pigs someone owned and the spells said against some intended victim, but because anyone who would dare to express their individuality in public would surely also do it in secret.

Implicit in the antinomy between the time of custom and the advent of bisnis was a relativization of the economy into those practices and perspectives that are good and hence should be advanced into the future; those aspects of custom that require recalibration; and those practices and perspectives, objects and places, that do not appear to be contemporaneous with themselves, "survivals" like fight stones, pearlshells, sacred groves, plus the dispositions of senior clansmen. The metamorphosis from shells to money was viewed as an index of a transition to a new concept of the past, a past that is no longer desirably reproduced in the present, but rather conceptualized as divided from it. It is the construction of the past as a symbolic resource that agents can invoke and deploy for the making of the present.

The other side of the invention of a past was an unqualified leap into the modern, and on this side of the break in the world few things were as salient as money. In short order, a number of social functions accrued to money. Its possession and use became an index of modernity, the objectification of the subject who had recalibrated his relationship to tradition. Part of the power of money, as with pearlshells, derived from its externality, but now this power was magnified by the manifest power of its source: the Westerners who had conquered the Maring and whose ability to pull goods appeared limitless. In this regard, money also allowed its owners to purchase imported goods, especially foods like rice and tinned meats that people conceptualized and served as the modern equivalents of taro and pork. Money was the only means by which people could buy those foods that would permit them to embody the modern even as its consumption signified their modernity.

As Strathern (1996) indicates for the Melpa, there is a set of generational issues sparked by the introduction of money. Not the least of these is that, in contrast to pearlshells, which were obtained through affinal linkages and exchange partners, money was "won" through the sale of coffee and the genre of labor performed by young men. Employees at the Anglican mission station, orderlies in the hospital, the manager and clerks at the trade store, teachers at the school, assistant station manager, all were required to have fluency in pidgin, some knowledge of English, as well as basic skills in the arts of writing and arithmetic. What separated the up-and-coming generation was that their dispositions and attitudes, perceptions of the world and the West (that is their habitus) had been shaped by an objective structure inflected by school lessons about money, calls for tithing by the Anglican mission, wage labor, cash cropping, and state production of a national currency, all of which were unknown to their parents and grandparents. So a central feature of the reshaping of their senses was a growing sensibility toward money—money as an object of desire and a means to status that dislodges the production and efficacy of exchange networks. As the manager of the trade store at Koinambe explained, "Men like my fathers need to make exchange partners because they don't make money; when I need something all I have to do is buy it."

This statement was a slight exaggeration in that his fathers' generation did indeed find a way to attract money, mainly through a restructuring of the domestic economy. Their ability to "pull" money lay primarily in their control over land and domestic labor, meaning that they could place garden lands into coffee production and increase the production of piglets that they could then sell for cash. The senior generation also extracted money from the junior generation, though this would increasingly become a bone of contention, the young generation asking why they should "back" those whose aims and ambitions were no longer in tune with the times. More than simply access to money, what separated the generations was their disposition toward its use, the senior generation treating it like a valuable that should be reserved for special occasions whereas their children used it to satisfy small, immediate, and personal desires. On the side of production, the senior generation seemed unable to grasp the spirit of calculation required to run a trade store. The acquisition and use of money was thus at the core of the growing rift between generations.

The most telling difference between pigs and pearlshells was that people raise pigs on their home territories or that of their affines. Pigs embody the mixed labor of both sexes and hence were signs of their complementary role in the reproduction of the clan and subclan. In acts of exchange, pigs mediated the relationship between husband and wife as much as they mediated the relationship between donor and recipient. The Maring, like other Highlanders, expressly connect pigs to specific localities, lands that were the material representation of lineality. Further, the compensation of pork was thought to replenish male grease (*imbana*), which in turn advanced the continuity of a male substance (LiPuma 1978:76) that defined clanship itself. The representational value of pigs thus centered on interiority and identity formation, relations that were the opposite of those representable by pearlshells or money.

But pearlshells, of course, neither disappeared entirely nor lost all of their symbolic potency. Rather, pearlshells were now confined to the ceremonial arena—primarily the kaiko—where they were valued because they shine like well-greased skin, the quality of a person's skin—its smoothness, gloss, and color—being a mirror of strength and vitality. The relocation of pearlshells to contexts that were themselves hallmarks of tradition brought a new semiotic politics into existence. Indeed, a symbolic opposition was quick to emerge between pearlshells and money in which the former was associated with kastam, interiority, and local identity while money became emblematic of modernity, exteriority, bisnis, and the emergence of a national identity. The representational value and force of the pearlshell transformed from being a signifier of the outside, of indigenous but not Maring society, to being a primary signifier of the inside and interiority, now mapped as the kastam world of Papua New Guineans versus the modern world of Westerners. In this relocation of value, the opposition between money and the pearlshell was mediated by pigs, the kastam inside value that has become modern.

Moses and the Commandment of Profit

Other than the trade store run by the Anglican mission there was only one successful, locally owned and operated store in the Jimi and Simbai Valleys. The trade store was founded and directed by one of the first young men to attend high school, gain fluency in English, see himself as a devout Christian, and more generally approximate the dispositions of the Western capitalist. Critical to the success and longevity of his store was his perspective and attitude toward money. Here is an excerpt from a conversation I had with Moses in which he discussed (in English salted with some pidgin) his views about business and money.

> Money is different from anything we [the Maring people generally and his clan members more specifically] have known about in the past. Because it is part of bisnis [Tok Pisin], money is meant to be saved and used to allow the business to grow. When anyone comes to the trade store they pay in cash even if they are one of my fathers or brothers. I have made it clear to everyone that it is wrong to extend credit—to allow someone to have something without paying for it immediately. This is how people did things in the past and it is okay if all we are doing is exchanging things with one another. This is not right for bisnis however. Some clanspeople are resentful and jealous about my store [its success] and say that I am greedy and selfish; but I tell them that their stores fizzle out because they don't know how to manage money. Money is not something that we can just give away freely like it was sugarcane or sweet potato. Money has power inside of it; you know that but people here do not grasp that yet. They still concentrate on pigs when they should be learning to focus on money as this is the basis of our development as a people. The right use of profit is to replant it [in the store] so that the bisnis will grow straight. To go on the "new road" is to use money all the time.

I have quoted Moses at length because he not only understood that money was the icon of the modern and a repository and index of wealth; he understood money as capital to be reinvested again and again in an increasing spiral of accumulation and growth. Whereas in an earlier time, the Maring treated money exclusively as a form of wealth—they did not imagine it as a factor of production—here Moses expressly makes the connection. Beyond that, he sees himself as a prophet of the modern whose mission (in his drive to develop his store) was to convince others that money was first of all capital to be ploughed back into the bisnis. His argument, repeated time and again to his clansmen who were shareholders in the trade store, was that neither the goods for sale nor the profits generated could be treated as though they were part of the indigenous exchange system. In this logic, the trade store, as a dimension of modern bisnis, was a new context for the production of sociality in that money should mediate every transaction, regardless of the kinship of the agents involved. What in other more traditional contexts would be a gift was here reclassified as "credit"; Moses, parroting the credo of the mission store, held that no one would be extended credit. This viewpoint also called forth a new logic of desire, Moses defining his refusal to share the store's goods and profits as a virtue. There were those kin who desired him to act according to traditional canons of redistribution and share his good fortune, to which Moses answered that they were smitten with jealousy and ignorant of how things are done in the age of development.

Fluent in English, a high school graduate, a devout Anglican and a successful businessman, certainly one of the leading figures of his generation, a rising star in the largest and most prominent subclan of the largest and most influential clan, Moses was tapped by the Anglican mission in 1980 to become the station manager at Koinambe. Father Bailey, the priest in charge who chose Moses for the post, explained to me that the mission station was, in his own words, "a complex financial business," and Moses understood money. The good father was at least and decidedly right on the last point (church finances being more discombobulated than complex). The local perception flowered that Moses, and a handful of other young men like him, had acquired the special knowledge of things Western, and this led their image of money and bisnis to become culturally canonized as the correct and modern view (see MacLean 1984:336–67 for some other examples). Moses understood modernity as entailing and requiring a new species of knowledge, a view shared by most of his generation, even if they were not always able to articulate it in concrete images. This was not the case for Moses, however, who put it this way:

> To know how to make exchanges, to give women, pigs, and pearlshells to other clansmen, requires *nomane* [the wisdom, social insight, and culture of the ancestor spirits that is transmitted to their descendants; in this respect, nomane announces the relationship between the living community and its ancestors]. To be good in bisnis, however, requires *save* [Tok Pijin]. If a person lacks save, he won't know how to buy and sell things in Hagen or how to use money. [In this regard, save defines and mediates the relationship between indigenous agents and the forms of Western knowledge that would enable local agents.] It takes save to

use money, which is why those of the senior generation—men who have plenty of nomane—often do not know how money works: they only know how to "line" the money [a patterned, public display mostly of two-kina notes] when people give bride wealth and the death payment. The people who are successful in bisnis have learned to think of money and to use it exactly as white people do. In the future, this will be the cause of our success. The people will realize that once they win money, they can get anything they desire—in places like Port Moresby even girls to go with you. You know that I'm an Anglican and don't do things like that, but there is no reason not to buy clothes, food, cigarettes, and . . . Believing in Jesus and learning to use money to make bisnis are what will allow us to develop ourselves.

These remarkable and perceptive comments, made but a quarter century after contact, contain a whole and novel worldview about the interconnections between people and money, the Maring and the West. The view spoken here is that to understand money as wealth is consistent with custom and by inference the use of pearlshells and other indigenous objects of trade. In turn, knowing how to operate in this context requires nomane, the customary form of knowledge. By clear contrast, to understand money as capital and to know how to use money to make money requires save—the Western form of knowing and knowledge. Embodied in this understanding is a set of dispositions about money, dispositions shared by most of Moses' generation. Indeed, the junior generation's take on money was one of the things that engendered and defined its distance from older generations. As revealed in Moses' remarks, this generation saw money not only as a lubricant of exchange, but as a technology of power that enabled its holder to engage and control the forces of modernity. Knowing about money was bisnis by the same name, and bisnis was the heart of local development. "Anything concerning money is bisnis" was a common sentiment, true because any practice that entailed the flow of money, be it bride payment or the sale of a pig, involved that commodity that can be exchanged for all other Western commodities. The picture Moses drew was also of a racially coded epistemology in which whites understand money in contrast to blacks who do not, and learning how to use money is the main key to local development, that is, acquiring the know-how to imitate the behavior of whites. In marked contrast to the senior generation, Moses's cohort did not believe that Westerners possess a magical and by inference secret knowledge. Having gone to school— where one of the primary goals was to "demystify" local notions of where Western goods and money came from, mainly through a lesson based on the mystified version of how Western goods are produced and circulated—

this generation was beginning to understand that the West dominates others less by hiding knowledge from them (although this is surely sometimes the case) than by inducing them to accept public knowledge about the nature of social reality. Part of this reality of money was that one can exchange it not only for goods or for help (in tending to a coffee plot, in carrying goods from the mission airfield to the village, etc.), but also for sex and the company of women. Money can be exchanged for a relationship that was formerly well beyond the compass of interpersonal exchange, never mind bisnis. So the double understanding—embodied in Moses' remarks as well as those of other men who had visited Port Moresby—was that people would do things for and with money that they would never do with customary objects of exchange, and that Western money had the ability to do things and "pull" others in ways that kastam objects did not and could not. To put this another way, men like Moses were beginning to inhabit an objective world and to have subjective dispositions toward that world that engendered a space between the concrete and abstract aspects of the money form. There has been a progressive layering of meaning: Moses and his generation have begun to grasp money not only as an index of modernity and a store of wealth but as capital.

Plantation Labor and Worker Experience

The Maring introduction to the Western world and structure of labor had its genesis in sojourns to mostly coastal plantations. These stays were valued, indeed they served as forms of initiation ceremonies into the modern, because they offered young men the opportunity for freedom, a temporary respite from the structured, overpowering demands of kinship and community. The potential to earn money for their bridewealth payment was also enticing, and senior clansmen encouraged them on these grounds. The plantation was time out of time, and space out of space. The plantation system enslaved workers to the clock, to specified hours of work whose rhythm and intensity had no comparable indigenous form. While the plantation itself conjured the sensations of independence, the work itself could not have been done under conditions of less autonomy. An overseer, sometimes aided by a *bosboi* (a local second in command), would cajole, threaten, beat, and bribe the young men to "put up a proper day's work" for their pay. The days were predictable, long, and grueling, the nights and Sundays animated by the tensions, solidarities, and violence of an interethnic, all male, spatially displaced community.

The plantation was a halfway house between two forms of labor. It differed from rural domestic production in that workers did not produce goods for themselves but exclusively for others. Especially in the early days, the Maring frequently assumed that it was the plantation manager who was the other they were producing for, as opposed to a market. This view served to imitate domestic production in that it personalized the object of production as, for example, when helping a kinsman or big-man. Given their instilled beliefs and dispositions, the young workers sought continually to draw plantation labor into a domestic orbit of meaning, to make it intelligible by locating it within a known landscape of values. The tendency was to conceptualize the food and shelter, the nurturing given by the manager, as the exchange for the labor they proffered. The workers' appreciation of the provisioning of food and shelter sailed a world apart from the business and its managers, as part of the wages and costs of production. Until independence, the fact that the company held the workers' money for them, paying them only when they were about to return home, further masked their actual location in the panorama of capitalist production. After independence, many of the plantations, as well as the more overtly commercial forms of work, began to pay people wages in a regular fashion. And several men of the junior generation opened businesses that compelled them to buy supplies and arrange transport by plane and truck from Western-run enterprises. In these forums, the Maring got an initial taste of what it was like to inhabit a society in which agents do not acquire the products of others through the sociality of kinship and community, but through the sale of their own labor, independent and abstracted of its concrete content (Postone 1993:149–50). The situationally specific character of the encounter shielded the Maring from the direct hand of the logic of capitalism. Nonetheless, these openings, grasped by the junior generation as forms of independence in a kinship-constrained world, bore that special trademark of capitalism: the exhilaration of subjective independence within the grip of increasing objective dependence on a system whose reproduction depended on a relaxation of consciousness. What makes laboring for wages and money critical is that they have been the hybrid and mediating forms in an economic field that they are partly responsible for creating.

Monetizing Agency and the World

The inflow of Western money into the Maring universe, and its absorption into local practices, have animated processes that are as transformative as they are incremental, embedded in the feature of everyday routines, and easy to misrecognize. For Maring as for other Highlands peoples, these processes are founded in the advent of the commodity form as both an index and virtue of modernity, as an imagined key to Western economic and political power over local practices. More than a carnival, capitalism brings a profusion of goods, from food to guns, that enhance the possibilities of power over a future defined by a Western world that is itself defined by commodities. And, for the Maring, no object represents the coming-to-be-understood commodity more than money. The commodity was also instrumental in the advance of Western epistemology, especially in the case of money. Of all the commodities, it stands in the most abstract relationship to time and labor. The introduction of Western money and what, in contrast to traditional money, can only be purchased with money (e.g., goods at the mission trade store) has also reorganized the terms of desire. Where the use of pearlshell was limited to specific contexts of exchange, where the pearlshell was invested with social relations (certain shells even had their own names), money has a much broader set of uses and more easily becomes detached from social relations (not, as the case of Moses illustrated, as some "natural" property of money but as part of a culture of use learned in their encounters with the agents of modernity such as ethnographers and missionaries). The appearance of money also created new situations and terms for the exercise of judgment about the production of values and meanings. In a total sense, the infiltration of the Western money form, by transforming the ground of people's beliefs, desires, and judgments, gradually and imperceptibly helps to shape the conditions for the production of intentionality and subjectivity. Thus the ethnography suggests that an understanding of the meaning and value of "local" money is intrinsically tied to an understanding of the culture and progress of modernity.

What emerges from the steady infiltration of Western money is a quasi-Western money form. This money form begins its local life history imbued with little formal, commodity value, but a plethora of social meanings whose center of gravity was the alterity between the Maring and the foreign other, and the local vision of the road to modernity. In the inscription of social meanings, the hybrid form resembled its Western counterpart, though these meanings were, of course, specific to the Maring. Money is a privileged index of modernity precisely because its socially signifying values are left open. The Westerners who introduced the currency assumed, following the tenets of their own commodity-driven ideology, that the social meanings of money are epiphenomenal and that its economic function is transparent. In the first rush of contact, then, money appeared as an empty signifier, a form devoid of intended effect: it was not a prayer designed to salvage the soul, or a food to strengthen the body, or clothes to shelter the self from the elements and eyes of others. In this respect, the social representational value of the Western money form became synonymous with modernity itself: use of pounds, dollars, and kina signifying the modernity of those who use them. For Westerners as well as Maring, the adoption of money was interpreted as an omen of progress.

But, historically, this was only the initial moment of what is a longer and more mediated process. Over time, the social meaning and morality of money would become more nuanced. By the early 1980s, the once positive, almost millenarian imagery had become colored with negative tonalities. More than pigs, pearlshells, or plumes, money was easier to conceal, and especially in conjunction with the adoption of individual family dwellings, appeared to encourage a philosophy of concealment. Not only did the physical properties of money—small, lightweight, paper—allow it to be hidden, but the Western enclave seemed to condone its concealment. The height of hiddenness was the passbook account at the local bank at Koinambe, the priest who managed the corresponding branch of the bank of New South Wales refusing, when asked by a person's kin, to divulge how much money that person had on deposit, citing "confidentiality" as an inviolate Western value and rule. In this way, everything, from changes in housing styles to the advent of money and the practices of the Anglican mission, allowed the flowering of inequalities, of forms of selfish and possessive individualism that always, even in the precontact era, people imagined lurked beneath the surface or "skin" of human behavior and intentionality, but could now be expressed more openly as practical and increasingly legitimate action. From a complementary angle, the generation then coming of age began to question why "white" people seemed to have the money, and to look at this disparity as an index of tangible inequalities of power, inequalities that seemed to be out of step with the rise of the nation and the emergence of a government run by "black" men. Whereas in the 1950s and 1960s, money was an unconditionally "good thing," by the late 1970s people began to grasp money as something that could also undermine and destroy—as harboring an element of evil, a sentiment that was, incidentally, echoed in the sermons of mission men.

As money slowly but surely penetrated the Maring universe and people discovered ways of obtaining it, the commodity character of money began to take hold. At the heart of this experience was the slowly evolving realization that their relationship to others need not be mediated by sociality—that is, overt relations of clanship, affinity, or enmity—but could be mediated by their willingness to sell their labor and goods created from that labor in exchange for money. Particularly for the younger generation and, especially for those who had attended the mission school, the possession of money began to emerge as an end in itself, an objective whose touchstone was the growing but secretive bank account. This generation began to incorporate the ownership of money into its image and construction of the person. In everyday speech, they began to extend terms of derision such as "rubbish man" to include individuals who had little money or potential access. People's conception of land and their perception of its worth also began to change. Land that was suitable for coffee-producing or panning for gold so soared in value that clansmen began to fight for rights over formerly unused (in the case of coffee) or unusable (in the case of gold) plots of land, this friction inspired by their desire to "win" money.

Not the least of the effects of money was that it changed the conditions for the nature and expression of agency. Traditionally, the power of a person was manifest through their ability to "pull" or influence the behavior/intentions of others and the ability to perform sorcery/magic. The first was exhibited most in the actions of big-men (and, more dramatically and marginally, "wild-men"), the second in the performance of shamans and more marginally sorcerers. Traditionally, these also represented the limited circumstance for expression of "individuality" in a relationally dominated society. The appearance of money engendered both an externalization of power in that the ability to influence others turns on a person's access to money, and a leveling of power inasmuch as more and more people have access to sources of money wealth. Those who have money have power analogous to big-men, shamans, and sorcerers. So it was that the influx of money into the Maring region added a new dimension to the production of big-man status and complemented the increasing use of sorcery.

This observation flies in the face of accounts that presume the opposition and exclusivity between Capitalism (with a large C) and principles of the traditional economy. The basic understanding is that capitalism universally operates in terms of markets, economic maximization, and the accumulation of personal wealth (principally in the money form). The traditional economy is conversely founded on reciprocity organized around forms of kinship and interpersonal domination. The problem with this view and the primary reason why it fails ethnographically, even for the West, is that it separates production from culture. The idea is that the market and class are the forms of organization that flow from capitalist relations of production whereas kinship, ritual, and community are the forms of human organization generated by culture. Unfortunately, within this framework, there is no way to account for differences between capitalist "societies" because the market, value, labor, and money are assumed to be transhistorical and transcultural categories—to be, in other words, external to culture. When transposed to Melanesia, this viewpoint makes it impossible to grasp the evolution and trajectory of these societies because it is precisely the internal and intrinsic connection between capitalist production and culture that determines their movement historically. Yes, it is true that capitalism preempts and subsumes social relations based on kinship and community, but it necessarily does so in a partial and social-historically specific manner. This is a theoretical way of saying that not only does the integration of Others not entail uniformity or even harmony, but by its very nature it engenders variability and disharmonic relations that are themselves determinant features of encompassment. This last point requires us to observe and honor the differences between Melanesia and the West because these differences are, rather ironically, the basis of their now inseparable, intertwined histories.

CHAPTER 7

The Magic of the Evangelical

Close in the tracks of the kiaps were the missionaries who, in the mid-1950s, saw the Simbai and Jimi Valleys as twice virgin terrain. Through their eyes, its people were innocent of Jesus and the message of his gospel. They needed to be awakened from their cultural and moral slumber, to be given the chance at redemption that is every human's birthright, by being introduced to the Good News. So, propelled by the canons of their ideology, the missionaries sought to "save" the Maring by introducing them to Christ's message. The encounter between the Church and local peoples could not be but evangelical. For the defining goal was always to entice, wean, and save the Maring from the paganism of their ancestors. Father Patrick Murphy, a noted missionary and evangelist, and an intellectual mentor to several of the priests who worked among the Maring, explains:

> This Gospel message is necessary. It is unique. There is no other gospel. It does not permit indifference, syncretism or accommodation [because] it is a question of people's salvation. (1976:2)

All that was wanting was the faith, perseverance, and surrender to God's will to preach the gospel that "by itself [could] stir up faith" (2). For the community of the evangelical willing to give up the comforts of a parish in the metropole, the Maring had souls that were waiting, and unknowingly wanting, to witness the grace of Jesus' message. In the hearts of the missionaries, they were making a sacrifice out of their love for God and their fellow man, and they were doing so on the conviction that all of God's children should have a chance to at least hear what He has to say. Those who had tasted the word of God had the obligation to preach that word—an obligation that defined for them what it was to be a good Christian. The missionaries believed that they were humble servants of God, minor though devoted messengers, in an undertaking that was beyond their ken to comprehend, question, or inject their own desires. More than anything else, Melanesia was a canvas on which they could save the souls of others while redeeming their own.

In the mid-1950s, the Maring terrain was also as virgin as much of its forest because it was open to all and any sects, and so there was a scramble to quickly plant a mission before rivals appeared on the scene. Animated by this silent incentive, which was only acknowledged in a curt and slightly embarrassed way (to be competing for souls as though they were trophies did not seem very Christlike), the Anglicans set up claims in the Simbai and Jimi Valleys literally months after the first government patrols swept these areas. Though it was taboo to exhibit too much of a competitive spirit, the Anglicans were conscious of the Lutheran mission and even more so of the Roman Catholics who were anxious to found a mission outpost at Ambulla (see map 2, chap. 1) in the eastern reaches of the Jimi. The trick was to negotiate a choice site, meaning a venue with enough level ground to support an airfield. There was one (and probably only one) such venue in the western Jimi on the western edge of Cenda land. So the Anglican Church quickly and quietly "purchased" (or so it thought) a patch of land from the Cenda—a "sleight of land" that was to prove troublesome when, twenty years down the modern road, the Cenda, their population swelling, demanded that the Anglican mission return their land.[1] Thus the Anglican mission among the Maring was born in what was the first but certainly not last misunderstanding.

The second moment was a magnificent trope and living symbol of what was to come—at least from the Christian perspective. In 1966, the Bible translators, the Woodwards, heard word that a Kauwatyi woman had given birth to fraternal twins. They also heard that, bewitched by superstition and fear, she contemplated infanticide for the smallest, a girl who would later be called Megan. So the missionaries stepped into the breach to save a "child of God," to accrue His grace on the road to redemption, and to teach the spirit of Christianity by example to the pagan soul. They "adopted" the young black girl and raised her as a white Christian Australian, periodically bringing her back to Koinambe so that the indigenous world might see what had become of her as a result of Western training and values. And, for the Woodwards, what was almost as tragic and barbaric as the willingness to commit infanticide was that Megan's birth mother demanded compensation—and received a small award after a protracted struggle. For the mission men, charity of this magnitude, living proof that Christ could implant a white soul and civilization within a black Melanesian body, would help deliver the Maring from the sins of superstition and false idols. Megan would be the most modern Maring and the West's most indigenous Christian emissary—if only our Lord in the person of her adopted parents could convince her that her best days lay in the hinterlands of the Bismarck mountains. Not the usual choice for a vibrant Australian girl.

In the Throes of the Evangelical

Although Pax vobiscum followed closely on the heels of Pax Britannica, and the literature on religion in Melanesia is large and growing, there are few analyses of the evangelical encounter and even fewer of its epistemological resonances. Until recently the stage had been cleared to entertain the form and function of indigenous belief systems.[2] Nevertheless, there is little doubt that Christianity, in all its many versions, has been a profound agent of transformation. From the national to local level, from towns to hinterlands, the influence of the Church is deeply felt. However influential, an ethnography of their missions remains in its infancy, Mary Huber's historical ethnography of the Catholic missionary experience on the Sepik (1988) being an exception and an ignored pioneering study. Most of the accounts penned by the missionaries themselves, increasingly in a quasi-anthropological vein, are remarkably sterile given the vibrancy of the interplay between Westerners and Melanesians. It is as though the mission men are so absorbed in converting people that they cannot reflect on the lives of the Melanesians or the character of the encounter.[3] For the most part, ethnographers have sought to bracket the effects of the Christianizing missions. The silent command inscribed in my (as well as others') upbringing as an ethnographer was to look beneath the waves of evangelically inspired changes to the older more profound waters of precontact culture. The result is that in my previous studies I placed the relation between the mission and the Maring in parentheses. The usual Melanesianist strategy has been to quickly note the presence of a Christian mission (or missions) in an early chapter of the monograph and then to refer to its effects on local practices in an ad hoc manner throughout the remainder of the text. It would be unfair to single out any particular ethnographers, as the omission of the missions was our collective perspective. But as Paul said in one of his epistles to the Corinthians, however much we may have sinned collectively we are responsible singularly; and all that is needed to set us on a better course is to see a sign. The rapid encompassment of Melanesia should be a sign that the time has come to make amends by writing a richer ethnography of the Christian missions. It is no slip of civility that the preface of almost every ethnography of Melanesia thanks some Christian missionary.

The result is that anthropology has not dealt with the complexity of missionization in the context of an encompassing process of which anthropology is itself a part. There is little discussion of the epistemology and perspectives of the clergy, although they are identified as critical agents of colonialism. Also missing is any word about the relationship between the churches and the state, though we know that as early as 1956, Peter Hasluck, the minister for territories, argued that an explicit objective of the Australian administration should be to replace pagan belief and ritual with the Christian faith (Hasluck 1956). There is equally little analysis of the relation between fieldworkers and Christian missionaries, either from the viewpoint of these agents or from that of Melanesians. What needs to be said is that the influence of missionaries lies in the fact that their civilizing mission, everything that passes as the process of conversion, is simultaneously pragmatic and symbolic. It involves the provision of foods that have come to represent the new road (fish and rice), education at the mission school, and hospital services, plus the inculcation of a set of symbols, epistemological concepts, and desires. Moreover, the civilizing mission was and is simultaneously theological and cultural, at times holding fast to Christian doctrines, at times tempering their message to fit Melanesian culture. Certainly it is in the signifying side of Christian practice—usually mundane material and everyday practice—that we begin to grasp the cultural agency of missionaries: how it is that the clergy, far from home, often on the nether side of social insight, preoccupied with its own internal machinations, helped to animate far-reaching social and political transformations (see Comaroff and Comaroff 1991:9).

As is always the case in ethnography, there are some critical exceptions that nurture the redirection of ethnography. These begin with Mary Huber's pioneering, though largely ignored, study of the experience of the Catholic mission on the Sepik (1988). Against the gravity of its own tradition, recent sparks of ethnography have begun to focus on the dialectical history of Christian missions in a Melanesian world. The writings of Gewertz and Errington (1991), Clark (1989), Young (1989), Barker (1990), and others have underlined three themes mirrored in the waters of Maring ethnography. The first is that Melanesian peoples often self-represent the coming of the mission as the dawning of a new form of society—as a kind of total and world reforming passage from a "traditional" moral polity to its modern one. A second theme is that the influence of the missions on local lifeways stems more from the shape, delivery, and persistence of the conversation than from the substance of the message itself. The Melanesian spin on the Christian message—a message that was coded in English and couched in metaphors and tropes indigenous to the West (e.g, parable), usually made it say both more and less than the church men ever intended. And finally, these accounts illustrate that the missions' encounter with Melanesians indigenized the churches in more ways than they could foresee, conceive, or admit.

While the missionaries imagined they were turning heathens into Christians and the Maring themselves imagined a great break between their heathen past and Christian future, the reality was more complex on both sides. On the Maring side of the encounter, conversion to Christianity was never a wholesale displacement of one religion by another. It is not just that indigenous beliefs and practices could not be fully laid aside and reappeared under the Christian label (such as food taboos), but that the character of Christianity—the forms of epistemology, desire, and interest it promoted—contributed to the efflorescence of certain heathen practices, the most notable and paradoxical of which was sorcery whose incidence increased dramatically with modernity. Moreover and predictably, the Maring could not but view modernity through the prism of indigenous categories. The meaning of Christianity and figure of Jesus necessarily unfolded against the meaning and memory of ancestor worship. Maring Christianity, if that is the proper term, is thus invariably a complex and evolving synthesis, a domestication and imbrication of indigenous and imported forms. This truism of the religious transformation of others merits underlining because the Maring contextually and the missionaries habitually operated in terms of an ideology of replacement: the view that Christian practices and morality would simply take the place of customary ones as the Maring people evolved toward the modern.

On the Western side of the encounter, the mission presented itself as offering an alternative to indigenous lifeways, the unprecedented near-miraculous appearance of a new, external source of power, control, spirituality, and meaning. Its self-image notwithstanding, the missionaries consciously and more often unconsciously modified Christianity. From the start, they tried to "strip Christianity down to its essentials"—meaning the gospel, sin, the Sacraments, and centrally, Christ as the savior of Mankind. They comforted themselves with the view that they were not denuding the Church's message, but returning to the more primitive and fundamental meaning of Jesus' gospel. But in the process, the mission men tended to emphasize those facets of Christianity that played well before their local audience. In particular, the story of Jesus as big-man and ancestor captured the Maring imagination. In their effort to get through to the Maring the churchmen could not help but become slightly more like them, a process of assimilation that took place behind their backs, so to speak. Over the years, the mission came gradually to define itself, its vision of Christianity, its success, and its promise against the Maring world. Despite an absolutist and universalist philosophy (the evangelical project driven by the belief that there is only one true religion for all Mankind), Melanesian lifeways began to color the Anglican habitus. It was especially the case that the Anglican mission had to learn about, and engage in, exchange and reciprocity, its torturous land deal with the Cenda being but one example. To be sure, the interrelations between the Maring, the mission, and the other encompassing agents and institutions were rather asymmetrical, but they were never simply a one-way street. Indeed, the secret to grasping the engagement between the Maring and the Church is to recognize that it was more the form and the delivery of the Western message than the message itself that was transformative, and that the processes of modernizing the Maring indigenized the mission in more ways than it ever knew. Or, to put this another way, in the last judgment, an anthropology of colonialism will only be as worthy as its theory of symbolic seduction.

The Mission Perceiving Itself

The missions sought to create a state of Christianity in its anticipation of the Christian state that Papua New Guinea would become (the preamble of its constitution pledges that its people will guard and pass on "our noble traditions and the Christian principles that are now ours"). Particularly in the case of the Highlands, long secluded from Western wisdoms, prone to warfare, cannibalism, and other atrocities of the human spirit, Christian missionaries felt the need to impress the word of God and story of Jesus. If people like the Maring could only hear the true word, see the power of the Almighty, and touch the Bible then they would both surrender to the will of God and will their own metamorphosis. This at least is the story the Western missionaries told themselves and taught to the indigenous clergy. The illusion and conceit was that the power of the state and its own economic power, as well as the infiltration of money and the commodification of village life, played only the most tangential role in gaining converts. This view was commanded by the nature of their cosmology, which set God apart from and above the hum of ordinary life, especially the grubby acts and avarice of seeking economic gains at others' expense. There was everything morally amiss in a world in which faith had a price; their own faith and project had no meaning if they were simply purchasing Christians like lots of sweet potatoes. So they were forced to dismiss the coupling of conversion and commodities as blasphemous, as a form of perversion that greater exposure to God's gospel and a deeper immersion in His message would eventually correct. As I and the Maring were told on more than one occasion, "It will take a long time for these people to become true Christians, but that is the job of the Church: to teach God's word till it is finally heard." Father Bailey was by no means alone in these sentiments: the missionaries understood this simply as the chorus of common sense occasioned by the tough work of planting Christian ideals in the slippery soil of heathen New Guinea.

Moved by the same spirit, the missionaries sought to write their own subjectivities out of the script by claiming that they were simply doing God's work. Hence a missionary explained, "I am not here to do what I want to do; I am here to do what God and the Church want me to." To further make the point, he added that left to his "druthers" he would try to better learn the language and be more "like an anthropologist." Another Anglican priest, this time from the Simbai station, said that his mission was to teach and convert, that he was only an instrument through which God "realized His will." Similarly, a sermon offered at a mass at St. John's Church by a visiting priest observed that the purpose of evangelicalism was not to change people but to simply open their eyes, "to let them see on their own." In this vision of themselves, the missionaries were earthly transmitters of God's message, their own culture and personal desires nothing more than a coat of many colors.

These twin views were to stand at the unreflective center of the missionary ethos: that if simply shown the light of God, the local populace would join willingly in their own conversion, and that the priest was the instrument of God whose own subjectivity was overshadowed by the sense of mission itself. In this vision, the power of the state and the capacity of the Church to attract or "pull" commodities were only the most marginal aspects of the missionizing effort. In the first thrust of contact, the ministries of both Father Peter Robin at Simbai and Father Peter Etterly at Koinambe underlined to the Maring that their primary purpose was to light the candle of Christianity, and to help them appreciate the values of the "civilized" body and soul. In working toward their own spiritual uplifting, in joining the body of the Church, the Maring would learn about and celebrate those forms of civility (such as monogamy, the renunciation of sorcery and the evil arts, mutual respect and trust among clans) that lead to a prosperous future. In this view, which members of the Church thought to be so godly and straightforward as to require little reflection and commentary, the lines of misrecognition are already visible: for the attraction of the mission from the perspective of the Maring was precisely that it was the religion of the conqueror, endowed with a mystical ability to "pull" all manner of goods, fluent in the ways of writing and air travel. The Maring and the Anglican Church struck a bargain in the clouds: in return for going along with the notions and taboos of the missionaries the Maring would (according to their ideas) receive what the missionaries defined as peripheral to their enterprise (material wealth and new forms and powers of value creation) and that, in any event, they were incapable of truly delivering. A match made in heaven. A match that would have repercussions in the years to come. All of this could come to pass only with the founding of a mission station—a base of operations called after its place name: Koinambe.

The Koinambe Mission

The mission station was a template of the western Christian enclave. The design was never a conscious undertaking on the part of its missionary builders but an expression of their habitus: the meeting ground of their vision of the rural community, their ideas of space and time, and their sense of mission. Near the middle of the Koinambe community at the top of a rise stood the house of the priest, a three-bedroom split level dwelling of Western design and materials (milled wood, plumbing, etc). At one end of the split level was a storeroom accessible by its own external door from which was run a corresponding branch of the Bank of New South Wales, a post office, and a shortwave radio station. The hope was that the availability of a bank would help the locals to learn the "art of saving" while the post office and radio station would show them the wonders of communication with other peoples. Immediately adjacent to the house was the mission trade store, and a bit further up the rise was the primary school, the houses (built in the local style and materials) of its Melanesian teachers (generally Papuan) plus a sports field. On another hillcrest across from that of the priest's house was the Western-style home of the Bible translator. In a saddle between the two rises were the airfield, the infirmary, and the Western-style house of the nurse. Interspersed throughout the settlement were small gardens planted by the Maring population (approximately 150) living there. To all of this was added the most prominent and imposing structure in the valley: the Church of Saint John.

As Father Bailey noted on more than one occasion, everything that one needed—food, shelter, medicine, schooling, and worship—was found at the mission station. True to Anglican principle, Koinambe was a self-contained unit, a kind of cultural space station exploring and civilizing the outermost reaches of the earth. It was connected to mission central by tenuous threads of communication—the wireless and the weekly air flights, both of which might be canceled by the flashing thunderstorms that swept through the valley or by the heavy blankets of fog. Each mission produced its own kind of evangelical tenor, its own religious experience. The self-containment of the mission station was a metaphor for the self-production of identity that was one of the hallmarks of the Christian bourgeois vision of the construction of the person.

In form and substance, Koinambe created and nurtured an image of power and capacity. In contrast to the dispersed compounds that characterize Maring settlements, mostly small knots of five or six households of kinsmen separated by the space of gardens and forest from like compounds, the mission was a huge conglomeration of many kinds of people who would consider living side by side in only one other context: the rite of passage of the modern era, the contract labor plantations of coastal New Guinea. Koinambe exuded a sense of the modern cross-clan, multicultural, interracial community; in spirit and substance, the epitome of the "new road" village. Thus a young Kauwatyi man, standing on the veranda of the mission trade store that he ran, swept out his arm across the

Koinambe hills and observed "that nothing like this was thinkable in the time before" when "all we knew was fighting and living in the bush, rather than how to be Christians and live together." This new world community for the Maring was also the site of economic power, as exemplified by the money in the hands of the church, the wealth of clothes and goods available, the air flights from Mt. Hagen, the opportunities for jobs for those who had finished primary school, not to mention the great comparative personal wealth of its Westerners. Koinambe also had the aura of municipal order, a regularity of planning and design, a calendrical tempo not found as such in local communities. Every morning a bell was rung at eight to signal a summons to mass, and at nine, the service completed, the trade store, school, coffee buying, and other activities would begin. Toward evening the same church bell would ring to announce the end of the business day and the call to vespers (evensong). There was lunchtime, teatime, and the weekend as time out of labor time. In contrast to the Maring, mission time was defined by Western habits and seemed to take little notice of the seasons or the rising and setting of the sun. Koinambe was run on time in every dimension of our naturalized word: time as an organizing principle of actions; time as an internal monitor of one's own acts; time as the objective regulation of one's subjectivity and internal states (such as the compulsion to finish on time); time as the measure of the worth of a person's labor. The temporal habits, dispositions, and sensibilities of the missionaries, much the product of Western culture and capitalism, could not have been in sharper contrast to the rhythms of village life. These conventions of time could not have been more naturalized, the missionaries conscious only of the fact that the locals seemed to have no respect for punctuality and deadlines. Their internal clocks seemed to have no hands. Koinambe was nothing less than a monument of sorts to the reorganizing of the time and space of a Highlands landscape according to Western views and values. Particularly from the air, when the plane banked and circled to approach for its landing, it was apparent how much the municipal orderliness of the Western mind was now literally engraved on the Maring landscape—a reality that local passengers would comment on, usually by pointing a finger at the various structures, reciting their name, and then shaking that hand in a display of astonishment.

In order for the Westerners to insure their privacy, a luxury to which they were umbilically attached, they had to practice a form of segregation. Rarely if ever were Maring invited through the front door of a Western house. Like spitting in church, there was never a sign saying "do not enter"; people simply didn't because they knew that the houses of the priest, VSO nurse, and the Bible translator were off-limits. From the missionary's position, they were merely trying to maintain a certain measure of privacy, and of sanity, in a world far from home and much more promiscuously social, a way of being uncaring in its respect for the individual. From the Maring position, by contrast, the treasuring of privacy was understood as a mark and quirk of modernity. It was a way in which people could shelter and hide what they owned and thus avoid the imperatives of reciprocity. As a young man working as an orderly at the hospital observed, "These missionaries say they are our brothers, they say the Bible says we are all brothers, but they certainly don't share like brothers. They hide their wealth behind closed doors and out of our sight." As we shall see, the notion of privacy was to become a metaphor for private property. It put a positive spin on the negative, antisocial connotations that suffused the indigenous notions of secrecy and the possessive person. It began to educate Maring in the epistemology of capitalism where money speaks louder than relationships.

The Religion of Economy

Anglican values and Western commerce were two clauses of the same, perhaps run-on, sentence. This gelled, culturally, with the indigenous worldview that would never have thought of separating technical from ritual actions, planting a garden from propitiating their ancestors for well-being and fecundity. The Anglican Church at Koinambe ran the best stocked and most successful trade store in both Jimi and Simbai Valleys. Rice, tinned meats and fish, peanut butter, powdered milk, crackers and cookies, sodas, kerosene lamps and fluid, and much more lined its shelves and floors. The store attracted buyers from as far away as the central Simbai and ran at a profit nearly sufficient to support the entire mission. The tie between Christ and commerce had an omen of predestination about it not only because of the fusion of economy and ritual in indigenous practice, but because the Maring continually misread the mission's metaphors, imbuing them with a literalness and immediacy that went far beyond what the mission men ever intended. They preached that "those who accepted the word of God would enjoy untold prosperity"; "believers would be rewarded on this earth and in heaven"; and the faithful would be "enriched in more ways than they could imagine." But the Maring, with the wealth of the Westerners clearly in view, could imagine just fine and they intended to hold the missionaries to what they construed as material promises. What the mission men refused to contemplate was that the exportation of these metaphors would invite a reinvention of their meaning. Certainly one of the principal presuppositions of missionization is the transparency of language: the idea is that because the word of God was born beyond the walls of culture and history, it is bound to no time, terrain, or terms. Existing prior to and outside of any specific language, it is perfectly translatable into all of them. But this theory of languages was deaf to difference and the realities of reference in a foreign universe. The irony doubled was that the churchmen did not see their own language as metaphorical. To them, the words of God were clear and straightforward. To comprehend the language of the gospel one had only to listen, to listen naturally with an ear that heard more than the sound of culture. But this was not to be the case, and so the missionaries would often end up shaking their heads and furrowing their brows in frustration at the material and literal spin the Maring gave God's message. The Maring, it should be understood, were not deliberately trying to subvert the message of the mission; their understanding simply lay at that point where the structures of encompassment touch the dispositions, ethos, and conceptions laid down in village lifeways. Though the mission men prayed often and otherwise, "Maring Christianity" could not help but be a highly blended product.

The Anglican mission looked upon the close connection between commerce and Christianity as an important if incestuous union, hence something to be worried about. Their well-grounded fear was that people would associate with the Church only on account of the economic and political benefits it might yield. When the Anglican bishop of New Guinea visited Koinambe in the summer of 1980 a good part of his sermon fixated on the need to be "spiritual," "to feel the touch of god" without expecting "material rewards." The worry was in the making of what the good pastor called "rice Christians" who adhered to Christianity only so long as rice, as the index and symbol of Western goods, was flowing their way, thereby augmenting their capacity to feast and present. To put this another way, the Church was worried that its Christianizing project would be sucked into the local economy of social intercourse. This was, naturally enough, what many Maring had in mind.

The Anglicans had their own long tradition of missionization in Melanesia reaching back to the nineteenth century; and though there was no formal training on how to be a missionary, they had evolved their own habitus about how to cultivate a culture and what was to be expected from pagan religions. The absence of training stemmed from the ethos that to be a missionary was a calling from God, and that in moments of uncertainty and self-doubt the missionary could turn to Him through prayer for guidance. Based on their tradition the missionaries anticipated and imagined that local and Christian visions of the spirit world would differ in sign, substance, and sophistication. This ingrained, they had honed their "evangelical tools" to introduce new signs (e.g., Christian cross) and practices (e.g., mass) to supplant local ones, and to increase sophistication through schooling and literacy. But unbeknownst to the missionary mind, there was another, doubled difference between Maring and Western worlds. The Maring epistemology of action, spiritual or otherwise, took wing from an altogether different conception of the character of persons. Not least that the life of a person was both intrinsically and immediately inseparable from the social relations (e.g., with affines) that self-define that person. Hand in hand with this was an absence among the Maring of the differentiation of fields of action (e.g., religion vs. economics) characteristic of capitalism and its Christian companion. The Anglicans, Catholics, and Nazarene missions were akin in this respect; they all imagined an abstract, mediated, and contingent connection between someone's belief in Christ and their earthly riches. Good fortune seemed to follow those who led "good" Christian lives, but (and the metaphor here is mine) the relation was more like the propensity of wood to burn than the absolute result of spiritual purity and worship. By contrast, most Maring conceived their relation to Jesus to be much more concrete, an exchange in which their "gift" of allegiance and recognition merited a tangible reply. The relation of reciprocity between the spiritual world and living community was indeed founded on the transformation of that which was immaterial (the memory and name of an ancestor) into material objects and materially improved social relations. It was, in fact, a practice to stop sacrificing pigs to an ancestor who granted nothing in return for offerings of pork. Those ancestors who rewarded their descendants proved their power and were thus the object of continuous, further propitiation. In return for prestations of ritual pig, the ancestors blessed the living community by insuring the health of children, the exchanges of the clan, the fertility of wives, the success of the hunts, the vitality of the pig herd, and the plenitude of the gardens. Given this logic, many Maring presumed that propitiation of Jesus Christ would lead to material returns in keeping with his Western nature: i.e., consumer goods. Not surprisingly, the priest in charge often rued that teaching the Maring the difference between material well-being and faith in Jesus was proving an uphill battle. It occurred only obliquely and fleetingly to the missionaries that there might be some foundational cultural differences at work. They accounted for Maring behavior mostly in terms of those "universal instincts" of greed and lust for material things.

But if the Anglican ministry feared that, in the belly of the Maring, Jesus and the flavor of rice and tinned meats and fish had become inseparable, they had only themselves to blame. The clergy fed the association through the active hand they took in the trade store and other economic matters, such as the buying and transport of coffee. They also fed the beast of their own discomfort by the way they lived: the food, furniture, and other amenities that they considered to be small reward for their sacrifice of living in the "bush," a sacrifice that the Maring did not understand, this bush being their own given terrain. To all Maring, the missionary life-style seemed to be characterized by its luxury, writ large and small. The running water, the electrical generator that lit up the house of the Bible translator each night, the stockpiles of goods, sitting in almost ceremonial display, on the airstrip after the biweekly Talair flight offloaded: the houses and life-styles of the missionary community, however sparse by Western standards, were for those who watched the parade of local carriers hauling the goods up the hill to the mission house an index of the connection between Christianity and economy. No deluge of words from the pulpit of St. John's could wash away what the Maring saw with their own eyes. This was significant in ways that the missionaries' own unreflective vision could not fathom. Maring epistemology has its own theory of the gaze in relationship to speech: whereas the gaze was a touchstone of truth, indeed the same word denotes knowing and seeing, speech was the art of dissembling, enchanting, and seducing the listener. The Maring were Spinozistic by temperament; like the philosopher, they classify "word of mouth" as the lowest and least reliable coin of knowledge. It should thus offer no surprise that many Maring understood the sermons of the priests on the separateness of Church and bisnis as rhetorical flashes, the sweet speech of big-men that masks the reality visible to the open eye.

Whether the missionaries liked it or not, the local populace saw the goods they had, the techniques they knew, and the services they offered as extensions of themselves. Missionary protests to the contrary were merely bits of white noise. Their personae—like those of other Westerners, including anthropologists—became linked to the economy of modernity. As repositories of goods, techniques, and services, the missionaries themselves became cherished values: having a full-service mission station in close proximity was a way for certain clan clusters, such as the Cenda and Kauwatyi, to step on the accelerator toward modernity. They easily recognized that the mission helped them to gain a march on rival clans, especially those inhabiting more "remote" areas—remote, that is, from what had become the center of the modernizing universe.

Unlike some of their more fundamentalist brethren,[4] Anglican missionaries were not Bible-thumping zealots who thought they were taming a godless and uncivilized people. They self-imagined their role in the humanistic terms of providing medicine, education, and economic opportunity, leavened, of course, with God's word. Olive Robin, for example, a nurse by training and the wife of the pastor of the Simbai station, labored relentlessly to improve the health of Maring children. Steven Kay, the manager of the Koinambe station, organized and ran a coffee cooperative that significantly improved pricing for local coffee-sellers. Amid all this, as it witnessed the meandering of its project and Maring reactions to Christianity, waves of doctrinal doubt would sometimes wash over the Anglican mission. The mission men had bursts of awareness of their imprint on local lifeways, and they realized that most Maring prized them for "material" reasons. In seconds of reflection they rued some of the consequences of the modernizing mission. But the fire of doubt was always doused by the cold fear that new sects, like the Nazarenes and Seventh-Day Adventists, which did not allow reflection or respect for the Other, would capture Anglican converts. Having arrived late to the land, a land already divided among the existing Christianities, they could not take time to wonder. So the Nazarene erected their church across the valley from Koinambe, outside of Maring territory, in what was a no-man's-land, unsuitable for gardening or airstrip. "Good only for mosquitos" my friend Gou explained. But my conversations with its foaming pastor left little doubt that he believed that Christ had commissioned him to invade Anglican territory—to teach the Maring what Bible Belt Christianity was really about. As though they didn't know. Though small in numbers, the new sects exerted a gravitational force on established Christianity to forgo reflection and become more evangelical. The Anglicans also dismissed their concerns with the palliative that change was the price for hearing Christ's message. Whatever changes were instigated, however seemingly good or bad, this was and had to be "part of God's infinite plan." Thus, they worried little about the effects of Christian religion itself, which, after all, was the Maring's "reward" for having to deal with such rapid changes. The unstated, unquestionable notion was that all of God's cultures had a backbone strong enough to bear the weight of His truth. So if the Maring had their narratives of transformation, their flight of the cassowary, the missionaries had their own myths that helped them to make sense of and sustain their project.

Conversion and Power

The West is the whale that swallowed us.
MOSES WINAI

The overriding aim and raison d'être of the Anglican mission was to convert Maring souls to Christianity, to "bring them to the God they had never known." To reach into the indigenous spirit it was necessary to reach into indigenous social organization, to use the local ways of defining relationships of power and authority to shepherd people toward God. Father Bailey, citing the ideas of an evangelical publication that had caught his imagination, explained to me that the trick to converting Melanesians was to discover and tap into those cultural and social "triggers" that would galvanize the local populace to participate in the Church. Close to the top of this list of imagined triggers were the Maring big-men, leaders who, in a Melanesian way, could sway others through their stature and influence. Thus from the beginning the missionaries tried to convince

local leaders of the wisdom of joining forces with the Church, a huge temptation given its material resources. There was however a deep thorn.

Buried in the encounter of missionary and big-man was an insoluble
contradiction, a contradiction that encapsulated the clash between Western views of virtue and local venues of power. Though the mission prided
itself on its willingness to acknowledge Maring culture, to display sensitivity toward the complexity, logic, and appeal of customary arrangements, it
could, among other practices, never come to terms with polygamy; there
was no way to accommodate having more than one wife within the cir-
cumference of the Church's light. The best it could do and imagine was to
banish polygamy to a heathen past, to see it as the relic of an increasingly
obsolete and unmodern past. The conceit was that marriage was natural,
not cultural. Monogamy was given in the natural order of God's chosen
world, and thus a man "fornicating and procreating" with more than one
woman was an abomination, a mortal sin for which one's culture by birth
was no excuse. The conception, shared by other Christian denominations,
was that Maring culture stood between and corrupted God's natural order
because the Maring had not been exposed to His gospel. The Catholic and
Nazarene missions concurred on the point (with the Nazarenes adding the
flourish of seeing customs such as polygamy as bearing the mark of Satan).
No matter how sympathetic the Church was to local custom there was
absolutely no way that an avowed and unrepentant adulterer (which
polygamy, in the stream of Christian logic, inevitably led to) could be baptized. So, Father Bailey asserted that "a polygamist can enter the Church
only if he gives up his other wife." Thus the big tent of Christianity could
not accommodate one of the most central aspects of Maring political culture. The best the mission could do was conceive an archaeology of
morals, to equate, as Father Bailey once did, polygamy with the stone axe,
a once-upon-a-time technology that had now given way to a more modern
understanding.

The Church's stance on polygamy all but excluded big-men from
Christianity. This was especially true in the Jimi Valley where the cult of
the big-man was much more developed and the influence they had more
pronounced. In 1980, fifteen of twenty-one known big-men had more than
one wife, and of these, four had more than two, with the two most powerful men having three and four wives respectively. That polygamy is as valued as it is difficult to negotiate defines it as an index of male/clan wealth
and power. It is through their multiple wives, and the alliances and kin
relations that follow in the wake, that big-men augment their power. Not
surprisingly, not a single big-man decided to "give up" one of his wives in
order to be baptized. The Anglican clergy was never aware of the extent of
the contradiction between the demands of Christly virtue and local sources
of status and power. The result is that the most significant big-men, such

as the councillors of the Kauwatyi and Tukmenga clan clusters, never converted to Christianity, and the Church was never able to capitalize on the legitimacy these conversions would have engendered. Moreover, this occasionally resulted in some serious backsliding, the most outstanding examples being two up-and-coming big-men who sloughed off their Christianity to marry a second time on their ascent to power. Unable to grasp the political instincts of adult society, out of their league in the whirls of local-level politics, the missionaries felt compelled to focus their ministry on the generation of schooled adolescents and school children.

But, it was not simply polygamy and the missionaries' erotic fantasy of culturally blessed "group sex"—as one of the more hard-spoken mission men once blurted out (to the sheer embarrassment of his brethren at that dinner table). No, the practice of marriage itself, even the simple union between, as the good Father said it, "two young virgins," tied the mission in moral and doctrinal knots. During one stay at Koinambe, Father Bailey kept me in conversation through that afternoon and the better part of the night in his attempt to write an encyclical on good and bad marriages, those the Church would "recognize and those it would reject," only to come up empty and more baffled by night's end. Missives sent to other clergy in Melanesia proved no more enlightening. The problem, at least from the missionary position, lay in the very nature of Maring marriage processes.

When talking about Maring marriage, process is not merely a good place to start. It is the only place because people conceptualize marriage as a process of progressive binding whose final moment is a woman's burial on the clan lands of her husband. Unlike Western unions that are legally speaking instantaneous, there is no way to say "I now pronounce you man and wife." Maring has no performative verbs whose felicitous utterance transforms a man and a woman into a husband and wife. They imagine marriage in the graphic metaphor of two converging lines that draw closer and closer over the life of the union. There is no event, ceremony, fanfare, that bridges pre- and postmarriage statuses. A marriage crystallizes over time as gardens are made, houses built, children arrive, bridewealth is given, mutual assistance is rendered at significant times (such as major exchange events), the community recognizes the marriage, and the couple so presents themselves to the community. Especially in the early years, the bond between the partners is very brittle and it is really not until a child is born that the union becomes more or less permanent—like the solid union dear to the Christian imagination.[5] In this respect, the goal of bridewealth is not to legitimize the ongoing conjugal relations; rather, it is the fruit of conjugal relations that legitimizes the payment of bridewealth.

Despite trying with all their might, the Anglicans could never come to terms with, or grasp, the character of Maring marriage and the local

Christians could not grasp what the Church was about on this issue. The two cultures had been blindly joined by the history of encompassment, and so the fruits of the union were commonly aborted missions of understanding. At one point the Church tried to shape a roster of diagnostic criteria to determine who was living out of wedlock, in sin, and therefore in dire, soul-threating need of the Sacraments. But this conceit never went further than a few scrapped notes, as they found it impossible to define at what point in this process a couple was truly married. From the Church's perspective the problem was as simple as it was disturbing. Either a marriage was no more than a casual and promiscuous fling or, if bridewealth payments were taken as marriage ceremonies, people lived routinely in sin and disregard for God's law. For their part, even the most Christian Maring viewed the concerns of the Church as one of those peculiar and bewildering Western notions that occasionally seemed to bubble up to the surface. Nevertheless, from the Church's view the issue was alive because Christian marriage was the cornerstone of the Christian family. And so the missionaries exerted pressure on young adults to marry early, during the initial phases of their liaison with a prospective spouse, and in the Church. But, to the frustration of the missionaries, even those Maring who openly professed Christianity ignored their desires.

The ultimatum to the polygamist to divest himself of his extra wives and the puzzled search for that magical point when a liaison becomes a bona fide marriage were representative of, and metaphors for, the Christian West's notion of others' cultures. The problem was ontological, the solution nowhere in sight, and the Christians themselves were in denial. From the start, the missionaries could not help but to amputate local practices from their social context and then subject them to moral judgment. The Church could parse the Maring way of life into those practices that were close to God and godliness, those that required moral tuning (such as marriage), and those that were tainted with a primitiveness bordering on the satanical. Polygamy and sorcery certainly fit the latter category. Moreover, the missionaries did not view these practices as fundamental to the integrity of the Maring as a people but as human weaknesses that had become embedded in their cultural practice. Polygamy and sorcery were little more than lust and greed writ socially large. The missionary view was that Maring culture was, and would be, primitive so long as sin itself was socially inscribed and hence given a good name. Especially with respect to marriage, the Maring did not see their own practices in this dark way, though the missionaries would seek to teach them to do so. The underlying premise of missionary behavior was that Maring culture, by encoding and thus sanctifying certain universal human sins, stood between people and the natural will of God. Where the West outlawed sin, rendering it a personal perversion,[6] Melanesia made sin social. Maring culture was itself a problem. Not only did it endorse immoral acts and practices, it was a barrier to Christianity. While the missionaries denied that there was anything wrong with Maring culture or those of Melanesia generally, their views presupposed the opposite. The missionaries dealt with the contradiction with a vision of progress that was no more than a surrogate for an ideology of social evolution. So the Anglicans believed that monogamy, Christianity, and medicine would displace polygamy, ancestor worship, and sorcery as Maring society learned and progressed into the modern age. For the missionaries, it was precisely those practices that distinguished Maring from Westerner that retarded their progress. Christianization thus entailed, and was synonymous with, an erasure of those differences that distinguished Westerners and Melanesians. What was happening, of course (and conversely), was that the mission was a key player in the gradual encompassment of the Maring within a Western system of distinctions, a system that could not but set the Maring near the bottom of this cultural-evolutionary ladder. And as they ascended upward, what the mission understood as the worst of their customs, polygamy, sorcery, and the idolatry of ancestor worship, would then be forever exiled to a fast retreating past. Though the Anglicans were correct about the demise of ancestor worship, they had little immediate impact on polygamy, and never did they imagine that sorcery accusations would explode or that they would be at the center of a firestorm.

Jesus among the Maring

Whatever the status of the Church or the depth of indigenous Christianity, the fact is that after a quarter century of Anglican mission activity every Maring knew of Jesus and many believed in him, at least to some degree. But he was the exception, the other stars of Christian cosmology, such as Satan and the Virgin Mary, having no appeal for the Maring. These figures and the values they represented did not resonate with the indigenous cosmos; the mighty Satan, for example, provoking more amusement than consternation. Of all the Christian deities, it was Jesus, first man and then ancestor, the gifted and faithful son who followed his father's wishes, a big-man killed by his enemies, who best fit the Maring image of the relation between the living community and the spirit realm.

Certainly Christian Maring asked Jesus to bless the land much the same as their parents had (and some still did) beseeched their own ancestor spirits. A circumstantial aspect of the conjuncture of Christianity and ancestor worship was that the pantheons of the two religions meshed. Christianity has Jesus, a manlike god long since dead who claimed to be the ancestor of all ancestors, remote in time and space from a Melanesian genealogy. For Maring, Jesus lived in the time before memory. From the standpoint of Christian Maring, the shining virtue of the Anglican mission is that it made them aware of the existence of an ancient ancestor that, although very powerful (revealed in the power of his descendants), they had not traditionally known about. This view was, of course, the view of the Church, summarized and sermonized in its claim that God was their father. The Maring pantheon, by contrast, devolved on close kin ancestors: the recently dead who are known by name and deed in the collective memory of the living. Three related views of Jesus evolved, views of the absorption of the Other's ghosts, views that will change over time and terrain in substance and intensity—the population of believers always in transition.

The view of many Maring, including those who were not active Christians, was that what they had learned from the Church is that Jesus Christ sits at the apex of their ancestral genealogy. As in other Highland cultures, Maring genealogies are relatively shallow and compact, embracing three or four generations at most. Beyond this point, they are both precise and nameless insofar as they are imagined as reduplicating themselves since the origins of the clan in time immemorial. No genealogical editing or manipulations were thus necessary to mount Jesus at the zenith of this hierarchy; all people had to accept was the notion that in this space before time all people were related. This claim of common brotherhood for all humans was, of course, a tenet and teaching of the Church, and for many Maring this new notion of brotherliness was a hallmark of the "new road."[7] But this syncretic view was not the only view. Some of the more evangelical and convinced Christians believed that the pantheon of ancestor figures entertained in the Old Testament were also part of the local genealogies. In this reconfigured history, there were the known ancestors of the Bible— Abraham, Solomon, and Moses followed by Jesus and his saintly disciples—then a timeless stretch of unknown and nameless ancestors, leading to the ancestor spirits known to the living community. Of this group, only Jesus Christ was a god, and thus he was the only one to be worshiped and propitiated. Finally, there was a more agnostic view of Jesus: to wit, we cannot know if Jesus is truly our ancestor, but we do know that his descendants, the whites, are now very much in charge. It thus makes sense to follow their religious practices as this might permit us to appropriate or "pull" their forms of power and wealth creation.

The Maring held none of these views with unshakable conviction or certainty: they were not the timeless and unquestionable truths of the sort that had characterized their belief system before contact (Rappaport 1979). The Maring gleaned these views from the tale of Jesus, his life, works, and death standing at the epicenter of the missionary presentation of Christianity. Jesus' life was a linear teleological narrative beginning with his birth and progressing in a preordained script toward his crucifixion and resurrection. He was represented as a highly individuated being, both by the nature of his godliness and the motivation of his actions; he was the one and only cause of his own actions. He was the unimaginable person, bereft of any brothers and sisters, defining himself in opposition to the social order of his time. The Church depicted his power as an uncanny ability to influence and control others, to make people take notice (the parables), sinners repent, and the heavens itself clash with thunder. Power is understood here as a possession, and a godly one at that. The emphasis was that Jesus' internal state, his love for his fellow man, was reflected in his behavior, and his behavior was an expression of this internal state. Thus the inner and outer dimensions of the Christly life were isomorphic in their goodness. This view of a life, coded into a biography, was a far cry from the "traditional" Maring perspective. And so they had to wade through the epistemology of personhood inscribed in this view of a life. The biography of Christ was a morality play, an origin myth that was simultaneously the celebration of Western bourgeois virtues. The missionaries intended this double effect. They sincerely believed (in a reversal of Durkheim's argument) that Christ had created Western society in his image, that society evolving to incorporate (however imperfectly) his virtues and values. Thus it was through the example and imitation of the life of Jesus as told by the Church that all people were led to God's goodness and grace. There was also, of course, an unintended contradiction, the Church claiming that religion was separate from culture and that it could thus freely export Christianity, and presupposing that the Western world and practices were privileged precisely because they encoded Christianity. For the churchmen, this created an enormous tension in their assessment of indigenous practices, especially those such as marriage that broached the civil/religious border. So, Father Elderly was opposed to indigenous marriage ceremonies while Father Bailey thought them acceptable if accompanied by a regular Western-style church service. Due to this underlying contradiction in the Church's posture, its actual stance in any given locale was always contingent on the head priest who happened to be there at the time. Which indigenous practices they should accept (and to what degree) was a matter of some debate and dispute among the missionaries.

Inscribed also in the Church's narrative of the life of Jesus was, for Maring, an unsolicited introduction to the Western images and ideology of personhood. The Church invariably presented Jesus as a self-contained, self-animating agent, standing over and above and against the society of his time. The story of Jesus valorized the actions of the person who is so individualistic that he stands against the wisdom and interests of the leaders of his time. From a Maring perspective, Jesus emerges on the biblical

scene socially naked. He is the true individual, having no brothers, clansmen or affines to help and defend him. Many Maring were both puzzled
and amazed by this re-presentation of his life, sometimes asking me if
Jesus had brothers and sisters that the text had somehow failed to communicate. In the same vein, the life of Christ presents him as autonomous
from the relations tying him to others. He chooses the twelve apostles, for
example, purely by dint of his own initiative (see Luke 6.12–18; Mark
3.13–19). Where Maring mostly see persons as the composite and plural
site of the relations that define them, the Christian God, Jesus Christ, is
precisely the opposite. He is defined not by his relations to others, but by
his power to define others in his own image. In the vision presented by the
Anglicans, Jesus was the individual par excellence, and while many Maring did not and could not grasp the epistemology of personhood embodied in their re-presentation of Jesus' life, it was part of a lengthening conversation with the Maring that, spread over many dimensions of life from
economy to medicine, progressively valorized, inculcated, and blessed the
Western ideology of the person. Christianity thus emerged as one of the
forces that would move the individual facet of personhood from the margins closer to the center of social life and legitimacy.

The entire process of grafting Christianity, an inclusive and predatory
religion, onto a cultural landscape founded on a kinship-based and hence
exclusive religion had many repercussions. A main effect was to relativize
belief, to breach the cloak of unquestionableness that had surrounded
worship prior to pacification. Whereas previously, people had simply
assumed that their beliefs, rituals, and relations to ancestors were the
exclusive shape of the world, they were now confronted by an empowered
alternative, the antiancestor bent on challenging and replacing customary
forms of worship. The advance of Christianity forced the Maring to contrast the power of the ancestors to help their descendants with the power
of Jesus to enrich his heirs. In the field of contrasts, Jesus was the symbol
and shepherd of modernity. And the Church stood for all the forms of
value creation, wealth, and powers of modernity. By the 1980s the sacrifice
of pigs for the ancestors had all but disappeared in the Jimi. The sacred
groves were no longer used and began to fall into decay as forest vegetation encroached from all sides.

Epistemology also encroached from all sides. For the Maring, religion is inseparable from knowledge and the ways of knowing the knowable world. The most important of the neglected features of Maring religion and Highlands religions generally is that their epicenter is not ritual,
sacrifice, or the mythos of the gods, but the earthly, pragmatic relationship
between knowledge and morality. Through an intermediary, the Smoke
Woman, the ancestor spirits let the shaman talk their wisdom. Rappaport
(1979) explains:

Smoke Woman . . . acts an intermediary between the living and all other categories of spirits. Shamans communicate with her in seances, conducted in darkened men's houses and often lasting all night, by "pulling smoke." They inhale deeply the smoke of strong native cigars and send their nomane (a term which . . . refers here to the conscious aspect of the self that survives death) out of their noses to fly to the house of the Smoke Woman and to escort her back to the seance. She enters the shaman's head through his nostrils and, speaking through his mouth, informs the living of the wishes of the dead. (103)

In this manner, the ancestors advise the living community on which allies to cultivate, how to balance relations of reciprocity, the "truth" of contemplated collective action (such as making war), the virtues of specific marriages, and more. For the Maring, this knowledge was sacred or divine. In contrast to ordinary knowledge the divine wisdom of the ancestors is neither mediated by the body nor based on sensory data. Sound, smell, and sight have little to do here with knowing. Unlike ordinary talk, which is intentionally layered, vulnerable to dissembling and evasion, and thus inherently uncertain, the ancestral voices are transparent and unquestionably true. This truth of knowing is the definition of divinity for the Maring. It is knowledge that transcends the bodily, spatial, and temporal limitations of mundane experience, what for the Christian God is the catechistic attribute of omniscience. And there is also a moral dimension here: for knowledge of the world is never simply right or wrong, true or false, it is always good or bad. There is an implicational logic that says that what is known with certainty to be true, extraordinary knowledge about ordinary things, is thus sacred, aesthetically pleasing, and moral. Sacred knowledge is no less worldly than worldly knowledge because the spirits inform the living about the timing of rituals, the creation of marriages, the worthiness of political alliances; in a word, the ordinary conduct of a clan. The ancestors do not traffic in abstract doctrines and lofty principles. The world is an epistemological ladder in which the ambiguous nature of local knowledge is resolved by consulting the sentient ancestors. That at least is how it used to be.

Given this relationship between knowledge and the sacred, the impact of Christianity was to forcefully displace the ancestors by desanctifying them. Under the colonial regime, the ancestors were no longer able to tell the "truth" about the world because the new world was beyond their ken. The encompassment of the Maring world removed much of the dynamic of social life from local hands. What the ancestors had to say about military and marriage alliances for example become progressively meaningless with pacification and the assertion of the rights of women to select their

marriage partners. The ancestors' ground of power and divinity was cut
out from under them. The *rawi mugi,* or red spirits, men who had given
their life for their clan in battle and who thereafter advised their clansmen
on social issues, could no longer hold the high ground against the evangelist's proclaimed "army of God." If the ancestors could no longer impart
extraordinary knowledge about social affairs, truths in a certainly uncertain world, then they had nothing to offer the living but memories.
Because the Maring world merged epistemology with ontology, a radical
break in the nature of knowledge and ways of knowing tears the cosmos
asunder. On the new road it was Jesus who had the answers, Jesus, that is,
and what an elderly Maring in a prophetic, slightly mocking voice called
his "White Smoke Women" or priestly go-betweens. Good advice produces good results, and so in a world encompassed it paid the Maring to
entertain the message of the Church. Even those people who had not been
baptized or had been rejected by the Anglicans, such as big-men, repeated
over and again the necessity of auditioning what the Church says on matters of economy, polity, and domestic life. Especially the younger and
more Christianized believe that what the West has bestowed on them is a
new and more authentic vision of the truth, and thus the true difference
between good and bad, right and wrong. A moral divide appears that is
also a historical disenfranchisement of the past and of course the ancestors
who inhabited this past. The Maring's own past comes to be re-presented
as an endless era of warfare and violence, pain and sickness, the poverty of
stone tools and "bush" clothes—what in "mission ideology" comes to
those who live in sin and darkness. But on the "new road" the ancestors
are little more than mute relics; they who have lost their ability to speak
social truths and hence their divinity. By contrast, the Western God and
his disciples now obviously possess the truth, this exemplified by the superiority of their knowledge and its results. To the Maring, Western society
is conflict-free and founded on law; its roads are wider, longer, straighter;
its technologies of housing, gardening, clothing, eating, transportation,
and communication are better and more easily acquired. The
desanctification of the ancestors meant that by 1980, "only a few oldtimers
still sacrificed pigs to the ancestors"—that, at least, is how one young man
put it, adding as a coda that these "oldtimers did it secretly and separately" even from their own clan members, Christians like him, who they
thought would disapprove.[8] It is worth noting that the disenfranchisement
of the ancestors was a pragmatic rather than theological decision; it is not
that people no longer believed in the existence of their ancestors, they simply no longer believed in their relevance.

A related aspect of change is that the advent of Christianity politi-
cized religion in a new sense. Never mind sacrificing pigs to the ancestors,
to simply choose not to be baptized, to continue to use a Maring name, to

court a second wife, to actively transmit religious knowledge from the past to the future generation was now understood as a political statement. This is nothing less than an embracing recontextualization of cultural life. A telling because ubiquitous example was the process of naming. Using a name such as Penga or Waiya, as opposed to Abraham or Moses, gained a different meaning than in the days before missionization. Where before names were given and easily passed into the background, now they are foregrounded. Each and every mention became an index of a person's relation to modernity. It is, of course, a hallmark of Christianity, this compulsion to rename people, to presume that the act of baptism is a rebirth of the person. A growing practice was for people to imitate Western naming customs by using their Maring name as their surname and their baptismal name as their first name. Whatever anomalies this created,[9] it was important for the younger generation to go by their Christian name, to signal to others that they were more literate and sophisticated than their ancestors and parents. For their part, the missionaries saw the renaming of the local population in the most positive and unreflective light: they were, they told me, surprised by my very questions and interest in, what for them, was these pilgrims' progress.

Literacy and Language

For the missionaries of Koinambe and beyond, the centerpiece of their evangelical directive was, in the most literal sense, the Word of God. Toward this end, they sought to establish the Bible as a truth and the truth. To do this it was necessary to separate the written and spoken word, to parse language into a spoken world where anything is possible and a written universe of more tangible and reliable truths. The Bible translator explained to me that if the Maring could read God's message then they would not need to be converted, they would convert themselves. Though they did not, of course, put it this way, the Holy Bible was, for the missionaries, a socially magical document. To receive scripture was to feel the ultimate life-transforming spark. Periodically, groups of "native evangelists" from the coast would sweep through the Jimi, spending several days with the young men of each of the clan clusters in an effort to ignite a round of conversions. Describing themselves as Pentecostal—meaning that they were rabidly evangelical—the groups invariably trumpeted the Bible. Here, for instance, is an excerpt from a talk given to some men gathered in front of my house.

> Everything that a man needs to know to be saved is in the Bible. Absolutely nothing is missing. So to be redeemed, you must read

and listen because the Bible contains Jesus' commands to you. If you believe in Jesus, and do what he tells you to do, good things will come to you. Before we heard the word of Jesus we were nothing but ignorant bush people. Now [and here the speaker thumps the Bible he is holding] we too have God's message.

Part of the story here is that Melanesian priests, deacons, and evangelists often rendered the message of their white teachers in less fussy, more dramatic language. Even in their attempts to duplicate the official discourse, they could not help but to place Christianity in a colonial context and to put a Melanesian spin on the message. Once again, anytime B.C. is conceptualized as a time of violence and ignorance, the redemption of local society brought about by the colonialism of Christianity.

On another occasion, a visiting evangelist who identified himself as James, spoke.

It is not enough to believe: to go to church and pray. You must hear the calling of Jesus and work actively to convert others to Him. This is the true way that black people will be saved. One of the taboos that Jesus places on people is not to be passive; we must make others hear his talk.

While no preaching ever had immediate and dramatic effects, miraculous, hosanna conversions were never in the Maring cultural repertoire, they were all sentences of a longer conversation that did not end. On this theme, Bishop S. Gaiut proclaimed that "the first priority" of our churches is "to evangelize" those who have not heard the Good News; and he added that the key to evangelical success was zeal and persistence (Gaiut 1976:1–2). Resistance on the part of local communities was the work of the devil and local demons, work that true witnesses to Jesus would overcome with his help. As Rev. J. K. Daimoi, the Executive Secretary of the Bible Society of Papua New Guinea, noted, it is "clearly stated in the Book of Acts" that to evangelize a people is to "turn their world upside down," a world turning for which the Church is to make "no apologies" (Daimoi 1976, 26). What these Church leaders underlined was that evangelical crusading at the village level was supported by, and a reflection of, a larger national interest. Indeed, in national political discourse, the spread of Christianity and a Christian life-style and the making of the Papua New Guinea nation are often braided together.

For the missionaries of the Maring, there were three steps to spreading the Good News and winning recruits to the army of Our Lord. From the start, the missionaries focused their energies on the youngest generation. This meant children, adolescents, young adults, and those who had recently married. The initial step was to create a literate populace who could read the Bible, minimally in pidgin and preferably in English. It is here, of course, that the school was central, and the Church had a stake in encouraging wide participation and good attendance. The local preference was to send only boys to school on the understanding that men were to be dominant in the modern economy (women had economically greater responsibility under the indigenous system of production) and the reality that young girls were needed to help their mothers in the garden. The Anglican mission urged the Maring to send both girls and boys for schooling and bemoaned the fact that "people didn't understand the need to educate everybody simply because they were all God's children." In this statement and in sermons, informal conversations, and other discussions, Father Bailey made it clear that education and conversion were inseparable in the eyes of the Church. Schooling, conversion, and the discipline of the jail and work Mondays: they were all pieces of the same model, all modeled on one another. They were facets of the moral reeducation of the Maring: respect for knowledge, God, law, and state were essential for the shaping of a good modern citizen as well as good citizens of modernity. Exposure to the best of Western institutions would lead people on that journey of self-improvement; they would learn self-control (i.e., to settle disputes legally not violently); they would learn self-sacrifice for the national good (i.e., the Monday work system), they would learn the self-advancement made possible by literacy (i.e., to use technology); and, they would learn about their own self-salvation by accepting Christ into their minds and hearts. A new subject would emerge, a morally and intellectually reconstructed person able to succeed in the world they were being thrown into. This was epitomized by the "native evangelist" who, literate in English and pidgin, mindful of his obligations to God and country, a pillar of the community and an example of the life given to God, and fluent in the ways of the modern, would convert his own people to Christianity. The crowning achievement of this progress toward a new Melanesian subject was ideally the ordination of indigenous priests.

But it was also at this point that the universal subject of God met the ethnographic subject. For, while it was allowed that anyone, regardless of their color or culture, could get a calling from God, the Western clergy believed that the Maring (and indeed most New Guineans) could not anytime soon become Anglican priests in the truest sense of that status. Although they spoke this way only in private, the Western clergy believed that there was a gap between the Melanesian priests' understanding of Christianity and that of those who had been steeped in the Western tradition. The local clergy might have the same transformation of spirit brought about by the calling, but they did not have the same knowledge or intuitive insight of those who lived the religion culturally. It was all too easy for the indigenous priests to let their heritage guide their thoughts, and to thus slip unknowingly into views and beliefs that crossed over into precisely the kinds of syncretism that Father Murphy had warned against (see the start of this chapter). While, as universal subject, Westerner and Melanesian were equal before the Almighty, as ethnographic subject of Christianity the Melanesian was hobbled by his culture. The theme expressed in the mission's reaction to polygamy is repeated here in another key: Melanesian culture as a barrier between God and the God-given potentialities of the universal subject. Several young Maring did go off to the Anglican seminary in Popondetta in the mid-1970s, but none returned as clergy. They did, however, return as people who were betwixt and between societies: one of these men was a Kauwatyi who became my friend and a principal informant for much that appears in this chapter.

A primary goal of the Koinambe mission was to establish the master narrative of the life of Christ. The story of the birth, sermons, miracles, crucifixion, and resurrection of Jesus was told over and again across many media. Sermons, hymns, picture books, recorded songs, and the cross itself all reiterated this theme of the life of Christ. Especially prior to national independence in 1974 (when the schooling system came under more direct government oversight), the curricula of the school and church overlapped to a great degree. Even after independence when there was an influx of Melanesian teachers, mostly from the long-missionized Anglican regions along the southeast coast of Papua, the school emphasized the life of Christ because most of the teachers were practicing Christians. Several, in fact, were evangelical and believed they were, to quote one of them, "doing Jesus' work in the classroom." In the early years, reading lessons in English were done from old catechisms sent from Australia, although by the late 1970s these had been replaced by other, more nationalistic but still somewhat religious materials. Physically, the church and the school were adjacent structures at Koinambe. The link between school and church was very clear to the eyes of the Maring who, for reasons that should be obvious, apprehended them as part and product of a single agency.

But the project of literacy as a road to redemption was not a smooth climb for the Anglican mission, for there was the vexing problem of language itself. In what language should the story of Jesus be told? The Maring could learn English, this indeed being the language used in the primary school. But the use of English was confined to the hours within the classroom, and few Maring had a good command of English or employed it on a regular basis. The result was that only a handful were ever able to absorb the Bible and learn of Christ's life in English. Thus, any sermon given in English always required a translator. From a practical viewpoint, the obvious choice was to use pidgin. A great many Maring, women as well as men, spoke pidgin, and there was already a translation of the Bible into pidgin. But the use of pidgin did not sit well with the Anglican priests who felt it was a bastard tongue, never capable of the subtle meaning and insight necessary to grasp the intricate truths of the gospel. The nuances of Christ's word would be lost under the thick grindstone of pidgin, with its very abbreviated grammar and clumsy vocabulary. That at least was the sound in Anglican ears. The third possibility was, of course, to speak in Maring. But the local tongue proved to be too difficult for the missionaries and for that matter the Bible translators as well. Like other Papuan languages, Maring has clause chaining, a set of noun phrases followed by a string of declined, interlinked verb forms. So the possibility of preaching in Maring required a local translator, which enhanced the chances of misinterpretations of God's message. Though the Anglican mission believed firmly in the cultural and linguistic neutrality of Christianity, it turned out that translating English into Maring was filled with numerous pitfalls. For example, while love of all sorts—love of God and Church, brotherly love, love for one's spouse—was central to the mission's message, translating that word *love* into Maring was a semantic nightmare. The multivocal, polysemic, highly relational term *love* had absolutely no equivalent in Maring. Translators searching for an equivalent often relied on the term *wumbi kana,* which means "domesticated," "cultural" (as opposed to natural), "tame," or "friendly" depending on the nature of the referent (human, animal, etc.). The term denotes the relationship between classes of beings (e.g., humans and pigs, one clan versus another); in no way does it convey the sense of warm and affectionate devotion between individuals. At no time did it occur to the missionaries that the Maring language might be unable to accommodate the social semantics of a Western Bible. Questions about the existence of the individual or the translatability of Western notions of sin and redemption were neither asked, answered, nor considered worth the trouble.

The necessity of translating the Bible into the local dialect was animated by the belief of the Summer Institute of Linguistics that Armageddon, the Final Judgment, could rain down on "Mankind" only once all of God's children had been introduced to His gospel. For them, this meant that the Bible must first be translated into every known language. We should be thankful to Melanesia on this score; what with its nearly one thousand languages, it alone will retard the Final Judgment for some hundreds of years. Given the difficulties of Maring for the Western ear, and having made little progress the first several years, the Bible translator hit upon a unique strategy. In the early 1960s, when the Maring were still reeling from the shock of contact, he and his wife adopted a baby boy of a Kauwatyi clan. He then raised this boy to be completely bilingual, sending him for a time to school in Australia. The result was that by 1977–78, the boy, now a young man, was ready to begin translating the Bible into his own language. The gospel of Luke was published in 1979 through his efforts (though nowhere is his contribution acknowledged). The pathetic irony is that, with the translators retired to Ukarumpa (the Summer Institute's base) and the educated Maring learning to read in pidgin and/or English, I was in 1980 probably the only person in the Jimi who could read the Maring Bible.

During the first twenty-five years of existence, the mission never reconciled its language problem, though by this time it had other more pressing concerns—not least of which were that Cenda elders were suing for the return of the mission station land, the church in Kompiai had been compelled to close down due to sorcery accusations, and the evangelical process as a whole had slowed to a crawl.

The Margins of Christianity

Anglican success in ringing up converts and establishing local area churches varied over place and generation. Those clan clusters who had suffered defeat in the early 1950s at the hands of other clusters showed the greatest and most uniform allegiance to the Church. In the Jimi, this was specially true of the Cenda and even more so of the Manamban. The Manamban had been defeated and driven from their clan lands by the Kauwatyi in alliance with the Tukmenga. They were restored to their land by the Australian administration. Sandwiched spatially between the two largest and most aggressive clan clusters, the Manamban bet on Pax Britannica or military peace and the message of peace preached by Christ and his emissaries. As a Manamban leader once told me, "Father Brian [Bailey] will help to cleanse people of their taste for violence: but if people don't obey him and begin fighting again the government will punish them." For the recently defeated clan clusters a commitment to Christianity, as the instrument of enrichment and power, was their strategy for regaining their lost stature in the age of modernity. Nevertheless, many of the senior clansmen even from the most marginal clusters would remain leery of the mission and the missionaries.

The most powerful and historically successful clan clusters—the Kauwatyi, Tukmenga, Kundagai, and Yomban—entertained a more ambiguous relationship with the missionaries and Christianity in general. They were less than enthusiastic about Church doctrine, such as the ban on polygamy, and attempts by the missionaries to intervene, however indirect and unintentional, in the affairs of the cluster. Moreover, because the clan leaders were unbaptized, unschooled, and beyond the radius of the Church, rarely did they comprehend the religious message of the Anglicans. If, as the missionaries observed with a shrug and a sigh, Maring

Christianity had shallow roots because most people did not grasp the true nature of God's message, nowhere was this more apparent than in their conversations with big-men. What the big-men did know beyond question was that economic power lay in the hands of the mission, so for their own political advantage they had to cooperate with the Anglicans and the more Christianized among them. A cultural compromise evolved. The big-men abstained from any personal relationship with the Church though they encouraged junior members of their clan to capitalize on the economic opportunities afforded by the Church. With a few exceptions, they were quiet agnostics, not knowing if Christ was for real, but knowing that their appropriation of Church powers was the realpolitik of the future. For their part, the missionaries confessed to me on many occasions that they were baffled by the actions and motives of the big-men who, it seemed, were guided by stars that they did not understand.

The most aggressive converts to Christianity were members of the up-and-coming generation, aged fifteen to mid-twenties. They envisioned Christianity as the modern religion, the belief system of business, technology, consumer goods, mass media, and forms of wealth creation that put kastam and its divinities to shame. To embrace the mission was also a means to elude the grasp of senior clansmen. An oft-repeated sentiment of this generation was that schooling and mission allowed them to "escape the village" and seize control. A dialectic had been set in motion whose ultimate consequences were unknown. Exposure to modernity—the school, Church, and English—bred deep dissatisfaction with local village life, senior clansmen appearing dated and impotent in relation to Westerners. At the same time, the language skills, education, and sensibilities of this generation placed them in a better position to capitalize on these new economic opportunities. The immediate result was the efflorescence of bisnis linked to the Church, this ranging from the scores of young Christian men who worked for the trade store, hospital, school, and church to village entrepreneurs who ran trade stores and coffee exporting operations using church-chartered planes.

Some of the senior clan members, especially those who had led full and powerful lives before the epoch of encompassment, openly rejected Anglican overtures. For them, to be truly Maring was to live and die according to their own religion and rituals. At the other end of the spectrum from these senior voices were those who unconditionally allied themselves with the mission, declaring the past dead and the future Western. However, the great majority of people fell somewhere between these two extremes, their positions changing over time according to occasion, their commitment to Christianity colored by uncertainty, their faith filtered through a cultural lens that routinely recast the message of the missions. The churchmen would express this reality to me by confiding that they did not really know where they stood with the Maring, whether or not they were making real headway. What was clear was that it was this large knot of people in the middle that would attempt to engage the mission, to negotiate a Christianity that met at least some of their own desires. However distasteful to Anglican sensibilities, the Christianity that was evolving was going to be syncretistic.

Part of the reason for this has already appeared: the Maring did not separate the overall success of the living community from its intercourse with the spirits. They were only on the brink of learning the Western lesson about the differentiation of religion and economy—a lesson about the separation of social fields that would come later, especially with the further infiltrations of capitalism. After a quarter century of contact, the Maring world was not cleaved into separate domains, each endowed and defined by its own form of practice. What missionaries separated into economy, politics, and religion were of a piece in the local universe; the kingdom of God was very much of this earth. Jesus, his religion, and his agents were, in the Maring imagination, quite inseparable from material success and the power of the modern.

Beyond the solidity of fields, there was another and equally profound reason why local Christianity would be thoroughly syncretistic. The Maring have a long history of importing rites, magic, and objects from other peoples. There is a belief that things of foreign origin are wild and thus capable of embodying great power, so much so that certain spells and chants are not even uttered in Maring, but in a foreign tongue (bastardized Kandawo) that no one can understand or identify. The power of these spells and chants derive from their "otherness" rather than their capacity to refer to and predicate about the world. The irony here is that a critical part of the cultural appeal of Christianity is precisely the fact that it is powerful and alien, yet fits in some key respects into the local religious life. Built into Maring religion was a basic cultural relativity (actually much the same as characterized Western Christianity during its first millennium). Though the Maring had mostly abandoned ancestor worship, they did this on practical grounds; never did they imagine that Christianity and custom were theologically mutually exclusive. The notion of exclusivity was the position of the missionaries; it was the cornerstone of their concept of conversion. For them, a Christian was someone who had shed their indigenous religious identity and, turning toward the West, had embraced Jesus. This was not, however, the position or practice of the Maring. For most, their adoption of Christianity did not preclude their involvement in other forms of belief, such as people's continuing faith in traditional curing rites, sorcery, and other forms of magic. It should be clear at this point that one reason I did not estimate the number of Maring Christians, or (worse) use the Anglicans' estimate, is that to count the converts presumes in advance a dominant epistemology of individualism that did not exist.

The Maring's initial reaction notwithstanding, the mission continued to focus on conversion, aiming its words at the generation coming of age. Mission preaching about the virtues of conversion had as its subtext the concept that the social world consisted of autonomous individuals who, based on their own free will, chose a primary religious identity. As he traveled from village to village, the Anglican bishop told groups of mostly young men that "it is up to each and every one of you to make the decision to accept Christ" into your life. The very fact that this generation would come to contemplate the issue of conversion, who was baptized and bore a Christian name and who did not, who still offered a pig to the ancestors and who had disowned them entirely, was part of the long interchange that began to inculcate the rudiments of Western epistemology.

Localizing the Mission and the Sacrament of Sorcery

By the tail end of the 1960s, the Anglicans at Koinambe had secured a permanent foothold in the Jimi. Once the main mission was galvanized, the Church took to establishing local churches in the Maring communities to the east. The Anglicans envisioned the local churches as simple extensions of the main mission. Manned by deacons (clergy ranking one step below that of priest) and lay catechists of Papuan descent, most of whom were educated to their calling at the seminary in Popondetta, the community-based church was to attend to people's daily religious needs, to carry out the small jobs of faith and devotion critical to the maintenance of a Christian life-style. Although Koinambe imagined that these local outposts were small-scale versions of the center, there were very significant differences that it did not anticipate or appreciate.

Not the least of these differences was that as the Anglicans localized the mission, the men of the cloth and the church itself became ensnared, sometimes unknowingly and usually hopelessly, in the webs and intrigues of local politics. The missionary premise that there is an ironclad separation between culture and Christianity, religion and politics, could barely be maintained at the Koinambe station, and then mostly due to its relative self-sufficiency and isolation from clan politics. The Koinambe men saw themselves as interested spectators of village politics; external and objective, they could lend impartial advice, counsel peace, and help mediate disputes. This was a moral geography punctuated by the fact that Koinambe lay on the western edge of Maring territory far from the heartbeat of indigenous power. The internal politics of Koinambe concerned the local big-men only insofar as events at the mission involved their protégés or flows of goods. It was one thing when Koinambe was a space out of space, the Christian enclave that was separate and different from other communities. However, once the Anglicans entered the local arena, secular entanglements were inescapable. MacLean (1984), speaking about the Tukmenga cluster, describes its Anglican evangelist as a big-man deeply immersed in local politics. He notes that on one occasion at a death compensation payment,

> the two sides confronted each other. Both sides were fully deco-
> rated for battle [as is the custom] and carried axes and bows and
> arrows. At what seemed like a critical moment, as the two sides
> virtually met, the Evangelist lost his temper. He is acknowledged
> to be a strong man with a short temper [a quality of the big-man].
> He stalked up and down between the two sides, yelling and rip-
> ping axes out of peoples' hands. (215)

Although evangelists, like the one at Tukmenga, were clearly enmeshed in local-level politics, as big-men fighting for status, as intermediaries in disputes, as centers of power, the Anglicans had no plan or strategy on how to engage the local political life. On this point, in response to my question the father explained that "some matters we have to leave in God's hands, to trust Him." The result was that the fate of the Church in any particular clan cluster depended on, and varied according to, the way its representative dealt with local politics and politicians. Because no clear policy or oversight existed, the history, involvement, and values of the local ministries varied, often dramatically, from one clan cluster to another. In some clusters, local ministries blossomed from their inception with no signs of letting up, while in other clusters the mission started strong and then became progressively less visible or retreated altogether.

The problems that beset the recruitment of local assistants were as much spiritual as political. These men could not help but be an incarnation of the conjuncture of Christian and local forms of veneration and verity. Deacons like Samson and Gabriel epitomized those who stood in the cultural breach between Melanesian and Anglican—believing simultaneously in Christ and the spirits, the codified commandments of the Bible and the inscribed conventions of practice, the mandate for monogamy and the power of polygamy, the spiritual omnipotence of God the Father and also the harms of sorcery. The contradiction lived by the mission took this shape. The churchmen felt that native evangelists were, by birth and betterment, more able to sound chords familiar and enticing to local ears. Thus to convert them by knowing them well. Yet in the folds of the same thought, the churchmen worried their beads that local talent would offer an unknowingly skewed or watered-down version of Christianity. Or worse—and here Father Bailey told me he refused to contemplate the possibility he had so frequently contemplated—that they offered a version of Christianity infected with local forms of spirituality, magic, and desire.

The fears of the priest were not unfounded, although the catechists, evangelists, and deacons never intended the miscegenation of faiths. But in the course of their business, the politics of the ordinary, they were compelled to present Christianity in opposition to sorcery and ancestor worship. By being placed in the same field, as a modern antidote to an older form of empowerment, Christianity became colored by its association. The evangelist among the Tsembaga urged his flock to turn away from the easy and obvious power of sorcery, to trust instead in the benefits, material and otherwise, that would flow "like water" from prayer and acceptance of the Almighty. Samuel, the traveling deacon, who spent much of his time at Gai in the Simbai Valley, reasoned and argued that Jesus would protect his children from the blackness of the sorcerer. There was a certain sort of epistemological covalence between Christian Sacraments and pagan sorcery. The burning issue, even as sorcery became more pronounced with modernity (a subject to which we shall return), was which was more powerful; how would they struggle against one another? This version of Christianity stripped away its pretense at universality and returned it to the quotidian, particularistic, scheming world of local politics. And once embedded, indigenized, handed over to all the creativity that local agents could muster, there was no end to the spiritual concoctions people might brew by combining the two faiths. Thus there emerged the strategy of calling upon God and his Sacraments to throw up a powerful defense in order to pursue an aggressive attack on one's enemies. Those whom the evangelist had smilingly ushered into church in the morning would later that night morph into beasts to stalk the dark in search of their clan enemies. Given the dramatic nature of sorcery, and how far it seems from the Christian ideal, the contradictions inherent in the missionary project float to the surface. As long as Christianity remained in its quasi-universal form, its local appeal remained limited by its cultural distance. But as soon as it was localized, and who better able to do this than indigenous evangelists, it became entrapped and transformed by the considerable powers of local agency.

The most important failure of the Anglican Church was in the Kauwatyi clan cluster, important because the Kauwatyi cluster was the largest and most powerful. I first realized there was change afoot during the construction of my house at Kompiai. The house seemed to be progressing faster than I had dared to imagine, wood for the walls and doors, crude-cut furniture, materializing out of thin air. I would have been less surprised had I known, as I was soon to find out, that my builders had cannibalized the church for parts. The pews, a few beams, the altar, and some six-inch nails all went into my "new" house. Before I understood anything about local politics—having arrived just a month earlier I was, to put it sympathetically, still feeling my way around—I became part of a political statement about the relationship between the Anglican Church and the Kauwatyi, and more pointedly about the competitive struggle between two powerful clans and two empowered big-men who used the mission for their own political ends.

The initiation of a mission among the Kauwatyi began in the mid-1970s when its largest and most aggressive clan, the Kamjepakai, requested the establishment of a local church and donated land for that purpose. If the Anglicans suspected that they were becoming enmeshed in a local political struggle, they looked the other way, only too glad to win such critical consent. And so an impressive church was built on Kamjepakai land, mostly with Kamjepakai labor, and staffed with a deacon from coastal New Guinea. The Kamjepakai conversion was animated by their general desire to take advantage of the mission's economic power and their specific desire to best rival clans. As might be surmised, attendance at church services was predominantly Kamjepakai, though there were a number of women and young men from other clans. Apparently taking their cue from their interpretation of the sermons delivered by the deacon, some Kamjepakai believed that, empowered by the Sacraments, they could use God's prayer to help vanquish their rivals. Unlike a Western reading of the Bible, the Maring interpretation failed to see the difference between magic and miracle, although it was explained to them as if the difference between Christ raising Lazarus from the dead and a shaman reviving someone comatose from malaria was self-evident. But to local shamans, the Christian claim was that Jesus was their most powerful magician, the ancestor who could heal the sick, walk on water, transform his bodily shape (e.g., appear as a dove), fly through the air (vividly depicted in his Easter ascent into heaven), and attract people (such as the apostles) and goods to him. In the logic of especially the older shamans, it followed that those who worshiped the Christian God and dutifully attended mass would have access to his almighty powers, and that God would reciprocate by helping the faithful to subdue their rivals. This was no more than the "biblically proven" evangelical promise that the faithful would triumph over their foes. Hanging in the house of one older man, apparently a present from a kin who had visited the coast, was a picture (exorcised from a Christian magazine) of Michael the Archangel in full medieval battle dress, his breastplate reflecting unearthly light, his sword sheathed to his side, his hand turned fast around a lance, his boyish face glowing with victory, and below the caption "Michael the Archangel leads God's Army against evil." Though it is hard (for ethnographer or local) to know the exact or cumulative weight of Christian mythos and metaphor on the way the Maring view their world, it is clear that in at least one interpretation embracing the Church was seen as the road, the new road, to greater power. So some shamans from the Kamjepakai clan aimed the magic of Christianity against their enemies. During mass, they prayed to Jesus to help them and harm those who vied with them for wives, money, goods, and jobs on the church station. Ill fortune would visit others while they pulled the fruits of modernity.

To hear the other four Kauwatyi clans, the Kamjepakai prayers were all too well answered. They had, in the words of the leading Kukupogai big-man, twisted the Sacraments into sorcery. This was revealed in a variety of ways. A disproportionate number of jobs at the Koinambe mission station had gone to Kamjepakai (including the main local translator of the Bible, manager and assistant manager of the mission's trade store, and assistant station manager—the highest ranking local position). A key reason for their success and, from the Church perspective, a just reward for their effort, was that the Kamjepakai more than others had been willing to embrace schooling. A Kamjepakai had the best and only truly successful trade store outside of the mission store. This store allowed them to "pull" money from other clans and then redistribute it within their own ranks, enriching them at others' expense. And finally, from 1976 to 1977, there was an "outbreak" of disease and misfortune that, accordingly to members of the other clans, disproportionately harmed them and miraculously spared the Kamjepakai. From the vantage of the other clans, their only play was to exorcise the demon of their misery. So when the local deacon went on holidays in the summer of 1978 he was told never to return, never, that is, if he valued his life. The demise of the Kauwatyi church was a blow to the progress of Christianity in the Jimi, although the Anglicans continued to gain ground along other fronts and to have more success in other clusters. What was more, the missionaries knew nothing of what happened among the Kauwatyi (until one evening I told them the story) nor did they evolve any insights into the intersection of the mission with local politics. Even after he discovered the peculiar genius of seeing sorcery in the Sacraments and understood why the Kauwatyi church failed after what appeared to be such an auspicious start, Father Bailey didn't try to resurrect the church or disentangle the role of the Anglicans in local politics. He simply shrugged his shoulders and reflected that it must be "God's will" that the missionization of the Jimi should test "our Christian resolve."

After the first quarter century of missionization, it became clear that the Maring had both accepted and rejected the Anglican Church in more ways than the Maring or Anglicans could understand. While almost everyone tagged themselves Christian, the contours of commitment and belief were extraordinarily uneven. Some people professed to be devout Christians yet appeared to understand next to nothing about Christianity. Others were Christian in name but agnostic by practice, paying little attention to the Church other than to its benefits in their interests. Still fewer made a sincere effort to study and practice Christianity even if they were aware of the material benefits of association. In addition, there was a dwindling number of senior clan members who saw Christianity as the preoccupation of the younger generations. The unevenness and variability of belief make it impossible to measure Christianity by the numbers. To note, for example, that by 1980 approximately 70 percent of all Jimi Maring had been baptized (and thus renamed) tells little about the character of their Christianity or the impact of the mission. It would certainly be a mistake to gauge the social influence of Christianity by either the enthusiasm or resistance shown by local agents: for the mission was part of a much larger complex of encompassing agents and institutions, and the mission's influence flowed well beyond the borders of the religious life to touch the threads of unthought epistemology and the experience of the everyday.

Exposure to the mission, though by no means only the mission, introduced Maring to the concept of an absolute standard of value and morality, of a single refractory form of knowledge. Exposure also began to instill in people a Western sense of time, abstract time as a measure of labor's worth and as an organizing principle of human action. In subtle and slight ways the daily life of the Church, from the constantly told story of Jesus to the way that it hired, treated, and paid workers, emphasized the individual aspect of personhood if not individualism itself. And the skills valued by and at the mission—knowledge of English, skill in arithmetic, aptitude for business, and, more generally, Western dispositions—gave the upper hand to the younger generation of men who had been in school and socialized with the mission personnel. The mission also help set in motion a long chain of influence by defining (more precisely, redefining) the terms of communication. The medium of and for modernity, and the privileged medium at that, would now be the written word. Epitomized and sanctified by the Holy Bible, it would not be viewed with the same suspicion as its spoken cousin (see chap. 5 for an example). The schooling process, the power invested in the text as a perceived source and product of Western power, the Christian mantra of the inviolate nature of God's word, the political leverage gained by those who could read, all served to help to establish the authority of the encoded word as against other forms of communication. Through its well-provisioned store and general encouragement of commerce and bisnis, the mission was instrumental in helping to transform the design of desire; people increasingly desired Western foods and clothing, the faster, more exciting pace of urban life, and modern material signs of success. So, a quarter century later, two young men whose fathers witnessed the arrival of the whites are waiting at the airstrip at Koinambe dressed in pleated shorts, sunglasses, wristwatches, broad beamed hats, and leather shoes, waiting for a plane that will take them to the seminary in Popondetta where, in their own words, they will become priests[10] and return "to teach these bush kanakas to know God and become civilized."

CHAPTER 8

Traditions of Medicine and the Miracle of Modernity

When the mission first came, the elders were displeased
because they refused to give us the medicine that would
bring cargo.

KAIYA, 1980

Though the missionaries prayed and promised the conversion of the Maring, searching heaven and earth for signs that their message was taking
root, they were also and painfully aware that the locals seemed less interested in the Good News than in God's power as revealed in the hospital
and trade store. For Maring, the desire for Western medicine was inseparable from the appropriation of the wellspring of the power of encompassing agents and institutions. Like tales of imported wealth and the affair of
money, it was part of their attempt to capture new and more compelling
sources of the production of value. As ancestors were instrumental in the
vitality of pigs and produce, so the combined forces of the Holy Trinity
would furnish the medicine for health and wealth. In the beginning, as the
epigram underlines, the Maring drew no distinction between technical and
ritual action, between spiritual and medical and economic realities, and
accordingly they entertained that mission and medicine were blood brothers in the construction of Western power, political, economic, and otherwise. The next quarter century would attempt to teach the Maring about
Western visions and divisions of body and society.

    Finding the nature of indigenous medicine obscure, convinced it was
a talisman of the primitive in the process, both the mission and the state
envisioned the provision of Western medicine as a touchstone of modernity—as a domain of life in which they had a clear and overwhelming
advantage. While the abstract nature of God and state might elude the
Maring, nothing was more real than the body, nothing more miraculous
than returning those on the cusp of death to good health. For the missionaries, the body embodied the communion of spirit, substance, and sociality. It was the temple of the to-be-redeemed soul. An earthly site where the
power of Christian faith was as visible "as sunlight after rain" and the portals of conversion ever more open. Though there was never a bull or even

a whisper from Canterbury on the virtues of medicine, on the frontier healing had the glow of a secular sacrament. But no less for being so. The premise, accepted as beyond question, was that biomedicine was the epitome and exemplar of Western ascendance. Its practical power showcased all of the virtues, verities, and authority of the Western mind. While people might imagine familial life, farming practices, education, and patterns of speech as matters of habit and habitat, no one could fail to grasp biomedicine as objectively superior to all other pretenders. Its virtues and advantages were not situational or a matter of personal perspective. They were inscribed in the body itself—in nature rather than culture. And in the recognition that beneath the social self there was a biological individual, a God-made container for the human soul. The Christian spirit and the desire for improvement could find its deepest roots only in a body that was sound and sentient. Both the soldiers of the Savior and the state would convert the Maring to modernity by healing and health care. As Christian leaders of all stripes would attest, it was Jesus himself who anointed medicine as a privileged site and testimony to the power of the Almighty. Certainly, the story of Jesus awakening Lazarus from the dead was a winning sermon, a crowd-pleaser that made a lot more local sense than walking on water or transforming it into a better beverage. So nowhere did the West mark and map its project of modernity more than in the field of medicine; nowhere did it encompass and subsume Others with greater peace of mind.

The insertion of a formalized Western medical system into the practical state of ethnomedicine ignited a set of transformations that began in local curing practices but rapidly, inevitably diffused throughout the social tissue. Vernacular visions and examples of the ordinary person who reclaimed the normalcy of health through the supranormal use of magic and spells transport us to the center of Melanesian images of power and potency as well as the ordinary practices whose enactment and values anchored the social. Thus the confluence of Western biomedicine and Maring ethnomedicine could not but bring to the fore all the issues surrounding the generation of generations, the forging of subjectivity, and the foundations of the power and authority to inflect collective action. As this suggests, the encounter between the two medicines unfolds across numerous planes at once, planes that imbricate and communicate through the bodies and acts of embodiment of those concerned. At the most immediate, the encounter materializes as the social history of medical practice, the character, trajectory, and stages of its evolution since contact. This encapsulates questions of change in the indigenous perception of accident and illness, the evaluation of healing, the goals of treatment, the terms of integration of the two medicines, and the emergence of medicine as a quasi-autonomous field. These questions have more reaching implications because the transfer of medical control from shamans to health personnel was a transformation in the locus of power. It reconfigured the relationship between the Maring and the mission/state, between generations, and invariably between men and women in that control over the body—which is inseparable from control over the processes of embodiment and personation—was at stake. Not only were these areas of transformation interrelated—Western medicine, the state, and Christianity arriving hand in hand—but the concepts that permeated biomedicine seeped into other practices. The Maring increasingly cited them as evidence and argument in village court cases, used them to divine Christ's interpretation of community behavior, and deployed them in the strategies and struggles of everyday politics. Because ethnomedicine and curing were not part of a restricted field of knowledge or desire, the advent of biomedicine would influence everything from religion to epistemology. In this respect, the confluence of bio- and ethnomedicine walked the same path as the genesis of scientific medicine in the West (see Porter 1992).

As always on the frontier, these transformations lie at the crossroads of the relationship between the objective structures of the two medicines and the cognitive and motivating structures that animate social action and sociality. Because these processes conjoin, as though by an unintended act of cultural summation, the dividual and individual dimensions of the person in respect to two medicines and three generations, analysis can be reduced to a single perspective (ecological, demographic, etc.) only at the cost of a serious loss of reality. First, each medicine has its own objective structure—structures that, differently designed, presume entirely different stances toward sociality and the body, and thus instill and presuppose their own forms of knowledge, disposition, and desire. But also, what "patients" believe and sense through the agency of their own body as a dimension of the social body influences the outcome of treatment and hence the efficacy ascribed to that intervention. For these reasons alone, no theory that assumes that biomedicine progressively replaces ethnomedicine because of its "objective" efficacy will ever suffice. The perspective adopted here, which is no more than an acknowledgment of the ethnography, is that the advance of Western medicine reshaped local attitudes and dispositions toward the use and usefulness of medicine, and also that indigenous attitudes and dispositions, as embedded in practice, inflected the circulation of biomedicine into the Maring region. Meaning and value lie at this intersection. It is thus essential to inquire both how the advent of Western health care was reshaping ethnomedicine (i.e., people's behavior, sensitivity, and practices) and how this determinate appearance of biomedicine under the auspices of the Anglican mission was inseparable from, because mutually determined by, ethnomedicine. Both the indigenous vision of medicine and the specific agents who delivered biomedicine to the Maring doorstep were midwives to the incorporation of Western science into local lifeways.

Another way of approaching these issues is to ask how analysis can grasp the meaning and functions of ethnomedical practice. How to interpret and account for the determinate shape of illness and cure, the symbolic and pragmatic functions that accrue to them, and the effectiveness of healing rituals? These are all concerns that have appeared in the Melanesian literature, and in italics with respect to the Maring. On this ground, I maintain that understanding ethnomedical practices is not a question of recovering their ecological, biopsychological, and/or physiological effects, but of restoring their practical necessity. In the context of modernity, this means that ethnography must come to terms with the significance and functions that people, embraced in an ongoing encounter with the West, confer on medical practice and experiences, given the protean forms of knowledge and desire that configure their conceptions of health and illness. Sometimes overdetermined, sometimes underdetermined, these practices and experiences are always immersed into a river of signification spiked with political intent. This alone should remind us that no transcultural vision of health care as a means to insure the well-being of individuals can even begin to explain indigenous curing. Nor can it explain Western medicine in either its domestic or exported appearance, which, however much it ideologizes itself as the objective and instrumentally driven diagnosis and treatment of the biological individual, has its own economy and politics of the body. Western medical practice seeks to commoditize a service for individual consumption, thus bracketing the social conditions for the production of illness and recovery even as the research community accumulates evidence demonstrating their organic linkage (that work-related stress promotes cancer, that AIDS patients who join supporting communities have a longer life expectancy and improved chances of remission, etc.). The result is that the meeting of medicines involves a triangulation, an interplay between the scientific field of medicine, Western medical practice, and ethnomedicine. This creates medical encounters of the third kind for Westerners as well as Melanesians: even as Western medical practitioners shun ethnomedicine as primitive witch-doctoring, medical investigation has been discovering some of its benefits that, through the rear door reserved for the exotic, are entering into the medical consciousness of Westerners.

What does this tell us? First, without understanding the character and use of ethnomedicine, it becomes impossible to grasp the product of the historical encounter. Western medicine no more simply replaces ethnomedicine than Christianity simply replaces indigenous spirituality. Second, scarcely more insight derives from analyses that, in the tradition of the ethnography of folk medicine, ignore the biomedical conditions against which agents shape and evaluate indigenous knowledge and practices. This folk viewpoint cannot shed light on the vulnerabilities of ethnomedicine that are evident to its own practitioners or, what amounts to the same thing, on the indigenous notions of efficacy in play when the encounter occurred.[1] Finally, Western conceptions of health and medical practices are themselves a historically unstable mixture of research and ideology. So what was exported to the Maring and Melanesia was an arbitrary confluence, defined by the state and delivered through kiaps, missionaries, and medical personnel. Only by dissecting, at the field hospital so to speak, the body of the two medicines can we recover the dialectic of encompassment.

Medicine in any context, and profoundly in the fields of encompassment, underlines the relationship between social epistemology and the body of persons. How do concepts of the body become inscribed in the body? And how does the inscription of the body in the world—which involves the mediated mediation between nature, the objective structures of sociality (always critically, the cultural construction of nature), and the embodied forms of knowledge, desire, and dispositions—shape the construction of the subject? How does the body as organic, the flesh and bone subject to death and decay, challenge the cultural construction of the person?—a challenge because, as Lévi-Strauss spent his life showing, cultures define themselves by conventionalizing nature. They also perpetuate themselves practically by the same means. For Maring and Melanesians generally, sickness, suffering, and death have always challenged their images of sociality. Sickness unto death calls forth the individual aspect of the person in a kind of public display because no one can assume another's pain or die for them other than by ritual transfer, which in its necessity (e.g., to perpetuate the continuity of the clan) cannot but acknowledge the reality that it seeks to transcend. Melanesian societies have used all the powers of ritual at their disposal—and formidable powers they are (Rappaport 1979)—to mask by transforming the expression of the individual aspect of personhood that is the reality of death. The modes of mourning and the rites of replacement all attempt to sustain social continuities in the face of personal loss and discontinuity. Western medicine, as advanced by state and the mission, in seeking to control the bodies of the Maring, could do so only through an exercise of power that imposed, among other things, its own epistemology of individuality. Just as the Protestant perspective thinks a one-to-one correspondence between God and person, so medicine assumes a one-to-one correspondence between medical treatment and the biological individual. The aim was to treat neither the whole person nor the community at large, simply to "eradicate the cause of infection, mend the broken part, or prevent bad outcomes"—as the VSO nurse put it. At one and the same time, the medical professionals did not know the Maring communities in great depth and also felt certain that such knowledge was irrelevant to treating the biological individual. This articulates the Western ideology—often and situationally contradicted by Western practices—that a person's body is separable from its sociality. In the nature of things they have an extrinsic relationship. Western notions of race and ethnicity, its theories of sociobiology and eugenics, standard medical texts on the diagnosis and treatment of disease, popular debates on whether a specific behavior (such as homosexuality) is environmentally or genetically determined, legal defenses for criminal behavior, and much more all exemplify the ideological impetus to separate biology and sociality. Simultaneously, Western views on the relationship also flow in the other direction, not least in the Christian notion of miracle and the interventions of God in the affairs of the body. The idea that if we all fold our hands and pray faithfully for the sick among us, God may answer by his healing powers. There was here a contradiction between mission and medicine, a contradiction inherent to the Western worldview, which was played out as a tension between the medical staff and the churchmen. The Anglicans desired to both separate themselves from the field of medicine and annunciate the inseparability of physical health from spiritual faith.

The relationship between biomedicine and indigenous Melanesia has been uncomfortable for anthropology because there is an enormous opposition between the acknowledged results of medical care and its political implications. On one hand, there was no doubt that health clinics, stricter sanitation measures, disease prevention programs (especially inoculations for children), and prenatal care have improved the health and life chances of Melanesians. This was anyway the Maring view. On the other hand, swallowing this biomedicine entailed their surrendering control over their bodies, living and dead, to the minions of mission and state, sometimes in ways that yielded more submission than remission. For the Maring, modernity placed everything from the way they were born and raised to the way they died and defecated under the auspices of agents and institutions over which they had little control. The use of biomedicine and belief in its authority also became a sign and weapon in the confrontation between generations. Better health care thus came at the expense of a fundamental realignment of power, the growing power of the junior generation in the context of overall disempowerment. And this is only the part of the story of power in the agentive mode. The infiltration of Western medicine also implanted an epistemology that began to transform people's senses of body and subject. A distinction between mind and body, the principle of the body as machine (composed of genetically defined semi-automatic systems), the premise of the biological individual, the very manner in which the agents of biomedicine interacted with the Maring could not but transform their categories of knowledge about subjects. The contradiction that anthropology must live with is that Western science—all science, social, medical, environmental—is both a dimension of domination and a resource of emancipation (for overturning imperial histories and perspectives, combating malaria and infant mortality, minimizing the suffering of natural disasters, etc.). In this context, the only sin worse than participating in the process of encompassment is not participating—that is denying Others the modern's technologies of self-direction. But the story gets ahead of itself. It begins with indigenous views of causation and illness.

Community and Curing

Though the Maring have always concerned themselves with divination and curing, it was never, as in some African societies, culturally underlined by elaborate ritual or the cultivation of specialists. Matters of medicine were routinely put in the hands of all-purpose shamans. Until pacification, the growth and decline of clan clusters was yoked to the relationship between the politics of war and incidence of disease. Lowman (1980) illustrates that too great military success as well as too little could force a clan cluster into decline. Repeated victory in war would escalate the influx of affines and refugees, causing environmental degradation and a depreciation in community health; repeated defeats made it difficult for a clan cluster to attract wives and forced them to seek the protection of nucleated settlements, leaving them more vulnerable to parasitic infection (Lowman 1980:16–17). The evidence further suggests that insofar as the Maring exploit the transition zone between lowland and highland habitats, they are exposed to a greater variety of diseases than people living exclusively in one habitat or another. Most pathologies found in the Maring region are water-related, the absence of strict sanitation and water management promoting their transmission. Some of the most common diseases were respiratory infections, influenza, measles, conjunctivitis, hepatitis, various forms of worms, and malaria. Lowman (1980:210–38) observes that immunity to malaria has always been marginal and that malaria's prevalence has increased with contact. Still, one indication that Western medicine was leading to better health was the robust population growth of the 1970s (LiPuma 1985). In the context of the increasing devotion of land to coffee growing, this was spawning problems of its own with respect to land tenure and dispute settlement. The comparative downward shift in the age of the population also increased the political power of the junior generation as indigenous politics had long correlated numbers with strength.

Especially in the early years of contact, the kiaps wore the crown of the health inspector. On their arrival, knowing the drill, the members of a cluster would line up, standing straight, arms pressed to their sides, hands open, palm forward, so that the kiap might determine their "general condition." The fear, enunciated in several of the annual reports, was that exposure to Westerners would lead to the decline of local populations, as it had in Africa, the West Indies, and the Americas (e.g., Annual Report, New Guinea 1956–57). All and everything should be done to prevent the catastrophes of other places, other times. For Maring communities, Western agents insisted that the critical measures for improving the health of local populations were the construction of latrines and the immediate internment of the dead. Part of the project of the mission and the enforcement procedures of the kiaps was to motivate the Maring to build and use latrines as opposed to the "bush." The ever-present model was the rest house, itself located on a clan cluster's principal dance ground, which featured an enclosure and deep-well latrine some seventy-five meters from the main dwelling. Some of the most senior clansmen officially endorsed the latrine as a matter of law while the junior generation began to use it as a matter of practice. By 1980, there were court cases in which people were fined for defecating too close to a settlement and for not building a proper latrine. For the state and the mission, and then for the junior generation, there was always more at issue than the germ theory of disease. There was also the moral governance of the body as an index of the morally sound social body. The segregation and containment of human waste was emblematic of a new sense of order, an emerging cleanliness, the concern of those "civilized" for that which passes in and out of the body. From the outset, the kiaps marked the construction and use of latrines as a mark of modernity. Where the "kanaka" would defecate willy-nilly in whatever bush was available, such seat-of-the-pants decision making oblivious to disease and ecological despoliation, the modern Maring respected proper sanitation. Hepatitis in particular was attributed to poor sanitary habits, though the building of latrines does not seem to have led to a decline in its incidence. All things considered, the most important factor in the increase in population was a reduction in infant mortality and a diet richer in protein.

The second major concern of sanitary improvement was less dramatic from a health standpoint but more so culturally. The state-created and state-enforced health code recommended the Maring revise the way they buried their dead. In the past, a raised outdoor platform was built of timber and lined with Cordyline, the sacred plant symbolizing the clan's territoriality in which clansmen invest their life spirit. The corpse was then laid out on the platform and exposed to the elements until rotted away to bare bone. In the damp, tropic weather of the rain forest this rarely took more than six weeks. During the body's exposure, women stood vigil because death, as a point of transition in the natural cycle, presented dangers to the living. Their attention to the platform was essential, especially the tending of night fires to protect the dead from evil spirits and sorcerers who may approach in the form of dogs, pigs, or birds of prey. As the corpse decayed, its agnatic substances slowly dripped back into the land that conceived and replenished them. The agnatic spirit found shelter in nearby trees; the bones that remained, the essence of the mother's contribution, would then be wrapped in leaves and later buried. Given the possibility of disease and contagion that surrounded such burial practices, and that the Maring themselves saw the attending of the dead as dangerous, a new practice developed in which the body was placed on a raised platform but now built underground. The mourners still wrapped the corpse in cloth, though now, in imitation of Western custom, it was set to rest in a roughly hewn wooden coffin. Kinsmen then placed the body on a raised underground platform by inserting it into a niche they had carved in the wall of the grave. In contrast to customary burial, there was no need to stand watch and no possibility of handling the corpse—a reality that women in particular supported wholeheartedly. By the early 1970s, both the execution and desire for the kastam arrangement seem to have expired. In the new practice, the Maring had found a way to navigate the rapids of modernity while preserving the calm of custom.

The Maring were also commanded to use the health clinic, to obey to the letter the instructions of the nurse, and to submit their bodies to new forms of equipment, typically with no explanation other than a generalized assertion of Western power. The imposition of biomedicine was inseparable from submission to the laws of an overarching authority named as the state and personified by the kiaps and medical personnel. Both thought it irrelevant that the methods, motives, and means of treatment lay beyond the walls of local knowledge. The indigenous need only grasp that their bodies were in better hands. In the early years especially, mothers were reluctant to bring their babies to be weighed and inoculated by the circulating nurse, posing a question that Western agents understood as an index of ignorance but which, from another logic, was precisely the question of those who live within the compass of kinship. What possible interest could another have in children not their own? By implicational logic, does such an interest imply that they will do to my child precisely what they would never do to their own? The issue pricked especially deep when the nurse, backed by the kiap, ordered a mother and child to report to the mission hospital for supplementary feeding. That a stranger would nurture one's child, and with foods gleaned from the land of a foreign clan, was as alien a concept as the Maring could tolerate. The Western premise, as far from Maring consciousness as could be imagined, was that the laser of law could penetrate into the nuclear relationship of mother and child and, moreover, there existed an institutional medical ethic and internalized occupational dispositions that, directed toward the categorical identity *patient,* transcended kinship in the name of universality. In the name of the modern.

Of course, the Maring (like other Melanesians) could only begin to grasp this from the perspective of their own universe. Though Western agents sometimes seemed to think otherwise, the Maring could not simply adopt a modern perspective in order to indulge in the benefits of modernity. Indeed, a tenet of Western individualism is that agents are able to self-transform their intellectual and emotional outlook independent of their material and cultural circumstances. This ideology divides the Other, including the "non-model" minorities of the West, into two camps: the handful of exceptional individuals who take the initiative to transform themselves and a vast majority who *allow* their material and cultural conditions to impede their progress. With respect to biomedicine, Westerners often sorted the Maring into those few who adopted a Western perspective and were thus able to enjoy its rewards and the majority who, shackled to local theories of illness and curing, often did not or did so only when pressured. As elsewhere, the Western cultural construction of the transcultural—that Christ and Christianity were culture-free, that all who had an economy could appreciate the money form, that the virtues of biomedicine were transparent, that defining and educating the mind was the key to cultural improvement—was a primary philosophy and psychology of encompassment.

Social and Natural Cycles

The first Westerners encountered a Maring society that rested firmly on an opposition and complementarity between natural and social cycles. The first centered around fertility, gardens, and women. Its logic was that of fecundity, procreation, and growth spoken in the language of death, decay, and rebirth. Associated especially with female ancestors, its practical philosophy was grounded in the mortality of the body, the harvest of the gardens, fruitful marriage, and the birth of children. The natural cycle imagined that there is a progression to all things living, a progression that was inseparable from the organism. So it was deemed absurd that sorcerers would attack the elderly, killing by mischief those who were already in decline. By contrast, the social cycle revolved around warfare and ancestors, ceremonial exchanges and military alliances (Rappaport 1968). Associated with warriors who had died in battle, with maleness and the "hotness" of the head, its logic was that of violence, reconciliation, and compensation. Its philosophy was grounded in the sociality of *nomane—*

the collective life force of the clan. Where the natural cycle slipped unnoticed into the house of modernity, the power of the colonial state interrupted the social cycle in the name of pacification, order, and civilization.

A practical distinction between social and natural types of illness mirrored the logic and language of these two cycles. They were the sources of the cause of illness and misfortune, the determination of cause more important in determining treatment than a patient's symptoms or medical history. Conceptions of the cause of social illness and misfortune revolved around generative schemes for the construction of the cosmos and human activity within it. The application of these schemes imbued order and disorder, well-being and affliction, with practical meaning. As the Maring have made clear to every ethnographer, their universe begins in a foundational opposition between the realm of sociality, the locus of social and symbolic organization, and the realm of nature, perceived as wild. Maring are mid-mountain horticulturalists whose settlements are suspended in the middle altitudes between the bushlands of high and low ground. Spatial arrangements, the rituals of war and peace, as well as most ordinary activities, articulated a continuum from sociality at the center of the settlement to wildness at the periphery. Between the two extremes were gardens and sacred groves, the first associated with woman and fertility and the latter with men and spiritual power. These generative schemes could be applied to the social order as well as the cosmos. The logic embodied in the generative schemes shaped concepts of the body, health, and illness, and gave substance to the causes of distress and the modes of healing. The categories were simultaneously opposed yet complementary, mutually threatening yet interdependent (Wagner 1972). Thus the cooperation of affines in the making of exchanges and alliances, the joining of the sexes in intercourse and gardening, the interplay of the social and wild in horticulture and warfare, were essential for clan reproduction. The disorderly or antisocial commingling of these elements caused illness, misfortune, and pollution. The categories were coupled because the generative schemes always applied to action and embodied knowledge: eating with enemy clansmen or sexual congress with the wrong person at an inauspicious time or place. Disorder in the universe was not so much a conceptual breakdown, though the most reflective informants, typically those who had attended school, could conceptualize this conceptual schism, as disorder in social action, improper social uses of the body. Hence, each set of symbolic relations, each generative scheme, could be used practically as an etiology. Behaviors that abridged the customs set down by the ancestors (for example, the commandment to share pork with one's clansmen) invited their retribution. Rivalry and bad blood among affines surfaced as sorcery (especially within the clan cluster). A disruption of proper relations between men and women resulted in pollution and ancestral wrath. The maintenance of improper conduct with enemy clans (such as eating forbidden food) also led to pollution, weakening the body, and leaving it more vulnerable to sorcery and resistant to healing. Finally, the confusion of social and natural domains (e.g., making a garden in the bush) could provoke the attack of wild spirits that lurked outside the dominion of humans. This is worth emphasizing because there is another anthropology to the contrary. The Maring did not determine the causes of illness by acts of cosmogony; rather, the generative schemes at their disposal continually referred them back to cosmological values.

As the Maring preoccupation with center and periphery suggests, place occupied a critical position in Maring cosmology and social geography. The clan lands literally embodied the substance and history of clansmen. The cycle of social reproduction interlinked food, land, procreation, and death with the formation of agnatic identity (LiPuma 1985). Clan territories were divided into discrete named parcels of land, each of which had its own character based on the history of residence and production in that locale. The special affinity between clansmen and place meant that when people traveled to foreign and thus alien places, they were liable to be taken ill. Since contact, men have gone to coastal plantations where they occasionally died or had bouts of serious illness. Maring linked these deaths and sicknesses to the hostility of the environment (including the presence of sorcery for which they possessed no countermagic). Medical rationality may observe that coastal environments were truly more hostile and unforgiving, especially to Highlands peoples. Just as Maring history elided people, places, and actions, so their concepts of illness also bundled these concepts. But this was only part of what Maring meant, for disease and misfortune were diagnostic of the disharmony between clansmen and land, not the cause. So when illness struck hard, clansmen typically shifted their settlement compound to a more auspicious site. The old houses were razed and new ones built on another territory, usually in the same vicinity. Residence shifts seemed especially common when an influenza epidemic broke out.

The disorderly confluence of elements was not the only basis of illnesses and afflictions. Maring recognized that in addition to social relations there were various natural diseases and ailments. The natural cycle was a perceived continuity between procreation, growth and development, and old age, followed by death, decomposition, and decay, leading to fertility and the rebirth of one's descendants. The natural register represented the orderly, inevitable, and unceasing progression of elements. People's residential arrangements, adherence to food and sexual taboos, and participation in ritual were conducted in terms of this cycle. Like other Melanesian peoples (see Herdt 1989), the Maring entertained a nurturing/atrophy theory of the body and its vital fluids. The body and fluids of children were built up through the nurturing acts of their kin and their own self-restraint (e.g., observance of taboos and, in the case of men, avoidance of sex) until they gained the full powers of adulthood after which the obligations of sociality (e.g., procreation, childbearing) diminished and exhausted their vital fluids and organs, leading to death, decay, and renewal. The young and old, far from the fullness of power, were the most susceptible to illness and the maladies of the natural cycle, whereas only sorcerers and evil spirits could fell adults at the height of their physical prowess. We can summarize Maring accounts of illness, curing, and cause as follows:

NATURAL CYCLE	SOCIAL CYCLE
Minor ailments	Life-threatening illnesses
Children and elders the most likely to be taken ill	Adults, especially mature and important men most likely to be stricken
Indicates progression of the natural cycle	Indicates social disharmony and disruption of the social cycle
Causation was natural	Caused by sorcerers and ancestors
Cured with local, everyday remedies	Cured through the diagnosis and magical healing of the shaman coupled with the sacrifice of pigs to the ancestors' spirits

Concepts of Illness and Health

Nowadays we have fewer shamans and more sorcerers.
TIPIKA, 1980

Social illness had the following appearance. A person's or a clan's behavior breached norms regarding the proper relationship between categories of social beings or, what amounted to the same thing, between persons and land: ceremonial food was stolen from the garden of another, at the moment of consumption ancestors and kin were denied by an act of selfishness (i.e., individualism), food was eaten or sex consummated with a taboo person (the Maring culturally specialize in taboos, having many and intricate varieties), or sorcery was employed on one's own clan members. Depending on the nature of the offense, this would incite the attack of ancestors, sorcerers, or wild spirits. These attacks caused physical disturbances of some kind. Food may blockade a critical body canal, such as the windpipe, or a poisoned object may be implanted in a vital organ (especially the liver). The result was a physical/spiritual transformation of the person, as characterized by pain and loss of min, implying a descent toward death. The disregard for the morality of relations at once material and social invited misfortune to body and soul, substance and spirit. On this reading of the world, the process of curing never begins by amputating body from mind, the person from society, in order to isolate and analyze the illness. It is no surprise then that this way of thinking-the-world read symptoms and named causes rather than diseases. The aim was to deploy a batch of schemes immanent in practice that, by opening the windpipe or removing the splinter, reversed by a kind of symmetry the social, spiritual, and bodily damage that the attack had done. The goal was not to isolate and analyze, but restore the wholeness that immorality ripped asunder. The tracks of this implicational logic run in both directions, the goal of the shaman to reverse the descent into death by triggering a flow in the opposite direction. And so a man who has consumed pork alone in the bush, angering the ancestors who oversee sociality, leading to the penetration of his liver by bamboo spikes that renders him delirious, invokes the shaman who by removing the offending splinters causes the victim to offer the compensation of pork to ancestors and affines, thereby restoring his sanity, sociality, and body. A collectively approved public denial, the rites of curing were designed to negate and neutralize the dangerous forces released by the transgression of limits. Their goal was to put the genie back in the bottle.

In this respect, the shaman was a mortal and moral contradiction. He was by character and circumstance an expression of the individuated aspect of the person, chosen, precisely because of this, to function as the authorized delegate of the community in the service of the restoration of sociality. Curing and sorcery, both shamanistic powers, were opposites joined at a deeper level: sorcery, a species of individualistic expression that enervated the social world in the interests of the separated self; curing, a species of individualistic expression that revealed, reversed, and restored the social world in the interests of the community. So the shaman was himself a sacrilege. A man who transgressed the limits of agents and agency in the process of resurrecting the limits transgressed. Shamans were, in Maring words, men who "stand apart" and "live by themselves" and are obsessed by secretiveness. Not surprisingly, given their ambiguous position in social space, they appear as both saviors and scapegoats—as heroes of curing and perpetrators of sorcery. The logic of practice and power could not but fuse the shaman and sorcerer, the practice of medicine with the art of harming. But far from disturbed by the liminality of the shaman, the essence of ethnomedicine was to harness position for purpose.

The shaman as a personification of the individual aspect of person-hood also had other expressions. Most people claimed that they did not know the methods of the shaman, or even if there were accepted tech-niques. For their part, the methods of the shamans I interviewed were amazingly individualistic and eclectic, a symphony of elements imported from other cultures, improvisations on existing themes and means, and the legacy of their own secretive and individualistic teachers. Aware that they could both harm and heal, that their intentions were impossible to divine, and that the distance between shaman and sorcerer was a matter of circumstance, people regarded such men with a mixture of fear, awe, and curiosity. The power to remove a curse or bamboo knife from the afflicted—with techniques as various as the shamans themselves—was also the power to levy or implant them. In fact, it may be said that the power of the shaman/sorcerer derived precisely from his acts of individ-uality meant to express the individuated aspect of the person. So the paradox of modernity that the elder statesman and shaman Tipika alluded to above. With the accelerating ascendance of biomedicine, there appeared to be no new shamans-in-training, no young healers learning and waiting offstage to assume the wisdom of their fathers (see Barker 1989), even as the incidence of sorcery and the presence of sorcerers were on the rise.

In contrast to its social counterpart, the Maring associated natural ill-ness with the developmental and aging process. This covered a broad range of pains and ailments from teething and tooth decay to the bowel and joint problems suffered by elders. For the most part, natural illnesses were associated with stages in the life cycle—certain diseases common to infants, or menstrual cramps for women. As long as an illness was consis-tent with the natural cycle, and within the more specific life cycle of the person, it was not thought to be the patient's fault or the result of sorcer-ers or angry ancestors (cf. Ngubane 1977). The line between social and natural illness was not, of course, always transparent; especially when an illness deepened, shamans were called upon to divine its status. In more than a few instances, shamans reclassified an illness originally thought to be of natural causes as having a social etiology. The assumption was that natural illnesses were mild and episodic, that those in the prime of life did not, could not, succumb to them. The classification system had less to do with the cause of an illness than with its consequences. Time and again, for example, agents would classify the flaring of chronic low-grade malaria as natural, as a small discomfort that ambled in and out of a person's life, whereas nothing was more obviously socially induced than a bout of life-threatening cerebral malaria. As illnesses, they had nothing in common of social import. Sorcery trials, whose touchstone was intentionally moti-vated disease and misfortune, did not center on natural illness, but on the socially defined asociality of sorcerer and victim. In this light, traditional curing had two main objectives: to eliminate the magical cause of physical death and to reconcile the troubles that engendered the attack in the first place, the assumption being that unless the victim's family placated the aggrieved ancestors, sorcerer, or wild spirit, then the assaults would continue until death arrived.

In general, a person who contracted an illness underwent a change in internal state. This could be either a natural part of the inevitable cycle, or else a socially induced transformation brought about by the intentional acts and intervention of spirits and sorcerers. Within this frame, health depended on two things: first, the harmony or balance (*kopla*) that a person maintained within the social and cosmological order; second, an individual's personal strength and recuperative powers. People's strength and regenerative powers were thought to diminish as they became older, as did their resistance to disease (see Lewis 1976:96–98). By 1980, people came to believe that Western medicines were superior in the treatment of natural illnesses and so they were seldom afraid to go to the health clinic to capitalize on the availability of Western drugs. By contrast, especially for the older generation, biomedicine was thought to have little effect on the outcome of socially induced harm, although it might be effective in relieving symptoms and assisting the body's normal regenerative powers. How the kinsmen of the stricken chose to treat an illness was also the site of confrontation between generations and medicines. These two processes were articulated in the mission hospital when a victim of sorcery suffering an illness received the dual care of a shaman who extracted the slivers of bamboo lodged in the liver while the nursing staff administered Western penicillin to check the infection. There was no sight more representative of the two medicines, the colliding epistemologies, than the Western nurse, her stethoscope suspended from her neck, standing on one side of the patient while an elder shaman, a small string bag dangling from his neck, stood on the other, all encircled by family members who took very different positions on the merits of treatment. The nursing staff and the man's educated son believed firmly in the virtues of biomedicine, the shaman in his powers to thwart the progress of the ailment and discover the troubled sociality at its source, while the majority held to a dual epistemology that sought to combine the medicines for whatever it might be worth.

Ethnographic Interlude

One day as I sat with the shaman Tipika, a man of renown who had taught me an extraordinary amount about his magic, and three young men in their early twenties who had attended the mission school, we talked, among other things, about my most recent match with malaria: an attack that lasted a few days until one of the members of the quinine family had put it back to sleep. One of the young men, repeating our earlier conversation on the same subject, observed, glancing at me to augment his authority, that when mosquitoes bite us they give us an invisible virus that causes malaria, all kinds of malaria—great fevers and small. This flew in the face of the local premise that illnesses of differing severity must have different causes, and it further implied that malaria belonged wholly to the natural cycle, a phenomenon within the province of biomedicine. The remark was contentious because it eroded the ground of the elders and the shamans. When I earlier talked with the young men, my sole intention had been to explain how Western medicine understood malaria, though clearly, in the Maring's ongoing struggle for understanding and between generations, even innocent comments, that is, seemingly objective because factual from my perspective, were potentially incendiary. Not to be so easily consigned to the fires of modernity, Tipika turned to me and asked, if I knew all about what he called the "fever," could I please explain why some mosquitos decided to only pester their victims whereas others wanted to kill them. And did I not I think it a bit strange that mosquitoes, small brainless creatures that they were, would be making such momentous decisions about the health of humans? Wasn't it more likely that the mosquito was really a transfigured sorcerer? Or that a sorcerer poisoned the person? It was clear that his magic was the vessel into which he poured himself. He was not about to give it up, to be reduced to simply playing an ancient part now rendered meaningless by the modern. I could, of course, have explained that being bitten and by an anopheles mosquito was largely a matter of probability and chance. But I doubt the notion that nature plays craps with human life would have offered more than the coldest comfort, intellectually or emotionally.

Tipika continued, the others listened. He said that men like him were especially dangerous nowadays because they have freedom and anger: the freedom to "gather" magic from anywhere and anger born of watching their world crumble. Tipika said that he did not care about the mission and did not want to be like the priest. He did not care about the health center and did not want to be a doctor. I realized that most of all he did not want the status and role assigned to him by modernity. He desired not to succeed at this status and role of shaman but to flee from it. To return to a promise in which the modern did not grow like a rind between him and his practical magic. A world in which the young men he called "sons" did not see him through the prism of the modern, which transformed his fight magic, his power to cure, into an emblem of what was being left behind, what his sons needed to forget to get on with their lives in a Westernizing world. What he was saying, and profoundly, is that to have a world imposed upon him in which he is seen as enacting his customs is to become estranged from his culture. As he said to me on an earlier occasion, "I might as well teach you my magic, no one else is interested," his hand sweeping out dismissively at a knot of young men gambling dice. What the shaman was saying subtly but audibly was that the very act and fact of recognizing him as an ethnomedical specialist, and the transmission of his knowledge to me, his satisfaction of my desire to know his culture, was part and parcel of the encompassing process. On another occasion in the same vein, Tipika said that the new road was neither inherently good, nor bad: simply what was. But that did not dispel a note of personal anger.

Medical Care and the Anglican Mission

The first plans of the Koinambe mission station (ca. 1966) drawn up by Father Etterley included a hospital. By the early 1970s, the mission had built the hospital with its own funds, complete with an outpatient clinic, sick ward, plus examination, supply, and operating rooms. The hospital was staffed with a head nurse from the Volunteer Service Organization (VSO) assisted by medical orderlies and local nurses from long-established Anglican areas. The mission also inaugurated a tradition of monthly village patrols by the VSO nurse to improve pre- and postnatal care, dispense medicine, and send those in need of acute care either to the mission hospital or to the regional medical center in Mt. Hagen. In addition, medical outposts staffed by a local trainee were established in almost every community. Inscribed in the division of labor between medicine and mission was a separation of church and science, a recognition that repairing the body was of a different order than redeeming the soul. Both required specialists who, occupying different positions in intellectual space and indeed embracing different visions of health and well-being, could not but exist in an uneasy tension. After a brief period of reluctance, the Maring developed a taste for Western medicine, pharmacopoeia, and techniques. It was a new and complementary source of power that the younger generation especially could tap in pursuit of its interests.

For the Maring, the hospital was to the church as the deed was to the word. Their view was that the truth was inalienable from action. No amount of preaching about the powers of the Almighty was meaningful without concrete observable acts of power. And, as noted earlier, the Maring motto was never "In language we trust." On this perspective, the health center was more powerful than church services though less than the trade store. The Anglican Church, like most mainstream churches in New Guinea, believed that providing medical services was part of its mission to serve the body, which keeps the soul. This dovetailed with a theme

repeated time and again at evangelical conferences: that traditional religions were dominated by fear whereas Christianity was rooted in love. The
local view that ancestors will cause death and illness lent support to the
idea of a religion of fear and trembling. Against this world radiant with
harm, the Church believed that to open people's hearts and minds to the
Good News of Christ's love, it must show that it could deliver the community from illness, that the Western God was not a master of punishment
to be feared, but one's ally in the quest for health and well-being.

During the late 1960s and early 1970s, a string of aid posts was established in most of the local territories. The aid posts were established in
terms of population densities rather than political boundaries. In some
cases, two clan clusters who had been opponents in the wars of the 1950s
and who currently opposed one another politically were assigned one post,
and the aid post was sited on the land of one of the clan clusters. This led
to situations in which a vanquished clan cluster had to visit an aid post
located on the land of their traditional enemy (in some cases the APO was
also from an enemy clan). The mission was only too aware of these political rifts but felt that the key to promoting a Christian spirit and to unifying the various groups lay in overcoming old animosities. In the same
image, the aid post like the main road and the mission station itself was to
be a modern public space that belonged to everyone because it belonged to
no one. As in the case of the modern system of justice, there was supposed
to be a transcendence of kinship—a notion of duty and commitment to the
sick that inhered in the position independent of the person. From the vantage point of the Westerners, the key to finding a good APO was to find
someone who could begin to appreciate Western ideas of science and who
would be immune to the "pull" of kinship and/or the demands of exchange
relations. Moreover, in order to relieve the burden placed on the mission
hospital and to distribute health care more widely, the mission in concert
with the state sought to empower local aid post personnel by placing more
resources, authority, and monies at their disposal. This also fit the overall
program of transferring oversight of rural medicine from Western to
Melanesian hands. The logic of the progress of medicine could not but
help to empower the junior generation as they alone were capable of meeting the requirements, objectively by virtue of their education and language
skills and subjectively because Westerners felt more comfortable dealing
with them.

There was a deep contradiction in the Anglican view of medicine, a
contradiction also present in its Western incarnation, which was part of
the stowaway baggage imported to Melanesia. On the one hand, they
wanted the Maring to subscribe to scientific theories of disease and treatment, thus demystifying the issue of health. This was thought necessary
because indigenous views of illness and curing were inseparable from

indigenous religion and cosmology. To destabilize and dislodge local notions of sorcery especially, people had to adopt, however rudimentarily, Western ideas of biomedicine. As one missionary explained, people had to realize that illness had to do more with germs and proper sanitation than with "incantations mumbled over the victim's fingernails." Here the Protestant ethic and the spirit of science were fellow travelers. Yet, simultaneously, the mission taught that health and sickness depended on the will of God—Who could be approached only with one's hands folded in prayer. The efficacy of pills and injections was in His hands. This view could only undermine the very biomedical view that Church personnel were instrumental in promoting. In the practice of everyday life at the mission station, this spawned an inherent conflict between the views of the priest and those of the VSO nurse: indeed, on one occasion when the priest called for prayer she called for an emergency plane to evacuate a desperate patient riddled with malaria. This was by no means an isolated event; simmering disdain was always just beneath the surface of the cordiality demanded in the frontier setting. The VSO volunteers and the physicians that occasionally visited in no way imagined that it was their task to assist the mission in converting the local populace.

Maring thought of Western health care as a new inventory of practices rather than as an alternative system. They overlooked its systematic aspect, conceptualizing it in the light of ethnomedicine, which, indeed, was not a natural or bounded system (see Comaroff and Comaroff 1991:367). By contrast, Western health workers and clergy viewed "traditional" and "modern" systems as diametrically opposed: the hospital fighting a battle for men's bodies just as the Church fought to redeem their souls. Like the Maring, Western health workers perceived all of medicine through the prism of their own system. Thus they imbued ethnomedicine with a systematicity and closure it could never possess. They believed the Maring had to choose between competing and alternative medical systems. In the eyes of mission-educated Maring, more than the Anglican mission itself, this choice was a referendum on modernity. And so an express goal of the junior generation, delivered formally as speeches at the weekly market and informally through their influence on their kin, was to urge people to use the aid post and mission hospital, not only when they were ill but for preventive care as well.

The Evolution of Pluralism

Maring initially perceived Western medicine as part of the enormous, yet incomprehensible powers of the West. They understood that biomedicine was strong but also fraught with danger. Thus in the early years of contact, fear led people to avoid the aid posts and the health center. During this period, roughly from the late 1950s to 1970, they did not perceive Western medicine as medicine, but as part of the conquering process at the hands of the Australians. Hospitals, examinations, and policies to maintain health were not in the inventory of Maring practices. The elder generation, then in power, could do nothing about the "visits" of medical personnel armed with the kiap, but they could rebuff the attempts by the Australian administration and the Church to get people to use the health facilities. But more than any deliberate policy, people avoided the clinic and health-care givers because their methods and sociality lay beyond the compass of indigenous epistemology.

This initial phase of contact gave way to a second phase in the early 1970s. Its principal artery was the steady incorporation of biomedicine into the distinction between social and natural illnesses. Biomedicine was thus seen to specialize in promoting the body's natural regenerative powers. People felt that it was a greatly enhanced version of their own natural treatments, such as rubbing with nettles or the ingestion of plants. While the elders continued to steer clear of Western medicine, the senior generation refined their epistemology into a hierarchy of resort (Romanucci-Ross 1977). The organizing principle was an implicational logic that, by deriving its first principles from sociality, bore no relationship to a Western medical logic. If the aid post or health clinic could treat an illness—and the Maring were openly receptive to inoculations and pill-taking, as these paralleled long-standing ethnomedical prescriptions—then that illness belonged to the natural cycle. It concerned only that person and was therefore minor—or, better, was minor because it did not signal a disruption of community. By contrast, serious intractable illnesses, resistant to biomedicine, were clearly the harming of sorcery and spelled a dissembling of community. Clansmen soon began to see that they could use Western and ethnomedicine in complementary fashion.

While the Maring conceptually harmonized the two species of medicine, they were still divided at the level of practice: for the local populace played no part whatsoever in administering Western medicine. It was still at this time presented as a foreign knowledge beyond their constricted capacity to manage or understand. The difference between simply receiving medical treatment and participating in its practice was inscribed in the social structure of medicine. The management of biomedicine had three tiers. At the top was a nurse from Volunteer Service Organization of England. During the 1970s, there was a succession of VSO nurses who organized and directed the health center at Koinambe. Assisting the VSO nurse were junior nurses, almost always from coastal areas where the Anglican mission had been operating for nearly a century. At the bottom of the hierarchy were local orderlies who did cleaning and carried heavy loads. The social hierarchy expressed the view that Westerners were more capable of administering biomedicine than coastal Papua New Guineans who in turn were more capable than Maring. Westerners, coastal New Guineans, and Maring all shared this viewpoint, which was objectified in levels of perceived competence (defined as length of medical training, knowledge of English, and ability to understand Western forms of reasoning).

An important though underestimated instrument of change was the medical patrol conducted by the VSO nurse. The road show moved the medical hierarchy from community to community, displaying the social order of medical care. Given their perspective that knowledge/power were inseparable from sociality/habitat, the Maring took it as axiomatic that Westerners knew more about the science of medicine than Melanesians knew or could know, reasoning, as one senior clansman phrased it, "that sorcery and the forest have secrets that belonged to us while your medicine has secrets that belonged you." More, the patrols were indoctrinations in Western medical values. For example, the questions addressed and the responses required of a mother when the nurse examined her children presumed and entailed that she assimilate Western medical concepts. The nurse's grading of the health of children (like her questions as to the degree of health/sickness) assumed health and illness existed on a continuum. This contrasted with the indigenous version that while there were various degrees of health and illness (i.e., those who were ill may improve or become worse; those who were healthy vary in strength), health and illness were opposing states: people were either sick or healthy. Similarly, the idea that every ailment had a natural cause and a medical therapy—first and final chapters in a tale of diagnosis, treatment, and recovery—was foreign to local values, which never isolated the biological individual.

In the 1980s, medical care began to enter a new phase that promised to accelerate the Maring adoption of biomedicine. The linchpin of change was the growing local participation in the health-care system. Local aid post orderlies, especially in the Jimi Valley, began to replace their coastal counterparts. On the same note, a Papua New Guinean was promoted to the position of head nurse at the Koinambe hospital, a point that greatly impressed many Maring. At this historical juncture, the junior generation paid little attention to ethnomedicine other than simple practical therapies, such as chewing ginger for a toothache or rubbing the skin with nettles to stimulate blood flow. Many of them assumed what the mission preached, that God had trumped the sorcerers and that biomedical regimes could best treat all illnesses, no matter their genesis. There emerged a close correlation between generation and how agents perceived illness and utilized therapies. The elder generation characteristically responded to serious illness by calling for a shaman and then, after he identified the social breach and the enraged ancestor, his kinsmen sacrificed a pig to the spirits to petition for recovery. Almost invariably, the elders refused to go to the mission hospital, spurning requests from their children and especially their grandchildren. The senior (middle) generation was most likely to take the most pluralistic approach to treatment, usually receiving both ethno- and biomedical care, though rarely did they sacrifice pigs to the ancestor spirits. Finally, the junior generation often went directly to biomedical care and Christian prayer, sometimes showing marked disdain for traditional remedies. Indeed, there emerged a kind of powerful cultural polarity in which the junior generation would openly criticize customary formulas whereas senior and elder generations would abstain from publicly criticizing Western medicine.

Symptoms of Change: A Case History

The following case history gives a sense of the reality of social change as experience. It also illustrates key elements of the Maring approach to sickness and health in the context of modernity—the tension, the ambiguity, and the clash between generations. The time was January 1980 and the setting is the Kauwatyi clan cluster, Punt being a leading big-man of the second most powerful clan. As noted, the Kauwatyi maintained a particularly ambiguous relationship with the Anglican mission. Nonetheless, due to the fact that they were land-poor, the Kauwatyi were leading exponents of modernity and had invested their own money and labor in the construction of larger and more sophisticated facilities for the local APO. In the continuing generational struggle, the senior Kauwatyi leaders believed that the junior generation was using the mission to challenge their authority and control. So in their desire to keep the mission at a distance, they expelled the Anglican evangelist and did not actively participate in festivals and other ceremonies organized by the Church. The result was a continuing tension between embracing modernity—medicine and education especially—and maintaining a Kauwatyi identity.

The Medical History

Punt, an important man in his mid-fifties, took seriously ill. He said that something was blocking his body's canals, causing fever, chills, slack skin, and a loss of spirit. He withdrew from all social life into the recesses of his hut, feeling that the weakening of his body rendered his *min* (life force) susceptible to further attack from sorcerers and evil spirits. Punt was in a state of physical and spiritual decline. His body was racked with fever, and he worried that he was losing his hotness and dryness. He avoided washing as the cold, damp water would only accelerate the process. He sat by the fire inhaling smoke to help restore his heat/dryness and rubbed his arms and back with stinging nettles to produce heat and excite the flow of blood.

But preliminary treatment was ineffective, and Punt became progressively sicker. He waxed hot and cold and appeared to be dying. His younger brother suggested the cause of the illness—ancestral anger over a long-past and nearly forgotten failure to sacrifice pigs in their honor. They had withdrawn their protection leaving Punt vulnerable to attack by sorcery. The logic was simple, unassailable, and implicational: if the illness was not natural than it must be social; if a strong and apparently healthy senior clansman like Punt could be so thoroughly decimated then his ancestors must have withdrawn their protection (and conversely, his long history of good health must have been due to their intercession on his behalf); if their protection was removed Punt would be vulnerable to sorcery; and if he was the subject of sorcery it must be because he had failed to repay a debt. On this logic, Punt had twice failed the test of exchange, once with his ancestors and then again with an exchange partner. The brother then planned a sacrifice to propitiate the disenchanted ancestors and to ask them, through the medium of the shaman, to identify who he had slighted in exchange. Some said the brother was anxious to make amends because he was party to the offensive actions and was now gripped with fear that he would be next. In any case, the subclan prepared to sacrifice a pig to the ancestors.

Punt's son, who lived at Koinambe and worked at the mission hospital, came back to the settlement to see his ailing father. He judged that earlier treatments, the rubbing with nettles and visits to the APO, had been ineffective. With scant ceremony or consultation he removed Punt to the Koinambe hospital. At the hospital, the nurse diagnosed the illness as cerebral malaria and directed a junior nurse to begin treatment. But Punt's son objected, saying that because his father was dying he wanted the white VSO nurse to administer the tablets herself. Later in the day, the nurse informed the Anglican priest that Punt was likely to die.

Punt's brother raved that he was furious with the ancestors. He noted that many clansmen were no longer making regular ritual offerings, and that, moreover, his previous sacrifices had produced little in the way of ancestral help. To darken matters, Christ was no help because he was unconcerned with sorcery. So now the ancestors were taking revenge. Stripped of protection, the man was easy prey for sorcerers who coveted his pigs—pigs that should have been sacrificed and given to ancestors and affines. The day following Punt's admission to the health center, a Kauwatyi shaman arrived with a small entourage. Shortly after arriving, he pronounced that a sliver of sorcerized bamboo had penetrated Punt's liver. While Punt was writhing on a small cot, delirious, making unintelligible sounds, the shaman took a bamboo tube filled with bespelled leaves, among other items, and worked a cure. The spell was not said in Maring but in bastardized Kalam, the language of the neighboring people.[2]

At the same time that Punt's brother was fetching a shaman, Punt's son, a loyal churchgoer, was telling the Anglican priest about his father's plight. That same day the priest announced from the pulpit that there was a dying man at the hospital who needed their prayers. He told the congregation that only the intercession of God could save him. For three days Punt hung on. On the fourth, his fever started to subside and his recuperation began. The Anglican priest proclaimed a miracle from the pulpit and over the shortwave to other missions. He rejoiced that God had seen fit to show the Maring his power. The shaman told me that his magic dissolved the bamboo and stopped the sorcery. The VSO nurse, Catherine Sutton, told me that the actions of Punt's son coupled with the administration of primaquine and the patient's generally sound health saved the day. She also confided in me that she did not know who was more absurd, the shaman or the priest, and then after a moment's reflection, she selected Father Bailey as the more absurd "because he should know better." But given the joy of the situation, there seemed more than enough credit to go around and no dearth of willing takers.

Responses to Illness

Here, as in numerous other instances from this period, Maring patients made use of both forms of medicine, separately and in tandem. While Punt's son favored Western therapy, he made no effort to halt the ethnomedical cure and indeed was present when the shaman performed his magical surgery. Somewhat uncertainly, he accepted the premise that when persons are gravely ill, their kin must tap all sources of power until they are cured. Throughout, treatment was plural and cumulative. A failure of the preliminary therapy of stinging nettles and fasting led to a visit to the aid post, which, proving ineffective, led to hospitalization and employment of a shaman. This was the progression of medical treatment, clearly a change from only a decade earlier when many fewer people used the hospital and consulted the shaman first. The example underscores the complementarity between Western and indigenous medicine, between focusing on its physiological versus its social causes. By 1980, most Maring believed that the treatments offered at the aid posts and health centers assisted the body's natural processes and were, in this respect, superior to ethnomedical remedies. There was an analogical transfer of schemes from ethnomedicine to biomedicine. If an indigenous medicine relieved pain by causing blood to rush, and a Western medicine better relieved the same pain, then the Western medicine must have achieved success by circulating blood more effectively than the indigenous one. The mainstream view was that Western medicine was a therapeutic magic that specialized in aiding the body's basic recuperative powers. It could not, however, counteract the ravages of sorcery or spiritual siege. The sorcerized bamboo sliver would cause death if not removed with techniques beyond the purview of Western medicine. Moved by an implicational logic, this fostered the notion that if biomedicine could not cure an illness then the illness must be the result of sorcery or malevolent spirits. In such cases the wisest course of action was to combine Western and indigenous treatments. So the malarial medicine was seen to strengthen the patient, a positive mobilization of power vested in the competence of Western medicine. The divination and magic was aimed at removing a continuous agent of death—the sliver of bamboo— thus eliminating an inevitable because unremedied cause of death (Glick 1967). And there was in all of this an air of practical experimentation. In one case, a young man who had attended school, worked for the mission, and aligned himself on the side of biomedicine called in a shaman when Western remedies failed to calm his illness. An opposite example was an elder clansman who sought Western medicine when, after receiving the help of a shaman, his condition continued to deteriorate.

The attitudes of Punt, his brother, and the shaman capture the indigenous conception that illnesses are specific to persons. There was not an entity, a given disease type, that attacked an individual, exhibiting its effects based on the physical state of the victim, the strength of the disease, and other factors. Rather, illness was a specific transformation of the person from a potentially identifiable cause. Within this framework, diagnosing the cause of the illness was less critical than the administration of treatment. In some cases, the initial cause of the illness (e.g., failure to make ritual sacrifices) was only divined after the patient has been treated (cf. Johannes 1980:51). Similarly, the means of sorcery, its reasons, or how the bamboo sliver entered the liver were not relevant to treatment. The case also illustrates the contradiction inherent in the Christian view, which both wanted to extol the virtues and value of medicine and the health center and, at the same time, wanted to oppose the separation of the science of healing from the Word of God. Certainly the priest's claim that only God's hand could cure Punt seeks to reunite them.

Medical History and Cultural Prognosis

It should not be ignored that the social organization of illness always fulfilled a political function by defining the limits of health, boundaries that differentiate healthy from sick people, the social limitations imposed on those who are ill, and the duties, responsibilities, and privileges of health. But medical pluralism among the Maring touches the social polity in another decisive way. The use of Western medicine and the uses made of it became enmeshed in social and political strategies and instigated generative changes in people's epistemology, desires, and dispositions—changes that stretched well beyond the limits of medicine. After a quarter century of encompassment, the local political structure, led by the senior generation, allowed a pluralism that combined ethno- and biomedicine, even as the evolution of medical care was gravitating rapidly toward the latter. A critical register of change was people's categorization of illness, these acts of classification simultaneously defining the appropriate treatment and reproducing a practice of medicine. In the hidden hand of history, people were progressively, gradually, and practically classifying more instances of illness as belonging to the natural cycle. Thus classified, they were amenable to Western therapy and outside the scope of ritual and magic; there was no need to call upon shamans to identify the social sources of the sickness, nor was there a reason to presume that anything was amiss socially. Thus agents saw little point or merit in, as one young man put it, "wasting pigs on the ancestors." Reciprocally, the successful treatment of an illness by Western medicine implied that the illness was natural rather than social. This was a point that the medical and mission personnel made often and in various ways, perhaps most dramatically when they preached, as they did repeatedly, that people died from infections not because they had been attacked by a wayward spirit or sorcerer, but because their kinsmen had not brought them to the clinic soon enough. To summarize the argument: the model of medicine being produced from the encounter between the Maring and mission was not the result of a logical combination of indigenous and imported brands because it was mediated by generations very differently constituted and positioned with respect to the social system.

The notion that the natural cycle was on the ascendency fit local concepts of modernity. The junior generation in particular believed that pacification and the turn toward law had all but extinguished the social cycle of war and peace. Accordingly, the "red ancestors" who had once presided over the cycle were increasingly irrelevant to the reproduction of the clan and the well-being of its members. In that same dimming light, relationships made with affines because they could serve as military allies and ports of refuge were diminishing in importance. Pacification, coupled with the new opportunities provided by modernity and the ascendency of women to determine their own future, allowed marriages to be made far and wide. This was part of a more general process in which things social were re-presented as natural even as a Western notion of the social—predicated in large part on the disenchantment of nature—began to take hold.

In this respect, biomedicine was part of the introduction of a notion of nature that imagined biology and environment, body and place, as extrinsic to the social.

The influence of the Western medical system was founded at least in part on the reality that it was a system, in contrast to ethnomedicine, that existed entirely in a practical state. From the standpoint of local healers, biomedicine was part of the overall weakening of Maring society, which they had come to accept as inevitable. Their authority had been founded on a monopoly on competence: their ability to remedy serious illness by divining its genesis, deploying the technologies of magical healing, and repairing the rents in the social fabric caused by the wanton transgression of limits. With the advance of the modern, the shamans lost their monopoly twice: once to Western medicine and again to a younger generation who had special competence in opening the corridors to biomedicine. Nothing illustrated this more than the dearth of shamans among the younger generation and their disposition that shamanism was part of the deadweight of the past. Beyond that, many members of the junior generation simply disregarded traditional notions of the transgression of limits, thereby redefining these limits and their implications for the construction of sociality. They especially ignored the elaborate catalog of food taboos, and the generative schemes whose enactment continually and practically divided the social field in respect to circumstances. Those who were more aggressive in their Christian faith even prided themselves on their willingness to forsake the food prohibitions specific to their clan and the taboos on eating the food from, or dining with, an enemy clan cluster. The circulation of food at the Koinambe station, which housed members of formerly warring clan clusters (e.g., the Cenda and Kauwatyi, traditional enemies, represented more than half the population), exemplified a new willingness to discard old limits in the interests of new realities. Spurred on by the mission men, they rejected the thought that eating alien foods could have medical consequences. The medical field was thus instrumental in a three-dimensional shift in power: from shamans to physicians and other health-care givers; from a customary set of social limits to a modern one; and from the senior generation to their juniors.

A characteristic of ethnomedicine generally and Melanesia specifically is that there is no separation between technical medical and ritual action. In this union, all treatment was on a case-by-case basis because Maring believed that the conditions of community, the behavioral history of those involved, and the action itself were all relevant. Healing passes from the specific illness and its causes to a specific cure, all of the while invoking symbolic means toward biomedical ends; the logic flows upstream implicationally from the symptoms and disease of a person to its cause—young men, for example, who are victims of malaria must have been the object of sorcery whereas old men who suffer the same disease may do so naturally. Moreover, there can be no field of medicine because there is no distinction between the person and position, between, for example, the shaman and the kinsman. Finally, for the same reasons, the practices of the shaman did not have a social space that corresponded to them. By contrast, the Koinambe mission station was an education in the definition and orchestration of fields. The religious sphere was commanded by the priest, housed in the church, and centered on the action of praying. The medical sphere was commanded by the nurse, located in the hospital, and centered on the actions of prescribing medicine, giving inoculations, and performing surgery. If the Church's domain was the soul and spirit of the person, the medical system concentrated on the body to the extent that often little or no social interaction passed between nurse and patient. The rotation of nurses also underlined that the persons were interchangeable because what mattered was that the position be occupied by a capable (i.e., medically authorized) individual. By 1980, the Maring had only begun to appreciate the construction and differences between fields, though the mission station served as a permanent model and its agent used the distinction between fields as a reason that was also a cause of action. Whenever anyone was seriously sick, this justified summoning the nurse immediately, almost ceremoniously. On several notable occasions, the Maring carried a sick man to the house of the priest and requested that he send the patient to the Mt. Hagen hospital, but the priest deferred that judgment on the grounds that it was the nurse's decision, she being the medical expert.

The infiltration of Western medicine also inflected the subjectivity of the Maring and the conditions of its construction. People came to believe in its power to help them and grew in their desire for its pharmacopoeia and technologies. Particularly those of the junior generation but also some seniors and a large cross section of women became disposed to use it as the medicine of first resort. No longer dependent on entangling kinship relations, and all the hierarchies and enduring obligations this entailed, the aid post and the mission clinic offered the opportunity for greater autonomy. This autonomy of the body became a metaphor for the expression of the individuated aspect of the person, part of the more general process in which the modern made individuality a progressively more acceptable form of being-in-the-world. Self-control over one's body meant that people were free to select their marriage partners, self-decide what food taboos they were going to respect, and self-orchestrate who their confidants/friends would be. The budding concept of friendship was bound to the autonomy of the body, as were ultimately all the acts of privacy that the West takes for granted, such as having a bank account, eating alone, or taking a solitary walk.

CHAPTER 9

Education and the
Discipline of Modernity

First the mission taught us that we have a mind, and then they
gave us thoughts to help fill it up. We also learned that time
exists, and this needs to be filled up as well. Otherwise we are
liable to sin.

GOU, 1980

For you [Westerners], time is a god.

MOSES, 1980

As the epigrams suggest, any account of education in Melanesia is inseparable from a discussion of the shape and influence of Christianity. More
rapidly than the state and with greater authority, Christian churches penetrated the hinterlands, setting themselves up as the primary instruments
and institutions of scholastic, civic, and moral education. Bundled
together in a kind of cultural porridge were a potpourri of lessons on citizenship and the New Testament, the embrace of a national history and the
reality of an afterlife, the rights of the individual and the one-to-one relationship we all have with our Maker. From the moment of their birth,
nongovernmental organizations such as the Christian churches were to
have a great hand in governing the countries of Melanesia. Not only were
the churchmen the major force in the initiation of new schools in remote
regions, but the elite who framed their national constitutions were loyal
sons of the Christianity that educated them. Many of these constitutions,
exemplified by that of Papua New Guinea, invoke Christianity as part of
their national heritage, assuming as a matter of faith that Christian and
national identities can be seamlessly threaded together. But the issue, as
colonial history knows well, is more complicated. Due to the internal divisions and divisiveness within a Christianity that, paradoxically, represents
itself as universal, Christian education could not but insinuate narratives
of identity that are both more local and more global than those of the
national state. The most educated Maring defined themselves as Anglican
in opposition to other and lesser species of Christianity, and also as
embracing a universal Christianity in opposition to all forms of paganism.
The shaping and inculcation of this Western set of imbricated identities

275

was inseparable from the missionary educational system. It would teach them that they were Anglicans, the virtues of this faith revealed in its material, social, and spiritual contributions to each of them as individuals. It would teach that their national identity was bound to Christianity and thus to the encompassing gesture itself so that ultimately colonialism disappeared into the bodies of the colonized. Finally it would teach them that they were all soldiers in a global Christianity that stood against not only paganism but also the satanic forces of immorality that vexed the modern world. So the reality under construction centered on the proliferation and dance of categorical identities—an Anglican Maring, a Christian citizen, and a member of world Christianity. Those schooled in the context of southern Africa will find this bumpy but charted terrain.

Until and through independence, Christian missions in Melanesia bore the educational burden with considerable assistance from first the colonial administration and later its postindependent successor. Mission and government segregated the colonial education system into "A" (Australian) and "T" (tribal) type schools. The A species, drafted for the expatriate population and taught by teachers imported from the south, taught the standard Australian syllabus—including of course lessons on Australian history. The T type, run by missionaries and generally staffed with "native" teachers, taught a rather different lesson, focusing primarily on English, counting, and the lineaments of Western sensibility and civilization. This was also a division between town and hinterland insofar as it was government policy not to compete with the evangelists by setting up schools in mission districts. Missionary and government imagined education as part of the order and systematicity of the modern world and as a set of values to be acquired by the student. Objectively, they saw education as a touchstone of modernity, an indispensable agent in the eclipse of tradition. Subjectively, the disposition to learn was a critical internal stance and discipline toward grasping the modern and developing the kind of mind that might do so. A symbiosis emerged in which the mission men maintained schools in remote regions, saving Australian/expatriate tax dollars and the difficulties of finding and retaining teachers, in return for the right to fuse education and salvation. For a long time, most Maring believed that the reason people learned to read was so that they could read the Bible in order to appropriate the source of its magical materialism. In the jagged puzzle that was modernity, reading and counting, the authority of Jesus, and a desired cornucopia of commodities were all interlocking pieces. The schools in the Maring region were always of the T type even when they were no longer so called.

Entering the school was a rite of civilization. And thus an encounter with the moral economy of Western thought. Dressing up for the occasion mattered—a point on which the Maring concurred absolutely. Given their intricately woven beetle bonnets, confections of bird plumes and possum · fur, shell necklaces and nose plugs, little could resonate more with their thinking of the world. So they were hardly surprised when the mission men argued that it was unthinkable that children should attend school in traditional garb. Father Etterley, the main architect of the school, explained to the Maring that there was something indecent and unnatural about the free exposure of flesh in the classroom. Only a covered body could uncover the mysteries of civilization, an education that could connect the dots between the economy of the body and that of the commodity. With more than a touch of magic, the missionaries also argued that it was more natural to learn Western knowledge in Western clothes. Thus they had clothes—shorts and T-shirts for the boys, frocks for the girls—ferried up from the south, clothing drives instigated in small parish churches around Australia to uplift local souls by clothing the bodies of these Christians in the making. The mission hoped that not only would the school children become imbued with the virtues of clothes but that they would carry this into adulthood and spread the spirit of decency until it became the *pasin belong ol* ("the trend," Tok pijin). This was important because the exposure of the body was both an invitation to the senses to feast improperly and a sign of the absence of propriety. There was a short step from skin to sin that clothes would lengthen by the magic of concealment. Therefore the mission awarded all of the schoolchildren gifts of clothes—reason enough, some Maring observed, to attend school at least for a while. That the clothes were almost always slightly too big for Maring bodies made them that much more fashionable, the runway to heaven emphasizing virtue at every turn. Through Maring eyes, the missionaries were certainly men of the cloth. Through missionary eyes, the Maring penchant for Western clothes expressed their progress—as several of the mission men explained to me in a self-satisfied way, glad to spy a sign of success in a sea of ambiguity.

The primary school at Koinambe, the secondary school in Mt. Hagen, and higher level education at, for instance, the Anglican mission seminary were all instrumental in producing a distinct field of education imbued with its own logic, spaces, temporalities, place in the developmental cycles of person and household, forms of reward and failure, boundaries, and relationships to other domains of practice. Where traditional forms of education were diffused throughout the constellation of local practices, the West would create and consecrate a distinct field of practice whose intent was to prepare individuals for real life. At a deeper level, the education system encapsulated all the epistemological values of a capitalist and democratic nation-state of autonomous individuals. It did this invisibly, shielded by the mask of what was functionally necessary to learn the modern world. The lessons in math, English, and geography were small compared to the lessons in personhood, the production of value, and the nature of knowledge itself. To arrive on time, to sit up straight in school and pay attention to the day's lesson, and to do this day after day in the company of others, supervised by the teacher and above him the headmaster, taking competitive exams to test one's personal knowledge, was a forced march into the heart of Western forms of knowledge, desire, and dispositions. The very existence of the schooling system invited an opposition between what was modern and what was traditional, and in this sense it helped to bring kastam into being as a category of thought. An opposition arose between forms of kastam knowledge transmitted from senior clan members to their junior kin and modern knowledge transmitted by strangers in service of the Church. Beneath this opposition was a realm of epistemological and dispositional contrasts that were even more striking. From the viewpoint of the missionaries, local teachers, and the education system generally, the indigenous methods of education, instruction, and training appeared diffuse, episodic, and casual. They seemed to be looking over their shoulder at the past rather than ahead to the future. Once it was presumed that there was a field of education founded on a set scientific body of knowledge and inculcated by means of a disciplined method of instruction, then the indigenous system came into relief as its opposite. More than new things to know, the Maring needed new ways to know things. As is often the case on the frontier between cultures, the content of the schooling system induced changes less telling than those animated by the way in which the lessons were taught.

Education in the Past Tense

Before the arm of encompassment touched the Maring, there was and could be no difference between education and socialization because there was no field of instruction distinct from practice. The training of the young was regular without being regularized, orchestrated without being systematized, their kin bearing a sense of responsibility to practically instruct them in the practice of everyday life. As food stood at the center of Maring life, the child's social, ethical, and moral education began in an attempt to instil the proper ways of eating, sharing, and nurturing others. The maxim was that children's upbringing began when they were weaned, and indeed the official naming ceremony for a child sometimes corresponded to this moment. In keeping with the simple mode of reproduction, adults and children all participated in the same culture, though in varying degrees corresponding to their station in the developmental cycle of the person. The upbringing of children thus flowed easily into social, economic, and political behavior of their kin, the aims and ambitions of the young confluent with those of their parents. Socialization was cyclical and rather determinate in that everything in the universe conspired to orient children toward the same reality as their elders. Accordingly, there were no special behaviors, rewards, punishments, and the like associated with socialization, parents needing to coerce children only after the doxic world had waned and the breach between generations had widened. By 1980, socialization had become more troubled because the objective structure of a now encompassed reality was no longer in sync with the cognitive and dispositional structures of the senior generation. Once a clan's reproduction was no longer cyclical, cloistered, and nearly determinate, once the future of its children was aimed at a world perpetually different from that of parents, then socialization became the politics of upbringing, a stage on which the bodies of children were introduced to the orthodoxies of their parents in the context of an ever widening public sphere that drew them in a very different direction. The encompassment of Melanesia probably changed parenting even more than it changed childhood.

In contrast to Western education, traditional learning was neither a text nor was it decontextualized. The cultural forms of knowledge, desire, and dispositions were not built up piece by piece during the progress of a child's life. Rather, the total pattern of practice was present as generative schemes from the beginning, the child coming to master that batch of pragmatic and productive actions in respect to others. The child learned to elicit or draw out of the world its potentialities, as a social relationship already present within the other, as a fruitfulness already present in the earth, as a spiritual blessing already present in the desires of the ancestors. As such, education was never about controlling or gaining the upper hand on others, nature, or spirits, rather about the continual appropriation and internalization of these potentialities. No one could ever teach these schemes of perception, appropriation, and so on because they were never the object of explicit representation, though they were, of course, inculcated in the socializing process. The category of teacher could not possess any functional autonomy because the field of education did not exist as such, there was no explicit body of knowledge, and learning did not have any gatekeeping functions (e.g., who would attain big-man status). Not surprisingly, the cultural metaphor for education was never the filling up of an empty space with objective objects, the house of culture built up brick by brick, story by story, but rather the development of the body itself. The release of potentialities that were always present. In this world, agents were never educationally finished since every social transaction begot another, every gift, every harvest, every act of propitiation completing one phase of an interaction even as it instigated another.

As the rainy season follows the dry, so this vision of sociality and nature, people and things, implies that socialization was never about formal methods for transmitting information about the objective world to possessive, self-contained individuals. The critical forms of disenchantment and contrast that animate the West—the division of an objectively conceived reality into nature, society, and individual, and the division of the subject into mind, body, and spirit—were never present as such in the Melanesian world. Other, that is, than as its inverse, a conceptual possibility made real by the modern.

The Gender of Education

In the indigenous world, gender was both a modality of agency and a stance toward that world. In this vision, the efficacy of women and men were not the same; women excelled at the forms of sociality and transaction constitutive of the domestic sphere while men excelled at those constitutive of interdomestic relations. The enterprise of men consisted of taking products created jointly with their spouse and/or sister, that is domestically, and transforming them into objects of interdomestic exchange. The distinction between the practice of men as husbands (or brothers) and the practice of men as clansmen becomes an idiom through which the possibility for acting on the world unfolds. Unlike in the West, the distinction between domestic and interdomestic does not implicate any distinction between the private life of the household and the public life of collective action. Each was equally relational and public. Where they differed was in the kinds of realities they engendered and the sociality they made visible.

In the context of education, the logic of this relationship clashed with the logic of Western schooling—at least Western schooling in its late-twentieth-century incarnation as an instrument of emancipation and egalitarianism. For senior clansmen, it was self-evident that only boys should attend school because its aim was to prepare them for the kinds of interdomestic relations characteristic of the modern. The coordinates of kastam located exchange relations and managing a trade store on the same plane: that of male action whose intent was to socially reproduce the clan. For senior women, it was equally self-evident that girls should attend to the interests of their mothers. These concerns, centering on domestic relations, such as the production of taro, pigs, coffee, string bags, and the like, allowed small need for the skills of schooling. There was also in place an age effect, as the skills of young girls were much more valuable than those of their brothers. True to this logic, most of the schoolgoers were young boys. The mission argued vehemently against this position and called upon the Maring families to send their daughters as well as their sons to school. The mission reasoned that all sexes were equally children of God and that every individual, no matter what gender, should be allowed to reach his/her natural potential. The mission saw in this, like in the practice of buying a wife, the oppression of tradition against the enlightenment of the modern.

Some key leaders of the junior generation agreed with them. They both won the approval of the Church and gained a stroke in their confrontation with the senior generation by sending their daughters to school. Almost invariably, it was recently married, educated, churchgoing men who sent their daughters to the mission school and applied pressure on others to do likewise. Most women of the junior generation applauded the move to send girls to school as part of a more general process of increasing personal freedom. The equation was simple and predictable, though certainly not absolute. The more a child's parents had been exposed to the agents and institutions of the modern—because of their age, education, and/or proximity to a mission school—the more likely they were to send their children to school, including a greater percentage of daughters. In particular, members of the junior generation living on the mission station believed that the West treated men and women the same. For them, the status of the nurse in charge of the hospital exemplified this rehearsal of Western ideology, though ironically she had, in her own words, "escaped" to Melanesia to avoid the sting of what she decried as "pervasive sex discrimination" in her homeland medical system. Again the ironic reversals of the frontier imbued the moderning process with its own peculiar character.

Lessons in Epistemology and Desire

Going to school required that the Maring learn a new set of correspondences between time, space, and forms of behavior. Schooling was a novel practice that not only combined these elements in unexpected ways, but created new forms of space and time and behavior in the process. As a foreign office of Western epistemology, the school system conceived time as having an externality and objectiveness that transcended, and in that process subordinated, practical and phenomenological time. The secondhand clock that hung on the school wall, the time-defined schedule of activities, the assumption that people should desire to conform to deadlines and appointments (and desire that desire as well), the revelation that human activity itself can be timed and measured, all these enshrined the modern god of time. Whereas, in the village, time existed in a practical and embodied state—the time to live an activity, such as harvesting taro once it had reached an edible size; the existential time of doing, which was inseparable from its sociality (e.g., the felt duration of a practice, such as building a fence or weeding a garden, depends on the company of the moment); and the seasonal time defined by the rhythms of sun and rain,

harvesting and planting. In this world, time was not an intangible commodity that appeared to possess a life and authority of its own. Talking
about time was no one's preoccupation. Time was not spent or saved like
money. It was not lost like a lousy investment or gained by working more
rapidly. There was no covert equation of time and economy, no metaphors
that assumed that time, and hence human action itself, was a commodity.
There was no disenchantment between nature and society because neither
term of the equation existed as such—only relations of collectivity and
sociality in nature. Against this indigenous sense of time—a sense that was
simultaneously objective and subjective at the same time—the schooling
system in concert with other Western institutions began to fix a notion of
objective time that existed independently of subjects. None of our covert
cultural metaphors captures this better than the idea that time is a container that agents fill up with actions—a point that my housemate Gou
made pointedly in the epigram above. In the same sense, the mission
sought to privatize time, to instill in its converts and pupils the value that
their time belonged to them and that its management was critical to the
construction of their subjectivity. The modern person conformed his/her
own private time to the strictures of objective time. And was proud of the
accomplishment. So one of the oft-repeated school lessons was how to
read a watch, and, more, to learn to determine how long it takes to complete a task as though, true to Western ideology, there was an intrinsic
connection between a task, how long it took to complete, and the underlying values that were represented. The modernist perspective takes this so
much for granted that it does not question the practice of timing intelligence tests, as though there was somehow a connection between a person's
intelligence and how fast they work. Not surprisingly, the commodity
most sought after by the junior generation was a wristwatch, the young
men sporting watches like badges and body decoration of their newfound
view of the world. The watches reported that they had the money and
mobility to buy an expensive good sold only in town and associated with
Westerners, that they possessed the knowledge to read the hands of time,
and that they subscribed—if only in principle—to a modern conception of
time, planning, and behavior. In this and other respects, the agents and
institutions of encompassment increasingly built objectivism into the
world by building it into the way that people viewed their world.

   If anything frustrated the Western mentality, it was the Maring's
seeming disregard for punctuality and planning. And the mission men,
especially the station manager, saw this promiscuous and "foggy" relationship to time as a barrier to advancement—which indeed it is in a Western-run world. He complained repeatedly that women and the senior generation were impossible; seemingly like clockwork they appeared late and
inappropriately. They appeared during lunch time to sell their coffee to a

station cooperative that kept only morning hours; they showed up on Tuesday for a Monday airplane flight and then simply waited for the Thursday departure. But even those with watches won with mission wages sometimes found it hard to eclipse the dispositions of customary time, the most intractable and trying example being their failure to report to work on time. That at least is the story the mission men told. Pejoratives aside, it was indeed the case that at this stage in the advance of modernity only a few Maring had internalized the disposition to conform to objective time, to feel a compulsion from within to meet the expectations of the clock, to hear its ticking as an insistent call to conformity. On more than a few occasions, the station manager, the priest in charge, and the Bible translator asked me when the Maring would learn time, as though this were an enigma so deep they were willing to chance a little anthropology.

Against the dispositions of kastam time, school and the mission generally thought that integral to its mandate was the inculcation of the modern sense of objective time and obedience to its artifacts, such as schedules. Students' time at the mission station was divided into church time, schooling time, lunch time, sports/play time, work time, and free time with specific forms of thought and action appropriate to each of these times. For the schoolgoers, their day began with morning services after which they filed into their classrooms. The school divided the morning session into two or three periods, featuring reading and English, alongside practical activities like learning the Gregorian calendar and the solar system. At noon by the clock's telling, students broke for lunch, returning for an afternoon session that included sports activities and a periodic work detail to clean the grounds. Specific activities, like playing soccer, done at an appointed time and day (Wednesday and Thursday afternoon), corresponded to specific spaces (the soccer field) and forms of social relations (a non-kinship-based team). The same held true with the morning prayer to begin classes, the classes themselves, and indeed every aspect of the organized school. Children learned that the schedule of activities did not depend on them or even on their teachers; they were not its author or cause. There was an external force that stood outside the sociality of the students and teachers that orchestrated their actions. As the poet Neruda observed: we live within the compass of the "clockface whose cadence utters our lifetimes" (1959). The coordinates of the modern were being set in place, slowly, variably, but inevitably as an incoming tide.

According to the priest in charge, the headmaster, and the European advisers who occasionally passed through, the organization of school should be a living artifact of the organization of mind in body. The distinction between the cerebral gestures of learning the curriculum and the physical exertions of sports and play ran, like an underground river, through the terrain of their statements, sometimes seeping up to the surface but even then written off as a natural occurrence. The organization of classroom instruction that sought to isolate the pupil's mind was insepara- ble from the goal of instilling knowledge in the abstract as well as abstract knowledge. True to the modernist epistemology of the person, the mission separated mind from body and both from the "human" spirit. This secular trinity of mind, body, and spirit was institutionally reflected in what West- erners took to be the primary purpose of the school, the hospital, and the church. The school concentrated on the life of the mind, the hospital on the biological individual, and the church on the spirit or soul. It was sub- liminally reflected in the Holy Trinity, the canon that there existed an omniscient God the Father, an incarnate Christ, and a Holy Spirit. In sum, the Western conception was that there not only existed a level of organi- zation above and beyond the physical brain—the mind—but that the mind had an ontological realness independent of both body and spirit. By con- trast, indigenous concepts such as *min* (life force, bodily consciousness), *nomane* (soul, culture, spirit), and *tep* (speech, sentience) began in the premise that mind, body, and spirit are fused in the first instance.

If Maring of all ages could concur on any one point, it was that prior to encompassment they did not know that they had minds, and that one of the advances of their contact with the mission was learning that, housed within their head, there was an invisible container that they could fill with information. Further, that some containers were more alert and easier to fill. This stood in contrast to the indigenous notion that knowledge was sit- uationally specific and relational, a performance of the thinking body to meet a social objective. It might be said of someone that they acted intelli- gently when speaking politically, but there was no linguistic construction to say that someone was intelligent as a general and abstract quality. Mis- sion education began to establish the notion of timeless internal states, constant properties of the person that agents express through their actions, these states appearing differentially across contexts for action. In the school curriculum, an underlying motif of the stories that the children read was whether an agent would or would not express a timeless internal state—such as their courage, honesty, or fidelity to their parents. In another of the ironic twists of the frontier, Maring schoolchildren were introduced to the myths of other Papua New Guineans through English translations that epistemologically transmuted the stories into morality tales based on the expression of internal states. Thus in addition to a mind that was filled with knowledge the school taught a body filled with timeless internal states.

A critical feature that distinguished Western schooling from the indigenous process of learning lay in their respective views of truth. Not least was the claim of certainty of knowledge on the part of Western edu- cation. From this perspective, the world can be taught precisely because it is organized and ordered, clarity of thought rendering the world unambiguous. There exists a canon of truths whose verity is independent of social relations, which is thus true for all people be they Western or Melanesian. By contrast, Melanesian truths, such as the existence of sorcerers, were so inseparable from their sociality that Westerners, as outsiders, were immune from their malevolence. By the same logic, the Maring universe was not organized and orderly throughout, animated by principles that inquiring minds could discover through the technologies of science. Rather there was order and organization at the center of the community, which gradually gave way to increasing entropy and disorder at the periphery. The domesticated and certain center opposed to the wildness and unpredictability of the bush. But more than this, Western epistemology separated the world into "objective reality"—what is out there, the tools agents use to grasp and measure what is real (numbers, measures of length and weight, etc.), and representations of that reality (e.g., written documents, photographs, recordings). Thus, technology and the commodities of the West engendered a reality that, appearing to exist independent of persons, could be measured (in terms of time saved, money gained, etc.) and then represented (by an entry in a passbook saving account, the trade store ledger, etc.). In other words, the school taught a reality that it was instrumental in creating. And insofar as this reality was not already inculcated within the schoolgoers, they had yet to internalize the underlying epistemology and dispositions that would allow them to grasp the lessons taught. What the mission men saw as the limits of local intelligence was actually the limits of Western intelligence about other realities.

Ethnographic Interlude

Sometimes a small hole in the universe would open and allow in a light that would suggest to the mission men that they did not know nearly enough of what needed to be known. On one occasion, I, the station manager, and his friend (another VSO recruit) tagged along with several Maring men to the lower bush to "look for" the bird of paradise. Off to discover the habitat and habits of these birds, the station manager and his friend asked the Maring questions about the birds and trees. The soft drizzling rain that filtered through the forest canopy was nothing next to the shower of information that Kaiya and his friends provided. They detailed how different trees changed from season to season, the insects that frequented the trees and their reproductive and eating habits, the birds that feed on these insects and those that competed with the insects for fruits, the calls of the birds, where they made their nests, how they treated their young, everything classified and named down to the subspecies level.

Astounded by this downpour of information, technical information, information learned by experience and education, the station manager commented that "each of them seemed to qualify for a Ph.D. in botany." "Why then," he asked me, himself, and the world in general, "were they so dismal and slow in school?" Why indeed!

The Subject and the Objective

The school was set apart in space and time so that a marked distinction could be constructed between the world and observing child. This reality was then arranged before the viewing subject and organized into a system of classification that was also a system of signification. This was exemplified in the lessons on geography, which were also lessons on nationalism, organized around a globe. The globe showed the Maring the collective world of nations, laid out before them in a manner that the organization of local territories never was or could be. This could not but project a sense of order—embodied in the codification of the relationship between territories and nations, and in the relationship between the observing child and the globe itself. In his work on the colonization of Egypt, Mitchell (1988) describes the relationship:

> The technique of . . . fixing an interior and exterior, and of positioning the observing subject, are what create an appearance of order, an order that works by appearance. The world is set up before an observing subject as though it were the picture of something. Its order occurs in the relationship between observer and picture, appearing and experienced in terms of the relationship between the picture and the plan or meaning it represents. It follows that the appearance of order is at the same time an order of appearance, a hierarchy. The world appears to the observer as a relationship between picture and reality, the one present but secondary, a mere representation, the other only represented, but prior, more original, more real. This order of appearance is what might be called the hierarchy of truth. (60)

A triangulation is set up between the subject, picture/description, and reality in which the truth and its apprehension depends on the iconographic relationship between the picture/description and the world, while the ability of agents to internalize the truth depends on the authenticity of this relationship in respect to their mental capacity. This is a historically determinate way of orchestrating the interrelationship between world, code, and subject—the modern way. It differs, first of all, from indigenous learning, which assumes an almost perfect intimacy between teaching and doing. People learned to plant taro, paint a war shield, sacrifice pigs, and almost everything else by the practical mimicry of their kin. Leading to the practical mastery of practice. But it was also and always that the appearance of order conformed to another logic, an implicational logic that centered on the way that the relationality of one action, object, or person animates, excites, elicits, influences another. By this logic, there was no difference between implication and causation; they were reciprocal. Because they were reciprocal and so entailed, the signs of the world were inseparable from that world. Maring epistemology was not a "code" for decoding the world—a description of reality extrinsic to that reality. Some examples. In the epoch of war, the uprooting of the rumbim plant implied/caused the deterioration of relations between clans, which, in turn, implied/caused the precipitation of mortal combat, which further implied/caused the assumption by men of food and sexual taboos, and so on. The secular and ritual actions were not commentaries about the world but actions performed upon it. The process of learning the world concentrated on learning how to excite, animate, elicit, and influence. Socialization was a matter of mastering the implicational chain triggered and presupposed by an action, object, or person. When a man dreamed that he had hunted wild pig in the haunts of the lower bush this implied that his life force, his min, had sojourned during the night, and further that he should, on waking, gather his bow and arrow to search for his prey. Differently but by the same logic, when a man bought a commodity (a bag of rice, a carton of canned of fish, etc.) and then removed it to the context of wealth exchange, such as a marriage payment, he was following a logic that said that the change of context implied that the object was attached to him in a new way, as a mediation of his sociality with others. Similarly, in the modern era people could use rice like taro not because rice symbolized what taro symbolized, but because they were both white and soft and swell when cooked. The relations of sameness and sympathy were what counted. In contrast to the West, there was no underlying quasi-autonomous epistemological domain of symbolic representations of the world. The representations were attached to both the world and the subject. Where the West is committed to seeing an ontological separation between the world, the intentions and interests of the subject, and the mechanics of knowing, the Maring assumed that they were inseparable in the first instance. Where the West committed all of its cultural resources—from the creation of the scientific method to its ideology of objectivity—to creating and preserving this separation, the Maring committed nothing other than a concern for the proper execution of their practices. In essence, because the Maring and Melanesians did not believe that the order of their world was based on an order of appearances, the character and content of socialization centered on doing and enacting. Or, to put this another way, persons need to have minds only if knowledge is separated ontologically from doing and agents are the cause of their own actions. And so the Maring learned they had minds in the process of learning a new reality.

Discipline and Order

Central to the process of encompassment was the creation of order, discipline, and regimentation. Recall the concern of the kiaps to create ordered villages that sparkled with sanitation. The same was true of education. Mission educators saw an undisputable linkage between the inculcation of order and discipline and the value of the education process itself. Central to the creation of order was to imbue the children with a respect for orderliness and cleanliness, to begin, as the headmaster noted, "to teach the children the importance of these things so that they could progress" (Dec. 1979). But this was no easy task, as the Western geometry of the body, the straight lines, even spacing, looking forward, shoulders back, did not resonate with kastam. As one teacher noted, just getting the students to line up properly was a small victory. But apparently a march worth taking as the school strived to teach its students that the properly aligned body in the proper clothes was essential to educating their newfound minds. Not the least of the lessons of modernity was that order was an end in itself, people should construct their subjectivity such that they can feel the accomplishment and taste the pride of creating order. To pursue the objective of order required a regime of constant surveillance, a long-established feature of the European schooling system. The indigenous concept of watching the behavior of others had its center of gravity in agents' sociality and intentionality. The goal of observing others was to uncloak the hierarchy of intentions that lay behind their actions, to go beyond the "skin" of the action to its underlying beliefs, desires, and judgments. The agency of surveillance was to elicit the sociality of the other(s) rather than to orchestrate the internal state of others. So where the Maring located order in the relational interaction itself, the school, following Western epistemology, located order in the collectively manifest but individually produced control of the self. Surveillance would insure that each child understood that he (and occasionally she) was the sole author of his own acts, and that good, successful, modern persons had aligned their internal states with their public behavior. Accordingly, the teachers scolded, reprimanded, and punished children for behaving as Maring children behaved. Especially the talking, banter, and laughing that seemed to accompany all ordinary interactions was, as the Maring phrased it, made taboo. The perception was that the classroom was a special type of ritual in which the participants had to assume an odd and uncustomary set of taboos.

The classroom was also unusual in that the physical confinement of the child seemed important. Where Maring education involved the body practically and instrumentally—in the act of planting, singing, talking—Western education sought to still the body, to quiet and contain its ordinary motion so to emphasize and elevate the mind. The child was expected to internalize this disposition both as a sign of respect for his teachers and fellow students and as a technique for his own self-improvement. Not surprisingly, the teachers in the school put great store in the virtues of self-control and self-respect, seeing in them the key dispositions in the Western acquisition of knowledge. They would tell the students that they would only acquire the cargo of the West when they had learned how to learn, though as one teacher pointed out in lamenting tones, progress was difficult because the children went home on the weekends, took extended periods of time off from school, and were surrounded by relatives who were too mired in the old ways.

As observed, Western education, in following the path of the modern, set great store in defining and refining ways to measure the real. Accordingly, a critical feature of school was counting, but more than this the use of number and quantity to identify value. Agents could identify, indicate, and assess the value of an object or a relationship, indeed all objects and relationships, by a numerical value. Thus the relationship between a student and the process of education could be reduced to a grade; the relationship between the owner of a business and workers could be reduced to a salary.

Education and Social Life

In this Western vision of education, the activities of school were distinct from practice and the motions of everyday life. What the sequestered child acquired through schooling was to be accumulated and stored for a later and larger purpose: when the individual now armed with the requisite forms of knowledge, disposition, and desire reentered the world. The Western model was applied even though it was far from clear that what children learned in school had any connection to the contours of the society they would reenter. This inspired a contradiction common to the world of the encompassed. On one side of the divide, the Maring conceived education as an escape route from the confinement of local life and community. The junior generation imagined that, once educated to the modern, they could sidestep the obligations of kinship, migrate to the towns beyond the domineering shouts of big-men and elders, and win prestige through a position in public service or with the Church. Education was a raffle in which the lucky won freedom and reward, the right to experiment with the modern world and enjoy its cargo. On this view, education was a means of disengaging from one community and entering another—and also a cultural journey from the bush, the indigenous metaphor of the periphery now returning to engulf all of indigenous life, to the freedom of urban civilization. On this score, Penga, the lapsed seminary student, was explicit.

> Boys go to primary and then high school to get away from their "fathers" [senior clansmen]. If they are lucky, a job with the government will come to them, allowing them to send gifts home [to maintain their kin ties and augment their status] but also do whatever they want. Once someone has enjoyed the life of the town, it becomes hard to return to the bush. It is everyone's wish who goes to school to find this government job, but few do and no one knows why. Men who are educated but do not get jobs either drift about or they become a raskol [the distinctive genre of bandit/delinquent common to Papua New Guinea].

For the Maring, the very process of attending high school instigated a progressive estrangement from the intimacy of community, a slowly evolving distance that also animated a disenchantment with the substance of local lifeways. In part this was because the high schools were located in either the Wahgi Valley or Mt. Hagen, meaning that schoolgoers lived away from home and in the company of other peoples. Moreover, the schools could not help but impart a distinction between urban, urbane life and the simplicity of a hinterlands of simple farmers.

On the other side of the divide, those who followed the star of education often came away empty-handed. Partially disengaged from their local communities but unable to matriculate into Western occupations, they could send home only their sense of shame and failure, even as all the commodities and excesses of urban life remained beyond their means. And also beyond their ken to understand, an unfulfilled promise, "no one knows why." MacLean (1994), echoing the views of Penga, makes this point from an interesting angle.

> The Highlands' critique of raskol makes the general critique of education particularly plain. Raskols are stereotypically understood as products of high school education who have failed to get jobs, an increasingly probable scenario these days. In many

ways they occupy a limbo in local conceptions. The have become disengaged from local society, but have also failed to make the leap into the institutionalized domain of freedom. They lack either specific anchorage, or any encapsulating structure to give form to the self. From the Jimi point of view they occupy the appropriate spatial limbo of the Sepik Wahgi Divide that separates the Jimi and Wahgi Valleys. (680)

What people also gradually realized was that many of those who attended high school wound up in a nether land somewhere between the certain tradition of community and the seductive hubs of development. Sadly, Penga said of himself what others said about him: that men who had learned to enjoy the taste of a Western life-style could not float back and forth between the rural village, the mission station, and the urban center. Intellectually, but even more as the emptiness of unfulfilled desire, they lived the schism between the hollow promise of freedom, wealth, and excitement and the grounding of identity in kinship and community. As for the community, it saw education in terms of a physics of finite relativity. Education could bring something to the community but was more likely to drain something away as those who were educated sought the urban world. Between the polar opposites of the rural and the urban, the educated were the mediating agents, neither secure and contributing to their communities nor successful and celebrated in the urban world.

In essence, the local view was that modernity had created a polar world. If the material riches of the West was the telos of the new road, that of education was an urban job unfettered by the awesome constraints of community life. The new road ran in both directions. Roads could not only be ports of entry for the goods, money, knowledge, and power that would elevate the local communities, but also sirens that could lure people away as they migrated to urban centers never to return, vacuums that could suck wealth out of local communities, and channels that demand the goods produced by local communities (particularly coffee) but return only piddling sums of money. In the physics of the finite relativity, the physical loss to the community created by the outflow of goods and people corresponds to, and engenders, the parasitic inflation of the other (MacLean 1994:678–79). The population, bisnis, and future of an other increase at the expense of the community devoured by the outflow until there is a loss of *kopla* (fairness and equality), of a balance that was once perceptible and reconcilable through exchange but under the reign of modernity is invisible and seemingly irreconcilable. In contrast to the precontact world, the agents who now drain the community have no address.

Epistemology and Sports

The Western distinctions between mind and body, and between practice and pastime, permit the concept and practice of exercise to come into existence in the modern sense. In the world before contact, exercise was exertion or work (*kongon*), activity of the mindful body gardening, fence-building, walking or running from place to place, dancing, hunting, plus the entire gamut of other routines that made up life as it was known. Not only were there few formalized games, other than children's games that replicated adult practices such as hunting and gardening, but no one exercised with the intention of improving their physique. People well recognized that the size of a muscle was indicative of its strength but put very little store in the appearance of muscle per se. They did not intimately associate muscular physique with social status, beauty, or eroticism and accordingly, did not attempt to develop their bodies. Agents grasped each other's body much more through the skin, eyes, and language, all of which they could alter without recourse to jogging, stretching, or weight lifting. Moreover, the notion of self-directed intention and management, that someone would willingly punish their body in order to please themselves with its appearance, struck the Maring as somewhere between amusing and bizarre. The Maring, like other Melanesians, were something of cultural specialists in body decoration, but never as a self-directed intention or as part of the project of producing one's own subjectivity. Rather, they decorated their bodies as a means of performing operations on themselves that transformed their sociality toward others. The body in relation to others was foregrounded in respect to the body in itself.

A significant, though little commented upon, aspect of the school's construction of the Western person was the introduction of sports. By this I mean less the character of physical activity or the rigors of a specific game than the forms of epistemology and desire that the school inculcated through pastimes such as soccer. If the priests and teachers imagined the school as a domain where the mind was visible, if the church was the home of spirituality and the suppression of carnal desires, then the sports field was the world given over wholly to the body. Whereas the body was supposed to be invisible in school and church, acting as a kind of placeholder for the mind and spirit, where the voice was highly regimented in school and church to the point of making silence a virtue in and of itself, the sports field was the expression of repressed voices and bodies. And just behind the school and church was a soccer field—quite a concession in light of the fact that in these extremely rugged environs it was hard to come by ground flat enough to support a building. Not surprisingly, the houses of the local teachers surrounded the field on two sides.

The segregation of the mindful, competitive, and indoor activity of learning from the bodily, team-oriented, outdoor activity of sports was a silent and powerful way of impressing Western values upon the students. The immanent lesson was that the space, temporality, sociality, and activities that defined the classroom versus the sports field reflected and reinforced the distinction between mind and body. It gave practical resonance to the distinction, a site for the ontological play on reality to take place. Equally compelling and far from the reach of consciousness was the premise that the movement of the body from inside (the classroom) to outside was homologous to the inner thinking mind in respect to the outward acting body. Sports as an aspect of schooling began to bring into existence new sets of oppositions that it sought to embody in the movements of agents' bodies. If the competitive individualism of test-taking was foreign to the Maring mind, the sports team was no less so. That teams come together to achieve an abstract and seemingly socially meaningless end, to defeat an arbitrary collection of others, was a puzzling but powerful dimension of the modern. Where traditional groups were composed of kin relations whose relationship transcended any specific task, the team was an admixture of persons whose relationship was specific to the game at hand. In that respect, the team replicated the multiethnic community that was Koinambe. And the team was supposed to exhibit teamwork in the abstract as opposed to the forms of practical cooperative activity that characterized ordinary life.

The Educated Individual

In order for all this to take place there needs to be a new, revised, or valued conception of the person. The educational system is not concerned with collectivities, but with individuals, such that it is surprised by the collective or group implications of schooling. The person must be first and foremost an individual,[1] the individuated dimension of local notions of personhood now elevated to ontological primacy. The individual must be the privileged site of the production and reception of knowledge. And this individual is understood as an agent who is self-moving, self-contained, an agent who will perceive and grasp the schooling situation as detached, decontextualized, and removed from other contexts for action. Learning becomes a process separate from life itself. Learning on the local view was not an objectified, detachable part of life but an inseparable part of growing, marrying, being a parent, dying, and afterlife. In the Western school model, knowledge is a kind of possession, and a person's power lies in an ability to control their destiny and other people. The notion was that information is a kind of property, it exists as a right of its owner rather than, as the Maring would have it, as a multiplicity of context-sensitive rights. Further, the person is divided into a physical body, producible through physical education programs (e.g., exercise), and a nonphysical entity called the mind, which in a racial-like way bore a particular mentality. In this vision, the best way for a person to realize his/her character was by being industrious, by maintaining a steady vigil and firm grip over his/her own body and mind.

If we reconstruct the Maring world prior to contact, we see that the system of social relations in which persons were embedded ordered the trajectory of their lives. They depended to a large extent on others for knowledge about themselves, the intrinsic relationship between persons and the things they had given as gifts, or the notion that people grow as beneficiaries of the actions of others acting in relation to still others. This stood in marked contrast to the notion promulgated by the education system that a person orders his/her life by making a plan, and that an orderly, progressive, and successful life is a question of the relationship between life, a plan, and its execution. This was, of course, laid out in the time sequence of going to primary school, then if a person is industrious enough to high school, and still further to college in Port Moresby. There was a spatial dimension in that a person moves further and further from their village, first to Mt. Hagen and then to a major city, so that geography recapitulates epistemology. Life was much more a matter of balance in the indigenous worldview. There was no notion of the future as a neutral space in terms of which one's lifetime may be arranged, nor any notion that a person's future can be determined in terms of individuality. In a word, a person's future does not confront him/her as an objectified but unfilled time that was made meaningful and productive through the imagination of a future in terms of a plan or goals or ambitions.

Conclusion

The system of education introduced by the missionaries began to transform the Maring world far less by the content of what was taught than by the underlying epistemological and ontological premises that were embedded in the form of instruction. Not least, the mission schooling system helped to canonize a representation of the modern world that all future representations and responses would have to take into consideration. Institutionally, the mission assumed that there was a field of education endowed with its own logic, spaces, boundaries, temporalities, and forms of reward. The model school was a model of the model society—a place where self-managing, self-contained individuals competed and cooperated in quest of the self-improvement of mind, body, and spirit. This schooling was related to nationness insofar as it was meant to produce the citizen individual whose identity formation was dominated by personal and national identities, with other forms of identity taking a subsumed place.

The mission, consistent with its vision of the person as a possessive, autonomous individual, insisted that persons be self-managing and that a principal goal of socialization was self-management skills. Under the regime of the modern, education becomes an extension of the political system insofar as it becomes directly implicated in the exercise of social control. One might add that in contrast to the West, where the extension of education to the disenfranchised (such as minority groups) is invariably accompanied by the strengthening of collateral forms of social control (e.g., judicial and prison systems), the senior and dominant generation of Maring, because they were also dominated, cannot exercise the option taken by the dominant class in the West. Mission education also could not help but promote encompassment and reinforce the generational rift in that a judgment on fitness for higher education, employment on the mission station, and so on was also a judgment on the use of a language that was the language of the West.

CHAPTER 10

The Conclusion of the Past and the Making of the Present

The scent of kastam. Like smoke from the cooking fires, it
lodges forever in the most ordinary things. Especially there. In
house rafters. In bananas of all degrees of ripeness. The shape
of animals and the color of yams. In the absence of war. And
of course in the thoughts of the ancestors.

From the perspective of the worlds not yet Westernized, the twentieth century is the age of encompassment. Like the inexorable rise of the oceans
during periods of global warming (when monsters inhabited the earth and
much of the island of New Guinea was underseas), the West has inundated
its others so that no corner of the globe has been left untouched by capitalism, the nation-state, and internationalized Western culture. The commodity form and state politics, the rule of law and the promise of science,
the discipline of the school and the wealth of biomedicine, the hallelujahs
of Christianity and the rhythms of rock, and with this the forms of knowledge and desire inscribed in Western practice, have all flowed across the
Highlands landscape. In the tradition of my people, I have tried to explore
how giant processes became manifest in specific instances. My understanding is that, if God now dwells in the mediations, so must our ethnography. The Highlands of New Guinea are exceptional only in that they
have been covered by this Western tide after the second of the world wars.
And so I have been able to tell an episode of this long story when the
memories of the transformation are still fresh, when it is possible to tell the
story from the beginning because still alive and sentient were those who
witnessed the initial encounter between Melanesians and Westerners. For
this reason, the Melanesian story is memorable and resonates with a larger
history. In terms of the number of people affected it hardly appears on the
radar screens of history; in terms of its proximity to the present it could
not be of more importance. That we, as creatures of the modern, inhabit a
kind of perpetual present, easily forgetting both our own past and that of
others, further amplifies its import. If the march of the West began with
the direct domination of colonialism, it is continuing with far less transparent and much more nuanced forms of domination. If the march began

in the age of self-confident imperialism, it is continuing in a time of uncertainty as to how these nations—or any nations—will fare in the face of the conjuncture of local and global forces.

Encompassment was not, of course, born full-size—though it is sometimes so imagined in local ideologies that re-present the past as the antechamber to a modern future. Listening to some of the junior generation speak socially, one would have thought that the Maring past was dissolving like a clump of red ochre tossed into the rage of the Jimi River. So, for example, members of the junior generation described violence as extinct, though there were signs that it was more like a sleeping volcano over which had grown a crust of cold gray ash. What there has been is more like an ideological civil war between generations, a contestation of power and epistemology. It pitted those who were raised before the modern against those raised in the shadow of its advent, and both against a junior generation that could not conceive the world in any other way. As the evidence speaks, the process of encompassment is not smooth, immediate, or transparent. Encompassment was episodic in that the influx of Westerners and practices obeys no logic other than the many scattered logics of evangelical operations, state policy, and business interests. Encompassment was gradual in that the relative isolation of the Maring—both geographically and in the vision of the West—meant that the weight of encompassment has been brought in small measures. Encompassment was nonconscious in that its greatest effects were at the level of knowledge, desires, and dispositions toward the world. Where Maring history previously was always defined by change within fixed horizons, encompassment has burned down the doxic world and fired the conception and possibility of change without limits. Modernity is a conversation between past and present held in the space shaped between the indigenous and Western worlds. We cannot underestimate the effect of moving from a cyclical and circumscribed history to a nonlinear and indeterminate history, that is, local history becoming a chapter of capitalist, nation-state, Western-driven world history.

I have used the term *encompassment* to register the dimension of power inherent in globalization. While local agency is alive and vibrant, as so many examples have illustrated, it is still the West that is imposing itself, not the other way around. The Maring have been compelled to deal with wage labor and the commodity; they have not and cannot compel us to adopt the philosophy of gifts. They have become Christians even as we have forsaken not only their ancestors but our own. I also use the term *encompassment* to register that what is now happening is part of a longer process and bears critical continuities with the past. In reality, globalization is the name of the process in which all the forces that the West unleashed to encompass others are now encompassing the West. The forces of capitalism, culture, and nationalism that the West unchained in the nineteenth century—when the encompassment of others began in earnest—have taken on a life of their own, now confronting their author as quasi-autonomous processes that seem to have no address. The encompassment of Melanesia begins at the end of the last century, though the missionaries, traders, colonial officials, and also anthropologists who came had long been schooled by their African and Indian experience.

To grasp what is happening in all its colors and complexities leads not only to an anthropology of encompassment but a recognition that the frontier between disciplines has been breached. When, for example, the concept of citizen implicates that of the person, the frontier between anthropology and political science is, to draw upon a now discarded anthropological terminology, a "survival" from the enlightenment. When our history and that of Melanesia become mutual, the divide between anthropology and history and politics betrays a logic without a home in reality. As socially mediating labor defines the citizen, and the IMF the policies of the state, the distinction between anthropology and history, politics, and economy becomes immaterial to the project of understanding. And so on and on. On the surface, I mean this to underline that the progress of future understandings of Melanesia depends upon a conjuncture of perspectives. On a deeper level, I have argued that grasping the character of encompassment is inherently comparative, meaning that there is no way to comprehend Melanesia without comprehending the West itself, without traveling beyond the forms of self-misrecognition and disguise that are the West's gift to world history. On a deeper level still, I have argued that we require a combined and comparative perspective whose logic is the same as that of encompassment. Because, as I have tried to show, encompassment *is* the context of its own understanding—the ethnographer an inherently double agent in that respect—it is necessary to focus on local details and mediations. Only this will allow us to grasp the contradiction that it is only from a culturally and historically specific perspective that we can determine the apparently transcultural and transhistorical construction of the world—what in another language is called globalization.

From the same standpoint, we must consider modernity a part of an emerging social imaginary whose shape is determined by the interplay between local and global circumstances. In Melanesia, Africa, and the world of Others generally, the appearance of the modern is simultaneously over- and underdetermined. As an impulse of transformation, modernity has an air of universality and inevitability yet is irremediably rooted in the concrete and particular existence of a cultural community. Further, because modernity is contested and opens up new horizons for actions, critical collective movements, such as the armed rebellion on Bougainville or a great conversion to a new religion, always contain the possibility of seizing the present and transforming the trajectory of the modern. Occurring in the breach between the local and the global, the outcome is determined and predictable neither from the structure of local circumstances nor from the impositions of the world community. But rather from their indeterminate interplay in determinate sociohistorical circumstances. Ethnographically, the objective must be to understand how the images of modernity circulating in a particular cultural community acquire multiple meanings, meanings that overlap, contradict, and contest for the same historical space. Here the story underlines the ways different generations struggle, forge coalitions, and pursue their own visions about what social reality is and the future should be. What matters is the (re)construction and circulation of the meaning of the past as well as the future among and across groups whose concepts, desires, and dispositions are no longer on the same path. So leaders of the junior generation clash with their seniors over the very nature of social relations and the forces that animate the world. Does sorcery still exist? Do gifts still make people? Do the ancestors count? The Melanesian example underlines the extent to which modernity has emerged as a universal form of society and also as a site of cultural particularism. Recognizing that modernity lies at the confluence of locality and encompassment is more than just another observation because it compels analysis to take account of the plurality of local concepts, desires, and dispositions without losing sight of the reality that encompassment as a global structure produces new and powerful similarities among the peoples encompassed. The argument and evidence from Melanesia expressly repudiates those theories that assume that globalization and increasing locality are antithetical phenomena. They are more like brothers-in-arms.

What makes theorization difficult is that an account adequate to its object must both make a space for the large scale epochal transformations in these societies and be sensitive to the reality that these transformations are local and indeterminate. The methodology must presuppose and take into account discursive changes in the foundations of social life and simultaneously center around intensive local ethnography that reveals the strategies and plurality of meanings inscribed in any event. This does not mandate, and I emphasize, that every account include a full analysis of all these levels. It does imply that our analyses should start with the understanding there is an intrinsic relationship between levels, even if all of them are not foregrounded simultaneously. In other words, an anthropology intent on giving an account of the globalization of modernity must be self-conscious about its search for a nonreductionist, multilevel notion of social change; it must be willing to give up some of its founding ethnographic strategies; and it must be able to award intellectual capital to those who study change, not only in the hinterlands of Papua New Guinea and the other famous anthropological haunts, but also in urban centers and other less "primitive" places, such as Port Moresby, Honiara, and downtown De Moines.

This book tells one moment of the larger story of the meeting of the West and Melanesia, the story of the West's contact with the Maring people of Highland New Guinea and the social changes shaped by this encounter. The story unfolding in these high valleys has happened before; it is a variation on a theme played out in the land of the others. This story is at once a history of the encounter and a sustained attempt to challenge the concepts that have shaped the study of modernity. By examining the agents and processes of pacification and first contact, the work of the Anglican missionaries, the infiltration of Western medicine, the advent of a system of schooling, and local response to capitalism and nationhood, it argues that the most critical and generative effect of modernity has been the transformation of the local social epistemology and the structures of desire and disposition. The evidence shows the Western practices embody Western designs of knowledge and desire, and that these structures interact with indigenous practices to generate new and mediated forms. These changes have most profoundly touched the generation coming of age in the late 1970s into the 1980s. The account traces ways in which modernity has promoted the individual aspect of personhood, led to the reshaping and enlargement of the public political sphere, authored new forms and functions for time, invented and defined a *human nature,* animated the use of money, created a carnival of new goods and services, and begun to establish labor (as opposed to kinship) as a critical means of social mediation. The account also shows how the encounter has led to a transformation in the way people grasped the nature of language (written and oral), their consciousness of themselves as a people, and their representation of their past and future. I have sought to tell the story from both sides, to illustrate the rationalities and motives that drove the Westerners as well as the Maring. I have sought to reinsert the anthropologist into the encompassing process. Arguing that the encounter between the Maring and the West is never a one-way street, the account testifies that the engagement of Westerners with people such as the Maring has indigenized the institutions and practices of these Westerners. In order to accomplish this, the book continually draws contrasts between the West's own understanding of itself and the way that it grasps the understanding of others.

The Maring and Melanesia have been encompassed by the West. The peoples of the islands we call Oceania have been "othered" by capitalism and Christianity, the nation-state and internationalized Western culture, interstate organization and new social movements. The West exports itself relentlessly in what has now become an old story. What is new is an understanding that honors the complexities of this process, that begins to tell both sides of the story in a nonmechanistic and nondeterministic way, so that the lives and people caught up in these processes retain their spirit. The quest to see peoples as they are and as they are becoming by virtue of their mutual interactions, must move along several fronts at once. To be adequate to its object, our analyses must connect the local level, life, and lives in village and hinterland, to the larger processes of encompassment— to nation and state, exploring the hyphen that draws them together, to the progress of capitalism and Western culture. The initial step in so contextualizing ethnography must be to locate it within the processes of encompassment. And to do this absent the postmodern conceits, especially the narcissism that takes the fieldworker's medical biography and emotional carriage as critical ethnographic data, or the false humility in which the anthropologist takes on and confesses for all of the sins of encompassment. For in the end, the postmodern conceits are also only part of our collective defense mechanism. The analysis must flesh out the mediations, the contestations, and the trepidations that bring these levels into conjuncture. It is, following a tide of recent ethnography, a call to rise above the local, the syndrome and security of talking about "my people," and address the mediations linking (now inextricably so) life in the village with world history. The conversation must be triangulated, embracing in the same theoretical sentence local structures and histories, the characters of the encompassing processes, and the mediating agents and institutions. Constructing this conversation inscribes the paradox of a science of Others in the age of encompassment. The greatest virtue and limitation of modern anthropology is its attachment to the local; positively, its knowledge of local life allows it to draw out these mediations in a way that no purely global perspective can ever achieve. Anthropology is essential to the construction of an adequate theory and history of the globalization of modernity because anthropology alone has the material and methods to mount a comparative account of localities. Let me reiterate this point because it gets to the essence of the matter. This triangulated conversation necessitates a comparative understanding of locality and community that is the hallmark of anthropology. Its tradition of a deep appreciation of local cultures and communities—embodied in ethnography—is indispensable. But it is also not enough; the mediations must be drawn out and they must be done so in the framework of a theory of encompassment.

Critical to understanding the process of mediation is an analysis of the transformation in the structure of knowledge and organization of desire inspired by the encounter between the Maring and encompassing institutions and agents. To do this requires that we locate with some precision what Melanesians and Westerners have in common and have in difference. This enterprise is difficult because it requires as much self-analysis, of moving beyond our own ideological vision of ourselves, as it does analysis of Melanesia. I have argued that one of the main problems with anthropological comparisons lies not in its understanding of Melanesia, but in our own self-understanding. Thus I have made, perhaps belabored, the point that economy, polity, and culture (of personhood, for example) are ontologically united, through separable in appearance, with this distinctiveness of social appearance intrinsic to the character of this ontological unity. Furthermore, to see the West in terms of the terms in which it wants to misrecognize itself—not least by separating economy from culture, the fetish of the commodity from our notions of the person—leads to an overemphasis of the differences between the West and Melanesia. There are cultural universals, which is why we can practice the religion we call ethnography, the well-grounded faith that we can grasp the intentionality of others through the instrument of our own mind and body. Once we have located ourselves in relation to Melanesia we can begin to fathom how encompassment transforms the character of knowing and desiring, how it animates changes that generate other changes that change the very nature of subjectivity and peoplehood. That allow the cassowary to fly.

Finally, I have argued for the construction of a theory of generation. Without one, an account of transformation will be inadequate. To do this requires that we construct the relational and dynamic space of generations in relation to other modes of sociality (such as gender and clanship). It requires that we detail the forms of collaboration and contestation between generations and within a generation. What was critical about the Maring junior generation was that it stood precisely at the conjuncture between the forms of knowing and desire immanent in their parents and those that were instilled partly by these parents and partly by a world that played no part in the creation of their parents' habitus, and that moreover must respond and adjust to the demands of a prevailing situation that increasingly exalts modern forms of knowledge and desire and disparages customary ones. In sum, what was (and still is), at stake in the tension between generations was the power to impose a vision and division of the social universe, to construct the reality that shapes the trajectory of Maring society as it pushes into its future. A future that is vastly different, objectively in its structure and subjectively in the forms of knowledge, desire, and dispositions inculcated within agents.

A key concept and stake in the contestation between generations, within a generation, and between the Maring and their Western encompassers, was the nature of kastam. This was played out as a struggle over the signs and substance of modernity: how the Maring signify and practice peace; the ways commercial goods, especially foods, become integrated into the economy of everyday life; what it means and entails to be a Christian, educated, and/or trilingual Maring. The current of exchanges, the polarity of tensions, between the encompassing agents and the local populace were defined by prior and determinate forms whose conjuncture was, however, unpredictable and open to all manner of serendipity and creativity. The shallow understanding that the missionaries and kiaps had of the Maring, and the Maring of the inflowing Western agents, all but guaranteed that communication would travel along the slenderest of threads. But, the fact that the Maring had to confront Western practices, practices that were presented to them as a challenge to their own, forced them to crystalize, objectify, and totalize their own customs. Western religion, medicine, and lifestyles became the ground and mirror against which the Maring began inventing themselves as a people. They began to see their own practices self-consciously, as distinct from those of others, as bearing a true coherence, as being coterminous with the Maring language and the emergent public political sphere. A new generative scheme took shape based on the categories of kastam, civilization, and bisnis in which the Maring began to reflect back to Westerners a transformed vision of the Western vision of them.

The junior generation's conception of its own past was a mixture of cultural vinegar and historical revelation, as they sought to both distance themselves from their own past, its incarnation in the elder generation in particular, and in the same breath invoke that past to define themselves against the West. Their encounter with modernity reconfigured old memories and inspired new forms of forgetting—the past becoming an object, a history that people both wanted to remove from their bodies and at the same time reclaim. Their uneven and contingent exposure to Western agents and institutions complicated the process, modernity at times seeming to possess all the stability of a windsock. Nonetheless, the junior generation quickly came to embody and lead the crusade for development. The mission and motto of the local government councils that they led was "to develop our place." The junior generation began to articulate development as a self-conscious category and program for how their once indigenous world was to be transformed, civilized, and uplifted into a new stratosphere of goods, services, and open-ended life trajectories. They acquired the notions of development and the great leap toward modernity inscribed in the discourse and dispositions of the clergy, educations, medical community, bureaucrats, urban capitalists, and others they came into contact with. Their worldview became an increasingly important social organizing force, particularly so through the image of progress as a ladder that would permit them to climb up out of their own past. The path of progress was structured according to languages learned, Christian affiliation, life experiences, modes of livelihood, technical know-how (that ranged from driving a truck to telling time), and much more. In this respect, the junior generation negotiated two frames of identity: the first based on kinship and community and obedient to the principles of sociality, the second focused outward to a modern, urbanizing, national world in which technical knowledge, individual initiative, capital savings, modern sector employment, and displays of accumulated wealth make the person. By 1980, a kind of moving, malleable, hybrid identity had begun to emerge, an identity forged in the space between an indigenous world that the junior generation could no longer want and a modern world that was not anxious to accept them, between an indigenous world they were pulling away from and a modern one that was pushing them away.

The Maring had a theory that what defined humans were their acts of self-control and resolve. Where pigs and dogs gorge on whatever food is set before them, humans eat slowly and carefully, never finishing and always sharing their meal. The same holds for our understanding of encompassment—it requires our analytical resolve and self-control. We must resist that romantic desire to believe that, against the tide of history and the awesome asymmetries of power, the Maring or any other people can truly resist. We must ward off the sentimentality that believes that somehow what is traditional can survive—that there is a preservation of practice and meaning that an archaeology of practice can recover. We must remove ourselves from the nostalgia for our own past and the demonization of our own present that imagines that Melanesians value their past in the same way that we do ours, as a counterweight to a modernity that values things over relations, the present over the past, the individual over community, and gratification over responsibility. This nostalgia forgets that this vision of the past is itself a necessary feature of and presupposes a Western conception of modernity. An anthropology of encompassment must also overcome the tendency to see colonialism, capitalism, and culture as machines of domination that simply steamroller other societies. Westernization has never been a monolithic process, but rather one that is characteristically contradictory and fragmented. The intentions of Christianity are not those of capitalism, and neither line up perfectly with those of the nation-state, in either its colonial or contemporary form. The agents of the Almighty, business, and the government seldom see eye to eye on the proper relationship between Westerners and Melanesians. Moreover, capitalism and Western culture embody their own forms of seduction, carnival, enchantment, and novel possibilities. In this context that will escape all reductionist readings, people come to desire things Western, to know them as their own, and to develop the dispositions to use them. The result is that the transformation of the Maring and Melanesia more generally wrought by encompassment is not simply the result of the importation of things Western or even a logical combination of indigenous and imported practices. Rather what results is the simultaneous appearance of a new form of indigenous-Western society, a hybrid, an indigenous modernity. Whatever the name, the Maring will never be the same, nor Western.

Being othered and being modernized is no easy task. Not for the Maring, nor for Melanesians generally, and not for Westerners when it was their turn earlier. One has only to recall the Reformation and Counter-Reformation in Spain and Germany, the fight against capitalism and its factories in England, the civil wars in Italy and the United States over the making of the nation-state, and the suppression of social movements (those advocating civil rights, universal suffrage, etc.) to realize that the West made itself modern in fits and starts, hip-deep in its own blood. Yet, the West has little trouble imagining that "others" are more primitive than the West ever was, and that those others will transform themselves into capitalist, democratic, God-fearing nation-states faster and more smoothly than we ever did. But, of course, their stars are better than ours. They have our help to instruct and jump-start them down the road to modernity. That, at least, is the tale the West told itself and used to justify the colonization of places like Melanesia and people like the Maring.

But the road to modernity could not help but be a struggle. The Maring, like Melanesians generally, had to make a space for identity and pride within the framework of encompassment, to create moments of self-definition and value so that they would not have to either capitulate or lose their identity in the crush of capitalism, Christianity, and internationalized Western culture or resist the modern whatever the consequences. To capitulate would lead to an effacement of identity; to resist would condemn them to economic and political marginalization. And so "combined strategies" of accommodation and self-creation began to emerge.

The consequence of all of this, I suggest, is that while the globalization of modernity is becoming increasingly critical—the "traditional" anthropological object is itself disappearing at an accelerating rate—and though globalization involves peoples that have stood at the core of ethnographic discourse, anthropology is but a minor player in the study of the globalization of modernity. The reason for this, I have suggested, lies in a marginalized and undertheorized notion of encompassment, a resistance against contextualizing ethnography in the complex set of mediations that link global processes to local transformations. Particularly in Melanesia (but by no means only in Melanesia), any turn to the study of encompassment signals a fundamental change in what anthropologists do and the way that they go about it. Analyzing encompassment requires more sophisticated theories of mediation and the state as well as a seachange in our concept of the anthropological subject. At the very least it determines that an anthropology adequate to its mission must come to terms with the interrelationship between structures of different genesis, internal organization, and orders of magnitude.

Encompassment has provoked a confrontation between an anthropology that joins their history to ours and an anthropology of Others which claims that the relationship of their encompassment can only be known if we first grasp their differences, an act of cultural transcendence that requires us to relativize our concepts. I have argued that a reading of the evidence tells us that neither the historical nor ethnographic approach is sufficient unto itself. Each refers back to the other. But their referral unfolds as a mutual borrowing on the condition of a mutual exclusion. On the one side, we can take up the interrogation of history only by bracketing the indigenous conditions for the production of what, to us, is their "otherness" or culture. This is a one way street. There is no way that by investigating the convergence of histories we can discover their otherness that confronts the West, and indeed motivated colonialism in the first place, nor can we climb toward some self-reflexivity concerning our epistemology of description. On the other side, the exploration of their cultures or otherness has always been on condition of encompassment. And there is nothing about these other cultures or even their response to encompassment that by itself explains the terms of the encounter. What is more, the very circumstance by which the fine-grained ethnography of local culture and community advances must be based on such an encounter whose vacant place is evident in every step of the relativist argument. If we leave the argument as a confrontation between those who favor history and those who favor relativist ethnography, anthropology quickly reaches an impasse. Metaphorically, breaking the impasse entails strategies that allow us to hold the coin of knowledge up to a mirror in such a way that we can see both sides at the same time. So the only way to resolve this impasse is to dissolve it. The referent of ethnography cannot be the internal logics of totalized sovereign cultures, rather our objective must be a comparative ethnography that unfolds historically. Not least a temporal ethnography of the agents and institutions of encompassment in respect to an ethnography of local lifeways. In this way it is possible to restore agency and subjectivities, experience and emotion, without forgetting that all of this is taking place under determinate sociohistorical conditions.

The Maring's encounter with the West transformed the terrain of meaning. In arguing with the mission over rights in land or what constituted a legitimate marriage in the eyes of the Church, in dealing with the demands of the kiaps about proper sanitation and the treatment of women under the law, in engaging in business negotiations with coffee buyers and also labor recruiters, the Maring could not avoid invoking, endorsing, and submitting to Western forms of discourse and logic. Whether they liked it or not, the Maring were engulfed into these forms of thinking. Especially members of the junior generation were apt to enter into rational argument about marriage and other issues; this rationality was worn as a kind of emblem of modernness and was in sharp contrast to the oldest generation that appeared immune to Western reason and sound argument. Local attempts at resistance also watered the seeds of seduction because they were unable to avoid internalizing the very terms by which they were being challenged. The assertion of "kastam," from the constitution of the category to some of the signs and images used to extol it, was, after all, done in modern terms. What the Maring would learn is that there is no way to escape the encompassing process; there are only more or less better ways to survive it. If anthropology has a meaning and mission in this context, it is to help preserve the force of their most elementary words by creating a stage on which we can learn to hear and understand them.

In Melanesia, it is as if the river of language and culture, overreaching its banks, flowed to the present down a thousand tributary channels, each unique, yet each of common water. The effect of modernity is to rejoin these tributaries into the common flow of the capitalist nation-state, to reverse the course of the nature of these cultures. One only hopes the project has some merit.

Notes

Chapter 1

1. As for myself, I am embarrassed by their embarrassment, and a feeling comes over me that wants them to better appreciate and respect their own past, their own grandparents. But who am I to want this for someone else? This thought flashes across me in the very next moment. But talking to these young men who have become my friends, in the special and strange sense that friendship is possible across cultures, it is hard for me to escape the feeling that they grossly overvalue Western lifeways and practice, that their enchantment and acceptance of things Western, however historically inevitable, involves losses that are never known except retrospectively. They have the reverse reaction, wondering why I am not more enthusiastic about my own culture.

2. On the flip side of this cultural logic, those of the senior generation would ask me why I worked—why, for example, I went to the trouble of making a food garden—if I could get things simply by magic. Why would I spend time on a garden when I could simply send a letter and receive food by the next delivery from Mt. Hagen or even America?

3. This is a paraphrase. The encounter took place many years ago when I was still a graduate student. I do not remember word for word what Cardoso said, though for many years I have believed that he said something like this.

4. Beneath its crisp analytical style and often dense prose, much of what is called the New Melanesian Ethnography is sentimental, tender, and nostalgic. For not only does it want to theorize the differences between Melanesians and Westerners, it desires these differences to persist, feeling that the world is a better place if left to its own diversity. I don't know whether this is right historically or theoretically, but I can't help but share the feeling—otherwise I would have become something other than an anthropologist.

5. A second temptation (which is more true of, say, Indonesian ethnography than Melanesian) is to be so enamored of the power of the "world system" that every local culture becomes just one more tragic footnote to a history not of its own making. This view, in saying correspondingly little about the local level, cannot but efface local forms of agency, forgetting that the Christianity and capitalism imported to Melanesia are fast becoming highly Melanesian brands of Christianity and capitalism.

6. This is somewhat of a misnomer. All modern anthropology is of modernity, while all studies of modernity cease to be anthropology in its most traditional cloth. But there is no point in fretting about this. It is simply anthropology follow-

ing in the footprints of those it studies: that is, seeking to deflect the impact of the modern even as it reconfigures itself.

7. Healey (1990), writing about the Maring, contends that "even into the 1980s" change "has been slight." He admits that the political encapsulation of the village into the nation-state has led to some modification of internal village politics, but then goes on to say that "these new alignments, however, have not engendered any major alterations in the organization of production and exchange" (xvii). Against this I would submit that the changes have engendered significant movement in the organization of meaning, representation, and desire. I have (somewhat unfairly) singled Healey out because he has spoken about the Maring, but he is by no means alone in taking this approach that cannot help but reduce Melanesian societies to islands immune to history and its implications.

Chapter 2

1. Marie Reay (1992), speaking about the Minj region adjacent to Maring territory, notes that the district officers were afraid of precisely this situation and therefore "dreaded any manifestation of 'antiadministration sentiment'" (141).

2. Samuel Beckett may well be the author of expatriatism. Like expatriates, his characters characteristically found themselves in grotesque situations within a world that is apparently normal to everyone around them.

3. Sinclair, for example, notes that "like many of my fellows, I had little time for the United Nations and I resented the carping, petty nature of much of the criticism that powerful sections of that August world body continually hurled at our administration of the Territory. It was hard to swallow this sanctimonious humbug" (1981:218). Black representatives from postcolonial states such as Nigeria and India especially grated on their nerves. Blacks judging whites seemed an inversion of reality that was, as one kiap put it, as though "the Abos [derogatory term for the aboriginal peoples of Australia] were running Australia."

4. My own fieldwork in the Maring region in 1974 began with a near confrontation with the district officer, raising the dismal prospect of ruining my field research even before it had begun. The DO (who shall remain nameless) had invited Georgeda Buchbinder—then a professor of anthropology at Queens College and a Maring fieldworker—and myself to stay with him before going to Tuguma in the Simbai valley. Prior to my moving to Chicago to attend the University of Chicago, I had lived for two years with Georgeda in New York. That evening after dinner, the DO became progressively more intoxicated and began to make suggestive remarks and then sexually harass Georgeda. I had grown up in the Bronx, had been in numerous fights in my life, and had the ominous sense that I was about to be in another. Knowing me and seeing that I was about to become unhinged, Georgeda pulled me aside when the DO announced that he was going to the loo and told me that we could not afford a confrontation and that she, as my superior, would handle the situation the best she knew how. And so she played along with him, kissing him, fondling him, and allowing him to remove her blouse, all the while filling up both their glasses with whiskey, until too drunk to perform

and growing angry at his impotency, he and Georgeda passed out. In the morning, I followed their lead and pretended that nothing had happened as the DO accompanied us halfway to Tuguma.

5. This was the advice that was given to me, but believe me I would have known it anyway from having listened to the stories of Meryvn Meggitt, Bob Glasse, Georgeda Buchbinder, Paula Brown, Ed Cook, Cherry Lowman, and other senior ethnographers.

6. Vividly imprinted on my mind is a night I spent with two former kiaps, one a civil servant in the provincial government, and four VSO members (two of whom were woman). The kiaps and one of the VSO men went on for at least an hour castigating a young nurse who it was presumed had had relations with a local man. Their attack was so visceral, out of control, and vicious that it was as if she had run her nails down the raw nerves of their psyches. In a seriously joking way, they sputtered between beers that she should be gang-raped and her partner castrated for what, in their eyes, was an unpardonable sin. They opined that they might understand it "if she was ugly and no one wanted her" (no one white, that is), but she was "more than acceptable." My observation that the nurse and the young man, an orderly at the local hospital, were consenting adults and that it wasn't as though someone had been harmed was met with a look of disgust and the reply that I simply didn't understand; that even though I did not look like an academic (i.e., I was a former football player and weight lifter in contrast to their image of what an academic was supposed to look like), I sure thought like one. As I got up to leave, I could see in their eyes and demeanor a new and obvious distrust toward me—a man's man, a patriot of his race, would support their ideology of miscegenation. That was not only the racist current that ran through them now. It was of long standing, back to the time when they first donned their khakis and began to tour the Highlands. Despite the obvious need, there is apparently no twelve-step program for former kiaps.

7. One night at a dinner in Port Moresby, a couple in their mid-thirties, an English businessman and his German wife, went on for some time how barbaric such practices as head-hunting and sorcery were, how these were telltale signs of the savage, of people lacking a sense of civilization and civility. I reminded the couple that mustard gas and gas chambers, V-2 rockets raining down on the civilian population of London and the firebombing of Hamburg in retaliation, not to mention the atomic bomb, were part of our civilization. The English businessman nodded his head and reluctantly said that was true, as though I had reminded him of his genetically deformed sibling that his parents kept in the basement, while his German wife replied that "she had forgotten all about that"—that wonderful shifter *that* rescuing her, rescuing us, from having to say that we did unspeakable things, and having done them what right do we have to look at Melanesia and claim the high moral ground as our birthright.

8. The missionaries were not sanguine about the future of Western civilization. Their reason was that its present period was one of a liberalization of values and actions that was nothing less than a socializing of sin. This was underscored by the legalization of abortion, pornography, and other sins, and the creation of social institutions to advance them.

9. James Watson is more genteel, gentlemanly, and dapper than I could ever hope to become. And the phrase "among other things" is, I would suggest, a most polite and euphemistic way to say that kiaps had little brief for local practices, both because they thought they understood them and because they thought understanding them didn't matter.

10. My translation is admittedly not totally faithful to the published texts in either French or English—both of which might be translated into their respective languages. I have broken up a run-on sentence, corrected two grammatical errors, eliminated an "overly" redundant phrase, and generally tried to make the text intelligible and accessible. My reason is that I think that what Bourdieu has to say here is important—too important to be buried beneath impenetrable prose.

11. Just as the West understands an action, such as an act of courage, as an expression of the underlying trait of courage, so we often see the men and women who make history and the institutions they forge as expression of larger, immanent historical forces. This appears philosophically as well as ideologically in the work of Hegel, and more historically concretely in notions such as "manifest destiny"— the idea that the agents and practices that displaced the Ameri-Indians were simply responding to this larger historical impetus. Colonialism itself takes its form and justification from the idea that its agents, such as missionaries, are simply parts of a grander and inevitable scheme.

12. If the Maring did not have a history as the West imagines history it was because they also did not live in nature as the West imagines nature. This is not to say that they did not know their environment. As farmers and hunters, they seemed to know every tree, plant, insect, and bird down to the subspecies level. And they knew so much about their interrelation—which insect bred in what tree and was preyed upon by what bird—that I thought that each of them probably qualified for a Ph.D. in botany (except Penga of course). What they did not encounter was nature as an entity that was independent of, and could stand against, culture and kinship. What was nature was not distinct from the organization of the spiritual universe, the ancestor spirits of the high ground versus the low, the spirits of the head and hotness and culture versus those of the lower body and coldness and fertility. The trees where the birds of plume lived were intrinsically related to the relations of exchange and kaiko that they made possible. It was for this reason, among others, that Maring stories of their past were never histories in the Western sense inasmuch as they elided people, actions, places, and environment.

13. I can vouch personally on this latter point as he made every attempt possible to manipulate me for his ends. From his perspective, I was a blessing and resource in the sense that I could furnish him with money to help him satisfy his political objectives. He continually raised a fuss if I assisted members of other clans, which, of course, I had to, inasmuch as my objectives entailed establishing and maintaining relations with members of all of the Kauwatyi clans and with a number of non-Kauwatyi clans as well. Living with him was a continual game, often involving brinkmanship, as he would threaten through emissaries (never directly) to have me expelled from Kauwatyi if I did not adhere to his desires, which invariably required me to act in a partisan political way on his behalf. Part

of my social education was learning to fend off his overtures and threats by thinking through a cultural logic that went like this: if through enriching him I suffered a loss then this would cause other people to have to share my sorrow, which would upset the balance of my relationships with others. These others would feel compelled to restore this balance by giving gifts to me, which, through the intermediary of my person, would create a reciprocal obligation for him, an obligation that he might not recognize because it was not on the "skin" of events, and thus failing to reciprocate properly or not recognizing the request of others for what that request truly was, might lead to sorcery. And as a Westerner, I was by my "nature" (or more precisely, my cultural species) outside the possibility of sorcery. There was in this what I have referred to as an implicational logic, which unlike Western logic is not a logic of things or even concepts, but one in which A relation implies B relation that in turn implies C relation, thereby creating an implication string that links persons together through the inevitable intentionality buried in their actions.

Chapter 3

1. I had come to the study of Melanesia and the Maring by chance, first through the influence of my teacher and lover, Georgeda Buchbinder, who had done biomedical ethnography among the Maring in the late 1960s, and then through my long and deep friendship with Cherry Lowman, the first to study the Kauwatyi, and Skip and Annie Rappaport. If Cherry was the best ethnographer of the five, Skip could combine theory and ethnography fluidly, and Annie pioneered the description of the Maring language. The trademark of this group was that, like the best of Melanesian life, kinship was always more important than competition. From as far back as I can remember, my father, an old-world dignified Sicilian gentleman, would repeat to me the Sicilian saying that "to have a family is to have the earth"—the earth here meaning literally and metaphorically all that there is, the ground of action, and land upon which to plant crops. The Maring share a similar ethos saying that "kinship lies at the root" and that "the bond between siblings is the cause and reason of action." In Skip and Annie, Cherry and Georgeda, I felt I had found not only an anthropology, but an intellectual family. From my years of conversation with them, from the exchange of notes and ideas, I am able to imbue this account with a depth and breadth that I could never have given it alone. More than that, there is a genuine joy in knowing that a better account of the Maring is all the gift I would ever need to repay them.

2. I will never forget now what I so long repressed. Victor Turner, who was a man of immense kindness as well as intelligence, held his graduate seminars on religion and ritual in his home. On the occasion of a stirring and poetic description of Ndembu ritual by his wife, Edith, he opened his scrapbook and showed a few of us who had lingered photographs of some initiands and their parents. I asked about one man who, seemingly out of context, was wearing a T-shirt and cap, to which Victor Turner replied that the inscription on the T-shirt and cap were of the mining union; the man in question was a union organizer. He was a Christian who

had used his position in the Church to rally people across cultures (the mines were, of course, ethnically omnivorous) to the union cause.

3. There are some interesting exceptions such as *The Pacification of Melanesia* (Rodman and Cooper 1979) that focus on the nature of capitalism and colonialism in this respect.

4. This notion of disciplinary valor was part of the unsaid of anthropology, though on certain occasions it did ooze to the surface. This was epitomized by G. P. Murdock's assertion that culture did not exist and Marshall Sahlins's stinging reply that not only called attention to Murdock's theoretical blunders based on flawed methodological individualism, but, in a powerful allusion to the French revolution, accused him of betrayal. Sahlins, the most influential anthropologist of his time, wrote, "In George Peter Murdock, anthropology may have already found its Robespierre" (1976:91).

5. The Maring believe, the Simbu hold, the Orakavia maintain, the Melpa claim . . . fill in the people, verb, and predicate. The ethnographies of Melanesia are replete with sentences of this order—the trope of totalization that all description relies on (even the statistical sampling of individuals common to Western polling, which embodies an element of totalization in the very structure of its questions) cannot help but set up totalized categories. In Melanesia, these are necessary acts of totalization, a kind of shorthand for saying that the dominant Maring belief is, the majority report among the Simbu is, most Orakavia maintain, or the Melpa generally . . . This way of talking about others takes for granted that the ethnographer has command of the entire society, which, in turn, rides on the assumption of a simple uniform mode of reproduction and clearly defined boundaries. The ethnographic sentence reads very differently if I say the Maring believe, though this belief wanes in border communities that are an admixture of Maring and Kalam clans . . . The sentence also reads differently if I say the Maring, depending on generation and gender, believe . . . The issue is how the evidence is to be heard and integrated into an ethnographic understanding. Are there socially meaningful relationships in these differences? One reason, if not *the* reason, the discussion about totalization has been confused is that anthropologists entertain two separate concepts of totality that, not coincidently, correspond to their two notions of culture. The first notion derives from the limits of awareness of agents in practice. About this Sahlins (1997) comments that "cultural life in its complexity, let alone its totality, involves reasons and relationship that no one who lives it can be expected to express" (273). From what philosophers call an ontic standpoint, Heidegger (1962) argues much the same: namely, that the present is the temporal space least likely to receive an authentic self-interpretation because people, by the character of consciousness, are preoccupied with the immediate and what is "ready to hand" (246–47). Because Maring, like people the world over, assume their cultural life is natural and presupposed, they ignore the structural, historically evolving relationship between, for example, birth rites and funerals (Buchbinder and Rappaport 1976). And there are no practical benefits to be gained from the kind of abstract reflection that would elevate this relationship to consciousness, least of all when kin are saddened by a death or celebrating the birth of a child. Given the necessi-

ties and limits of practical awareness, any science of social life must engage in acts of totalization in order to grasp the character of structures and practices.

6. The primary reason that Melanesian ethnographers ignored studies of discourse and ethnographic speech events was that these materials require a high degree of linguistic sophistication. The concepts and language are sufficiently complex that only a substantial exposure to linguistics makes the materials comprehensible. Here, for example, is an account of the relationship between the production of an ethnographic text about a past event by two of the foremost sociolinguists.

[The aim is] to recover the co(n)texts from which the text-artifacts were produced in transduction-inscription. To be sure, the decontextualized text, understood as a meaningful building block of culture may have a narrative time line when evaluated purely for its literal denotational content, that is, when it is viewed simply as cohering denotational text. But does a denotational text preserve in any sense the durational contingency, the interactional "real time" of its originary entextualization? Does it preserve, for example, the temporality of emergence of intersubjective entextualization—moments of presupposed mutual (mis)understanding of what was happening—during the event of inscribing its artifact? (Silverstein and Urban 1996:4–5)

Ethnographers will be forgiven if such texts make them blind. Nonetheless, the point still holds that descriptions of the past are never ontologically authentic or transparent, though they are of course culturally real and meaningful. What the linguists are saying is that while the ethnographic interview that becomes text captures quite a bit of referential information, what escapes is the actual process of constructing the speech event. This process includes not only substance but spaces and lapses, for example. And it turns out that one of the most important aspects of Melanesian speech events is silence, which is the sine qua non of a nonreferential function of speech. This follows incidentally from the relational nature of Melanesian persons. The argument, which I will make here only in passing, is that because Melanesians externalize their subjectivity in the response they elicit from others, silence is a form of self-understanding or reflection. To put this another way, the act of being silent after speaking that signals the evaluation of the response of others is a far cry from being mute.

7. The notion of "my people," which has its origins in the fieldwork of Malinowski, is part of the oral culture of ethnography, spoken at conferences in response to other ethnographers' examples from "their" people but never to my knowledge used in print. The possessive pronoun *my* is double-edged: on one hand, it indicates that the ethnographers have conflated their own individuality with the identity of those they studied; on the other hand, it is an index of deep ethnographic understanding because this level of personal identification is necessary to bridge the social separation to which all ethnography in Melanesia is condemned. The progress from stranger to insider, more than a move in status, is a journey across a psychological landscape of self and others. Born of the delusions

of the person who is in-between, Malinowski thought he had invented the Tro-brianders when, in reality, they had not only invented him but gave him the opportunity to reinvent himself.

8. A computer-aided search of bibliographic references on some sixty books and over 400 articles on the New Guinea Highlands since 1990 indicates that, with the exception of Wagner himself, this article had never been cited, not even by his students and those that explicitly use his theories. Ironically, Wagner noted in a conversation that he thought that this was perhaps his best article.

9. Besides making certain theories and evidence invisible, which is why transformations of paradigm in a social science usually entail the resurrection and/or reconceptualization of its ancestors—that is the re-appearance of what has been made invisible—another defense mechanism is the maintenance of a gap between grand and small theory. The assumption of totality is an interesting case in point. At a grand level, most anthropologists subscribe to the proposition, and openly endorse the theory, that an account of non-Western societies should avoid totalization and the forms of essentialization on the back of which it must ride. Taken axiomatically as a theoretical gain, there is no argument about this. This understanding notwithstanding, at the level of small theory, the specific concerns that animate a particular analysis or comparative generalization may presuppose that totality exists. The gap is so important because it allows analysts to deflect and deflate criticism by being able to point with confidence at the grand theory.

10. The ethnographers included but are not limited to Roy and Anne Rappaport, Peter Vayda, Cherry Lowman, Georgeda Buchbinder, John Street, William Clarke, Alison Jablot, Chris Healey, Neil Maclean, Robin McKenzie, and myself. Data was also collected on shorter visits by other anthropologists including Douglas Chen, Ralph Bulmer, and Sarah Meltzoff. In addition, Father Brian Bailey professed an interest in anthropology and sought to collect information on a variety of local subjects while the Bible translator and wife interviewed people on their language.

11. It is at this point in the ethnographic journey that postmodernism falls into logical decay. Amselle 1998 provides an instructive example. He argues persuasively that it is impossible to distill traditional African culture after centuries of Islamic influence and that colonial officials, anthropologists, and missionaries were responsible for fixing the boundaries of African cultures. But under the spell of postmodernism, he cannot resist the claim that these limits as well as the production of identity itself occur independently of the cultural understandings, logics, and concepts of those encompassed. Thus, Amselle argues that it is "absurd to even pose the question of Fulani identity" (47). As to why certain "unities" like the Fulani appear, Amselle writes that a cultural identity emerges because these unities appeal "to social actors who share a common response to its symbolism" (31). I can hear Marshall Sahlins—whom Amselle has already taken to the woodshed for his adherence to a concept of culture—chuckling. And Geertz and others join in. For in one fell swoop, Amselle has conceded his entire argument without apparently being notified of his own surrender. The reason is that we have a name for this common response and understanding of symbols: namely, culture. And lo and behold, only a chapter later we learn that there is indeed "a local theory of identity" that links the religion of the Fulani "to their ethnic particularity" (76). My

aim here is not to offer curbside assistance to a disabled theory, only to point out that the postmodern strategy of omitting local theories of ethnicity precludes the possibility of understanding the making of borders.

12. In the ethnography of Melanesia, language has always been something of a scandal. Ethnographers have ignored both language and the processes of encompassment because it was the encompassment of the Other that made ethnography linguistically possible. Whatever the difficulties of especially the Highland languages, ethnographic investigation has been dependent on pidgin as the contact language through which the ethnographer learned the indigenous tongue, as the language used to confirm the interpretation of local dialogue, as a language of investigation when the local idiom proved impossible, and as the language of modernity adopted by local agents. This pidgin is itself both a product of, and inculcated through, contact with the West. So Melanesian ethnography has presupposed the condition that it has bracketed. This avoidance is evident in the fact that few ethnographies say anything about the linguistic conditions of their own production even when they are avowedly talking about such obviously linguistic phenomena as myth (two examples among many are Gillison 1993 and Weiner 1995).

13. One of the most difficult things to learn and appreciate in fieldwork is that apparently simple statements, everyday run-of-the-mill statements of no monumental importance, often contain a complex epistemology. Statements like "take the aspirin I'm giving you, it will relieve your headache" embody an entire philosophy about the capacity of the I to cause change, about the relationship between empowered external objects (e.g., pill) and states of being in the world (e.g., in pain), and about the relationship between interpersonal action and personal biography.

14. Again, ethnographers, from Vayda and Rappaport to Healey and myself, have been willing to overlook their own words to preserve the integrity of the sovereign culture. At different points, we have all noted that Maring clusters only make war with other Maring groups, and that some clusters made war with the Manga. Both clauses of this sentence cannot, of course, be true. The reality is that because warfare was a mode of sociality the conflict between the Manga and Yonbam suggests that there was no cultural difference prior to pacification.

15. Cesare Pavese, exiled to Calabria by the Fascists, dispossessed of his identity, compares in a poem called "Agonia" (Agony) the forms of identity lost and regained, the perpetual search, to a quest for the most basic elements of the senses: colors. He writes, "desidero solo colori" (all I desire is colors). Then, "questo corpo dopo tanto pallore riavra la sua vita" (this body of mine will live again after all those colorless years).

> Sentiro intorno a me scivolare gli sguardi
> e sapro d'esser io: gettando un'occhiata,
> mi vedro tra la gente. Ogni nuovo mattino,
> usciro per le strade cercano i colori.

> [I'll feel within the glances of men go gliding around me,
> and I will know that I am me. Just a look and I will know

I am there like my others. In the new morning,
I will step out on the street and go searching for colors.]
(my translation)

16. Antonio Benitez-Rojo's *Mar de las lentejas* (*The Sea of Lentils*) (1985) is a marriage of history and fiction that courts the Spanish colonization of the Americas. Drawn from the annals of the first encounters, *The Sea of Lentils* navigates the myths by which the Spanish, the indigenous peoples, and the Africans brought in slavery constituted each other through the stories they spoke, the fantasies they repressed, till there appeared a grotesque composite of mutual otherness— grotesque because its violent imagery paled before its violent reality. There is here a razor's edge between ethnographically true fiction and fictionally described ethnography.

Chapter 4

1. I mean this distinction between white and black metaphorically as the simulacrum for a raciology that is intrinsically intertwined with colonialism, power, and production and validation of regimes of subjectivity.

2. In Marilyn Strathern's words, to understand local practice, we need to adopt techniques that permit us to overcome the "tenacity of our own intervening metaphors" (1988:175).

3. This includes, of course, (partially) Westernized others such as non-Western academics and scientists.

4. See LiPuma 1990 for a discussion of the linguistic terminology used here.

5. This goes a long way in explaining why studies of personhood in Melanesia (such as Munn 1986) sidestep the issue of modernity and attempt to bracket the contexts and effects of the encompassment of Melanesia by the West, one of the primary effects being that Melanesians are the subject of Western understanding.

6. See LiPuma and Meltzoff 1989 for a more detailed description of the relation between culture and capitalism as well as the very theoretical work in Postone 1993.

7. Analysts who think an incommensurability between Melanesia and the West cannot help but overestimate difference. For example, in *The Gender of the Gift,* Marilyn Strathern notes that "gift exchange has always been a conundrum to the Western imagination [because it is] the circulation of objects in relations in order to make relations in which objects can circulate" (1988:221). But while this is certainly the culture of gift exchange, it is hardly unimaginable for Westerners such as ethnographers. Suppose, for example, I rewrote her sentence to read: dinner parties (among colleagues, members of a family, etc.) circulate foods and words in relations in order to create relations in which foods and words can circulate. There is little here that is mysterious or hard to imagine. The difference between gift and commodity-based societies, I would submit, is not (perhaps never) absolute; they do not rely on fully incommensurable epistemologies. The difference is that in gift-exchange societies, commodity-like transactions occur only on the social margins

(with, for example, Westerners), where in commodity-exchange (capitalist) societies, gift exchange is reserved for the small, nonpublic, and intimate spaces where kinship and community still have a voice.

8. Such duality is an inherent aspect of any social practice that objectifies persons through objects produced. This is as true for the anthropologist as for the Melanesian gift-giver. For instance, the paper that an anthropologist presents at a colloquium, though presented individually and bound by the norms of individual responsibility, embodies the labors of others, directly and/or indirectly. The paper is detachable and publishable under the sole name of the author because the author has extracted him/herself from the set of social relations without which that paper could not have come into being. So, what I write here inscribes not only my own labor, but that of numerous others, in the absence of whose labor in relation to me, my paper would look very different. In the ideology of the commodity form, this matrix of relations is externalized under the euphemisms of "influence," "assistance," and other things that, conventionally, appear in footnotes, brackets, and prefaces—lest the individual and individuality of the author be compromised. In this way, our commitment to the ideology of the individual and the commodity form guarantee that this product (the paper) will appear to be extrinsic both to its producer and to the set of relations that produce him/her. From the standpoint of the audience that focuses on the content of the paper ("what it has to say"), the meanings of the paper for its author (e.g., the memories of the "field" that it arouses) and the set of relations it embodies are tangential—so much so that this is hardly obligatory or presupposed information. The paper comes to the audience as evidence of its author's intent, knowledge, ethnographic research, analytical insights, etc. For the audience, it is the author's prestige, or intellectual capital, that is at stake. By reverse action, what an author derives from the presentation (besides a small amount of money) is the author transformed in regard to others which the author attaches to him/herself as prestige and intellectual capital. The author thereby depends on others for evidence of his/her own fame and intellectual identity. In this respect, the dividual aspects of the person can be uncovered buried as they are beneath the ideology of the fully individual person and the paper as a pure commodity.

9. For example, it is more than possible to conclude from a truly relativist viewpoint that it is impossible to make any independent determination of a person's rights. On this view, there is no critical position or leverage from which to conclude that a person from another culture has been deprived of their rights since the notion of right itself is culture-bound. This is the case whatever these rights may be (the right to life, right to be free of foreign domination, right of freedom from slavery, etc.). Thus, there are no grounds to conclude that the Western colonization of Africa and Latin America, policies of apartheid, enslavement, and genocide by a nation against one of its ethnic or religious minorities, and so on, abridge these victims' "rights." Truly relativistic positions are ultimately politically highly conservative even if they appear to be scientifically rather radical. Two disturbing (at least for me) consequences follow from this relativism. First, we have little or no obligation to help members of other cultures since we do not know if they have rights to violate; second, the "truth" of a position is ultimately no more

or less than the power to enforce a particular image of reality. The very notions of "human" rights or "women's" rights (as opposed to culturally specific rights such as Enga, Catalan, Ndembu, Apache, or Kurdish rights) presume that there are sites of commensurability of personhood across cultures.

10. In fact, the status of names in a given society is a critical index of the relationship between dividual and individual aspects of personhood.

11. It should also be observed that cross-contextual regularities in ascribed intentionality are inseparable from the metapragmatic regimentation of speech. The reason for this is that what I call metapragmatics is nothing more than the system of signs for stipulating the use and meaning of signs in context. That is to say, we know that the use of language to convey an intention in social context A (e.g., a shaman's intent to heal) is the same as context B (e.g., a nurse's perceived intent to heal) because the metapragmatics of the language stipulates that the use of certain speech forms in A can carry the same meaning when used in B.

12. See Rappaport 1968 and LiPuma 1988 for further background material.

13. Other Melanesian societies also create comparative discourses about persons. The Paiela, for example, characterize some people as having spirits that are straight and good and other people as having no spirit or bad spirit, with the result that these agents act crookedly and badly (Biersack 1991:234).

14. The vision of misrecognition entertained by Marilyn Strathern in *The Gender of the Gift* is rather problematic. She asserts that the Western notion that society is authored is an "illusion," but she fails to ground her account by articulating the character of illusion or misrecognition. In fact, the whole tone of the word *illusion* would seem to be a mistake in that it suggests simply a false belief, a sensory error correctable by sight and insight. On my view, a theory of the appearance and power of forms of misrecognition in social life should move along the following lines. It must begin in the understanding that these forms are socially constructed. That is, they are genuine cultural products having as much ontological authority as any others. Further, the forms of misrecognition are socially necessary. That is, the way that the forms inflect social action is essential to the reproduction of a society in its current, specific historical form. Hence, a given way of misrecognition will transform only when the society of which it is a part also transforms. And finally, analysis is able to grasp the genesis and source of misrecognition (and also establish the ground of social critique) through the analysis of the contradictions within the sociocultural system. Failure to come to terms with the terms of misrecognition forces the writer to adopt a universalizing logic in order to shape a relativistic position—which is precisely what Strathern does (Josephides 1991:148–49 drives home this point).

15. There are analogues to sorcery in other societies that stress the dividual element of personhood. In Hindu and Buddhist cultures, for example, world renunciation and other forms of ascetic retreat permit persons to declare their independence from society and thus express their individuality in respect to the social body. To put this another way, societies that feature the dividual facet of the person can permit the full-fledged appearance of the individual on only the margins of society—that is, as either profane or sacred.

16. Weiss (1998), focusing on Africa, notes that Haya notions of the practice

of sorcerers have changed in respect to capitalism, specifically that family farms, where the dead are interred, can now be bought and sold for cash. So Haya sorcerers are now more likely to disinter and cannibalize corpses than in the past. Indeed, I would suggest that it is possible to construct, for both Melanesia and Africa, a model of contemporary sorcery as the reconstruction or reimagination of "tradition" in the context of the modern.

17. Those who opt for an unalloyed theory of dividuality forget that many Melanesian societies have a conception of selfishness, meaning situations in which a person remains unpartible, refusing willfully to give in to the pull of the relations in which he/she is enmeshed (e.g., Biersack 1991:248).

18. I was only able to get four or five known cases of "wild man" behavior in which a person runs amok striking people irrespective of kin relation or distance.

Chapter 5

The names and locations of the participants in the trial have been changed to protect their identity. I would also like to thank Andrew Strathern, Cherry Lowman, and Roy Rappaport for their helpful suggestions on this chapter.

1. Maring leadership was independent of spiritual and magical powers or access to them; in contrast to some lowland societies (Stephen 1987), having access to ancestor spirits or being able to magically cure and curse conferred leadership only within the circumscribed field of that specific practice.

2. By metapragmatics, I mean the use of language to organize how people do things with speech (e.g., report the speech of others or create boundaries on the speech event) and to define the context for the interpretation of discourse. Such rules of use delineate the different types of culturally recognized speech/social events such as gift-giving, addressing the ancestor spirits, performing magic, reporting an illness, giving an explanation, etc.

3. There is an entire linguistic dimension to the trial, as each trial is comprised of series of speech events that both presuppose and construct Maring cultural reality. Speakers use a whole range of "metapragmatic" devices to present and represent the truth in speech events. This ranges from informal speech events such as a greeting to more formalized events such as trials and invocations of the ancestor spirits. Within the trials, there are two levels of metapragmatic structuring. The first includes the general norms and conventions governing use of speech in this setting. For example, witnesses may talk for as long as they like, as often as they like, and on any topic they like even if it appears to bear little connection to the issues at hand. The second level is the use of speech to report about speech within the trial framework. People characterize each other's speech in order not only to present its referential content but to represent the emotional, ontological, and validity state of the speaker. For example, in one trial, the witness noted that "the person I met on the path that night asked about my pigs [referential, descriptive content] with the nervous laugh of a sorcerer [thereby characterizing the emotional, ontological status of the speaker]." A growing body of Oceania-based research on culture and language (e.g., Feld 1982; Goldman 1983) supports this

notion of speaking, illustrating that all speech events are doubly mediated and determined—by the structure of the grammar and the pragmatic structure of the speech event.

4. Note that catechists in other cultures, such as Ambrym (Tonkinson 1981), have initiated antisorcery campaigns (though mostly on the premise that sorcery is destructive, not that it does not exist).

5. At the time of the trial, the exchange rate was US$1.30 for each kina.

6. Though there is no way that I can prove the point, I would also suggest that this notion of the individual is indicated by people's increasing acceptance of private (as opposed to merely personal) property and of privacy.

Chapter 7

1. The Anglicans had assumed that Koinambe could be bought like any other material thing, and the Cenda would be willing to sell this land because of their desire to hear about Jesus. The Cenda assumed that the land could not be alienated because their ancestors, not those of the Anglicans, were buried on this land, and that, for letting the Church use their land, they deserved a real material return commensurate with the wealth of the Church. An equilibrium rather than a settlement transpired. The Koinambe mission claimed ownership of the land but made some concessions to the Cenda; the Cenda did not renounce claim to the land but took no action against the mission. They did not have the know-how or muscle to remove the mission from their land, and in any case, the mission was a rather valuable resource.

2. Some of the more recent ethnography, such as that of Brison (1992), deals more explicitly with the Christian missions. But anthropological habits are hard to break. When anthropologists write about Melanesian religions, they still mostly write about indigenous, presumably precontact belief systems. For instance, a recent volume on the religious imagination in New Guinea (Herdt and Stephen 1989) has only one article (by D. Tuzin) that broaches the relationship between the mission and the religious imagination, set last in the volume (with the exception of the conclusion). None of the remaining ethnographic accounts even mentions Christianity let alone its impact on local ways of thinking and knowing.

3. Most of the accounts that appear in strictly mission journals feature three main concerns: the success of a mission in tallying up souls, Melanesian cultural barriers to Christianity and how to overcome them by winning over the locals, and urging those on the front lines to revitalize their own faith in order that they may evangelize others with renewed zest.

4. Several fundamentalist evangelical missionaries who I met in Mt. Hagen come immediately to mind. One of these, Thomas Jackson of the Tilibi Church in the Wola area, stands out. He excoriated both the intractable heathenism of the Wola as well as that of my colleague, Paul Sillitoe, who worked in the area in the 1970s.

5. As is so often the case for the Maring, a more detailed account of the stages of this process can be found in Rappaport 1969 and LiPuma 1988:172–86.

6. The missionaries were not sanguine about the future of Western civilization. Their reasoning was that its present period was one of a liberalization of values and actions that was nothing less than a socializing of sin. This was underscored by the legalization of abortion, pornography, and other sins, and by the creation of social institutions to advance them.

7. Some people were fascinated with the prospect of having a white ancestor, and more than one person even asked why, if their founding ancestor was white, were they black—a good question.

8. The Maring are, of course, by no means alone in the demise of customary religious ways. Men's cults throughout Melanesia, for example, have collapsed under the weight of Westernization, their trade secrets revealed to women and outsiders, the practices now reduced to relics of a heathen past (see Tuzin 1989).

9. This produced the anomaly that if two people had the same last name the one certain fact about them was that they were unrelated; conversely, no true brothers ever had the same last name since they were always given different Maring names at birth.

10. While all of mankind was said to be able to receive the call of God, it was still the case that European priests believed that the Maring did not now, and would not anytime soon, have the true sophistication to become "real" priests. This view didn't square easily with the official position that since everyone was made in God's image, hence all had the same core of possibility. The Melanesians, however, could not become real priests because their culture got in the way. There were remnants of belief in sorcery and magic, for example, that were not present in Christianity and seemed impossible to expunge. Custom apparently turned the inner core in every direction but heavenward.

Chapter 8

1. This stance is especially true of ecological and demographic anthropology, which frequently sees local medicine as central to the life of the community only insofar as it presents an obstacle to the adoption of biomedicine. Paradoxically, this viewpoint, which reduces anthropology to a species of life science, systematically overlooks (because it has not developed the resources to grasp them) the sociomedical conditions that lead to the incorporation of biomedicine. Moreover, in drawing its vision of medicine from the logic of science, it has no way to address the practical functioning of any medicine, bio- or other.

2. Any account of ethnomedicine and local healing practices raises the question of their physiological and social efficacy: why healing succeeded even when local practitioners knew little about scientific disease types or appropriate remedies. Theories of the existence of indigenous medical practices have operated along several complementary lines. One thesis is that processes of natural remission generate healing on their own independent of medical intervention. Many patients would recover whether or not they received treatment of any kind, although shamans as well as Western healers may claim credit. This thesis can be further supported with the recognition that cultural responses to illness can help to

promote recovery. Greenwood (1981:219) notes that from the perspective of biomedicine, the value of cultural response lies in its social acknowledgment of illness, restoration of ontological wholeness and creation of optimal conditions for natural recovery. Anthropologists can cite medical studies conducted both in Western and non-Western societies to support this viewpoint. The elaborate emotionally moving, ritual events that frequently surround curing strengthen this argument. Finally, analysts may reinforce both these views by noting that ethnomedical treatments can have pharmacological, nutritional, or physiotherapeutic value. To cite a famous Maring example, feeding ritual pork to the sick may add quality protein to their diet at a critical time, helping to replace nutrients and to assist the body's natural defenses. Johannes (1980:62) explains with respect to the Nekematigi of the Eastern Highlands:

> As a placebo, pork is likely to be highly effective because of Nekematigi values and benefits about its salubrious qualities. Killing a pig for someone communicates to him not only the acknowledged seriousness of his condition but also the fact that others, who value his life, are doing something about it.
>
> In addition, pork may function as an important dietary boost. Added dietary intake of high quality protein during times of stress or infection helps to restore physiological equilibrium by replacing lost nutrients and or providing the excel necessary for the formation of antibodies and phagocytes.

Although all of these factors may contribute to the health of the patient, they are neither an explanation nor a description of ethnomedicine. Singularly or together, the views operate in terms of the functions of practice: the creation of optimal conditions for recovery. But there is no door that leads from the functions of psychology or dietary habits to the structure of practice. The functions can engross the phenomena because they are abstract, but they cannot specify the determinate forms of ethnomedical practices. This argument holds for the adoption of Western medical practice; nothing in the improved efficacy of biomedicine in treating certain types of illness can explain the structure and evolution of pluralism.

Chapter 9

1. See chapters 4 and 5 for further discussion on the construction of the person in Melanesia.

References

Abercrombie, Thomas
   1991   To Be Indian, to Be Bolivian: "Ethnic" and "National" Discourses of
          Identity. In *Nation-States and Indians in Latin America,* ed. G. Urban
          and J. Sherzer, 95–130. Austin: University of Texas Press.
Akin, David
   1996   Cash and Shell Money in Kwaio, Solomon Islands. Paper presented at
          ASAO conference on Indigenous Currencies and Changing Exchange
          Spheres in Melanesia. Kona, Hawaii, 1966.
Amselle, Jean-Loup
   1998   *Mestizo Logics: Anthropology of Identity in Africa and Elsewhere.*
          Stanford: Stanford University Press.
Anderson, Benedict
   1983   *Imagined Communities.* London: Verso.
Appadurai, Arjun
   1990   Disjuncture and Difference in the Global Cultural Economy. *Public
          Culture* 2:1–24.
Attenborough, David
   1960   *Quest in Paradise.* London: Butterworth Press.
Barker, John
   1989   Western Medicine and the Continuity of Belief: The Maisin of Colling-
          wood Bay, Oro Province. In *A Continuing Trial of Treatment,* ed. S.
          Frankel and G. Lewis, 69–93. London: Kluwer Academic.
   1990   Encounters with Evil: Christianity and the Response to Sorcery among
          the Maisin of Papua New Guinea. *Oceania* 61: 139–54.
Beidelman, Thomas
   1982   *Colonial Evangelism: A Socio-Historical Study of an East African Mis-
          sion at the Grassroots.* Bloomington: Indiana University Press.
Benitez-Rojo, Antonio
   1985   *Sea of Lentils.* Amherst: University of Massachusetts Press.
Biersack, Aletta
   1991   Prisoners of Time. In *Clio in Oceania,* ed. Aletta Biersack, 231–95.
          Washington, D.C.: Smithsonian Institution Press.
Bourdieu, Pierre
   1972   [1962]The Disenchantment of the World. In *Algeria 1960.* Paris: Edi-
          tions de la Maison des Sciences de L'Homme.
   1977   *Outline of a Theory of Practice.* Cambridge: Cambridge University
          Press.
   1984   *Distinction.* Cambridge: Harvard University Press.

1987 What Makes a Social Class? On the Theoretical and Practical Existence of Groups. *Berkeley Journal of Sociology* 32:1–17.
1991 Language and Symbolic Power. Cambridge: Harvard University Press.

Briggs, Charles
1986 *Learning How to Ask: A Sociolinguistic Appraisal of the Role of the Interview in Social Science Research.* Cambridge: Cambridge University Press.

Brison, Karen
1992 *Just Talk: Gossip, Meetings, and Power in a Papua New Guinea Village.* Los Angeles: University of California Press.

Buchbinder, Georgeda
1973 Maring Microadaptation: A Study of Demographic, Nutritional, Genetic, and Phenotypic Variation in a Highland New Guinea Population. Doctoral dissertation, Columbia University.

Buchbinder, Georgeda, and Roy Rappaport
1976 Fertility and Death among the Maring. In *Man and Woman in the New Guinea Highlands,* ed. Paula Brown and Georgeda Buchbinder, 13–35. Special Publications of the American Anthropological Association, no 8.

Bulmer, Ralph
1965 The Kyaka of the Western Highlands. In *Gods, Ghosts and Men in Melanesia,* ed. P. Lawrence and M. Meggitt, 132–61. Melbourne: Oxford University Press.

Bunn G., and P. Scott
1962 *Languages of the Mount Hagen Sub-District.* The Summer Institute of Linguistics. Ukarumpa, Eastern Highlands: Terrace of New Guinea.

Carrier, James
1992 Occidentalism: The World Turned Upside-Down. *American Ethnologist* 19:195–212.

Clark, Jeffery
1989 God, Ghosts and People: Christianity and Social Organization Among Takuru Wiru. In *Family and Gender in the Pacific,* ed. M. Jolly and M. Macintyre, 170–92. London: Cambridge University Press.

Comaroff, Jean, and John Comaroff
1991 *Of Revelation and Revolution.* Vol. 1. Chicago: University of Chicago Press.

Comaroff, John
1996 Ethnicity, Nationalism, and the Politics of Difference in the Age of Revolution. In *The Politics of Difference,* ed. E. Wilmsen and P. McAllister, 162–84. Chicago: University of Chicago Press.

Comaroff, John, and Jean Comaroff
1992 *Ethnography and Historical Imagination.* Boulder: Westview Press.
1997 *Of Revelation and Revolution.* Vol. 2. Chicago: University of Chicago Press.

Cook, Ed
1967 Manga Social Organization. Ph.D. dissertation, Yale University.

Daimoi, J. K.
1976   *Evangelism in the Early Church.* Lae: National Seminar on Evangelism, Papua New Guinea.

Durkheim, Émile
1915   *Elementary Forms of the Religious Life.* London: George Allen and
Unwin.

Errington, Fred, and Deborah Gewertz
1996   The Individuation of Tradition in a Papua New Guinean Modernity.
American Anthropologist 98:114–26.

Fabian, Johannes
1983   *Time and the Other.* New York: Columbia University Press.

Feil, Daryl
1987   *The Evolution of Highland Papua New Guinea Societies.* Cambridge:
Cambridge University Press.

Feld, Steven
1982   *Sound and Sentiment.* Philadelphia: University of Pennsylvania Press.

Foley, William
1986   *The Papua Languages of New Guinea.* Cambridge: Cambridge University Press.

Foster, Robert
1991   Making National Cultures in the Global Ecumene. *Annual Review of
Anthropology* 20:235–60.

1992   Take Care of Public Telephones: Moral Education and the Nation-
State Formation in Papua New Guinea. *Public Culture* 4:31–45.

1993   Bodies, Commodities, and the Nation-State in Papua New Guinea.
Paper presented at the University of Chicago, Department of Anthropology Conference on Culturalism, Nationalism, and Transnational-
ism, 1–2 November.

1995a Print Advertisements and Nation Making in Metropolitan Papua New
Guinea. In *Nation Making: Emergent Identities in Postcolonial
Melanesia,* ed. R. Foster, 151–84. Ann Arbor: University of Michigan
Press.

1995b *Social Reproduction and History in Melanesia.* Cambridge: Cambridge
University Press.

Frankel, Stephen
1986   *The Huli Response to Illness.* Cambridge: Cambridge University Press.

Franklin, Karl
1981   *Syntax and Semantics in New Guinea Languages.* Ukarumpa: Summer
Institute of Linguistics.

Gaius, Simon
1976   *Preparing the Local Church for Evangelism.* Lae: National Seminar on
Evangelism in Papua New Guinea.

Gee, James
1985   The Narrativization of Experience in the Oral Style. *Journal of Education* 167:9–35.

Geertz, Clifford
1983   Culture and Social Change: The Indonesian Case. *Man* 19:511–32.

Gellner, Ernest
1987 *Culture, Identity, and Politics.* Cambridge: Cambridge University Press.
Gewertz, Deborah
1983 *Sepik River Societies.* New Haven: Yale University Press.
Gewertz, Deborah, and Fred Errington
1991 *Twisted Histories, Altered Contexts: Representing the Chambri in a World System.* Cambridge: Cambridge University Press.
1995 *Articulating Change in the "Last" Unknown.* Boulder: Westview Press.
Gillison, Gillian
1993 *Between Culture and Fantasy: A New Guinea Highlands Mythology.* Chicago: University of Chicago Press.
Glick, L.
1967 Medicine as an Ethnographic Category: The Gimi of the New Guinea Highlands. *Ethnology* 6:31–56.
Gluckman, Max
1965 Foreword to *The Lineage System of the Mae Enga,* v–xiii. New York: Barnes and Noble.
Godelier, Maurice
1986 *The Making of Great Men: Male Dominance and Power among the New Guinea Baruya.* Cambridge: Cambridge University Press.
Goldman, Lawrence
1983 *Talk Never Dies.* London: Tavistock.
1993 *The Culture of Coincidence.* Oxford: Clarendon Press.
Gordon, Robert, and M. Meggitt
1985 *Law and Order in the New Guinea Highlands.* Hanover: University Press of New England.
Greenwood, B.
1981 Cold or Spirits? Choice and Ambiguity in Morocco's Pluralistic Medical System. *Social Science and Medicine* 15B:219–35.
Gumperz, John
1982 *Discourse Strategies.* Cambridge: Cambridge University Press.
Hanks, William
1996 Exorcism and the Description of Participants' Roles. In *Natural Histories of Discourse,* ed. M. Silverstein and G. Urban, 160–202. Chicago: University of Chicago Press.
Hannerz, Ulf
1989 Notes on the Global Ecumene. *Public Culture* 1:66–75.
1992 *Cultural Complexity.* New York: Columbia University Press.
Harrison, Simon
1995 Transformations of Identity in Sepik Warfare. In *Shifting Contexts,* ed. Marilyn Strathern, 81–97. London: Routledge.
Hasluck, Peter
1956 Australian Policy in Papua and New Guinea. George Cohen Memorial Lecture, University of Sydney.

Hays, Terrance
    1992   A Historical Background to Anthropology in the Papua New Guinea
            Highlands. In *Ethnographic Presents,* ed. T. Hays, 1–36. Berkeley:
            University of California Press.
Healey, Christopher
    1990   *Maring Hunters and Traders.* Berkeley: University of California Press.
Heidegger, Martin
    1962   [1927] *Being and Time.* New York: Harper and Row.
Held, David
    1987   *Models of Democracy.* Cambridge: Polity Press.
Herdt, Gilbert
    1989   Doktas and Shamans among the Sambia of Papua New Guinea. In *A
            Continuing Trial of Treatment,* ed. S. Frankel and G. Lewis, 95–114.
            London: Kluwer Academic.
Herdt, Gilbert, and M. Stephen, eds.
    1989   *The Religious Imagination in New Guinea.* New Brunswick: Rutgers
            University Press.
Hill, Jane, and Judith Irvine
    1993   Introduction. *In Responsibility and Evidence in Oral Discourse,* ed. J.
            Hill and J. Irvine, 1–23. Cambridge: Cambridge University Press.
Hobsbawm, Eric
    1994   *The Age of Extremes.* New York: Vintage Books.
Hopkins, Terrance, and E. Wallerstein
    1987   Capitalism and the Incorporation of New Zones into the World Econ-
            omy. *Review* 10:763–79.
Huber, M. T.
    1988   *The Bishop's Progress: A Historical Ethnography of Catholic Mission-
            ary Experience on the Sepik Frontier.* Washington: Smithsonian Insti-
            tution Press.
Iteanu, Andre
    1988   The Concept of the Person and the Ritual System: An Orokaiva View.
            Man 25:35–53.
Johannes, A.
    1980   Many Medicines in One: Curing in the Eastern Highlands of Papua
            New Guinea. *Culture, Medicine, and Psychiatry* 4:43–70.
Jorgensen, Dan
    1996   Regional History and Ethnic Identity in the Hub of New Guinea: The
            Emergence of the Min. *Oceania* 66:189–210.
Josephides, Lisette
    1985   The Production of Inequality: Gender and Exchange among the
            Kewa. London: Tavistock.
    1991   Metaphors, Metathemes, and the Construction of Sociality: A Cri-
            tique of the New Melanesian Ethnography. *Man* 26:145–61.
Keesing, Roger
    1989   Anthropology in Oceania: Problems and Prospects. *Oceania* 60:55–59.

Kelly, Raymond
    1993   *Constructing Inequality: The Fabrication of a Hierarchy of Virtue among the Etoro.* Ann Arbor: University of Michigan Press.

Knauft, Bruce
    1985a *Good Company and Violence.* Berkeley: University of California Press.
    1985b Ritual Form and Permutation in New Guinea: Implications of Symbolic Process for Socio-Political Evolution. *American Ethnologist* 12:321–40.

Kulick, Don
    1992   *Language Shift and Cultural Reproduction.* Cambridge: Cambridge University Press.

Kurtzman, Joel
    1993   *The Death of Money.* New York: Simon and Schuster.

Lambek, Michael
    1993   *Knowledge and Practice in Mayotte: Local Discourses of Islam, Sorcery, and Spirit Possession.* Toronto: University of Toronto Press.

Lattas, Andrew
    1993   Sorcery and Colonialism: Illness, Dreams and Death as Political Languages in West New Britain. *Man* 28:51–77.
    1996   Introduction: Mnemonic Regimes and Strategies of Subversion. *Oceania* 66:257–65.

Lederman, Rena
    1981   Sorcery and Social Change in Mendi. *Social Analysis* 8:15–27.
    1991   'Interests' in Exchange: Increment, Equivalence and the Limits of Big-Manship. In *Big Men and Great Men,* ed. M. Godelier and M. Strathern, 215–33. Cambridge: Cambridge University Press.

Leenhardt, Maurice
    1947   *Do Kamo: Person and Myth in the Melanesian World,* trans. B. Gulati (1979). Chicago: University of Chicago Press.
    1982   *Do Kamo: Person and Myth in the Melanesian World,* ed. James Clifford. Berkeley: University of California Press.

Le Roy Ladurie, E.
    1989   *Jasmin's Witch.* London: Scholar Press.

Lewis, Gilbert
    1976   A View of Sickness in New Guinea. In *Social Anthropology and Medicine,* ed. J. Loudon. London: Academic Press.

Liep, John
    1996   Means of Distinction: Currencies, Spheres and Localization in the Massim. Paper presented at ASAO conference on Indigenous Currencies and Changing Exchange Spheres in Melanesia. Kona, Hawaii, 1966.

Linnekin, Jocelyn, and Lynn Poyer
    1990   *Cultural Identity and Ethnicity in the Pacific.* Honolulu: University of Hawaii Press.

LiPuma, Edward
    1980   Sexual Asymmetry and Social Reproduction among the Maring of Papua New Guinea. *Ethnos* 1–2:34–57.

1981   Cosmology and Economy among the Maring of Highland New Guinea. *Oceania* 61: 266–85.

1983   On the Preference for Marriage Rules: A Melanesian Example. *Man* 18:766–85.

1985   The Social and Cultural Factors That Influence Aggression. In *Aggression: Functions and Causes,* ed. J. Maring Ramirez and P. Brain, 49–66. Sevilla: Universidad de Sevilla Press.

1988   *The Gift of Kinship.* Cambridge: Cambridge University Press.

1989   Modernity and Medicine among the Maring. In *A Continuing Trial of Treatment: Medical Pluralism in Papua New Guinea,* ed. Stephen Frankel and G. Lewis, 295–310. Boston: Kluwer Academic.

1990   The Terms of Change: Linguistic Mediation and Reaffiliation among the Maring. *Journal of the Polynesian Society* 99:93–121.

1993   Closure in the New Guinea Highlands: A Response to Hays. *Current Anthropology* 34:154–55.

1994   The Sorcery of Words and Evidence of Speech in Maring Justice. *Ethnology* 33:1–17.

1995   The Making of Nation States and National Cultures in Oceania. In *Nation Making: Emergent Identities in Postcolonial Melanesia,* ed. R. Foster, 33–68. Ann Arbor: University of Michigan Press.

1996   Democratization in the Age of Encompassment. Paper presented at the conference on Globalization and Democracy, University of Chicago and the Center for Transnational Studies, Nov. 4–6.

1997   History, Encompassment, and Identity: Nation-Making in the Solomon Islands. *Identities* 4:47–76.

N.d.   The Encompassment of Others: Capitalism, the Nation-State, and Western Culture in the Post-Colonial World.

LiPuma, Edward, and Sarah Meltzoff

1989   Towards a Theory of Culture and Class: An Iberian Example. *American Ethnologist* 16:313–34.

1990   Ceremonies of Independence and Public Culture in the Solomon Islands. *Public Culture* 3:72–97.

1994   Economic Mediation and the Power of Associations. *American Anthropologist* 96:31–51.

Lowman, Cherry

1968   Maring Big-Men. *Anthropological Forum* 2:199–243.

1980   Environment, Society, and Health: Ecological Bases of Community Growth and Decline in the Maring Region of Papua New Guinea. Doctoral dissertation, Columbia University.

Lynch, John

1998   *Pacific Languages.* Honolulu: University of Hawaii Press.

MacIlwain, R.

1955   Minj Patrol Report No. 2. of 1955/56. Minj Subdistrict, Western Highlands District, Territory of New Guinea.

MacLean, Neil

1984   To Develop Our Place: A Political Economy of the Maring. Ph.D. dissertation, the University of Adelaide.

1994 Freedom or Autonomy: A Modern Melanesian Dilemma. *Man* 29:667–88.

Mann, A.
1966 Some Reflections on Current Constitutional Issues. *Journal of the Papua and New Guinea Society* 1:83–94.

McKaughan, Howard
1973 *The Languages of the Eastern Family of the East New Guinea Highland Stock. Anthropological Studies in the Eastern Highlands of New Guinea,* vol. 2. Seattle: University of Washington Press.

Meggitt, Mervyn
1977 *Blood Is Their Argument: Warfare among the Mae Enga Tribesmen of the New Guinea Highlands.* Palo Alto, Calif., Mayfield.

Meltzoff, Sarah, and Edward LiPuma
1983 A Japanese Fishing Joint Venture: Worker Experience and National Development in the Solomon Islands. Manila: Rockefeller Foundation.
1986 Hunting for Tuna and Cash in the Solomons: A Rebirth of Artisanal Fishing in Malaita. *Human Organization* 45:53–62.

Mertz, Elizabeth
1988 The Uses of History: Language, Ideology, and Law in the United States and South Africa. *Law and Society Review* 22:661–85.

Mitchell, Timothy
1988 *Colonising Egypt.* Cambridge: Cambridge University Press.

Mosko, Mark
1992 Motherless Sons: 'Divine Kings' and 'Partible Persons' in Melanesia and Polynesia. *Man* 27:693–717.

Munn, Nancy
1986 *The Fame of Gawa.* Cambridge: Cambridge University Press.

Murphy, P.
1976 Proclamation in a Melanesian Setting. Lae: National Seminar on Evangelism, Papua New Guinea. Pp. 1–23.

Nachman, S.
1981 Bual: Expressions of Sorcery in the Dance. *Social Analysis* 8:42–57.

Ngubane, Harriet
1977 *Body and Mind in Zulu Medicine.* London: Academic Press.

Otto, Thomas, and Nicholas Thomas
1997 *Narratives of Nation in the South Pacific.* Amsterdam: Harwood Academic Publishers.

Parmentier, Richard
1989 Naturalization of Convention: A Process in Social Theory and Social Reality. *Comparative Social Research* 11:279–99.
1993 The Political Function of Reported Speech. In *Reflexive Language: Reported Speech and Metapragmatics,* ed. J. Lucy, 261–86. Cambridge: Cambridge University Press.
1994 *Signs in Society.* Bloomington: Indiana University Press.

Parry, Jonathan, and Maurice Bloch
1989 Introduction: Money and the Morality of Exchange. In *Money and the*

Morality of Exchange, ed. J. Parry and M. Bloch, 1–32. Cambridge: Cambridge University Press.

Patterson, Mary
  1974–75 Sorcery and Witchcraft in Oceania. *Oceania* 45 (2, 3): 132–60; 212–34.

Pavese, Cesare
  1979 *Hard Labor (Lavorare stanca).* Baltimore: Johns Hopkins University Press.

Polier, Nicole
  1994 A View from the Cyanide Room: Politics and Culture in a Mining Township in Papua New Guinea. *Identities* 1:63–84.

Porter, Roy
  1992 *The Popularization of Medicine, 1650–1850.* London: Routledge.

Postone, Moishe
  1986 Towards a Reconstruction of the Marxian Culture of Modernity. Chicago: Working Papers and Proceedings of the Center for Transcultural Studies, no. 3.
  1993 *Time, Labor, and Social Domination.* Cambridge: Cambridge University Press.

Price, David
  1990 *Atlas of World Cultures.* New York: Sage Publications.

Rappaport, Roy
  1967 Ritual Regulation of Environmental Relations among a New Guinea People. *Ethnology* 6:17–30.
  1968 *Pigs for the Ancestors.* New Haven: Yale University Press.
  1969 Marriage among the Maring. In *Pigs, Pearlshells, and Women,* ed. R. Glasse and M. Meggitt, 117–37. Englewood Cliffs, N.J.: Prentice Hall.
  1977 Ecology, Adaptation and the Ills of Functionalism (being, among other things, a response to Jonathan Friedman). *Michigan Discussions in Anthropology* 2:138–90.
  1979 *Ecology, Meaning, and Religion.* Richmond: North Atlantic Books.

Reay, Marie
  1992 An Innocent in the Garden of Eden. In *Ethnographic Presents,* ed. T. Hays, 137–66. Berkeley: University of California Press.

Riebe, Inge
  1974 . . . And Then We Killed: An Attempt to Understand the Fighting History of Upper Kaironk Valley Kalam from 1914–1962. M.A. thesis, University of Sydney.
  1987 Kalam Witchcraft: A Historical Perspective. In *Sorcerer and Witch in Melanesia,* ed. M. Stephen, 211–48. New Brunswick: Rutgers University Press.

Robbins, Sterling
  1982 *Auyana: Those Who Held onto Home.* Seattle: University of Washington Press.

Robertson, Roland
  1992 *Globalization: Social Theory and Global Culture.* London: Sage.

Rodman, Margaret, and Matthew Cooper, eds.
    1979   *The Pacification of Melanesia.* Ann Arbor: University of Michigan
            Press.
Romanucci-Ross, L.
    1977   The Hierarchy of Resort in Curative Practices: The Admiralty Islands,
            Melanesia. *Culture, Disease and Healing: Studies in Medical Anthro-
            pology,* ed. D. Landy, 481–86. New York: Macmillan.
Rostow, Walter
    1978   *The World Economy: History and Prospects.* Austin: University of
            Texas Press.
Sahlins, Marshall
    1976   *Culture and Practical Reason.* Chicago: University of Chicago Press.
    1981   *Historical Metaphors and Mythical Realities.* Ann Arbor: University of
            Michigan Press.
    1985   *Islands of History.* Chicago: University of Chicago Press.
    1997   Reply to Borofsky. *Current Anthropology* 38:272–76.
Salamone, Frank
    1977   Anthropologists and Missionaries: Competition or Reciprocity?
            Human Organization 36:407—12.
Schama, Simon
    1988   *The Embarrassment of Riches.* Los Angeles: University of California
            Press.
Schwimmer, E.
    1979   Reciprocity and Structure: A Semiotic Analysis of Some Orakavia
            Exchange Data. *Man* 14:271–85.
Silverstein, Michael
    1979   Language Structure and Linguistic Ideology. In *The Elements: A
            Parasession on Linguistic Units and Levels,* ed. P. Clyne, W. Hanks,
            and C. Hofbauer, 193–247. Chicago: Chicago Linguistic Society.
    1981   *The Limits of Awareness.* Working Papers in Sociolinguistics, no. 84.
            Austin: Southwest Educational Development Laboratory.
    1987   The Three Faces of "Function." In *Social and Functional Approaches
            to Language and Thought,* ed. Maya Hickmann, 17–38. Orlando: Aca-
            demic Press.
    1996   The Secret Life of Texts. In *Natural Histories of Discourse,* ed. Michael
            Silverstein and G. Urban, 81–105. Chicago: University of Chicago
            Press.
Silverstein, Michael, and G. Urban, eds.
    1996   *Natural Histories of Discourse.* Chicago: University of Chicago Press.
Sinclair, James
    1981   *Kiap: Australian Patrol Officers in Papua New Guinea.* Sydney: Pacific
            Publications.
Souter, Gavin
    1963   *New Guinea: The Last Unknown.* Sydney: Angus and Robertson.
Stephen, Michele, ed.
    1987   *Sorcerer and Witch in Melanesia.* New Brunswick: Rutgers University
            Press.

Stocking, George
1987 *Victorian Anthropology.* Chicago: University of Chicago Press.
Strathern, Andrew
1975 Veiled Speech in Mt. Hagen. In *Political Language and Oratory in Traditional Societies,* ed. M. Block, 185–204. London: Academic Press.
1977 Why Is Shame on the Skin? In *The Anthropology of the Body,* ed. J. Blacking, 99–110. London: Academic Press.
1979 *Ongka: A Self Account by a New Guinea Big-Man.* London: Duckworth.
1981 "Noman": Representations of Identity in Mount Hagen. In *The Structure of Folk Models,* ed. L. Holy and M. Stuchlik, 281–303. London:Academic Press.
1996 *Body Thoughts.* Ann Arbor: University of Michigan Press.
Strathern, A., and M. Strathern
1971 *Self-Decoration in Mt. Hagen.* London: Duckworth.
Strathern, Marilyn
1980 No Nature, No Culture: The Hagen Case. In *Nature, Culture, and Gender,* ed. C. MacCormak and M. Strathern. Cambridge: Cambridge University Press.
1984 Subject or Object? Women and the Circulation of Valuables in Highlands New Guinea. In *Women and Property, Women as Property,* ed. R. Hirschon. London: Croom Helm.
1988 *The Gender of the Gift.* Cambridge: Cambridge University Press.
1990 Negative Strategies in Melanesia. In *Localizing Strategies,* ed. R. Fardon. Edinburgh: Scottish Academic Press.
Tambiah, Stanley
1984 *The Magical Power of Words. Man* 3: 175–206.
1990 *Magic, Science, Religion, and the Scope of Rationality.* Cambridge: Cambridge University Press.
Taussig, Michael
1980 *The Devil and Commodity Fetishism in South America.* Chapel Hill: University of North Carolina Press.
Tonkinson, R.
1981 Sorcery and Social Change in Southeast Ambrym, Vanuatu. *Social Analysis* 8:77–100.
Turner, V.
1967 *The Forest of Symbols.* Ithaca: Cornell University Press.
Tuzin, Donald
1989 Vision, Prophecies, and the Rise of Christian Consciousness. In *The Religious Imagination in New Guinea,* ed. G. Herdt and M. Stephen, 161–87. New Brunswick: Rutgers University Press.
Van Meijl, Toon, and P. van der Grijp
1994 *European Imagery and Colonial History in the Pacific.* Saarbrucken: Vergal fur Entwichlungspolitik Breitenbach.
Vayda, Andrew
1971 Phases and Processes of War and Peace among the Maring of New Guinea. *Oceania* 42:1–24.

Wagner, Roy
    1972   *Habu: The Invention of Meaning in the Daribi Religion.* Chicago: University of Chicago Press.
    1988   Visible Sociality: The Daribi Community. In *Mountain Papuans,* ed. J. Weiner, 39–72. Ann Arbor: University of Michigan Press.

Wallerstein, Emmanuel
    1974   *The Modern World System.* New York: Academic Press.
    1990   Culture as the Ideological Battleground of the Modern World System. *Culture, Theory and Society* 7:31–55.

Watson, James
    1960   A New Guinea "Opening Man." In *In the Company of Man: Twenty Portraits by Anthropologists,* ed. J. Casagrande, 127–73. New York: Harper and Brothers.
    1983   *Tairora Culture: Contingency and Pragmatism.* Seattle: University of Washington Press.
    1992   Kainantu: Recollections of a First Encounter. In *Ethnographic Presents,* ed. T. Hays, 167–98. Berkeley: University of California Press.

Weiner, James
    1995   *The Lost Drum: The Myth of Sexuality in Papua New Guinea and Beyond.* Madison: University of Wisconsin Press.

Weiss, Brad
    1998   Electric Vampires: Haya Rumors of the Commodified Body. In *Bodies and Persons,* ed. Michael Lambek and Andrew Strathern, 172–96. Cambridge: Cambridge University Press.

Westermark, George
    1981   Sorcery and Economic Change in Agarabi. *Social Analysis* 8:88–100.

Wilmsen, Edwin
    1989   *Land Filled with Flies.* Chicago: University of Chicago Press.

Wolf, Eric
    1982   *Europe and the People Without History.* Berkeley: University of California Press.

Wurm, S., and D. Laycock
    1961   The Question of Language and Dialect in New Guinea. *Oceania* 32:128–243.

Young, Michael
    1989   Suffer the Children: Wesleyans in the D'Entrecasteaux. In *Family and Gender in the Pacific,* ed. M. Jolly and M. Macintyre, 108–33. London: Cambridge University Press.
    1997   Commemorating Missionary Heroes: Local Christianity and Narratives of the Nation. In *Narratives of the Nation in the South Pacific,* ed. T. Otto and N. Thomas, 91–132. Amsterdam: Harwood Academic Publishers.

Zelenietz, Stephen
    1981   Sorcery and Social Change: An Introduction. *Social Analysis* 8:3–14.

Zelizer, Viviana
    1994   *The Social Meaning of Money.* New York: Basic Books.

Index